Hindu Mythology And The Critique Of Sacrifice

The Head Beneath The Altar

Hindu Tradition Series

The Hindu Tradition Series aims to bring together books of the higest academic standard that critically interrogate Hindu tradition in the widest sense. Its focus is on cultural and religious history, including relevant political and social developments. The interaction with other traditions, whether originally from inside or outside the Indian subcontinent, will figure prominently among its volumes.

Number 7

Hindu Mythology And The Critique Of Sacrifice

Edited and Translated by
BRIAN COLLINS

The Head Beneath The Altar

MOTILAL BANARASIDASS PUBLISHERS
PRIVATE LIMITED • DELHI (INDIA)

Hindu Mythology and the Critique of Sacrifice
The Head Beneath The Altar
Hindu Tradition Series,
Number 7

ISBN : 978-81-208-4190-1

First Indian Edition : Delhi, 2018
Earlier published under the title *The Head Beneath the Altar: Hindu Mythology and the Critique of Sacrifice*
by Michigan State Univesity Press, East Lansing

Book design and composition by Charlie Sharp, Sharp Designs, Lansing, Michigan

Also available at
MOTILAL BANARSIDASS
40-41 U.A. Bungalow Road, Jawahar Nagar, Delhi 110 007
1 B, J.S. Compound, Kennedy Bridge, Nana Chowk, Mumbai 400 007
203 Royapettah High Road, Mylapore, Chennai 600 004
236, 9th Main III Block, Jayanagar, Bengaluru 560 011
8 Camac Street, Kolkata 700 017
Ashok Rajpath, Patna 800 004
Chowk, Varanasi 221001

Library Of Congress Cataloging-In-Publication Data
Hindu Mythology and the Critique of Sacrifice:
The Head Beneath the Altar by
Brian Collins in HINDU TRADITION SERIES, No. 7
Pages cm.–(Studies in violence, mimesis and culture)
Includes Bibliographical references, and Index.
ISBN: 978-81-208-4190-1
1. Hindu mythology. II. Sacrifice—Hinduism.
III. Violence—Religious aspect—Hinduism.
IV. Girard, Renè, 1923–I. Title.
BL 1135. P6213 294.5'925 77-92643

Published by
Motilal Banarsidass Publishers (P.) Ltd.
www.mlbd.com • mlbd@mlbd.com
Printed by Imprint Books, New Delhi - 110085

For my grandfather, Dewey Wade Johnson

DECEMBER 10, 1927–FEBRUARY 3, 2012

Foreword by the General Editor

The writings of René Girard have been and remain a challenge and source of inspiration for scholars of sacrifice and of violence in religion. Unfortunately, Girard did not write much about India, in spite of its rich and well-documented sacrificial tradition. Girard's ideas have therefore not received the attention they deserve among scholars of Indian religions. This may change with Brian Collins' book, which presents a well-informed yet critical analysis of Indian religious practices in the light of Girard's theory. We can only hope that this book will open up new horizons in the study of Indian religion.

Johannes Bronkhorst

Contents

ix ACKNOWLEDGMENTS

1 Introduction

43 Rivalries

83 Priests and Kings, Oaths and Duels

137 Epic Variations on a Mimetic Theme

181 Meaning: The Secret Heart of the Sacred

237 Yajñānta: The End of Sacrifice

253 NOTES

287 BIBLIOGRAPHY

303 INDEX

Acknowledgments

There are many people without whom this book would not have been possible. The foremost of these is Bill Johnsen of Michigan State University, whom I met fortuitously at the American Academy of Religion's annual meeting in Montréal in 2009 when the manuscript of the English translation of Girard's *Sacrifice* was still in preparation. Following that very brief meeting in the vendors' hall, Bill generously invited me to Palo Alto for a conference, where I met Girard and two other people who were instrumental in getting this monograph published. The first is Robert Hamerton-Kelly, who was commissioning monographs at the time and encouraged me to submit a proposal to Imitatio. The second is David Dawson, who was in the midst of finishing his own monograph as well as moving his family to Costa Rica but still found time to read, reread, and provide crucial feedback first on the proposal and then on the monograph itself. Through email and Skype, David was my primary interlocutor as I wrote these pages.

Others from the Colloquium on Violence and Religion, Imitatio, and the Thiel Foundation who provided one kind of support or another for this project are Isak de Vries, Lindy Fishburne, Jimmy Kaltreider, Andrew McKenna, and Martha Reineke, who also was a great help during the search for employment that coincided with the writing of this book. I would also like to acknowledge the input of Noel Sheth of the Jnana-Deepa Vidyapeeth Pontifical Institute of Philosophy and Religion in Pune, whom I spoke with at the symposium on René Girard and World Religions in Berkeley in April 2011, and express my gratitude to the North Carolina Consortium for South Asian Studies, especially David Gilmartin and Anna Bigelow of NC State University and Afroz Taj and John Caldwell of UNC–Chapel Hill, for a helpful discussion of chapter four at a colloquium in September of 2011.

While I take full responsibility for any and all mistakes, I would have made many more of them without the help of Kate McKinney Maddalena, who assisted in my translations from French, and Wendy Doniger, for whose continuing help and support there is not enough *gurudakṣiṇā* in the three worlds to repay. Finally, this book would probably never have been completed without the support of my parents Darrow Johnson and Jean Hagen-Johnson, my uncle and aunt Dave Lenat and Georgia Hagen, my grandmother Stella Johnson, and my wife Jennifer Ellen Woody Collins, all of whom kept asking about "the book."

Introduction

I wander afield, thriving in sturdy thought,
Through unpathed haunts of the Pierides,
Trodden by step of none before. I joy
To come on undefiled fountains there,
To drain them deep; I joy to pluck new flowers,
To seek for this my head a signal crown
From regions where the Muses never yet
Have garlanded the temples of a man:
First, since I teach concerning mighty things,
And go right on to loose from round the mind
The tightened coils of dread religion;
Next, since, concerning themes so dark, I frame
Songs so pellucid, touching all throughout . . .

—Lucretius, *On the Nature of Things*, Book I,
"The Infinity of the Universe"

But although his fury and sarcasm leave the Vedic seers unscathed, he takes aim at modern anthropologists with exuberant zeal . . . In their presence, Girard incessantly repeats "Molière's inexhaustible comment, '*Ah! qu'en termes galants ces choses-là sont mises*!' ['How elegantly those things are phrased!']."

—Roberto Calasso, *The Ruin of Kasch*

India is the birthplace of the religious traditions of Buddhism, Hinduism, Jainism, and Sikhism. It has served as a pilgrimage place and source of spiritual renewal for Chinese monks in the fifth century, Tibetan royalty in the tenth century, and the Western counterculture since at least the early twentieth century. India's gift to the world, in the words of the nineteenth century Hindu reformer Swami Vivekananda, is religion.[1] But India is also the site of some of the last century's worst episodes of violent conflict, including the bloody 1947 partition of India and Pakistan and the successive wars between the two nations over the next 25 years; the political murders of Mahatma Gandhi (by a Hindu), Indira Gandhi (by her Sikh bodyguards), and Rajiv Gandhi (by a Tamil separatist); the deadliest man-made ecological disaster in history at the Union Carbide plant in Bhopal in 1985; the periodic outbreaks of communal violence against Hindus, Muslims, Sikhs, and Christians; and the nuclear armament of India and Pakistan. Religion, in addition to India's gift to the world, is also often the scapegoat for India's violence.

Hindu mythology reflects this mixture of otherworldly spiritualism and worldly violence. Like most mythologies, it is full of images of cosmic wars, apocalyptic destruction, and tragic heroes. But it is also the repository of as many stories about courtly love, self-sacrifice, ethical quandaries, and sophisticated philosophical edifices to rival (or even surpass) Augustine and Aquinas. And unlike Greek or Scandinavian mythology, Hindu mythology is also connected to a living religious tradition and helps to define the religious identity of hundreds of millions of Hindus. As scholars of Hinduism have learned, one is far more likely to draw protests when writing about Gaṇeśa or Śiva than when writing about Loki or Aphrodite. Indeed, as we shall see, scholars of Hindu mythology have recently found themselves enmeshed or implicated in India's religious conflicts.

Many books have been written about the violence of religion, the religions of India, and the violence of the religions of India. But René Girard, who has spent the last four decades thinking and writing about religion and violence, has had virtually nothing to say about it until his lectures on the Sanskrit Brāhmaṇas at the *Bibliothèque nationale de France* in October of 2002. This book will make a study of those lectures, published in English in 2011 as *Sacrifice*, in light of the rest of Girard's work, current Indological scholarship, and primary texts from the Hindu tradition. Along the way, we will also visit the work of Girard's predecessors, heirs, rivals, and critics, examine some well-known and some frequently overlooked Hindu myths and rituals, and take some sidelong glances into Christian theology, contemporary philosophy, and Greek, Iranian, and Scandinavian literature. In the end, we will come to some conclusions about what it means for him and for us that Girard has finally turned to India so late in his long and distinguished career and how a Girardian reading of Hindu myth might contribute to a new universal history built on humanity's shared future rather than its diffused pasts.

From Mimetic Theory to Hinduism . . .

This book has two separate but related aims. First, I want to see to what extent René Girard's "mimetic theory" of the sacrificial origin of religion and culture can enrich our understanding of Hinduism. More specifically, I am interested in using Girard's theory and the hypotheses it engenders to understand what is happening in Indian myth and ritual between 500 B.C.E. and 500 C.E., a time frame roughly covering the periods of religious development that Axel Michaels calls the epochs of "Vedic Religions," "Ascetic Reformism," and "Classical Hinduism."[2]

This is a rather large stretch of history that covers some significant changes, including the development of the Indian state, the successive rise and fall of Hindu and Buddhist empires, and cultural impact from Central Asian newcomers. But this book is about Hindu myth, not Indian history. While I will be referring to historical events occasionally to provide context, my primary mode of analysis will be textual, not historical, proceeding from Brian K. Smith's argument that "*Hinduism is the religion of those humans who create, perpetuate, and transform traditions with legitimizing reference to the authority of the Veda.*"[3] Accordingly the Veda will always be in the background of my analysis, and more so the commentarial tradition of the Brāhmaṇas. I will also be spending a significant amount of time on the later heroic epic the *Mahābhārata*, sometimes granted the honorary title of "Fifth Veda."

For the benefit of the nonspecialist, it may be useful at this point to explain exactly what a Veda and a Brāhmaṇa are. Both of these words have multiple overlapping meanings that can confuse those encountering Indian religions for the first time. "Veda" is a Sanskrit word that means "knowledge" and is cognate with the English *wit* and the German *wissen*. It refers to a class of revealed canonical literature that has the status of ultimate authority in the later Hindu tradition, which is why calling the *Mahābhārata* the "Fifth Veda" is so significant. But the Veda also refers more specifically to the top "layer" of the Vedic literary tradition, the four original Vedic Saṃhitās. In this book, when the term appears in italics and is preceded by *Ṛg*, *Yajur*, *Sāma*, or *Atharva*, I am speaking of one of the four Saṃhitās, or "collections," that comprise the top layer of the Veda and when I use the term without italics, I am referring to the class of Vedic literature as a whole. The Brāhmaṇas are commentarial texts belonging to the second layer of this Vedic corpus. Unfortunately, the word "Brāhmaṇa" also refers to the class of priests responsible for passing on the Vedic tradition and performing its rites. To avoid confusion on this point, I will abandon transliteration when using the latter sense of the word and use "Brāhmaṇas" to refer to the texts and "Brahmins" to refer to the people.[4]

To make matters worse, there is another word that is synonymous with Veda in the collective sense: *śruti*. *Śruti* or "heard" texts, unlike those of the *smṛti* or "remembered" variety, are *apauruṣeya*, that is, "without human [authorship]," and thus the ultimate and unquestionable authority over men and even gods, at least according to some schools of thought. Though the texts have no authors per se, they were revealed, through ecstatic states brought on by the ingestion of the sacred *soma* juice, to Vedic priest-poets who then memorized them and passed them along orally. An array of ingenious mnemonic devices aided the oral transmission of knowledge in ancient India and kept the integrity of the texts remarkably intact. As proof, Indologists have discovered separate oral traditions hundreds of miles apart that have maintained the same text word for word over a period of centuries without losing or changing a syllable. The Vedic scholar Michael Witzel has called the Vedic oral tradition, "something like a *tape-recording* of ca. 1500–500 B.C.E."[5]

The Veda is a sprawling multiplicity of oral traditions comprising primary texts and commentaries of many different Vedic lineages, some still extant, some lost to time. This vast body of texts is divided into four classes or layers. The first, as we have seen, consists of the Saṃhitās or the Vedas proper, which are themselves divided into four: the aforementioned *Ṛg, Sāma, Yajur* (which is further divided into Black and White branches), and *Atharva*. The *Ṛg Veda* is the largest, comprising 1028 poetic hymns celebrating the exploits of the Vedic gods, which were recited at the community's rituals. The *Yajur* is made up of prose mantras to be chanted at specific points in the rituals and the *Sāma* is a collection of Vedic hymns presented in complex metrical forms, all but seventy-five of which are also found in the eighth and ninth books of the *Ṛg*. The *Atharva* is the youngest Veda and is characterized by its collection of magic spells and charms.

The earliest stratum of the Vedas (generally agreed to be books two through seven of the ten books of the *Ṛg Veda*) dates to sometime between 1500 and 1100 B.C.E., around the time the nomadic and pastoral Vedic people that produced them entered what we now call India, bringing their mobile sacrificial tradition with them. The language and culture of the Vedic people belong to a larger linguistic and cultural family called the Indo-European, which also includes the ancient cultures of Greece, Rome, Scandinavia, and Central Europe. The Vedic language and culture are most closely related to those of ancient Iran, leading some scholars to speak of an "Indo-Iranian" subgroup. By around 800 B.C.E., the Vedic people had left the Indo-Iranian world behind and were settling in the Ganges River Valley, where what had been a collection of tribes and clans began to develop into a stratified and hierarchical society consisting of four classes or *varṇas* (literally, "colors"). Brahmin priests were at the top. Below them was the martial and royal Kṣatriya class. The agricultural and mercantile Vaiśya class was below the Kṣatriya, and at the bottom were the Śūdras, or slaves. This well-ordered picture, of course, comes to us from the very Brahmin-centered world of the textual tradition and should be taken with a grain (if not a five-pound bag) of salt. Recent evidence from the study of population genetics indicates that people in India were mixing across every conceivable ethnic and class barrier until around the second century C.E.[6]

Indologists refer to the period of social upheaval that gave rise to this class ideology as the Second Urbanization, the First Urbanization being the pre-Vedic Harappan civilization that thrived between 2200 and 1500 B.C.E. in what is now Pakistan. By the time of the Second Urbanization, at least according to the idealized vision of the Vedic world portrayed in the text, the institution of *yajña*, or sacrifice, had become the central feature of the society. Wealthy patrons sponsored elaborate rituals performed by dozens of Brahmins, sometimes working for days on end. And as they became more established as the class with the exclusive right to perform the sacrifice, Brahmin lineages began to develop their own commentarial traditions to make sure that the rites were performed properly and to elucidate the often-obscure Vedic hymns with mythical and proto-philosophical explanations. These commentarial texts were the Brāhmaṇas, the second class of Vedic literature, and each one developed into a "branch" connected to one of the four Vedas and with its own commentarial tradition in the form of the more esoterically inclined Āraṇyakas and Upaniṣads, which comprise the third and fourth classes of Veda, or are sometimes combined into a single third class.[7] As the final layer, the Upaniṣads (or the Āraṇyakas and Upaniṣads together) are frequently referred to collectively as the repository for the philosophical body of knowledge called the Vedānta or "The End of the Veda."

To the four Saṃhitās (*Ṛg, Sāma, Yajur,* and *Atharva*) and other three classes of Vedic literature (Brāhmaṇas, Āraṇyakas, and Upaniṣads), we should also add the Sūtras, technical explanations of the Vedic rituals contained in the *Yajur Veda*, which are not granted the status of Veda themselves but are considered *smṛti*, or "remembered." The category of *smṛti* literature also includes a wide variety of ritual texts, theological and philosophical treatises, myths, and histories that do not possess the Brahmin-sanctioned authority of the Vedas but have had considerable influence over religious development in India. The ones that we will be concerned with are the Sūtras, the *Rāmāyaṇa* and *Mahābhārata* epics, and the Purāṇas (encyclopedic compendia that are the sources of classical Indian mythology).

Having had a cursory glance over the massive body of Hindu scripture, we now come to the regrettably unavoidable question of whether or not the term "Hindu" has any coherent meaning that would justify looking at such a wide array of material as expressions of a whole. As many scholars have pointed out, "Hinduism" is an English word with no real counterpart in any Indian language. More than that, it doesn't appear anywhere in print before the nineteenth century. With this in mind, there are at least two reasons (both of which have merit) why some scholars, many of them influenced by the Islamicist Wilfred Cantwell Smith (notorious critic of the category of "Religion"), argue that Hinduism is a colonial or scholarly construction that does not correspond to any coherent religious tradition. First there is the postcolonial critique with its imperative to unmask any and all ideas presented as self-evident and examine the power structures and inequalities that produced them. This critique has revealed the political uses of the term "Hinduism" to legitimize certain forms of political order in the colonial period. Second is the sometimes-bewildering multiplicity of distinct practices and sects that are all lumped together in the category of Hinduism, which begs the question of whether we ought not consider them as separate traditions. But, even in the face of these challenges, there are good reasons to accept the notion of Hinduism, if only provisionally. In his 2006 essay, "Who Invented Hinduism?," David Lorenzen challenges the claim that "Hinduism was invented or constructed by European colonizers, mostly British, sometime after 1800" and notes that the first documented appearance of "Hinduism," though it does come at the recent date of 1816, is in a text by Rammohan Roy, the Hindu reformer and founder of the Brahmo Samaj, a society dedicated to making Hinduism a world religion.[8] Despite Roy's Indian nationality, this fact taken alone may be more evidence in favor of the xenonymic nature of the word, since Roy was consciously remodeling Hinduism in light of his engagement with Unitarianism.[9] But before the term enters English, we can find many more instances, in various forms, of a word that denotes the traditions of the Brahmins and the sects devoted to Vishnu, Śiva, and the Goddess (Vaiṣṇavas, Śaivas, and Śāktas, respectively) in Spanish, Italian, and Persian sources as well as native accounts dating to the fifteenth century. From this and other evidence, Lorenzen concludes that something recognizable as Hinduism, displaying "many continuities with the earlier Vedic religion" is discernible from the period of the composition of the earliest Purāṇas, which served as focal texts for the temple-based Hindu sects between the fourth and the seventh centuries C.E.[10]

Although Lorenzen and Brian K. Smith both define Hinduism by its relation to the earlier Vedic religion, it is surely the case that some strains of Hinduism are as different from Vedic religion as the Church of England is from Second Temple Judaism. And, more to the point, applying an idea as alien as mimetic theory—derived from Girard's reading of Shakespeare, the

Bible, and Greek drama—to such an array of disparate sects and traditions would seem to exacerbate the distortion that comes from lumping together the traditions of twentieth century Śāktism in Śri Lanka and tenth century B.C.E. Horse Sacrifices in the Panjab. Keeping that in mind, in this book I will focus on the aspects of Hinduism that are directly and demonstrably related to the Vedic tradition. Along with the Vedas themselves, especially the *Ṛg Veda* and the *Yajur Veda*, I will also look at the commentarial tradition contained in the Brāhmaṇas, the ritual speculations of the Mīmāṃsā philosophers, and the Sanskrit epics. And in order to illuminate the multiple connections between Hinduism and the archaic religions on which Girard's work has been mainly focused, I will also look at materials from other Indo-European cultures, including Greece and Scandinavia.

We will conclude that there is such a thing as Hinduism, which undergoes some profound changes from its beginnings in the nomadic culture that produced the *Ṛg Veda* to the transformations and innovations of the subsequent commentarial traditions but maintains an internal consistency and has a familial relationship to other Indo-European traditions. The next question to ask is why one needs to bring René Girard into a book about Hinduism at all.

. . . and Back

This brings us to the book's second aim, which is to see what kind of corrections or nuances the Hindu tradition can offer to Girard's theory of religion, based as it is on his reading of the Western canon from Genesis to *À la recherche du temps perdu*. A brief timeline of the development of Girard's thought will be useful here. After beginning with the pure literary theory of *Deceit, Desire and the Novel*,[11] in which he introduces the triangle of mimetic desire, Girard's work takes an anthropological turn in his seminal *Violence and the Sacred*.[12] It is in this work that he begins to look closely at the myths and rituals of what he calls "archaic religion" and constructs his theory of the violent nature of the sacred and the generative power of the scapegoat mechanism through which sacrifice gives birth to human society. In *Things Hidden since the Foundation of the World*,[13] Girard opposes Christianity and Prophetic Judaism to archaic religions and argues that the "anti-mythology" of the Gospels unmasks the violent sacred and the sacrificial order it has engendered in all cultures. And more recently Girard has turned his attention to the subject of politics in *Battling to the End*,[14] his discussion of the apocalyptic total war envisioned by the nineteenth century Prussian military theorist Carl von Clausewitz, and to the subject of the Brāhmaṇas in *Sacrifice*, his engagement with the work of Sylvain Lévi.

This is the argument that runs through Girard's work in a nutshell, presented here as a kind of mimetic "primal scene." It begins with the idea that humans are separated from other animals by our instinctive mimeticism, through which we learn by imitating other humans (or other types of animals). Like all animals, we have instinctual needs for things like food, water, and sex, but we also have what Mark Johnston has elegantly described as "a surplus of indeterminate yearning," an inner emptiness that our imitative instinct translates into desire.[15] Because desire itself is not therefore instinctual, but a second-order phenomenon, we have no inner instinctual voice telling us *what* to desire in the same way that a grumbling stomach tells us we need food or certain other physiological signs tell us to have sex. In the absence of an intrinsically identifiable object, our imitative or mimetic instinct has to fill in the gap. We learn what to desire the same way we learn how to make tools, namely, by imitating others. And because we only know what to desire by seeing what other people desire, everyone becomes models for imitation for everyone else. On the positive side, this mimesis allows us to learn complex behaviors. On the negative side, it leads to inevitable violence when our desire for the same thing turns our models first into obstacles and then into rivals. The example Girardians frequently use to illustrate this is the room full of children fighting over the same toy despite the presence of other, unused toys in the room that are identical to the toy in dispute. The toy, like every other desired object, has nothing intrinsically desirable about it. It is only desirable because others desire it. If I am a child in that room, my instinct is to imitate some model and if that model is holding a certain toy, then that is the toy I want to be holding too. Objects of desire, then, are incidental and are quickly forgotten when the rivalry they engender escalates.

Rivalry is pure mimesis because it does away with the mediation of a desired object. After all, all objects of desire are in this scheme nothing but substitutes for the impossible thing that can fill our deep unnamable lack, a "plenitude of being," as Girard puts it. As rivalry takes hold, the formerly desired objects become inconsequential and the rivals become more and more like each other until they become doubles, an undifferentiated crowd turning against one another in a war of all against all. The word "undifferentiated" is crucial here because the fact of undifferentiation escalates the violence to its highest pitch and simultaneously opens up the possibility for the event that will bring about its end. With the rivalries no longer mediated (and held together) by objects of desire, they break apart and people begin to turn against each other indiscriminately. In this random movement of aggression, one person inevitably becomes the target of more than one aggressor. And now that more than one person is doing the same thing, order begins to return because there is something to imitate again: there is a crowd.[16] The same mimetic instinct that began the violent escalation begins to take hold again and, in imitation of the two (or more) aggressors who have randomly ganged up on one, a group forms around that one unlucky member of the group. No longer torn apart by fighting over objects of contention that they cannot share, the group now finds cohesion as they become united *against* a target—or, more precisely, a victim—whom they wish not to share, but to destroy.

And so, spontaneously, there is an event: the violence of the mob turns on a single victim, whom they kill or perhaps drive out, experiencing their first taste of unanimity as a result. The death or expulsion of the victim becomes the first mechanism for generating difference. This is significant because Girard insists on this basis that the primary mode of difference is not binary, as the structuralists would have it, but the logic of the exception. The victim is the *e pluribus unum* in two senses, representing the transformation of many individuals into a single community ("from many, one") as well as the expulsion of one from the group ("one out of the many").

Now comes the aftermath. With perfect logic, the pacified crowd reasons that that victim must have caused the chaotic violence that preceded his death and ended immediately after. Alive, he was the cause of the violence. Dead, he is its cure. And this victim is also the first "victim," since up to this point no human or animal has been killed for anything other than the instinctual struggles for food or sex or to establish animal dominance patterns. According to the *Oxford English Dictionary*, the word "victim" is first attested in 1497, when J. Alcock uses the term to refer specifically to sacrificial victims: "Obedyence excellith al vyctyms [printed vyayms] and holocaustis in the whiche was sacrefyced ye flesshe of other creatures." We also find the word *victima* used the same way in Latin. *Victima* and the Modern English "witch" are both related to the Germanic word cluster derived from the Proto-Indo-European **weik*, "consecrate," which includes *wig*, "idol," in Old English; *weihs*, "holy," in Gothic; and *weihen*, "consecrate" in German and has the sense of setting something apart.[17] Through a double transference that is the birth of the sacred, the victim becomes the transcendental signifier, identified by the now peaceful human community as both the cause and cure of the violence. The term "transcendental signifier" is an important one. With this terminology, Girard is responding to Jacques Derrida's rejection of the idea of a "transcendental signified" that exists outside of language and anchors its meaning.[18]

Girard makes plain his differences (no pun intended) with Derrida when he puts forward the victim as the transcendental signifier. But never does he completely dismiss Derrida, as this conversation with his interlocutor Jean-Michel Oughourlian from *Things Hidden* shows:

R.G.: Because of the victim, in so far as it seems to emerge from the community and the community seems to emerge from it, for the first time there can be something like an inside and an outside, a before and after, a community and the sacred. We have already noted that the victim appears to be simultaneously good and evil, peaceable and violent, a life that brings death and a death that guarantees life. Every possible significant element seems to have its outline in the sacred and at the same time to be transcended by it. In this sense the victim does seem to constitute a universal signifier.

J.-M.O.: Are you referring to the idea of a transcendental signifier which has been energetically rejected by current thought?

R.G.: I am not saying that we have found the *true* transcendental signifier. So far we have only discovered what functions in that capacity for human beings.

J.-M.O.: Should not the reference be to a transcendental signified rather than signifier?

R.G.: The signifier is the victim. The signified constitutes all actual and potential meaning the community confers on the victim and, through its intermediacy, on to all victims.[19]

Girard is arguing that before the emergence of language the victim opens the possibility of signification, standing at once for war and peace, life and death. Anyone familiar with the deconstruction of the "transcendental signified" and Derrida's radical critique of origins should note Girard's deft reversal of the linguistic terms by which the victim, as transcendental *signifier*, becomes the origin precisely of all the most basic distinctions of human thought—of space (inside and outside the community) and time (before and after the event), of group identity and the sacred order that transcends it. Neither Girard nor Derrida argues that there has ever been a time in our history in which something or other has not functioned as a transcendental signifier. Indisputably, human culture has operated under the sign of God, Being, Presence, Truth, Emptiness, and so on, but Girard argues that it first operated under the sign of the Victim. And Girard agrees with Derrida that the history of Western thought has been the expulsion of one transcendental signifier by thinkers like Plato, Descartes, and Heidegger only to replace it with another equally unsatisfactory one.

Girard goes on to explain how the transcendental signifier of the victim and the transcendental signified together make the sign of the "reconciliatory victim":

> Since we understand that human beings wish to remain reconciled after the conclusion of the crisis, we can also understand their penchant for reproducing the sign, or in other words for reproducing the language of the sacred by substituting, in ritual, new victims for the original victim, in order to assure the maintenance of that miraculous peace.[20]

Upon this founding murder, "*la fondation du monde*," all culture rests. The first instruments of culture are *ritual*, the repetition (with substitutes) of the founding murder to regain the peace that it brought; *myth*, narratives misconstruing the death of an innocent victim and bearing the general structure of 1) Primal chaos, 2) Accusations against the victim, 3) Death of the victim, and 4) Founding of culture; and *prohibition*, rules designed to circumvent the mimetic rivalries or vengeful cycles that could bring about another crisis, such as prohibitions against twins, who are terrifying reminders of the crisis of undifferentiation.

Myth, ritual, and prohibition provide the structure of all archaic religion. In turn, archaic religion is irrevocably destroyed by the singular revelation of the Gospels, which reveal the scapegoating mechanism of culture by insisting on the innocence, not just of Jesus, but also of all victims of mob persecution and violence. Christianity gives us the idea of the scapegoat, which refers to the paradoxical situation of being conscious of an unconscious process.[21] In light of the narrative of Jesus's death and resurrection, we can no longer be taken in by myth or ritual; we can no longer believe that the victim has done something to deserve his or her fate or that killing the victim has any prophylactic power. This revelation takes away the power of archaic religion by making the scapegoat mechanism visible, after which people begin to take the side of the victims in what Nietzsche calls the "slave revolt" of Christianity. Religions that continue to tell myths of the guilty victim are still locked in the sacrificial system. Christianity, which places all the responsibility on the angry mob and none on its victim, which stubbornly (and perhaps unreasonably) rejects Caiaphas's argument in John 18:14 that it is "expedient that one man should die for the people," is in reality the end of religion, not just a new subspecies.

Had Girard begun with a study of Kālidāsa instead of Shakespeare, or the *Kathāsaritsāgara* instead of *Don Quixote*, the theory described above might have taken on a different shape, especially his conclusion that the revelation of the Gospels alone spells the death of sacrificial religion. Girard himself confesses an ignorance of the Indian tradition in *Sacrifice*, choosing to rely exclusively on one scholarly work written over a century ago by Sylvain Lévi (I will look more closely at this decision in the next chapter).[22] And even in *Sacrifice*, he returns, as ever, to his argument about the intellectual breakthrough of the Gospels, writing, "Wherever the Gospels take root, blood sacrifices disappear forever."[23] One cannot take this too literally, of course. While he is arguing that cults of animal sacrifice, which had long replaced human sacrifice in most places, began to dwindle very quickly after conversion of the Roman Empire to Christianity (a fact that Alan Cameron has recently chalked up to imperial defunding),[24] Girard also notes the many ways in which sacrificial thinking persists in the Christian world. What he means is that *the power of blood sacrifices to stem communal violence disappears.* It is important to note the way in which Girard's trenchant critique of Christianity trumps what some see as his Christian triumphalism. To take Girard seriously is to see Christendom as a thing that should not be, a sacrificial culture based on a misinterpretation of a non-sacrificial event. And because the non-violent Kingdom of God has yet to be created on earth, all the Christian revelation really does is open the floodgates for communal violence. For Girard, unmasking the scapegoat mechanism at the basis of culture is a good thing in absolute terms, but a bad thing in relative terms because it removes an effective safety valve and creates the possibility for truly cataclysmic violence to be unleashed.

Now that we have roughly sketched out Girard's theory, we can move on to the question: to what extent do the Gospels "take root" in India, the part of the world with which this book is concerned? According to the apocryphal *Acts of Saint Thomas*, a Syriac Gnostic text dating to the third century, the disciple Thomas (who bears the very Girardian epithet of Thomas Didymus or "Thomas the Twin" because he was said to have been the twin brother of Jesus) was sent to South India after he was sold into indenture to a trader. There he supposedly preached in the court of the Indo-Parthian King Gondophares. In a second mission, Thomas is said to have visited the land ruled by Mahadeva on the Malabar Coast, where he was martyred.[25]

The historicity of these accounts aside, the Syrian Christian community in India dates back to at least the fourth century (maybe even the second) and still survives today. The state of Goa, where a quarter of the population identifies as Catholic and where the remains of Society of Jesus founder Francis Xavier are interred, was settled by the Portuguese in the early sixteenth century. It was also the last outpost of the Inquisition. We also have evidence of a South Indian Jewish presence dating back to the tenth century in the form of some golden plates inscribed in Tamil. There is also evidence of regular contact with the region in Biblical times. The land of Ophir with which King Solomon trades in 1 Kings 10:11 and 2 Chronicles 9:11 is generally accepted to be the Malabar Coast.[26] Some scholars have even suggested that certain elements from Aśvaghosha's first or second century Buddhist hagiography the *Buddhacarita*, including the temptation by the god of death Māra, found their way into the stories of the life of Christ.[27]

In various more or less indigenous forms, Christianity in India precedes the incursions of the Muslim Mughals, the Catholic Portuguese, and the Protestant British. Ironically (or perhaps not), the region of India where the Gospels took root is also the region where Vedic sacrificial religion is still holding out today. The Malayalam-speaking state of Kerala, home to the oldest Christian communities in India, is also the place where the conservative Nambudiri Brahmins completed the Vedic Agnicayana ritual ("The Piling up of the Fire") with the help of the late Dutch Indologist Frits Staal in April of 2011. It is worth noting that, at least since its modern revival in 1975 and probably long before that, the Agnicayana ritual as performed by the Nambudiris is done without killing.

But for our purposes, the impact of Indian forms of Christianity on Hinduism is beside the point. The question we are trying to answer is whether Girard's theory works outside of the Christian context. Is the Gospels' introduction of the epistemology of the victim the only event capable of undermining the sacrificial system of archaic religion? Is Hindu myth capable of developing a critique of sacrifice on its own? This last question is further complicated by the very real presence in India of regular blood sacrifice made in goddess temples throughout the subcontinent. But before we take this point as an indication that Hinduism fails to critique the sacrificial system, we should see what Girard himself says at the end of *Sacrifice*.

> I cannot conclude these lectures without mentioning certain developments essential to our theme, even if we are unable to treat them at greater length. They have to do, of course—my audience suspects it—with *the presence of an anti-sacrificial and even non-sacrificial inspiration in the most advanced parts of the Vedic tradition*, those which announce the great Indian mysticism of the Upanishads, as well as those which, leaving India, ultimately give rise to Buddhism.[28]

Using Girard's own hermeneutical process, I will argue that there is an "anti-sacrificial and even non-sacrificial inspiration," a robust critique of sacrifice, not only in the late Vedic tradition, but also in the *Mahābhārata* epic and certain strains of philosophical thought. This critique of sacrifice, I will demonstrate, presents itself in a form different than that found in the Gospels and invites some new reflections on mimetic theory.

Examining the Hindu traditions through a Girardian lens over the course of this book, we will see close parallels between Hinduism and other religions, including Christianity, along with some striking differences. What will be most surprising are the ways in which the parallels at first appear to be differences and the differences at first appear to be parallels, like the rope that at first appears to be a snake (or vice versa) in an Indian metaphor that we find, among other places, in the *Yogavāsiṣṭha*: "As when the truth that a rope is a rope is seen and the fear generated by the misunderstanding that it is a snake disappears, the study of this scripture frees one from sorrow, born of saṃsāra [the cycle of rebirth]."[29] Now that we have laid out the first aim of this book, reading Hinduism through mimetic theory, and the second aim, reading mimetic theory through Hinduism, we will move on to the third and final aim, a reexamination of mimetic theory for scholars to whom it might be of good use.

Mimetic Theory and the Study of Religion: Ideological Concerns

The tertiary aim of this book, coming out of the second, is to "rehabilitate" mimetic theory for scholars working in the field of religious studies, where Girard has been dismissed for so long that his name has largely disappeared from mainstream academic discourse except as a historical footnote. From the standpoint of a historian of religions, criticisms of Girard's work boil down to a few major points. First, it is Christocentric, creating an anthropological philosophy that privileges a specifically Christian understanding of religion. Second, his theory attempts to explain cultural phenomena like myths and rituals plucked from various traditions without first understanding them in situ. Third, Girard's readings are too selective and speculative, predictably concluding that each myth he examines is the disguised story of a collective murder and that all indications otherwise are obfuscations.

Some of Girard's bad press has to do with his being branded a reactionary, beginning with Hayden White's review of *Violence and the Sacred*, which compares Girard's thought to that of the Counter-Enlightenment thinker Joseph de Maistre, whose political theology accepts the sacrifice of individuals for the greater good and espouses the "noble lie" that conceals the illegitimate origins of power.[30] In *The Headless Republic*, Jesse Goldhammer picks up this argument again, handing down the judgment that

"Girard's conservative theory of sacrifice is thoroughly Maistrian in political orientation."[31] Countering this rather superficial misreading, Ivan Strenski has given a much more nuanced critique of Girard's work, opposing it to de Maistre's utterly:

> Girard's theory of sacrifice should be seen as *rejection* of a view of sacrifice originally developed in the seventeenth-century Eucharistic theology of the Roman Catholic reaction to the Reformation in France . . . This theology of sacrifice was agent in shaping French spirituality not only in the critical period of the Counter-Reformation, but also enjoyed special revivals in the works of Joseph de Maistre.[32]

Elsewhere, Strenski picks up on the specific ethical concerns in Girard:

> Girard's concern with the violence of sacrifice seems driven then by heated contemporary public concern having to do with the everyday, systematic exploitation—read "victimization"—of people as a result of their disadvantaged class, gender, economic status, or location in the third world . . . Witness to the moral salience of Girard's theory of sacrifice, one should note how his work has entered into the discourse of Latin American liberation theologians and social justice activists.[33]

Strenski identifies five main elements that oppose his thought to reactionary Roman Catholicism, all of which would be familiar to anyone who has read any of Girard's books. First, while the reactionary point of view accepts as a necessity the violence of the sacrifice, Girard deplores it, memorably excoriating Georges Bataille for being "primarily inclined to treat violence as some rare and precious condiment, the only spice still capable of stimulating the jaded appetite of modern man."[34] Second, the reactionary point of view sees violence as foundational to all human institutions, even Christianity, while Girard argues that it is foundational to all human institutions *except* Christianity (though it is perhaps foundational to Christendom). Third, the reactionary point of view affirms the continuing expiatory power of the sacrifice while Girard denies it. Fourth, Girard and the reactionary Roman Catholics both see Jesus's death as a focal point of history. But while the reactionary explanation is that the crucifixion is the culmination of sacrifice, Girard argues that it is the non-sacrificial act that destroys sacrifice forever. Finally, the reactionary Roman Catholics see the Eucharist as a repetition of Christ's sacrifice while Girard sees it as an act of remembrance and an opportunity to imitate Christ without mimetic rivalry.[35]

One needs only to read any of Girard's work to see the groundlessness of those arguments condemning him as a reactionary and a naïve Christian apologist. But even if Girard came out in interviews as a raving right-wing Christian triumphalist (he does not), scholars would probably have no objection to appropriating his theories on those grounds alone. If that were so, the works of Heidegger and Carl Schmitt would not be the perennial topics of dissertations, books, and articles that they are today. So we must also take up the more important and difficult task of answering objections to Girard's work on methodological grounds.

Mimetic Theory and the Study of Religion: Methodological Concerns

Leaving aside the ideological implication of Girard's theory, there are those who object on the grounds that it is ahistorical and places an undertheorized and uncritically received model of religion at the foundation of human culture. David Frankfurter, to take a recent example, refers to the idea that "religion and the sacred might give rise to *every* conceivable act" as "a rather self-indulgent line of speculation encouraged by the writings of René Girard and Mircea Eliade."[36]

More problematic still for historians of religions is Girard's crypto-theological insistence that the Gospels are the absolute revelation of mimetic desire, the scapegoat mechanism, and the founding murder and that all myths are exercises in obscuring or effacing the same. Girard presents this argument in a particularly strong form in *Sacrifice*:

> They are completely deceived, who say it is the Gospels and the Bible that think in terms of scapegoats and covert persecutions because they speak openly of these things whereas myths never speak of them. Myths never speak of them because they are entirely possessed by them. They are completely deceived, who hold that myths are too luminous, too sunlit, too Greek to be guilty of secret persecutions.[37]

Simply put, Girard argues that myths, like the crowd that crucified Christ, "know not what they do," while the Gospels know what they do.

There are two issues to address with this claim. The first is the uniqueness of the Gospels, which we must separate from the superiority of the Gospels. The second is Girard's assumption of the sameness of myth, from Sophocles's version of Oedipus to Livy's Romulus and Remus to the Vedic hymn of Prajāpati to the Milomaki story told by the Ojibway tribe of North America. The Girardian theologian Raymund Schwager, after attempting to reconcile the theological problem of the "Wrath of God" with Girard's reading of the Christian Bible, concludes that "[a] comprehensive method is necessary, which assesses both pagan and Judeo-Christian narratives by the same criteria."[38] But when it comes to his reading of myths and the Gospels, it is by no means clear that this is what Girard himself is doing. It seems rather that Girard is ruthless in his readings of myths, while he reads the Gospels through rose-colored lenses.

To take an example, we will look at Girard's attempted non-mythological reading of the birth of Jesus, whose superficial similarities to the stories of the Hindu god Kṛṣṇa's birth have been the occasion for more than one misguided and distorted comparison. Many have commented on the mythic elements in the story of Jesus's virgin birth: the mating of a god with a human woman, unnatural occurrences that accompany the birth (like a guiding star), and the presence of a vengeful enemy who is seeking to destroy the child. Girard recognizes this and explains:

> To put its message across, no doubt the virgin birth of Jesus still resorts to the same 'code' as do the monstrous births of mythology . . . The Gospels can make use of this 'code' without being brought down to the level of the clumsy mystification and 'mystical naivety,' which our philosophers customarily see in them.[39]

Despite its uncomfortable resemblance to a myth, the immaculate conception of Jesus is, for Girard, essential to the Gospels since it locates him outside of the taint of human violence and the brotherhood of Cain.[40] Then why, we may ask, do Matthew and Luke make such a point to establish his descent from the earthly King David? More puzzling still, why does Matthew trace his descent through Joseph, who is not even Jesus's true father?

Girard remarks on the lack of violence and mimetic doubling in the story of Jesus's birth.[41] This is true enough, but how can we forget this story from Matthew 2:16:

> When Herod saw that he had been tricked by the wise men, he was infuriated, and he sent and killed all the children in and around Bethlehem who were two years old or under, according to the time that he had learned from the wise men.[42]

What is this if not an infanticide to eliminate a rival king, as well as an analogue to the sacrificial death of the Egyptian first-born in Exodus? And what is John the Baptist if not a mimetic rival whose violent death by decapitation is the occasion for the beginning of Jesus's ministry? Can we not chalk up the absence of overt rivalry between John and Jesus as just the kind of obfuscation and erasure that myths always perform to conceal violence?

Girard would argue that there is no rivalry between Jesus and John and no violence. But he does not let the absence of violence in other stories stop him from positing its hidden existence in them. The following passage from *Sacrifice* is a case in point. Girard has just finished analyzing the myth of the cosmic giant Puruṣa's willing dismemberment to create the universe:

> This is essential, and I shall summarize it once more: somewhere in an indeterminate past there must have been a crime attributed to Purusha. It was of course only a projection—imaginary but necessary for the fabrication of a really odious scapegoat. If Purusha no longer appears guilty, it must be due to the extreme age of the myth, which has effaced everything that in the genesis of the religious order is unsettling, anything that might potentially reveal the founding violence.[43]

If the Brahmins could efface the signs of mimetic violence from their myths, could the Gospel writers not do the same?

Girard's reading of every text but the Gospels is relentless in the search for the mythic account of the founding murder. And although he has given us elaborate justifications for why the Gospels are exempt from such a critique, none of them is especially satisfying. In the end there is no way to justify the sharp distinction Girard makes between the Gospels and myths without first granting the Gospels the status of transcendent revelation. And I am not prepared to do that any more than I am prepared to accept the *apauruṣeya* or "non-human" origin of the Vedas. We must conclude then that the revelation that is at the heart of mimetic theory is not in the Gospels, but in Girard's brilliant reading of them.[44]

On the status of the Gospels, hardcore Girardians will vehemently object to my assessment. Others who are suspicious of Girard to begin with will wonder why this does not disqualify mimetic theory as rigorous scholarship. In answer to the former objection, let me be clear that I care nothing for maintaining the integrity of or defending the mimetic theory. As far as I am concerned, Girard's legacy to religious studies and the humanities in general is not some theoretical edifice, but rather a set of reading practices that share with the best work of Derrida the goal of unmasking the violence that is so cleverly concealed in texts. In answer to the latter objection: the proof is in the pudding. Having addressed some of the potential methodological and ideological concerns about using mimetic theory, we will now see how Girard himself sounds a note of caution.

Tiresias and the *Ṛṣi*

At the end of his trenchant critique of Girard's non-sacrificial reading of the Gospels, Lucien Scubla concludes with this charitable caveat: "All those who have had the opportunity to converse with [Girard] have been able to appreciate his extreme modesty and know that he never fails to point out the partial and lacunary nature of his research and his results."[45] On this point, although he has not said it in print, Girard has recently reflected that he should never have called mimetic theory a "theory" at all, but that he did so because at the time he was beginning his work "every Frenchman needed to have a theory." If it's not a theory, he was asked by Robert Hamerton-Kelly, then what is it? "Just some observations on human nature," replied Girard.[46]

It is in light of this disclosure that I turn to Girard's very early essay, "Tiresias and the Critic," which he delivered as an introduction to the infamous conference held at the Johns Hopkins Humanities Center in October of 1966 that simultaneously introduced structuralism and post-structuralism to the United States. The paper contains what I think is some of Girard's most elegant writing. In it he sketches out some "observations about human nature" in the form of a warning about the pitfalls of theory that we should read alongside his later pronouncements about the archaic and the Christian.

> The blind prophet may well take such pride in having uncovered the illusions of his fellowmen, the demystificator may be so satisfied with his demystification that he, himself, may fall, ultimately, into an illusion almost identical to that of his adversary. At this point, everything Oedipus says of Tiresias will become as true as Tiresias's interpretation of Oedipus. Reciprocity is perfect; reciprocity, in the myth, is always perfect. Tiresias, losing sight of the fact that no God, really, speaks through him; forgetting that his truth, partial and limited, bears the imprint of its true origin which is the heated debates and battles of men as well as the imbrication of converging desires; Tiresias will think he incarnates the truth and he will abandon himself to oracular vaticinations. He, too, will believe that all riddles are solved, that all pitfalls are in the past.[47]

Not all riddles are solved. Not all pitfalls are in the past. Girard's warning not to forget "the heated debates and battles of men" and "the imbrication of converging desires" that are the origins of our truths is an appropriate one at this juncture, as we begin to examine how mimetic theory might fit into the study of Hindu myths. Not only is Girard's truth the product of intellectual debates involving scholars like Sylvain Lévi, Georges Dumézil, and Marcel Mauss (debates we will examine in the next chapter), the Sanskrit texts that have come down to us are also products of centuries of battles, intellectual and otherwise. As we enter the world of words of the Vedic seers, we must not make the mistake of the old Theban oracle and take partial and limited truths for transcendent and universal ones.

We scholars may not be as blind as Tiresias, but we are certainly subject to a tunnel vision that shows us what we want to see, a myopic distortion that lends everything a fuzzy sameness, and a farsightedness that only allows us to see the differences over there and not the similarities over here. Not without reason is cultural myopia the charge that critics have frequently hurled at Girard as well as the one that has haunted Indology for the last thirty years or so. To try and clear our vision a bit, it will be useful to spend some time with the highly mimetic game of ethnocentrism.

Ethnocentrism, Christocentrism, and Hinduphobia

Responding to Robert Jewett in a discussion recorded in *Violent Origins*, Girard complains that he is nauseated by arguments against Christianity that make reference to its bloody past.

> Never before in history have people spent so much time throwing victims at one another's heads as a substitute for other weapons. This can only happen in a world that though far from Christian, to be sure, is totally permeated by the values of the gospel. Nietzsche was correct in saying this.[48]

Girard is referring, of course, to the argument Nietzsche makes in the first essay of *The Genealogy of Morals* about the "slave revolt" and the consequent imposition of slave morality that accompanies Christianity's triumph over the pagan world. In Girard's theory, the morality of Christianity even underlies the arguments *against* Christianity. For Girard, the critique of Western scholarly constructions of the "Orient" begun by Edward Said in 1978 and subsequently taken up by a whole generation of scholars is another example of taking the side of the victim against the aggressors. In the pre-Christian world, Girard might argue, no one would even think to question the position that might makes right. But he also makes a more controversial point when he says that what appears to be ethnocentrism may not be a bad thing, or even a socially constructed thing. It may be an objective truth.

> The question I wish to put to modern anthropology concerning the Bible is why the privilege granted the Bible by Western people is to be considered only the result of ethnocentrism. Could there not be a good substantive reason for that privilege—reason arising out of the Bible's power to disclose the truth about human society?[49]

Here Girard leaves his chin out, opening himself up for a knockout blow. Behind his question is a host of assumptions that Girard states outright in the next few sentences. He paints a picture of an academic conspiracy, beginning with one of the fathers of comparative religion, J. G. Frazer, to discredit the revelation of the Gospels by pointing out that they are nothing but warmed-over retellings of the myth of the dying and rising god.

> [The] same anthropologists who do not want to consider murder an important element in the creation of mythology, when they start talking about the Bible, curiously agree that the proof that the Gospels are the same thing as mythology is the Passion. Thus, rather curiously, they express precisely what I contend: that at the center of all myth, at the center of all culture, stands the same great event, the event of the scapegoat. This the New Testament discloses.[50]

There are some major problems here whose exposition can also help us to address Girard's general critique of comparative religion. The first is the assumption that identifying the Passion as a mytheme is some kind of admission that collective murder is at the heart of culture. Frazer aside, the scholar who identifies Jesus's death and resurrection as a mythic trope is only saying that the death and resurrection of a god is one mytheme among many, not the cornerstone of culture.

But, returning to Frazer, we must note that Girard is not the first to accuse him of attempting to turn the crucifixion into an Orphic myth. In Frazer's own time, his most savage critic was the anthropologist Andrew Lang, who reviewed *The Golden Bough* four times, once in an essay devoted solely to dismantling Frazer's picture of the crucifixion, and wrote an entire book, 1901's *Magic and Religion*, to systematically dispute Frazer's thesis. Frazer's biographer Robert Ackerman reproduces a letter Lang wrote to a friend while working on *Magic and Religion* in which Lang compares criticizing Frazer to "hitting a child" and writes mockingly, "[The] gifted author thinks he has exploded all of Christianity . . . One laughs out loud at the absurdity of it."[51] On the matter of the success or failure of Frazer's project, I stand with J. Z. Smith, who argues that Frazer deliberately sets himself up to fail, that in the end there are no answers because there are no questions, only a meandering journey through "the long tragedy of human folly and suffering."[52] Smith writes: "The *Bough* is broken and all that it cradled has fallen. It has been broken not only by subsequent scholars, but also by the deliberate action of its author."[53]

But we must also look at Frazer's own attitude toward the relationship between comparative religion and Christianity. In an April 1904 letter to a friend, Frazer expresses his reservations about accepting his friend James Hope Moulton's invitation to teach at Didsbury College, a Methodist seminary in Manchester.

> I should be implicitly bound to conceal my own belief in the falseness of Christianity, and, I suppose, not to put before students facts which might tend to undermine their faith . . . But the facts of comparative religion appear to me subversive of Christian theology; and in putting them before my students without any express reference to Christianity, I should still feel as if I were undermining their faith, contrary to my implied promise not to do so.[54]

It looks like Frazer's attitude is a perfect example of the anti-Biblical slant of comparative religion Girard is complaining about in *Sacrifice*, where he makes the rather strident claim that the "comparative study of religion . . . has no interest, ultimately, but to demonstrate the banality of the Gospels in the context of world religion."[55]

But here I must object. Even if it were the main interest of comparative religion (it is not), the banalization of Christianity is certainly not its lasting legacy. Rather, comparative religion has long served the interest of the liberal democracy and capitalism that are the legacies of Christianity, effectively normalizing and secularizing the Christian values of the individual with its attendant liberties and obligations. Girard clearly thinks of himself as an outsider to the discipline and often appears hostile to its aims. He has a deep suspicion of those who do comparative religion that sometimes comes off as downright reactionary, at which time he deserves a robust challenge. Girard complains, "If we questioned the good faith of Indian mysticism or Buddhist scripture in the manner in which we do the Gospels, we would be suspected of an 'ethnocentric' bias."[56]

On this count, he is both right and very wrong. Scholars who study Hindu texts with any variety of the hermeneutics of suspicion (and surely mimetic theory qualifies) have indeed come under fire for their "ethnocentrism," but not from the academy, as Girard would expect. Since India's leap into global prominence following economic liberalization in 1991, a movement has begun among American Hindus to combat what they see as a skewed portrayal of Hinduism in high schools and universities. Picking up the arguments of postcolonial studies, these groups have attacked American scholarship as "Hinduphobic," written by outsiders who are bent on undermining their tradition. And the ongoing deadlock between secular scholars (both Western and Indian) and right-wing Hindus is yet another example of mimesis, in which Hindu "fundamentalist" politics have become a reflection of the politics of their school board-controlling Christian counterparts in Kansas, waging wars to get Darwin and hippies out of their textbooks.

The introduction to *Invading the Sacred*, a volume of essays attacking Western scholarship on Hinduism, catalogs the academy's offenses:

> India, once a major civilizational and economic power that suffered centuries of decline, is now newly resurgent in business, geopolitics and culture. However, a powerful counterforce within the American academy is systematically undermining core icons and ideals of Indic culture and thought. For instance, scholars of this counterforce have disparaged the *Bhagavad Gita* as a dishonest book; declared Ganesha's trunk a limp phallus; classified Devi as the mother with a penis and Shiva as a notorious womanizer who incites violence in India.[57]

Over the last several years, these Hindu critics have pushed back hard against the scholarly community, petitioning for the removal of books, disrupting academic talks, and publishing their own polemical indictments of American scholarship on Hinduism, especially that done by Rice University's Jeff Kripal and other scholars counted among "Wendy's children," the large number of contemporary academics trained by the University of Chicago's Wendy Doniger. Since the publication in 2009 of Doniger's *The Hindus*, which topped the nonfiction best-seller list in India, these attacks have taken the form of a petition to have the book withdrawn by Penguin and a coordinated campaign of polemical negative reviews on Amazon.com.

In his article on the conflict, McComas Taylor describes a demonstration intended to put pressure on the National Book Critics Circle to withdraw *The Hindus* from consideration for its annual award:

> On a chilly evening in March 2010, demonstrators converged on the New School, a university in downtown New York. Mobilised by the United States Hindu Alliance (USHA) and the Hindu Janajagruti Samiti, they paraded behind barricades holding placards that read "Support fairness," "Don't reward mediocrity," and "Her book is a work of fiction." The participants had been required to register with the alliance beforehand, and were asked to "adhere to the high standards of USHA and Hindu Scriptures." They were advised that "the use of any profane, indecent or uncharitable language is strictly prohibited," and that vegetarian samosas would be served after the march.[58]

One reviewer of *The Hindus* on Amazon.com (who has clearly never heard of Bart Ehrman) even seems to present a mirror image of Girard's "ethnocentric bias" comment, implying that the Western academy would never tolerate any of its *own* religions being dragged through the mud with such slanderous lies and brazen impiety. H. Nagarajao, who has reviewed *The Hindus* on Amazon.com, writes:

> As expected, dissappointing [*sic*] and full of inaccuracies and manipulated lies to show Hinduism down. If one would truly understand Hinduism one would not write a book like this. Wonder what would be the reviews like if the author write [*sic*] something similar on Islam or Christianity or on Jews??[59]

Mounting a more coherent if just as distorted attack is an article by Aseem Shukla for the *Washington Post* blog with the rather possessive title "Whose History Is It Anyway?" It begins with the line, "History empowers and history emasculates," and since he is as an assistant professor of urologic surgery, we can be assured Dr. Shukla knows whereof he speaks when he talks about emasculation. He takes issue with the playful tone of Doniger's writing (she is fond of wordplay), her choice of subject matter (he accuses her of "privileging the absurd," putting himself in the strange position of pointing out absurdities in Hindu scriptures), and her lack of the "restraint and sensitivity, if not deference" with which a scholar should approach religion.[60] Between the Hindu right's accusations of ethnocentrism and Girard's accusations of reverse ethnocentrism, historians of religions are wrong at every turn. But at this point I must protest again. It is no more a question of ethnocentrism when we ask whether the Brahmin authors of certain Vedic texts are trying to reify their position of privilege than it is when we ask if "the text of Luke was modified by preoccupations of a modern, propagandistic nature" (the specific line of inquiry to which Girard is objecting with his "ethnocentric" comment).[61]

One of the ugliest incidents in this ongoing conflict happened in Pune on December 22, 2003. Led by city unit chief Rambhau Parekh, a group of activists from the Hindu identity organization the Shiv Sena protested the publication of James Laine's highly controversial *Shivājī: A Hindu King in Islamic India* (Oxford: Oxford University Press, 2003). Although the book had already been withdrawn by the publisher, the protestors attacked Sanskrit scholar Shrikant Bahulkar for his involvement with the book, dragging him into the street and blackening his face.[62] But it is misleading to associate these protests with an angry mob looking for a scapegoat like something out of the Girardian primal scene. The voices of protest against Doniger and "Wendy's children" are neither coming from an angry mob nor a *fatwa*-issuing ayatollah. They are coming from a well educated and affluent diasporic community that is taking advantage of the self-imposed instability in which the discipline of religious studies has been mired as a direct result of its engagement with continental philosophy filtered through the postcolonial lens. Their goal is to buy and bully their way into a seat at the table and gain control over the discourse of Hinduism in order to impose their own version of history.

With the idea that the poison is also the cure, at this point I will turn to the recent work of the French philosopher Alain Badiou, a stern critic of identity politics and much postmodern thought. With his Marxist-atheist reading of Paul's letter to the Romans as the foundation of universalism, Badiou provides us with, to use the terminology of Clifford Geertz, both a "model of" and a "model for" reading Hindu texts in the face of opposition from their self-appointed guardians. Badiou's reading of Romans is a "model of" in that he declares at the outset that he approaches the work of Paul caring nothing for "the Good News he declares or the cult dedicated to him" but as a complete outsider who sees in Paul's writing something of profound importance.[63] It is a "model for" because of what Badiou sees in Paul's message, namely "a case of mobilizing a universal singularity both against the prevailing abstractions (legal then, economic now), and against communitarian or particularist protest."[64] In the well-funded movement against "Wendy's children" we see at work the twin pincers Badiou identifies as abstract homogeneity of capital and identitarian protest working together to obliterate the possibility of truth claims made by those whom the vocal Hindu activists would silence.

Writing about Paul's disagreements with the apostles, whose claims to authority as eyewitnesses to Jesus's life and guardians of his tradition Paul rejects completely, Badiou throws down the gauntlet: "At a time when the importance of 'memory' as the guardian of meaning and of historical consciousness as a substitute for politics is being urged on us by all sides, the strength of Paul's position cannot fail to escape us."[65] It is true that the just rejection of colonial domination, especially in India, where stories of the practices of widow-burning and human sacrifice were used to justify governing and "enlightening" the benighted Hindus, has left us with an unwillingness to impose our truths on another. But, as Slavoj Žižek reminds us in *Living in the End Times* (following, appropriately enough, some quoted material from Doniger's introduction to the *Laws of Manu*), "One should reject the idea that globalization threatens local traditions, that it flattens differences: sometimes it threatens them, more often it keeps them alive, resuscitates them, or even creates them by way of ex-apting them to new conditions."[66]

Transfigured by postcolonialism and globalization, the scholarly study of religion has limited itself to the point where broad humanistic claims like Girard's are virtually unthinkable. But as thinkers like Badiou and Žižek are showing us, this self-conscious circumspection is a fraud.[67] Forbidding oneself to make universal claims is not the same as being unable to make them. In this era, when the morbid self-absorption that followed the collapse of imperial arrogance has allowed ideologues like those who would define India, a secular democracy with a twenty percent Muslim population, as a "Hindu nation," to make inroads into academic discourse, we have good reason to give Girard a retrial. We can only use the study of religion to understand the human, Girard insists, if we do so out of ethical responsibility toward the victim—past, present, and future.

René Girard and the Temple of Doom; or, Did They Really Kill People?

Now a new question arises: If we accept Girard's theory as a useful one, why look at the Hindu tradition at all, other than to perform the rather banal exercise of multiplying Girardian readings ad nauseam? For one reason, because in *Sacrifice* Girard himself suggests that this would be a worthy project that he is unable to undertake. For another reason, the number of texts on sacrifice (ritual, mythological, philosophical) from the Hindu and Vedic traditions dwarfs all others. And scholars have barely scratched the surface of this textual tradition. But more important, the institution of human sacrifice is uniquely present in the Hindu tradition in a way that illuminates its connection to the other Indo-European cultures of antiquity as well as the indigenous practices of India's tribal people, some of whose linguistic family ties extend through Polynesia to Australia.

To give an example of how comparative readings within the Hindu tradition can shed light on the ideas of sacrifice, let us briefly look at the work of Roy E. Jordaan and Robert Wessing, who utilize textual and archaeological research to demonstrate the presence of actual human sacrifice in Hinduism, beginning with the discovery of two human skeletons along with a number of animal skeletons at a Śaiva temple complex in Prambanan, Central Java, that dates to the ninth century.[68] Jordaan and Wessing challenge the popular idea that the Puruṣamedha, or human sacrifice, was never much more than a story in India, and that if it were ever real it would certainly have been long gone by the time of the Hindu-Buddhist conversion of Java. Following this assumption, scholars would have to conclude that whatever caused those skeletons to be buried under the temple must have been some indigenous Javanese practice unrelated to Hinduism. This is a tenuous argument, Jordaan and Wessing point out, since "[considering] the enormous quantity of material that still has to be translated and examined, the claim that human sacrifice is but a fantasy seems rather premature. . . ."[69] To answer the question of its "Hindu-ness" they point out that the Javanese temple is constructed according to the specification of the Śilpaśāstra, a ritual and architectural system for temple-building that received a fixed form around the eighth century C.E. but is based on oral traditions much older than that. One Śilpaśāstra text, the medieval Orissan *Śilpa Prakāśa*, calls for making *bali* ("offering") to the terrifying goddesses Durgā, Kālī, Raudrī, and Bhuvaneśvarī, who are known for receiving blood offerings.[70] Jordaan and Wessing also point out that some of the Śilpaśāstra texts, referring to special rituals that must be performed in the night, suggest a more violent esoteric tradition that supplements the exoteric rites done in daylight.

The discovery of the human and animal skeletons in Java raises some important questions: How are we to conceive of the relationship between Hindu text and Hindu practice? How do we understand the relationship between Sanskrit-based translocal forms of religion and vernacular-based local forms? Is there any evidence for a religious substrate underlying specific practices like human sacrifice observed from western Asia to Indonesia? Opposing nineteenth and early twentieth century Indologists' overemphasis on sanitized forms of Vedic religion and their offhand dismissal of the scandal of human sacrifice, Jordaan and Wessing conclude that "[a] more promising avenue of approach is presented by the relatively recent work by Girard, [Walter] Burkert and others in which phenomena like violence and ritual killing are recognized as ever recurring elements in religious practice generally."[71] The reality of human sacrifice is not a question at all for Girard, but an Indologist cannot be so hasty. In the final two sections of this introduction, we will examine the arguments for and against real institutional human sacrifice in Indian history.

The Astika *Position: Biblical Hermeneutics and Colonial Interventions*[72]

The European colonial powers' treatment of religious violence in India has oscillated between ignoring or marginalizing it and sensationalizing it for political purposes. Since at least the beginning of the nineteenth century, human sacrifice in India has remained a topic of interest for scholars. The most wide-ranging and complete survey of its instances in the literature came when Albrecht Weber, a close friend of F. Max Müller (another one of the fathers of comparative religion), published his essay "Uber Menschenopfer bei den Indern der vedischen Zeit" in 1864 (and enlarged it in 1868). Weber's study covers every instance of human sacrifice in Vedic literature, including the story of Manu's wife that Girard examines in *Sacrifice*.[73] In 1876, the Indian scholar Rājendralāla Mitra published "On Human Sacrifices in Ancient India" in *The Journal of the Asiatic Society of Bengal*, in which he argued that there were human sacrifices in ancient times that have continued up to the recent past. An officer in (and critic of) the Indian Civil Service as well as a pioneer in the study of Indian folklore, William Crooke lent more support to the argument for the reality of human sacrifices in *The Popular Religion and Folklore of Northern India*, published in 1896. Doing fieldwork in the districts of Etah, Saharanpur, Gorakhpur, and Mirzapur, Crooke studied the local sects devoted to the fierce goddess Durgā and her associated guardian deities and found numerous references to human sacrifice in ethnographic reports as well as official records. On the textual side, Willem Caland made a significant contribution to the ongoing discussion in 1926–1928 with his translation and publication of fragments of a previously unknown ritual text called the *Vādhūla-Sūtra*, which we will examine in chapter five.

The idea of human sacrifice still occurring in India made it a particularly good example of the barbarism of non-Christian religions for Christian apologists. In volume two of his *The Character of Moses Established for Veracity as an Historian, Recording Events from the Creation to the Deluge*, published in 1816, the Anglican vicar, physician, geologist, and amateur historian Joseph Townsend sets India alongside the classical world and pre-Christian Europe as an example of the persistence of the ancient institution of human sacrifice in the dark corners of the empire. In the fourth section, "Of Sacrifice," Townsend rattles off some gory examples of the practice from Greece, Troy, Carthage, Gaul, Germany, Sweden, Russia, Denmark, and Peru before he gets to India.

> Among the sacred books of the Hindoos [*sic*], the Ramayuna [*sic*] demands particular attention, because of its antiquity, the extent of country through which it is revered, and the view which it exhibits of the religion, doctrine, mythology, customs, and manners of their remote progenitors.
>
> In this we have a golden age of short duration, succeeded by a state of universal wickedness and violence, which continued till the deity, incarnate, slew the oppressors of the human race, and thus restored the reign of piety and virtue.
>
> This poem contains a description of the Ushwamedha [*sic*], or most solemn sacrifice of the white horse, instituted by Swuymbhoo [*sic*], that is,

> by the self-existent. At the celebration of this festival, the monarch, as the representative of the whole nation, acknowledged his transgressions; and when the offerings were consumed by the sacrificial fire, he was considered as perfectly absolved from his offences. Then follows a particular account of a human sacrifice, in which the victim, distinguished for filial piety, for resignation to his father's will, and for purity of heart, was bound by the king himself and delivered to the priest; but at the very instant when his blood was to have been shed, this illustrious youth was by miracle delivered; and the monarch, as the reward of his intended sacrifice, received virtue, prosperity, and fame.
>
> *It is well known that the Brahmins have in all ages had their human victims, and that even in our days thousands have voluntarily perished under the wheels of their god Jaghernaut* [*sic*].[74]

This lengthy quotation is worth reproducing because it gives us a quick overview of the highlights of sensationalist colonial Indology. In his reading of the ever-popular Sanskrit epic, the *Rāmāyaṇa*, Taylor seems to conflate the plot with a truncated version of the Purāṇic conception of time as a series of successively worsening ages or *yugas*, named after the four throws of the dice in the sacrificial ritual. Roughly analogous to the Golden, Silver, Bronze, and Iron Ages described in Ovid's *Metamorphoses* 1.89–150, they begin with the Golden Age (Kṛta Yuga), then on to the Age of the Trey (Treta Yuga), the Age of the Deuce (Dvāpara Yuga), and finally the Dark Age (Kali Yuga), which ends in apocalyptic violence and then the cosmic dissolution (*mahāpralaya*) that ushers in a new Golden Age.

Next Townsend describes the most elaborate of all the Vedic rituals, the Aśvamedha or Horse Sacrifice, a ceremony performed to consecrate a king's reign that requires a horse to roam free for one year. Followed by the king's army, the horse's circuit marks the ritual boundary of the new kingdom. And since anyone who tries to stop the horse would have to defeat the king's army to do it, it becomes the de facto boundary as well. The Horse Sacrifice performed at the end of some versions of the *Rāmāyaṇa* by the victorious divine King Rāma to consecrate his kingdom of Ayodhya is interrupted when the twins Lava and Kuśa—the sons of Rāma living (unknown to their father) with their exiled mother and Valmīki, the sage who is author of the epic—capture the horse and defeat Rāma's army. Hearing that two young warriors have defeated his best men, Rāma comes himself to the village where Lava and Kuśa have his sacrificial horse and engages them in an Oedipal battle (and in the popular Bengali version of the epic composed by Kṛttibāsa, he loses).

From there, Townsend continues to the story of Śunaḥśepa, the Brahmin boy who is offered to the god Varuṇa in place of the son of King Hariścandra (more about which in chapter two). And finally he moves on to contemporary accounts of the Jagannāth ("Lord of the World"), a deity identified with the Vaiṣṇava god Kṛṣṇa and represented by a face painted on a giant wooden disc that is wheeled on a cart through the streets in *ratha yatras* or "cart festivals" in the northeastern states of Bengal and Orissa. The most famous of these festivals occurs in June or July in the Orissan Vaiṣṇava center of Puri, where three giant carts carrying Jagannāth, his brother Balarāma, and their sister Subhādra are pulled two kilometers through the streets to the Gundicha Temple. The largest of the carts, the one carrying Jagannāth, is forty-five feet high and forty-five feet square, resting on sixteen wheels, each of them seven feet in diameter, a vehicle whose immensity and seeming unstoppability caused the name of the god to enter the English language as "juggernaut." Townsend's account of modern day deaths under the wheels of the cart stems from the fact that the British colonial administrators had alarming reports of devotees throwing themselves under the wheels of Jagannāth's car in the belief that being crushed by the god would send them straight to Heaven. The sixteenth century *Caitanya Caritāmṛta*, the central text of Gauḍiya Vaiṣṇavism (the source of ISKCON, the International Society for Krishna Consciousness or "Hare Krishnas") records an instance of the practice in which a low-caste and leprous devotee of the Lord Caitanya (an incarnation of Kṛṣṇa and his consort Rādhā fused into one body) is resolved to throw himself under the wheels of Jagannāth until he is advised about the impiety of suicide by Caitanya himself.[75]

Townsend's account of "Hindoo" sacrifice from the pages of the *Rāmāyaṇa* to the streets of Puri is quoted in full in the Methodist theologian Adam Clarke's gloss on Romans 9:33 ("As it is written, Behold, I lay in Zion a stumbling stone and rock of offence: and whosoever believeth on him shall not be ashamed") in his six-thousand-page 1831 Biblical commentary. The Townsend quotation is introduced with, "On the subject of vicarious punishment, or rather the case of one becoming an anathema or sacrifice for the public good, in illustration of Romans 9:3 ['For I could wish that I myself were accursed, separated from Christ for the sake of my brethren, my kinsmen according to the flesh'], I shall make no apology for the following extracts, taken from an author whose learning is vast, and whose piety is unblemished."[76] Also included in the quotation is Townsend's lamentation about the iniquity into which humans fell after losing sight of the true God:

> How much was it to be lamented, that even civilized natures should forget the intention for which sacrifices were originally instituted! The bad effects, however, would not have been either so extensive or so great, had they not wholly lost the knowledge of Jehovah; and taken, as the object of their fear, that evil and apostate spirit whose name, with the utmost propriety is called Apollyon, or the destroyer, and whose worship has been universally diffused at different periods among all the nations of the earth.[77]

Apollyon, or Abbadon in Hebrew, is described in Revelations 9:11 as the "angel of the abyss" and is identified by Townsend as the bloodthirsty demon of which "Jaghernaut" is but an avatar (so to speak). For Clarke, it is Apollyon who is the chief beneficiary of the spread of the Calvinist heresy. The gist of Clarke's commentary is a refutation of Calvinist predestination in favor of a Wesleyan-Arminian view. He concludes that anyone who propagates Calvinism, "far from producing *glory to God in the highest, and peace and good will among men*, [has] filled the Church of God with contention, set every man's sword against his brother, and thus done the work of *Apollyon* in the name of *Christ*."[78]

The sacrificial religion of the Hindus has been used as a pawn in more than just theological disputes. The discourse of human sacrifice in India has also been part of the language of colonial domination and resistance. Perhaps the most famous example is the case of the Thugee cult in the early nineteenth century. It was Colonel William Sleeman who began investigating a mysterious gang of highway robbers known for strangling their victims in 1818 and soon became convinced that the Thugees were a type of pan-Indian Mafia-cum-cult devoted to the goddess Kālī and intent on undermining the foundations of human society.[79] In a wave of mass hysteria and scapegoating akin to the witch-hunts, the Red Scare, and the Satanic Panic of the 1980s, Sleeman began branding nearly every petty criminal the authorities arrested as a Thugee. One criminal, Feringhea (a name very close to the Urdu word for "foreigner"), confessed, almost certainly with a lot of persuasion from Sleeman, to being the chief of the Thugees and revealed their cultic "secrets," which Sleeman dutifully recorded. The evil rituals depicted in the Thugees' confessions recall British colonial stereotypes of the black magic of Tantric religion as well as persecution texts like the ones Girard examines in *The Scapegoat.*

Girard lists three stereotyped accusations leveled against persecuted groups: crimes against "those people whom it is most criminal to attack," either because they are held in high esteem or because they are weak and defenseless; sexual crimes like rape, incest, and bestiality; and religious crimes that break the strictest taboos.[80] Girard notes that the imagined crimes of the scapegoat must threaten to destroy a community's social distinctions by undermining its foundation and utterly destroying all social bonds.[81] In colonial accounts, Thugees are "a growing evil," and "common enemies of mankind," a representation of the completely corrupt and decadent state of India as a whole. And while we do not see the Thugees committing outright blasphemy against the Christian religion, their rites are tantamount to sacrilege. The newspapers in Madras printed accounts of a ritual feast held by the Thugees on their victims' graves after every murder, with "coarse sugar [in] the place of the Christian communion bread and wine."[82]

While they were hunting the Thugees, the colonial government in Madras also had to deal with the issues of Adivasis, or the tribal groups that practice non-Hindu traditions throughout India. In 1837, they set up a special agency specifically to deal with the practice of human sacrifice among a Central Indian tribe called the Gōndi (or Kond), the largest in the region. Following the conquest of the region during the Ghumsur Wars of 1835–1837, the British set up the Meriah Agency, named for the Gōndi word used to describe the victim of their human sacrifice, in order to wipe out the practice. Felix Padel's 2000 study of the British involvement with the Gōndi people, *The Sacrifice of Human Being*, is a good example of the pitfalls of postcolonialism and cultural relativism. Padel's argument (more Maistrian in political orientation than anything Girard ever wrote) is that the violence of the Gōndi's sacrificial rituals was nothing next to the violence perpetrated by the British to stamp it out. Paragraphs like this one exemplify the occasional lapses in critical engagement that one finds in postcolonial studies:

> As I understand it, the difference between 'objective' and 'subjective' knowledge corresponds to the difference between 'scientific,' 'empirical' or 'rational' modes of knowledge, and 'artistic,' 'poetic,' or 'intuitive' knowledge. Western society privileges the former over the latter. . . . Most non-Western societies could be said to privilege the latter, or to have more of a balance between the two modes, recognizing the fundamental importance of things that are not susceptible to rational understanding—as shown by the entirely different concerns of Eastern from Western philosophy, or the importance of knowledge that comes from dreams and trance in tribal societies.[83]

And Eskimos have a hundred words for snow.

We need not accept Padel's uncritical account of the Gōndi situation to make use of his data. What is important for us to see is that the Gōndi, living in relation to but not under the Brahminical hegemony, maintained an indigenous form of human sacrifice well into the nineteenth century. Certain aspects of Gōndi religion, like their use of the Buffalo Sacrifice, seem to be related to the practices of goddess-worshippers. And since their territory is in the state of Orissa, Gōndi also become involved in the Orissan Jagannāth festival described above. The Gōndi deity who receives the sacrifice is their earth goddess Tari Pennu. The village headman purchases the victim, or *meriah*, from kidnappers that belong to a very low-caste group called the Doms. If the Doms, who live among the Gōndi in their villages, are unable to provide victims by kidnapping then they have to pledge their own children as *meriah*s, creating an economy of substitution in which the Doms themselves look like victims who buy back their lives by kidnapping outsiders. The Doms also act as revenue collectors for local Hindu landowners.

Before being sacrificed, usually during a full moon in the dead of winter (which is also, coincidentally, the time of the Vrātyas' Sattra sacrifice, which we will look at in chapter two) the *meriah* lives as an equal among the Gōndi, often as a member of the headman's household. But just before the ritual, the victim is removed from the host family and bound in chains or rope. And in the days leading up to the sacrifice, the victim is set apart by having his or her head shaved, being feasted by the tribe, and being led around the village for the Gōndi to touch and decorate with garlands and sandalwood paste. Just before the killing, the victim is drugged with opium or wine and is either bound to the killing post or has his or her arms and legs broken. The priest then disclaims guilt for the killing by intoning the words, "We bought you with a price and did not seize you; now we sacrifice you according to our custom, and no sin rests on us."[84] There is also a dialogue between the victim and the priest that recalls certain features of Vedic ritual. The actual manner of the killing varies from burning alive to suffocating in a pit of pig's blood. The most common description, which is also reflected in legal records of certain "sacrificial murders" in the region from the 1930s and 1940s, is reminiscent of the Dionysian frenzy Pentheus faces in *The Bacchae*: a crowd descends on the victim with axes and knives and hacks him or her to pieces, then scatters the parts of the victim in the fields of the village. The amount of tears the *meriah* cries during the immolation predicts the amount of rain the Gōndi can expect in the next year. The next day, the entire village goes into mourning for the victim.[85]

Padel correctly identifies the forms of sacrifice on which Western civilization is founded, including the various systems of exclusion and victimization that defined the British Empire, but his rationalization of the violence of Gōndi sacrifice is problematic to say the least. Examining material from the colonial context demands that one neither succumb to cultural relativism nor uncritically adopt the forced perspective of the dominant culture.

But Tantric and tribal religion were not the only targets of the British colonial reformers and there are more intellectually rigorous methods of interrogating the British discourse on India than Padel's, as is demonstrated in Lata Mani's analysis of the debate about the controversial practice of *sati* or "widow-burning." Analyzing the debates between colonial officials, missionaries, and Bengali intellectuals leading up to the official prohibition of *sati* in 1829, Mani argues that, "[although] *sati* became an alibi for the colonial civilizing mission on the one hand, and on the other hand, a significant occasion for indigenous autocritique, the women who burned were neither subjects nor even the primary objects of concern in the debate on its prohibition."[86] What was truly at stake in this debate, Mani demonstrates, was not the ever-popular chestnut of "women and children first" but the authority of the Sanskrit canon and who would wield it. Then and now, it is all too easy for the political inequalities between Western academics and Indian Pandits to distort the conversation between them to the point that the real victims are completely forgotten. Girard's dogged insistence on the reality of the human scapegoat cuts through these distortions like a knife, never letting us lose sight of the victim. With this in mind, we can now examine the arguments of those who try to deny the existence of violence in the tradition.

The Nāstika*/Gnostic Position: Looking for the Light of Asia*

The first study of human sacrifice in the Vedas was done in 1805 by Henry Thomas Colebrooke, one-time president of the Royal Asiatic Society and professor of Hindu Law and Sanskrit at the college of Fort William in Calcutta. Colebrooke, after reading the descriptions of the Aśvamedha and the Puruṣamedha in the Brāhmaṇas, came to this conclusion:

> In the [Puruṣamedha], a hundred and eighty-five men of various specified tribes, characters, and professions, are bound to eleven posts; and, after the hymn concerning the allegorical immolation of Narayana has been recited, these human victims are liberated unhurt; and oblations of butter are made on the sacrificial fire. This mode of performing the *Aśwamed'ha* and *Purushamed'ha*, as emblematic ceremonies, not as real sacrifices, is taught in this *Veda*: and the interpretation is fully confirmed by the rituals, and by commentators on the *Sanhita* and *Brahmand*; one of whom assigns as the reason, 'because the flesh of victims which have been actually sacrificed at a *Yajnya* must be eaten by the persons who offer the sacrifice: but a man cannot be allowed, much less required, to eat human flesh.' It may be hence inferred, or conjectured at least, that human sacrifices were not authorised by the *Veda* itself; but were either then abrogated, and an emblematical ceremony substituted in their place; or they must have been introduced in later times, on the authority of certain *Puranas* or *Tantras*, fabricated by persons who, in this as in other matters, established many unjustifiable practices, on the foundation of emblems and allegories which they misunderstood.[87]

Like certain other Orientalists of his day, Colebrooke admired the Vedas and tended to ascribe everything that contradicted his rationalist model of ancient Indian Vedic civilization either to savage prehistory or to the corrupting influences of the medieval Purāṇas and Tantras—especially the

Tantras, which were filled with more grotesqueries and absurdities than the British thought possible. Even so, Tantra was not universally scapegoated among the British as the source of all that was evil in Hinduism. It had its admirers too. On the scholarly spectrum that stretches from those like James Talboys Wheeler who saw Tantra as debased, orgiastic demon-worship and those like Sir John Woodruffe who rationalized Tantra's sexual and violent aspects and emphasize its continuity with the Vedic tradition, Colebrooke is much closer to Wheeler's blanket condemnation.[88]

Another example of scholarship that actively tries to minimize the role of sacrifice in Indian religion is the work of Moritz Winternitz, the father of the German text-critical school.[89] In the first volume of *A History of Indian Literature*, Winternitz is suspicious of the scale and symbolic nature of the 184 victims called for in the Puruṣamedha as described in the tenth century B.C.E. *Vājasaneyī Saṃhitā*. The list includes a thief sacrificed to darkness, a murderer sacrificed to Hell, a singer to sound, a warrior to martial honor, and a priest to priestly virtue. For Winternitz, this neatly formulaic roster identifies the rite as "perhaps only a symbolic act which represents a sort of 'human sacrifice' by which the great horse sacrifice must be surpassed which however existed only as a constituent of the sacrificial-mystical and sacrificial theory, but which in reality hardly ever happened."[90] To support his argument he cites A. B. Keith's confident assertion that "[there] can be no doubt that the [Puruṣamedha] ritual is a mere priestly invention to fill up the apparent gap in the sacrificial system that provided no place for man."[91] The "apparent gap" to which Keith refers comes from the fact the human is one of the five sacrificable animals listed throughout the Vedic literature, but is not sacrificed in practice (or at least not public practice). And although Keith lists many instances of the ritual killing of humans throughout the Vedas, his narrow definition of "sacrifice" precludes him from calling any of them sacrificial.[92]

Later Winternitz turns to the famous story of the thwarted sacrifice of the Brahmin boy Śunaḥśepa from the *Aitareya Brāhmaṇa*, speculating that it must have been old even to the composer of the text.

> [How] old must the legend itself be! It must be very old for this reason also that in it is preserved the memory of human sacrifice which must have been offered during the Rājasūya [Royal Consecration] in

> prehistoric times, although otherwise there is no talk of human sacrifices at the time of the king's coronation anywhere in the Brāhmaṇas or in the ritual books. . . .[93]

The Śunaḥśepa story is also the subject of a debate between F. Max Müller and the Sanskritist H. H. Wilson in the mid-nineteenth century.[94] Both Müller and Wilson compare the story of Śunaḥśepa to the Aqedah, the binding of Isaac in chapter twenty-two of Genesis, but while Wilson sees the story as proof positive that human sacrifice *was* practiced at the time in which the text was composed, Müller retorts that the story of Śunaḥśepa is no more evidence of human sacrifice among the Brahmins than the Aqedah is evidence for rampant filicidal sacrifices among the Jews.[95]

In the end, whether scholars are minimizing sacrificial violence or sensationalizing it, both treatments give us a distorted picture. Recent scholarship by people like Jan Heesterman, Madeleine Biardeau, Alf Hiltebeitel, and Hugh Urban have done a great deal to clear things up, but what has been missing is a systematic analysis of some key texts using the unique reading practices developed by Girard to ask precisely the question of sacrifice. Having laid out the cases for and against actual human sacrifices in ancient India and expressed some ideological and methodological reservations about Girard's mimetic theory, in the following chapters I will demonstrate the power of mimetic theory to provide penetrating analyses of some otherwise obscure texts.

Antādi, "The End of the Beginning"

In this introductory chapter, I have stated my intention to read Hindu mythology through Girard and read Girard through Hindu mythology. I have laid out Girard's mimetic theory in a nutshell and given some background for the major texts and traditions that we will be exploring throughout this book. To address, if not allay, suspicions about Girard's utility for reading Hindu myth, I have examined the major ideological and methodological objections to Girard, including an implicit objection Girard himself makes in his very early work, and explained why none of them has convinced me not to go forward with this project. Next, I have looked at some of the current controversies and criticisms surrounding the study of Hinduism in the Western academy, to provide some context for the ongoing discussion to which I am submitting the argument of this book, but also to stand as a rebuttal to the distorted picture of "the comparative study of religion" Girard seems to have in mind in *Sacrifice*.[96] Finally, I have asked the question that the mention of Girard's name in connection with religion always brings to the fore: What evidence do we have for the actual ritual killing of human beings? I have presented some of this evidence, archaeological and ethnographic, and looked at the roles this question has played in the study of Hinduism from the colonial period to the present day. I will use the following chapter to focus attention on Girard's *Sacrifice*, examining the references to other thinkers I see at work in the book and treating some of the myths Girard analyzes in its pages.

Rivalries

Our world believes in the spontaneity of desire, especially our human sciences, ever faithful to the optimism of the Enlightenment. This, in my opinion, is the principal reason for the hostility of the nineteenth century Indianists toward the Brahmanas, and of the established sciences toward mimetic theory.

—René Girard, *Sacrifice*

The general character of these works is marked by shallow and insipid grandiloquence, by priestly conceit, and antiquarian pedantry. These works deserve to be studied as the physician studies the twaddle of idiots, and the raving of madmen.

—F. Max Müller, *A History of Ancient Sanskrit Literature so Far as It Illustrates the Primitive Religion of the Brahmans*

Rivalry is at the center of Girard's work. Some would say that rivalry also characterizes Girard's relationship to the rest of the academy. It also plays a central role in the mythology of the Brāhmaṇas, in which the gods and the demons are locked in a continuous struggle for supremacy.

In this chapter we will focus on the issue of rivalry as we follow two parallel narratives, one historical and one mythological. Both of these narratives lead to Girard's engagement with the Brāhmaṇas, whose reviled status he clearly sees as analogous to that of his own work.

First we will look at the Sanskrit texts themselves and their reception in German and British Indology and, later, in the work of Sylvain Lévi and Girard. Then we will examine the rivalries that shaped the development of mimetic theory, beginning with the French-British conflict that serves as the background for Indology in France. We will continue on to the strained relationship between philologists like Lévi and sociologists like Émile Durkheim in the burgeoning field of the study of religion at the *fin de siècle* and see how Girard's project is a product of this rivalry. Then we will turn to the Vedas and Brāhmaṇas themselves and begin to look at the mimetic rivalry of the gods and the demons and the emergence of the divine king Indra out of this struggle. From there we will shift to the rivalry of the waning Vedic god Indra and the rising sectarian god Viṣṇu and how this mythological conflict relates to the changing status of the sacrifice in classical India. At the end it will be clear how Girard's turn to the Brāhmaṇas, specifically as they appear through the lens of Lévi's work, closes the circle on his intellectual project and gives us a new perspective on mimetic theory's place among the theories of religion.

Scapegoated Texts: The Place of the Brāhmaṇas in the Study of Hinduism

When European scholars first discovered the Brāhmaṇas they reacted with a rather surprising amount of disgust and derision.[1] According to F. Max Müller they were "twaddle, and what is worse, theological twaddle."[2] Another Sanskritist, Arthur A. MacDonnell, dismissed the Brāhmaṇas as "an aggregate of shallow and pedantic discussions, full of sacerdotal conceits, and fanciful, or even absurd, identifications."[3] William Dwight Whitney, whose 1885 work *The Roots, Verb-forms and Primary Derivatives of the Sanskrit Language* is still an indispensable resource for students of Sanskrit, wrote of them, "Here we have one of the aberrations of the human mind. . . . Their tedious inanity . . . will soon satiate, if it does not disgust, the general reader."[4] Even Julius Eggeling, whose unsurpassed diligence and scholarship resulted in a monumental five-volume translation with notes of the most famous of the Brāhmaṇas, the *Śatapatha Brāhmaṇa* of the White branch of the *Yajur Veda*, is dismissive of its significance:

> In the whole range of literature few works are probably less calculated to excite the interest of any outside the very limited number of specialists, than the ancient theological writings of the Hindus, known by the name of Brâhma*n*as. For wearisome prolixity of exposition, characterised by dogmatic assertion and a flimsy symbolism rather than by serious reasoning, these works are perhaps not equaled anywhere; unless, indeed, it be by the speculative vapourings of the Gnostics, than which, in the opinion of the learned translators of Irenæus, "nothing more absurd has probably ever been imagined by rational beings."[5]

Eggeling joins all the other detractors of the Brāhmaṇas in taking issue above all with what he sees as its haphazard and unsystematic use of equivalences and connections (e.g., the moon is the mind, is the Soma, is the god Varuṇa, etc.). The source of these scholars' initial frustration will become apparent when we try to decipher the Brāhmaṇic interpretation of the Pravargya ritual in chapter four. But despite what was seen as their propensity for flimsy and absurd correlations and associations, the Brāhmaṇas still held Eggeling's and Müller's interest as evidence of what they cynically understood as the priestly manipulations of the Brahmin class. Eggeling confidently writes:

> The Brâhma*n*as, it is well known, form our chief, if not our only, source of information regarding one of the most important periods in the social and mental development of India. They represent the intellectual activity of a sacerdotal caste that, by turning to account the religious instincts of a gifted and naturally devout race, had succeeded in transforming a primitive worship of the powers of nature into a highly artificial system of sacrificial ceremonies, and was ever intent on deepening and extending its hold on the minds of the people by surrounding its own vocation with the halo of sanctity and divine inspiration.[6]

Ever wary of an angry mob, Girard is rightly suspicious of this blanket condemnation and is quick to interrogate the accusations these Indologists make against the Brāhmaṇas and their authors. On the negative reaction to the Brāhmaṇas and to Sylvain Lévi's work on them Girard writes:

> [Lévi's book] dates to an era (1898) when the most famous Indianists of Europe and America not only scorned the Brahmanas but heaped them with insults. They did not hesitate to treat their authors as feebleminded, as saboteurs of their own culture. Sylvain Lévi believes, on the contrary, in the coherence of these books and that is why he strives to render them accessible to simple amateurs like myself.[7]

For Girard, not only are the Brāhmaṇas coherent, they represent a highly intellectualized form of archaic religion that gives rise to a self-critique. By arguing that the Brāhmaṇas "transcend themselves . . . in some later texts that radically criticize sacrifice" and vindicating Lévi's "confidence in the intellectual power of the great Vedic texts," Girard demands that we take seriously the system of correlations and equivalences that nineteenth century scholars dismissed as nonsense.

But perhaps we should stop acting as if Girard has given us some new interpretation of the Brāhmaṇas. He has not. *Sacrifice* is not an interpretation of the Brāhmaṇas at all. "It is not the original Sanskrit that I interpret," the author admits, "but Sylvain Lévi's book."[8] And neither is it anything particularly new. In fact, twenty-two of the English translation's ninety-five pages are devoted to a presentation of the theory Girard more or less completely formulated more than forty years ago. But he conceals none of this from us. What, then, is the importance of *Sacrifice* for the Girardian and the Indologist? For the Girardian, *Sacrifice* is unique because in it Girard turns his attention to a non-Christian tradition not only with the intent to seek out traces of violent origins in its myths but also with an openness to learn something from it. He discards the easy parochialism evident in some brands of mimetic theory in favor of a more ecumenical viewpoint, a move that enriches the theory immensely. For Indologists, *Sacrifice* is important because it gives us a new set of tools with which to reassess the unresolved Indological dispute over the "meaninglessness of ritual."

Indologist Frits Staal, who spent his career in an intense engagement not only with the Sanskrit texts but with the actualities of the rarely performed solemn Vedic rites themselves, which he began observing and recording in the 1960s,[9] puts forward the idea of the "meaninglessness of ritual" in its strongest form in his programmatic work *Rules Without Meaning: Ritual, Mantras, and the Human Sciences*. By the "meaninglessness of ritual," Staal intends the idea that ritual is rule-governed behavior performed for its own sake rather than practical behavior performed to achieve a certain result. In a 1982 article reviewing recent developments in classical Indology he explains his thesis in regard to the Brāhmaṇic understanding of the Vedic solemn rites:[10]

> In the case of the *śrauta* or solemn rites, my argument was directed primarily against the ancient authors of the Brahmana literature and against contemporary anthropologists and scholars of religion who had provided rites with numerous inconsistent and ad hoc interpretations, attempting to show that they were symbolic and represented something else. In contrast with these obvious rationalizations, I emphasized that ritual was *activity* and was performed for its own sake.[11]

Without fully accepting it, we can hear in this argument echoes of Girard's negative assessment of Marcel Mauss and Claude Lévi-Strauss's theory of sacrifice as mediation. If we conceive of sacrifice as mediation with an imaginary supernatural being as they do, Girard contends, then "sacrificial rites have no basis in reality, [and] we have every reason to label them meaningless."[12] Girard argues against seeing sacrifice in terms of communication between humans and an imaginary divinity and insists that we must look at the phenomenon in purely human terms and therefore as meaningful. To demonstrate his point, he also brings out a number of sacrificial stories (Isaac and Esau, Odysseus and the Cyclops) in which there is a sacrificial substitution but no deity present. In the case of the Vedic texts, we can find stories of sacrifice in which only gods or demons are present and humans are absent, which also serves to problematize the idea of sacrifice as a means to communicate with the gods.

Mounting a slightly different kind of defense for the Brāhmaṇas, Brian K. Smith argues that "Vedic 'equations' are neither absurd nor random but are rather systematic expressions made possible (and logical) by fundamental

Vedic principles of metaphysics and epistemology" and that "there is a philosophical center upon which all Vedic thought revolves," which he calls "resemblance."[13] He places the work of J. C. Heesterman along with that of Staal under the rubric of what he calls "The Meaningless Theory" (an association against which I will argue in the next chapter) and concludes against them both, countering that "any thesis for the meaninglessness of any human creation is a meaningful interpretation of what is regarded as a previously improperly understood phenomenon—and thus is itself a paradox that cries for a solution."[14]

To maintain the assessment of the Vedic rituals as meaningless, it would be necessary to disparage or at least discredit the Brāhmaṇas, the main purpose of which is to explicate the meaning of those rituals. In the epigraph that begins this chapter, Girard presents his own view of why nineteenth (and twentieth) century Indologists are so hostile toward the Brāhmaṇas. For him, it all goes back to the Enlightenment, with its cherished assumption of the "spontaneity of desire." But is this an accurate assessment? What have the Brāhmaṇas to do with the spontaneity of desire? The answer to this question is more apparent in Girard's essay, "The Evangelical Subversion of Myth" than it is in *Sacrifice*. Analyzing the proto-martyrdom of Saint Stephen described in Acts 6, where the apostle is dragged out of the courtroom during his trial and stoned to death after he announces he is having a vision of "the Son of Man standing at the right hand of God," Girard notes the episode's "inextricable mixture of legal and illegal elements, of ritual and spontaneous elements."[15]

> We are told that ritual and spontaneity are poles apart; in our text, they are so much the same thing that they cannot be distinguished.... The scholars' hesitation between the most spontaneous and the most ritualized form suggests that the second may well be the scrupulous copy and mimicry of the first. The ritual form can always provide a satisfactory channel for a spontaneous outburst; it can become de-ritualized, so to speak, without important changes, because it is nothing but the ritualization of a first such outburst that has proved so successful in reestablishing the peace that its forms are carefully remembered and reproduced.[16]

Here Girard is interrogating the connection between ritual and spontaneity in a way that bears directly on our discussion of the Vedic rituals. In Girard's argument, "ritual" and "spontaneity" roughly correspond to the "form" and the "content" of the sacrifice, and since the "meaning" of the sacrifice is so clearly reflected in its form it is difficult to tell where a ritual killing ends and a lynching begins. If the secret of the sacrifice is the founding murder, then it is a secret that lies hidden in plain sight like Poe's purloined letter. But we also know that the sacrifice hides a double secret: Along with the founding murder comes the peace and equilibrium that the community experiences. Girard locates this missing link between collective violence and group cohesion in a word from the Biblical passage that appears as *homothumadon* in the Greek and *unanimiter* in the Vulgate. "The unanimity of the participants is a quasi-technical detail here," he writes. "[It] is required by the scapegoat ritual and it is the result of the intolerable words uttered by Stephen, of the enormous scandal they provoke."[17] In this particular case, what seems like spontaneous rage is actually part of a ritual script.

Let us return to Girard's treatment of the Brāhmaṇas in *Sacrifice*. As evidence of the ecumenical nature of his argument, he comes to the unexpected conclusion that "[mimetic] theory sees . . . what the Brahmanas also see," namely, the mimetic nature of desire. It is on this point that Girard critiques the great models of Freud and Hegel to which his own thought is indebted.[18] But now we see what Roberto Calasso means when he writes that Girard's "fury and sarcasm leave the Vedic seers unscathed."[19] Girard continues, "Many indications confirm that everything in the Brahmanas is organized by the principle of mimetic desire."[20] It is noteworthy that he attributes to the Brāhmaṇas the crucial insight of his theory. And it is at this point in the argument that we can begin to make the connection between a reading of the Brāhmaṇas and a critique of the Enlightenment. Later we will see that this connection is also present in the work of Sylvain Lévi.

Bringing up the subject of the Enlightenment, we have entered the cycles of European intellectual and political history Girard explores in *Battling to the End.* In that work Girard's attention is focused on the rise of Romanticism in the wake of the Enlightenment and the mimetic, rivalrous fascination between France and Germany in the nineteenth century. But I would like to explore another rivalry that bears on the matter at hand—the rivalry between France and England as the two colonial powers struggled for control of India in the eighteenth century. In the wake of the dissolution of the Mughal Empire, the global conflict between the colonial powers of

France and England found another theater in South Asia, and the two men whose rivalry defined the conflict for colonial historians are France's Joseph François Dupleix and Britain's Robert Clive.

Dupleix and Clive

French contact with India may date back to as early as the sixteenth century, but it was with Louis XIV's charter of the French East India Company in 1646 that it began in earnest. France was late to the table. Elizabeth I had chartered the British East India Company in 1600 and the Dutch had quickly followed suit by forming their own East India Company in 1602, followed by the Danes in 1616 and the Portuguese in 1628. The call for the creation of a company in France came in the form of a tract penned by the archaeologist and champion of the French language François Charpentier, at the behest of Controller General of Finance Jean-Baptiste Colbert.[21] The language of the tract is significant:

> It is from [the East Indies] that we bring back what is the most precious among men, and what contributes both to the sweetness of life and its flash of brilliance. Henceforth it is imperative to acquire all this ourselves; I see no reason why we should continue to receive it from another's hand, or why we should refuse hereafter to gain for our citizens what foreigners have so far gained from us. Why should the Portuguese, the Dutch and the English go to the East Indies every day, possess shops and fortresses there and the French be deprived of the one and the other?[22]

The reason for Colbert and Charpentier's rabble-rousing language was the need they saw to introduce a common enemy (represented at this point by the combined forces of the Portuguese, the Dutch, and the English) in order to diffuse the rivalry between French mercantile concerns that, along with its lack of a shipping port, was crippling France's trade with India. The French shipping companies had been refusing to enter into an association for nearly thirty years. This call to unite against an outside force, helped by the large amount of money Colbert was able to get out of the growing French economy through forced loans, resulted in the French finally setting up their own East India Company nearly half a century after the British.

To compete with the other European powers on the subcontinent, the French set themselves up on the west coast, where they fought with the Dutch for trading rights before they established their mercantile center at the port of Pondicherry.[23] Up until the middle of the eighteenth century, the French carried on the business of colonial exploitation just as the Dutch, Portuguese, and British were doing elsewhere on the subcontinent, through trade agreements with the Mughal emperors. But by 1740, the Portuguese and Dutch trading empires had gone into decline, leaving France and England as the two rivals vying for control of India.

In 1742, French Governor General Joseph François Dupleix arrived in Pondicherry. After a failed attempt to stop the global Anglo-French conflict from spilling into India, he plotted to take advantage of the Mughal Empire's disintegration and extend the empire. To that end he fortified Pondicherry and built up a native army of sepoys, a move quickly copied by the British. From 1746 to 1748 the French and English fought for colonial domination over India in the First Carnatic War. With the help of the French navy led by the Admiral La Bourdonnais, Dupleix handed the British a defeat, even capturing the British center of Madras (now Chennai), although he was made to give it back as a condition of the Treaty of Aix-la-Chapelle. The Second Carnatic War broke out when the French and British joined opposite sides in the war of succession following the death of the Nizam of Hyderabad in 1748. In this conflict Britain's Robert Clive defeated Dupleix and his general La Bussy at the Battle of Plassey. Subsequently the French East India Company fired Dupleix for disrupting their business with excessive warmongering.

In *A History of India*, Hermann Kulke and Dietmar Rothermund describe the fate of the would-be architects of "*L'Inde Française*" in telling terms: "The warmongers were made scapegoats, La Bourdonnais was imprisoned; Dupleix died a pauper in France; only De Bussy stayed on in India—but his military potential was now greatly restricted."[24] During the Seven Years' War (1756–1763), the British dealt the French dream of an Indian Empire its deathblow, taking their centers of power at Pondicherry and Chandernagore and decisively defeating the French army at the Battle of Wandiwash. After this last paroxysm of struggle, the French, as per the terms of the Treaty of Paris, confined their colonial enterprises to the five unarmed trading settlements, or *comptoires*, of Pondicherry, Chandernagore, Karekal, Mahe, and Yanam.

On the Side of the Victims: French Indology after the Seven Years' War

In 1786, the philologist William "Oriental" Jones famously delivered an address to the Asiatic Society of Bengal that forever changed the way that Europe thought of India. Jones strongly suggested that Sanskrit, Latin, and Greek all developed from a mysterious ancestral language now commonly referred to as Proto-Indo-European.[25] He also posited a familial relationship between the classical cultures of the Mediterranean, Northern Europe, and South Asia.[26] Jones's project, a marriage of Linnean taxonomy and the philological aspiration to trace all human ancestry according to the chronology of the Bible, continued in yearly lectures until his death in 1794 and went on to influence the work of researchers like Jacob Grimm, Franz Bopp, and Émile Benveniste.[27] Jones was working from Calcutta, in the heart of British India, where he sat on the Supreme Court of Bengal and was actively engaged in colonial administration. The Asiatic Society he founded to study the history of the Hindus was closed to the Hindus themselves, politicizing British Indology from the very start.

From its beginning French Indology was also politicized, though in a way different from that of the dominant colonial power, the British Empire. The first introduction of Sanskrit texts to French readers came in 1770 in the form of *Histoire philosophique et politique des établissements et du commerce des Européens dans les deux Indes*, a massive work edited by Guillaume-Thomas François Raynal that preceded James Mill's influential *The History of British India* by nearly fifty years. Written in the wake of French defeat and with major contributions by Denis Diderot, *Histoire* was the first text of its kind to privilege Sanskrit sources over the accounts of European missionaries, and used this position to condemn British interventions in Bengal. In 1777 Jean-Sylvain Bailly, the revolutionary intellectual and first Mayor of Paris (before being guillotined during the Terror), concluded from his studies of Indian texts that "the Brahmans are the teachers of Pythagoras, the instructors of Greece, and through her the whole of Europe."[28] In agreement with Bailly, Voltaire read Indian history against Church history by placing Indian culture at the dawn of human civilization, a chronology to which the naturalist Pierre Sonnerat added his endorsement in 1782.[29] In 1788, a translation of the *Bhāgavata Purāṇa*, made working from the Sanskrit text and a Tamil abridgement, was published in France and introduced the French to the eroticized mythology of the youthful god Kṛṣṇa. The "savior" of India, they discovered, was light years away from the asexual and ascetic savior of Christian Europe. The translation had been commissioned by Foucher d'Obsonville and completed in 1768 by Maridâs Poullé, the son of an Indian Catholic convert. Poullé's *Bhāgavata Purāṇa* was one of the last works of French Indology to manifest "the Voltairian impulse to tear away Indian subject matter from missionary discourse."[30] But if French Indology became less concerned with toppling a Christian hegemony, in the wake of France's defeat in the Seven Years' War it became ever more concerned with toppling a British hegemony.

In 1857, after the bloody mutiny of the Sepoy Rebellion caused Queen Victoria to take the Subcontinent away from the British East India Company and put it under the direct control of the Crown, French republicans were jubilant at what they saw as evidence of the mercantile British Empire's fragility. Evidence of this attitude appears in Frédéric-Florentin Billot's 1857 political tract *L'Inde, l'Angleterre et la France* and in Jules Verne's lesser known 1880 novel *La maison à vapeur: voyage à travers l'Inde septentrionale*. Set ten years after the mutiny, Verne's novel describes the rising tensions between natives and colonizers, climaxing in a horrific battle between the forces of Colonel Edward Munro and the rebel leader Nana Sahib in which the British achieve a pyrrhic victory that paints them as tyrannical oppressors.

From 1880 to 1906, French rule in the five *comptoires* came up against a kind of mutiny of its own in the form of the Hindu mystic and Vellaja caste leader Chanemougam. Dubbed the "Black Louis XI" by the colonial press, Chanemougam led a powerful resistance against attempts to assimilate the local culture to French ideals under the new colonial policies of the Third Republic. In the absence of Kṣatriya (the warrior class) or Brahmin castes, Chanemougam's Vellaja caste became the dominant group in Pondicherry.[31] Chanemougam's resistance was more akin to Chicago-style machine politics than the open warfare of the Sepoy Rebellion, using bribery to influence elections and strong-arm tactics to keep the outcastes who would benefit from the French reforms out of polling places. In 1908 Chanemougam's control of colonial politics was finally broken when his puppet candidate for governor of Pondicherry unexpectedly died during the campaign and his opponent won the election.[32]

The changed attitude of the French toward traditional Indian cultural forms that had taken place between Voltaire's day and the Third Republic is summed up by this statement made by Governor Angoulvant, promising to prevent any more Chanemougam-style strongmen from rising up:

> The issue is to prevent the rise of other Chanemougams among the Europeans or the natives. It is not that a desire to emulate him does not exist and the Hindu rushes easily towards servitude. But the 'comptoir' can count on me to destroy, in its embryonic form, any such attempts to revive a distressing past which fortunately is no longer with us.[33]

For Angoulvant the main thing the French had to be concerned about was a desire on the part of the natives to "emulate" or "revive" their own past, for which the French apparently no longer had the kind of esteem once exhibited by people like Bailly and Voltaire. Another colonial administrator, one Captain Goumain, located the root cause of France's problems in India in the French desire to force assimilation on the institutional level while misunderstanding persisted at the cultural level. Expressing regret at France's abandoning its project to understand India and allowing knowledge of its culture to become relegated to a handful of academics, he opined, "We opened for [the Indian] the doors of the Parliament when we should have given him access to the university."[34]

The French may have "lost" India to the British in the eighteenth century, but the rivalry between the two powers stretched into the twentieth, where it continued to shape French Indology as well as British colonial policy. In 1902, under the vice-regency of George Curzon, two years after a massive famine claimed between six and nine million Indian lives, the Indian Education Reform Commission abolished the teaching of French in Indian universities (except in the case of women) while English remained compulsory. The British deemed French thought "dangerous" in India, their fears best expressed by the words of Counsel-General of Calcutta Charles

Coutouly: "[The] most forthright and best informed criticism of English rule in India is made by the alert pen of the French."[35] Coutouly is right to pick up on the inchoate anti-imperialism born out of hurt national pride that lies at the foundation of French Indology, separating it from its British counterpart. It is important to recognize the difference between the two in order to understand how Girard's engagement with the Brāhmaṇas fits in with the rest of his work: India has a much different place in the French *imaginaire* than it does in that of the British or German scholars who were so quick to condemn the Brāhmaṇas in the nineteenth century. After India gained its independence from Britain in 1947, France was one of the first European nations to send an ambassador, a man who would oversee the first stages of decolonization in French India. That man was Daniel Lévi, the son of Sylvain Lévi.

Sylvain Lévi and *La doctrine du sacrifice dans les Brahmanas*

No scholar truly works alone. And Girard, whose most penetrating insights have come in conversations with Jean-Michel Oughourlian, Guy Lefort, J. Z. Smith, Walter Burkert, Burton Mack, and Benoît Chantre, would be the last to claim that his work comes out of a vacuum. To appreciate the texture of Girard's theory and responsibly apply it to the Indian materials we must first explore the genealogy of his thought and its multiple intersections with the development of Indology, sociology, and structuralism in France.

"Without being truly close to Sylvain Lévi's," Girard writes, "my interpretation of the Brahmanas—through his book—vindicates his confidence in the intellectual power of the great Vedic texts. It is therefore to the memory of this researcher that I dedicate the present work, as a token of admiration and gratitude."[36] *Sacrifice* is thus as much a commentary on the work of Sylvain Lévi as it is an interpretation of the Brāhmaṇas. The turn to Lévi so late[37] in Girard's career ties together several of the strains of thought that have influenced mimetic theory from the beginning. It is fitting, therefore, that we should spend some time looking into Lévi's place in the discourses, not only of French Indology, but also of French sociology and structuralism, which are so crucial to understanding Girard's work.

Sylvain Lévi was born in Paris on March 28, 1863, into a Jewish family originating in Alsace, near the French-German border. He studied German and classics at the Lycée Charlemagne and received his baccalaureate in 1881. Lévi had an academic setback when he was rejected by the École Normale Supérieure[38] and so he went to the Sorbonne as a scholarship student and graduated second in his class. Published in 1890, his doctoral dissertation, *Le théâtre indien*, has since become an authoritative study of the subject. At the time of Lévi's matriculation, Jewish education in France was undergoing a major change as Hebrew schools began adopting French language instruction. Like other French secular Jews, Lévi had abandoned the religion of Judaism as a young man but embraced a kind of progressive and cultural (rather than political) Zionism. He shared with other French Jewish intellectuals the modern tenets of agnosticism and belief in the emancipatory power of education and in 1888 he joined the assimilationist and anti-Zionist Alliance Israelite Universelle, organized in 1860 to advance the status of Middle Eastern Jews through French education and culture.

In the world of scholarship Lévi proved to be a wunderkind. And because of his talent as a philologist and some well-timed faculty retirements, he rapidly rose through the ranks of the French academy to become a lecturer at the École Pratique des Hautes Études in 1886. After he was elected to the Collège de France in 1894, Lévi's home became a salon for Orientalists and his influence on French Orientalism and Indology steadily increased. He traveled widely in China, Japan, and the Middle East and studied the extinct Indo-European language of Tocharian, the first samples of which, inscribed on manuscripts preserved in the Buddhist monasteries of arid Central Asia, began to appear in France in the 1890s. Between 1895 and 1897, Lévi's work sparked the interest of the father of French sociology (and a major influence on Girard), Émile Durkheim.

At the time, Durkheim was frustrated with the sharp division between the new science of sociology and the study of religion in the French academy, and he saw courting Lévi as a way to attract scholars of religion to his field. More important, it was from Lévi that Durkheim picked up the idea of analyzing rituals to construct his theory of religion and it was under Lévi's influence that he formed what Ivan Strenski describes as the "Durkheimian view that the sacred was itself an impersonal force [as well as] concrete or material."[39] On Lévi's influence, Roland Lardinois writes:

> Postulating the fundamental unity of [the Brāhmaṇic] corpus considered in an autonomous way, Lévi sums up its doctrinal coherence founded on the idea of sacrifice. If Durkheim's sociology of religion is distinguished by its focus on the analysis of rituals, as Ivan Strenski has shown, this bias appears with full clarity in this work, before it was explicated, first by Hubert and Mauss and then by Durkheim.[40]

By placing sacrificial ritual at the center of Vedic religion and Hinduism in general, Lévi provided the theoretical groundwork for the subsequent researches of Durkheim and the other French sociologists and, later, for Girard's project.

But Lévi's work on ritual was more than just scholarly. Committed to improving life for Jews in France after the Dreyfus affair and for Russian Jews fleeing czarist persecution, he wrote several ritual manuals for Jewish practice, including "Rituel du Judaisme" and "La Régéneration Religieuse," both published in 1900.[41] In 1917 and 1918 he visited Palestine, where he applauded the revival of Hebrew and the way in which Jewish intellectuals were developing a relationship to the land through their agricultural projects. But he parted ways with Zionism on the question of a Jewish state, which he regarded as the work of "sectarians."[42]

Lévi also used his knowledge of Indology to undermine the position of Aryan superiority maintained by those European scholars who held up Vedic civilization as both more ancient and more venerable than that of the Hebrews. In the timeline of Aryan civilization put forward by these anti-Semitic scholars, Vedic culture was originally a rational monotheism corrupted into the abominable idolatry and priestcraft of Hinduism through contact with inferior dark-skinned people. But then in 600 B.C.E. the Buddha, like some South Asian Martin Luther, restored the pure Aryan spiritual heritage with his rejection of rituals and priests and his insistence that his words never be translated into Sanskrit but maintained in the languages of the *volk*. Lévi challenged this regnant model by suggesting that Buddhism itself was non-Aryan and had to come from a foreign source since none of its key concepts could be found in the Vedic corpus.[43] This claim is problematic for many reasons, but what is important here is the way that Lévi attacks the anti-Semitic conventional wisdom of Aryan superiority in scholarship on Indian religion.

Lévi tackled another Indological issue in a way that seemed to also be addressing "the Jewish question"—how to account for the survival of Hinduism and the complete destruction of Buddhism after the Muslim conquest of South Asia. For Lévi, the answer lay in the "embodied" aspects of Hinduism, especially ritual and caste. Like the distinctive Jewish patterns of dress and diet, these embodied traditions made Hinduism more resistant to cultural annihilation, while the universalizing claims of Buddhism were swallowed up by the similarly universalizing religion of Islam.[44] It is ironic that, as a French liberal with Enlightenment values, Lévi was dedicated personally and politically to the kind of universal values that he believed had doomed Indian Buddhism. Taking parallel tracks in his political and scholarly projects, Lévi tried to understand how Buddhism's transition to a universal religion and consequent spread beyond its Indian homeland paradoxically precluded its survival there. The answer to this question, he felt, could help formulate a way to save Judaism in Europe without resorting to a political Zionism.

But Lévi's understanding of religious change was not a simplistic Darwinian survival of the fittest. He did not see the "universalistic" religions of Buddhism and Christianity and the "embodied" religions of Hinduism and Judaism as interchangeable members of the species *religio omnimodus* and *religio proprius*, respectively. Lévi's understanding of religion was based rather on a polythetic model. In the case of Judaism, he recognized the validity of both particularistic "Mosaic" Judaism with its concern for the survival of "the chosen people" and universalistic prophetic Judaism of the kind that inspired the work of Leibniz and Levinas. Lévi himself oscillated between these two poles, embracing universalism as a French liberal intellectual and affirming an embodied particularism as a Jew facing a rising tide of anti-Semitism. It was with this conflicted view that he approached the Brāhmaṇas and it was this same conflicted view that he passed on to the developing field of sociology in France.

The same tension between universalism and particularism with which Lévi struggled in his ethical-political and scholarly lives exists in the work of Girard. Despite what some of his more polemical remarks might suggest, Girard has never dismissed the need to examine data in its cultural context or tried to efface the realities of particularity.[45] I would suggest that both Girard and Lévi share a passion, born of ethical concern, for the "big questions," as well as a commitment to rigor and humility in scholarship, and that this common ground is part of what draws Girard to Lévi's *La doctrine du sacrifice dans les Brahmanas.*

The Second Uncle of Marcel Mauss

Marcel Mauss came to study with Lévi, the man he would soon call his "second uncle," in 1895 on the suggestion of his first uncle, Durkheim. Mauss had just completed a course of study in Bordeaux with Durkheim's close friend, the idealist philosopher Octave Hamelin. Hamelin, who drowned while trying to save a relative in 1907 (a death described by more than one commentator as "sacrificial"), died before he had produced a great amount of work.[46] But what he did leave behind was a model of idealism influenced by Fichte and Hegel that was vastly different from Durkheim's refined Comtean positivism. And under Hamelin's tutelage, Mauss had absorbed this idealist theoretical model completely. It was within the framework of Hamelin's philosophy that Mauss first conceived of the project that would become his and Henri Hubert's *Sacrifice: Its Nature and Functions.*

Mauss was working on this project in 1895 and he meant to use Lévi as a human encyclopedia to get some quick facts about Hinduism and plug them into the elaborate intellectual edifice he was constructing. But when he mentioned this idea to Lévi, the older man was indignant and took Mauss down a peg or two, chiding him for his naively abstract "grand theory" tendencies and dragging him back to earth by insisting that he had to learn Indian culture from the bottom up. In a letter to Durkheim, Mauss recalls his tutelage under Lévi:

> The first meeting was hard. Lévi made fun of me: "Sanskrit will take you three years, Vedic Sanskrit a year more, at least, and your focus hasn't given you any familiarity with it. Throw yourself into some second-hand knowledge. Max Müller is already in your head, and you [social scientists] compare everything with ethnography." After that he wasn't so harsh. "We're going to do a kind of guided reading. Read *Vedic Religion* by [Abel] Bergaigne, and tell me what you think of it." That was the first time I had heard of Bergaigne. In three days, I had read everything. I went back to his office. I told him that if Bergaigne was right, everybody else was wrong,

> and that I wanted to be sure of one or the other. It was the reaction he was looking for from me, and he was supportive after that.[47]

Soon after, Mauss developed a strong interest in Hindu liturgy and started a sort of methodological apprenticeship with Lévi during which he began his never-completed essay *On Prayer*. This unpublished text is significant for a number of reasons. For one thing it gave Durkheim cause to regret sending Mauss to Lévi, since he considered the philology to which his nephew was being introduced a form of "vain erudition." More importantly, Mauss began *On Prayer* at a time when the methodology of the study of religions was undergoing a paradigm shift as a result of two new developments. First, scholars were abandoning the evolutionary models of J. G. Frazer and E. B. Tylor in favor of a contextualized approach to religious phenomena as products of a particular culture. Second, they were no longer relying on the haphazard reports of colonial administrators in places like South Asia and Australia for data, but were turning to systematic fieldwork done by trained anthropologists like Franz Boas and Baldwin Spencer.[48] Using Australian, Indian, and Semitic materials, *On Prayer* presents Mauss's reflections on the dialectical relation between methodology and the object of study in light of these developments.[49] He never completed *On Prayer*, but three years after meeting Lévi, Mauss collaborated with Henri Hubert to systematize Lévi's insights into a general theory of ritual in *Sacrifice: Its Nature and Functions.*

Mauss's time studying with Lévi had as much effect on the teacher as it did on the student, as Mauss discovered when he first read his teacher's work on the Brāhmaṇas in 1896–1897, on the eve of Lévi's departure for Nepal. After reading *La doctrine du sacrifice dans les Brahmanas*, Mauss came to the justifiable conclusion that his study with Lévi was the impetus for the work.

> Lévi's course on the *Brahmanas* was personally designed for me. His *Idée du sacrifice dans les Brahmanas* [*sic*], which is a masterpiece, was done because of me. With its first words, it gave me the joy of a decisive discovery: "*L'entrée dans le mond des Dieux*," was the beginning of Hubert's and my work on sacrifice.[50]

It is important to remember that Lévi made his career as a Buddhologist and *La doctrine du sacrifice dans les Brahmanas* is the only sustained treatment he ever did of Vedic religion. Despite this, *La doctrine* quickly became the most authoritative work on the subject the whole world over. The argument Lévi makes in it can be broken down into three insights. First, he notes that the interpretation of sacrifice is a source of contention among the various schools of Brahmins who composed the Brāhmaṇas. Second, Lévi understands that the internal logic of the texts and the rituals they interpret are based on homologies between the human world and the world of the gods. Finally, he notices a transformation of the forms of sacrificial ritual in the text beginning with the sacrifice of the self, then moving on to a vicarious human sacrifice, and finally to animal sacrifice:

> The only truly authentic sacrifice would be suicide. The Brāhmaṇas don't concern themselves with suicide, maybe deliberately. Such a violent form of sacrifice broke violently with the ritual minutiae the Brāhmaṇas delight in putting on display. However, it is safe to say that religious suicide by starvation, by drowning, or by smothering—recognized and practiced in India in all epochs—was practiced by its adepts and devotees in the period of the Brāhmaṇas. Elsewhere, older texts retain the positive and formal memory of a practice no less savage, closely related to sacrificial suicide: human sacrifice. A man stands as the redeemer for a man. The human sacrifice is conscientiously marked and ordered in the traits of ritual. The man is the victim *par excellence*.[51]

Lévi discovered in the Brāhmaṇas an explication of the religious basis of the extreme forms of Indian asceticism as well as the Vedic practices of human sacrifice. And more than that, he saw this doctrine of substitution as the key to the coherence of the texts, which eluded the other scholars of his day. One of the aspects of Lévi's work that harmonizes with Girard's is the notion that the force underlying the sacrifice is "impalpable and irresistible" and that "once released [it] acts blindly; he who does not know how to tame it is broken by it."[52] Lévi identifies this force with *brahman*, the Sanskrit word that denotes both the Brahmin-ness of a Brahmin and, in later philosophical developments, the ultimate and ineffable ground of all being. It is also the word that gives the Brāhmaṇas their name.

Lévi and Girard on the *Devas* and the *Asuras*

Much of Lévi's (and, needless to say, Girard's) work on the Brāhmaṇas is spent describing the never-ending war between the gods, or *devas*, and the demons, or *asuras* (often compared to the Greek titans). This war seems to define the gods and the demons; Doniger argues that the gods and the demons establish their respective identities precisely by virtue of their conflict:

> The one invariable characteristic of the gods is that they are the enemies of the demons, and the one invariable characteristic of the demons is that they are the enemies of the gods. . . . By nature, gods and demons are alike; by function, however, they are as different as day and night. In fact, one reason for their perpetual conflict is the simple fact that they only become distinct—and therefore real to the Hindus hearing the myths—when they are engaged in battle.[53]

In other words, it is their endless struggle against one another that transforms them from an undifferentiated collection of beings into two cohesive, if warring, communities. And this cosmic struggle that creates, sustains, and sometimes threatens to destroy the communities takes the form of ritual competition, an ongoing agonistic sacrifice. But for Girard, taking for granted that the gods and the demons are alike and *then* become different through a dialectical struggle is to miss the mimetic element of the myth. Girard would have us reverse the order of events: gods and demons are alike because mimetic rivalry has drawn them together, bringing about a sacrificial crisis. He writes:

> What interests me in these rivalries is the mimicry that obviously provokes them and which, becoming reciprocal, forces their escalation. To find the source of these rivalries, we must examine the beginning of each episode, for it is always the same: the two groups are separated but they never cease observing one another; as soon as one of the two reaches for an object, the second anxiously follows suit; soon there are two desires in place of one, two desires bound to collide since they have the same object. Everywhere, imitation is the motor of rivalry.

> This imitation accounts for all the symmetries, all the reciprocities that mark our narratives *before* the intervention of sacrifice, and sacrifice produces a decisive difference, always in favor of the gods. The demons are shown to be almost as clever as the gods, almost as precise in ritual practice, but not quite; this is the sole reason for their repeated collapse into the demonic and for the gods' ascension toward the divine.[54]

It is not hard to see why Girard is so enamored of this mythos. It almost perfectly reflects his belief in the sacrifice as the producer of difference in culture, or at least the ritual substitute for the real producer of difference in culture, which is spontaneous mob violence. The competitive sacrifices of the gods and the demons are not necessarily portrayed in violent terms, but instead as contests to see who can come closest to ritual perfection. As we shall see in a later chapter, this obsession with ritual detail is itself a symptom of the Brahminical repression of sacrificial violence.

Difference is not the only thing the sacrificial struggle of the gods and the demons produces. As Lévi notes, it also produces the divine kingship of Indra, king of the gods. Using as his sources the *Aitareya*, *Taittirīya*, *Gopatha*, and *Śatapatha* Brāhmaṇas and the *Maitrāyaṇī Saṃhitā*, Lévi tells the story of Indra's ascension to the leadership of the gods:

> The social organization of the gods begins as a federation of clans, each commanded by a chief. But rivalries between the groups soon break out and civil war breaks out among the gods. They begin to quarrel and divide into four parties, each unwilling to give recognition to the others. Agni leads the Vasus, Soma leads the Rudras, Varuṇa leads the Ādityas, and Indra leads the Maruts. . . . As they are in discord, the demons and the goblins began to pursue them. The gods then come to understand something: "Look at our empire! The demons and the goblins are catching up to us. We serve the interests of our enemies. Come, let us agree and obey the authority of a single leader." Then they recognize Indra as their king. But once the danger is passed, the royal office loses its *raison d'être* and the leader returns to the ranks. The title and the authority of king move from one god to another according to circumstance. "Who will be our king?" they ask. "Who will lead us into battle?" "I will be your king," Agni answers. "I will lead you. With Agni for your king, with Agni in command,

> the gods will be victors." The war recommences, and the gods look for a new leader. Varuṇa offers to lead them to the victory and then it is Indra's turn. Another time they take Soma as their king, and under King Soma, they conquer the regions of space. Educated by their experience, the gods are making progress. By unanimous consent, they settle on a definitive sovereign. Indra, proclaimed king of the gods, is consecrated in a solemn ceremony with all the pomp that is appropriate to his majesty. The gods in the company of Prajāpati call out, "He is the strongest of the gods, the strongest, most resistant, the best, the most energetic, that sacred king." They enthrone him with sacred chants, and he takes his throne pronouncing the holy formulas.[55]

First in *Violence and the Sacred* and then in *Things Hidden*, Girard argues that we can only understand kingship as a function of sacrifice: "The king is at first nothing but a victim with a suspended sentence, and this demonstrates that the victim is made responsible for the transformation that moves the community from mimetic violence to the order of ritual."[56] The story of the gods determining that Indra, rather than Varuṇa or Agni, is the perfect king could easily be seen as the determination of which victim is most perfect for the sacrifice. And since the war between the gods and the demons is a war of sacrifice, Indra is not so much a war chief here as he is a chief sacrificer, for whom the sacrificial victim is really only a substitute. We will continue to look at the ways Indra serves as a scapegoat and at his connection with other figures that serve as victims with suspended sentences later in the chapter. But first, we should "tarry with the negative" and spend a little time with the demons.

Indra and the *Asuras*

Asura, the word for "demon," has an etymology worth considering because of the light it sheds on Girard's conception of the gods and the demons as "an undecidable case of twins."[57] The meaning of *asura* as "demon" is unique to India. Its close cognate *ahura* has a positive meaning in the Iranian Gāthas, where it applies to the chief god Ahura Mazdā as well as to great men. The earliest strata of Vedic literature, the "family books" of the

Ṛg Veda, know the word *asura* as another word for *deva* ("god") and only use it in the singular and dual forms: there is as yet no class of being called *asuras*.[58] In *Ṛg Veda* 5.42.11, the god Rudra, the Vedic antecedent of Śiva, is addressed with the appositive *deva asura*, providing strong evidence that the terms for god and demon are interchangeable. As in the later Iranian texts, the term is also used for humans. *Asura* is used in the *Ṛg Veda* to refer to humans four times, twice in hostile contexts and twice in friendly contexts. The word for an evil deity, specifically the demonic Svarbhānu who attacks the sun during a solar eclipse, is *āsura*, or *asura* plus the alpha privative "a-," which translates to "non-*asura*."[59] In the later books of the *Ṛg Veda*, *asura* continues to be a synonym for *deva*, but when we finally see *asura* used in the plural it refers to human, not divine, enemies. It is not until the *Artharva Veda*, composed around 1200 B.C.E. along with book ten of the *Ṛg Veda* and the earliest Brāhmaṇas, that we see *asura* as a completely negative term used for the collective enemies of the dragon-slaying storm deity Indra. Trying to explain how the word *asura* came to refer to the enemies of the gods, Wash Edward Hale argues that the answer lies with Indra, known in the Vedas both as Asurahan ("Killer of *Asuras*") and Daśyuhan ("Killer of Non-Aryans").[60] As the Aryans, as the people of the Vedic culture called themselves, abandoned their nomadic life and settled in northern India, the *daśyus* they had opposed (with the help of their *soma*-swilling divine chieftain Indra) in their days as cattle-raiding tribes turned into demonic beings in their mythology. Thus, after the word *asura* began appearing in the plural to name the enemies of Indra in the *Artharva Veda*, the word *daśyu* disappeared almost completely from use.[61] Another interesting etymological development occurred in the late Vedic and epic literature, when the poets wrongly began to take the initial *a-* in *asura* as an alpha privative. Reading *asura* as "non-*sura*," the poets made up the word *sura* to be used as a synonym for *deva* so they could have the very logical if etymologically spurious duality of *sura-asura*.

Etymologies aside, the Vedic mythological roots of the cosmic war are found in two hymns from the *Ṛg Veda*. The first is 10.124, which tells the story of Indra convincing the fire deity Agni to join the gods against the demons. The second is 1.32, which tells the story of Indra slaying Vṛtra, long recognized as a prototypical dragon-slaying myth of the Indo-European type.[62] We will examine both of these myths in the next section.

Soma and Stoma*: Indra in* Ṛg Veda *10.124 and 1.32*

By the time of the composition of the tenth book of the *Ṛg Veda* [*ṚV*], the sense of *asura* as "demon" was firmly in place, setting the scene for an early sacrificial struggle between the gods and the demons. The famous hymn 10.124 begins with Indra calling Agni to leave the side of the *asuras*, who are being led by Indra's enemy, the serpent-demon Vṛtra, and asking him to join the gods as oblation-bearer. Agni agrees to defect from the side of Vṛtra and the demons in favor of the gods. And when his fellow demons Varuṇa and Soma see Agni defecting they decide to go over to the gods as well, leaving the demons without the means to perform sacrifice. The hymn reads:

1. [INDRA:] 'Agni! Come to this sacrifice of ours, that has five roads, three layers, and seven threads. Be our oblation-bearer and go before us. For far too long you have lain in darkness.'
2. [AGNI:] 'Secretly going away from the non-god, being a god and seeing ahead I go to immortality. Unkindly I desert him who was kind to me, as I go from my own friends to a foreign tribe.'
3. [VARUṆA:] 'When I see the guest of the other branch, I measure out the many forms of the Law. I give a friendly warning to the Asura father: I am going from the place where there is no sacrifice to the portion that has the sacrifice.'
4. [SOMA:] 'I have spent many years within him. Now I choose Indra and desert the father. Agni, Soma, Varuṇa—they fall away. The power of kingship has turned around; therefore I have come to help.'
5. [INDRA:] 'Varuṇa, these Asuras have lost their magic powers, since you love me. O king who separates false from true, come and rule my kingdom.
6. 'This was the sunlight, this the blessing, this the light and the broad middle realm of space. Come out, Soma, and let us two kill Vṛtra. With the oblation we sacrifice to you who are the oblation.'
7. The poet through his vision fixed his form in the sky; Varuṇa let the waters flow out without using force. Like his wives, the shining rivers make him comfortable; they swirl his color along their current.
8. They follow his supreme Indra-power; he dwells in those who rejoice in their own nature. Choosing him as all the people choose a king, they have deserted Vṛtra whom they loathe.

9. They say that the yoke-mate of those full of loathing is a swan who glides in friendship with the divine waters. The poets through their meditation have seen Indra dancing to the Anuṣṭubh [meter].[63]

The presence of the Vedic gods Agni, Soma, and Varuṇa on the side of the demons in this story is something of a mystery. Doniger links the hymn, in which Agni is clearly *inside* Vṛtra in some way, to *ṚV* 10.51's story of Agni being coaxed out of the waters by the gods, where he hides when he fears for his life after his three brothers have been killed in the gods' sacrifices. The gods finally draw him out of the water to serve as their oblation-bearer by offering him immortality and a share in the sacrifice. In 10.124, it would seem that the water where Agni hides in 10.51 has been transposed with Vṛtra, whose association with the waters goes back to the story of Indra's slaying Vṛtra to release the waters he has swallowed up in 1.32.[64]

Like many other Vedic hymns, *ṚV* 10.124 begins *in medias res*. It appears to be a fragment of a larger mythological cycle, much of which is lost to us.[65] We do not know whether Agni and Soma have fled to the side of the demons in fear for their lives and Indra is coaxing them to return or whether they began on the side of the demons and are defecting to the gods. We do not know whether this story is part of a constant switching of sides by the sacrificial deities Agni and Soma, who are sometimes with the demons, sometimes with the gods, just as in the *Mahābhārata* the goddess of victory, Śrī, always goes to the side of the winners. One piece of evidence that Agni may have gone to Vṛtra for protection is the fact that Indra names Agni as an *atithi* ("guest") of the demons, which means that Agni is under their protection. The presence of Varuṇa is also mysterious. Bergaigne (whose work Lévi directed Mauss to read) argues that in this hymn, Varuṇa and Vṛtra are one and the same figure and that it is part of the larger myth cycle of the Indra-Varuṇa conflict, which we will also look at more closely in the next chapter.[66] According to this reading, the description in line seven of Varuṇa "[letting] the waters flow out without using force" is a retelling of Indra releasing the waters from Vṛtra's stomach in *ṚV* 1.32. That hymn goes as follows:

1. Let me now sing the heroic deeds of Indra, the first that the thunderbolt-wielder performed. He killed the dragon and pierced an opening for the waters; he split open the bellies of mountains.
2. He killed the dragon who lay upon the mountain; Tvaṣṭṛ[67] fashioned

the roaring thunderbolt for him. Like lowing cows, the flowing waters rushed straight down to the sea.

3. Wildly excited like a bull, he took the Soma for himself and drank the extract from the three bowls in the three-day Soma ceremony. Indra the Generous seized his thunderbolt to hurl it as a weapon; he killed the firstborn of dragons.
4. Indra, when you killed the firstborn of dragons and overcame by your own magic the magic of the magicians, at that very moment you brought forth the sun, the sky, and dawn. Since then you have found no enemy to conquer you.
5. With his great weapon, the thunderbolt, Indra killed the shoulderless Vṛtra, his greatest enemy. Like the trunk of a tree whose branches have been lopped off by an axe, the dragon lies flat upon the ground.
6. For, muddled by drunkenness like one who is no soldier, Vṛtra challenged the great hero who had overcome the mighty and who drank Soma to the dregs. Unable to withstand the onslaught of his weapons, he found Indra an enemy to conquer him and was shattered, his nose crushed.
7. Without feet or hands he fought against Indra, who struck him on the nape of the neck with his thunderbolt. The steer who wished to become the equal of the bull bursting with seed, Vṛtra lay broken in many places.
8. Over him as he lay there like a broken reed the swelling waters flowed for man. Those waters that Vṛtra had enclosed with his power—the dragon now lay at their feet.
9. The vital energy of Vṛtra's mother ebbed away, for Indra had hurled his deadly weapon at her. Above was the mother, below was the son; Dānu lay down like a cow with her calf.
10. In the midst of the channels of the waters which never stood still or rested, the body was hidden. The waters flow over Vṛtra's secret place; he who found Indra an enemy to conquer him sank into long darkness.
11. The waters who had the Dāsa for their husband, the dragon for their protector, were imprisoned like the cows imprisoned by the Paṇis. When he killed Vṛtra he split open the outlet of the waters that had been closed.
12. Indra, you became a hair of a horse's tail when Vṛtra struck you on the corner of the mouth. You, the one god, the brave one, you won the cows; you won the Soma; you released the seven streams so that they could flow.

13. No use was the lightning and thunder, fog and hail that he had scattered about, when the dragon and Indra fought. Indra the Generous remained victorious for all time to come.
14. What avenger of the dragon did you see, Indra, that fear entered your heart when you had killed him? Then you crossed the ninety-nine streams like the frightened eagle crossing the realms of earth and air.
15. Indra, who wields the thunderbolt in his hand, is the king of that which moves and that which rests, of the tame and of the horned. He rules the people as their king, encircling all this as a rim encircles spokes.

Reading the description of Indra coaxing Agni away from the demons in *ṚV* 10.124 alongside the slaying of Vṛtra in *ṚV* 1.32, we can see Indra's overtures to Agni in the first hymn as part of a verbal contest that serves as a counterpart to a physical contest in the second hymn. And in both episodes, the gods win something back from the demons. In the physical contest, where Indra earns the title of Vṛtrahan ("Killer of Vṛtra"), the aspect of intoxication is central. As they are described in verse six when the battle begins, both Indra and Vṛtra have partaken of the Soma, but while Vṛtra is "muddled by drunkenness like one who is no soldier," Indra is "the great hero who has overcome the mighty and who drank Soma to the dregs."[68] This characterization of Soma ingestion as central to the battle goes along with Girard's treatment of the sacrificial role of the sacred (and almost certainly hallucinogenic) drink:

> The disequilibrium, the mental confusion brought about by the mimetic crisis, facilitates sacrificial substitution, making it easier for members of the community to replace their mimetic rivals with the one on his way to becoming a unanimous scapegoat. A certain drunkenness, therefore, a certain vertigo, is favorable to the success of the sacrificial operation.[69]

We have in these two stories of Indra, the great sacrificer with whom all human sacrificers identify, the two aspects of his personality: warrior and sovereign, corresponding to the powers of Soma on the one hand and *stoma*, or "praise," on the other. Indra's slaying of Vṛtra to release the waters (also imagined as cattle) through the power of Soma is analogous to his coaxing Agni away from Vṛtra through *stoma*. This reading reveals in the hymns two of the important elements of Vedic sacrifice: verbal contest and cattle raid, both of which are present in real form at an early stage and later routinized into scripted ritual actions. It is also important to note the strange events described in 1.32.14, when Indra flees in terror from some unknown figure coming to avenge Vṛtra's death. Hubert and Mauss ("searching rather too deep" in the judgment of Hermann Oldenberg) see this event as a parallel to the defeats of Herakles after he kills Typhon and Castor after he kills Lynkeus,[70] arguing that the dragon-slaying hero must always be slain in turn.[71] The presence of this "avenger of the dragon" might also be evidence that Indra and Vṛtra's duel is just a part of a feud in which the demon the gods have killed will be avenged in the next round. The word used for this figure, *yātár*, comes from the Vedic root *yā*, which some scholars take to mean, "to attack" or "to avenge." We will revisit this disputed verbal root in connection to Indra in the next chapter.[72]

Finally, there is the spatial element of *ṚV* 10.124, which gives us a picture of the gods and the demons facing one another as opposing groups for some unknown reason while Agni, Soma, and Varuṇa cross from one side to the other. This picture of the armies of the gods and the demons arrayed against one another like mirror images is reminiscent of a duel. In the *Mahābhārata* this *tête-à-tête* formation becomes the *mise-en-scène* for the famous *Bhagavad Gītā*, Kṛṣṇa's battlefield speech to Arjuna between the opposing armies of the Pāṇḍavas and the Kauravas before the fighting commences. The spatial opposition between gods and demons that is implied in *ṚV* 10.124 has its fullest expression in the Purāṇic myth of the churning of the ocean of milk, which we will examine in chapter three.

The contest between the gods and the demons begins to appear as a central theme in the early Brāhmaṇa texts. Along with it comes another major shift in the conception of Indra that coincides with the rise of the god Viṣṇu, who begins first to be paired with Indra before overtaking him in status and popularity. Although he becomes one of the three major cultic divinities in post-Vedic India, Viṣṇu is a minor figure in the Vedas, known in *ṚV* 1.154 as the god who takes three steps. These three steps win back the universe from the demons, according to the later tradition of the Brāhmaṇas, but the *Ṛg Veda* is more vague about their meaning. The nearest antecedent to the Brāhmaṇic myth of three steps as a means of recovering the three worlds for the gods (which we will examine later) is *ṚV* 6.49.13, in which Viṣṇu "measures out the earth three times for the sake of the suffering of man." Also in the *Ṛg Veda*, Viṣṇu and Indra are paired together as enemies of the demons. *ṚV* 5.5 has them defeating the demon Varcin and destroying his ninety-nine forts while 7.99 describes their victory over the demon Vṛṣaśirpa and 6.20 and 4.18 give credit to Indra and Viṣṇu together for slaying Vṛtra. Madeleine Biardeau argues, convincingly, that Viṣṇu's growing association with the great deeds of Indra is a function of Viṣṇu becoming identified with the Vedic gods of the sacrifice, Puruṣa and Prajāpati, and thus with the sacrifice itself.[73]

Prajāpati and Puruṣa, Indra and Viṣṇu

Prajāpati, "Lord of Creatures," is the creator and father of the gods in early Vedic mythology, reduced to a demiurge or a common noun used to denote members of a class of creator beings in the classical era.[74] Prajāpati creates the gods through his yogic austerities and through the ritual incantations that they reveal to him, as in this passage from *Śatapatha-Brāhmaṇa* [*ŚB*] 3.1.1.1:

> Prajāpati desired to have offspring. He performed austerities and he created the serpents. Prajāpati desired again to have offspring. He performed austerities a second time and he created the birds. Prajāpati desired again to have offspring a third time. He performed austerities again and he saw the Incantation of the Initiated One. He pronounced it and then did he truly create offspring. In the same way, after performing austerities and pronouncing the Incantation of the Initiated One, the sacrificer too creates offspring.

Since all beings are his children, Prajāpati is in a situation in which he cannot have sex without committing incest. So, in a perfect example of a scapegoat myth, when Prajāpati couples with his daughter Uṣas, "Dawn," in the form of an antelope, the gods decide to punish him and send the outsider god Rudra to pierce him with an arrow.

> Prajāpati conceived a passion for his own daughter, Uṣas. Desiring to couple with Uṣas, he slept with her. This was a sure sin in the eyes of the gods. They thought: "Anyone who acts this way towards his own daughter, our sister, is a sinner!" The gods then said to Rudra, "This one is surely

committing a sin, acting this way towards his own daughter, our sister. Shoot him!" Rudra took aim and shot Prajāpati. Half of his seed fell to the ground. And thus the Ṛṣi says of that incident, "When the father embraced his daughter, uniting with her, he dropped his seed on the earth." This became the chant called Āgnimāruta. This is the explanation of how the gods caused that seed to come out.

When the anger of the gods subsided, they cured Prajāpati and cut out Rudra's dart, for Prajāpati is nothing less than the sacrifice itself. The gods said to one another, "Let us think of some way that the part of the sacrifice torn out by the dart may not be lost, and how it can be made a portion of the offering itself." They said, "Take it to the sun god Savitṛ, who sits on the south side of the sacrificial ground: He will eat it a little bit so that it will look as though it has been offered." They accordingly took it round to Savitṛ, who sat on the south side. But when he looked at it, it burnt out his eyes. And that is why they now say that Savitṛ is blind.

The gods said, "It has not yet become appeased here. Take it instead to the moon god Pūṣan!" So they took it to Pūṣan. Pūṣan tasted it and it knocked out his teeth. And that is why they now say that Pūṣan is toothless. Therefore, when they prepare a pot of boiled rice pudding for Pūṣan, they prepare it from ground rice, as one does for a toothless person.

The gods said, "It has not yet become appeased here. Take it instead to Bṛhaspati!" So they took it to Bṛhaspati. Bṛhaspati hurried to Savitṛ to enchant it (*prasava*), because Savitṛ is the enchanter (*prasavitṛ*) of the gods.[75] "Enchant this for me!" he said. Savitṛ, as the enchanter, accordingly enchanted it for him, and being thus enchanted by Savitṛ, it did not injure him: and thus it was appeased.[76]

Puruṣa, the cosmic giant whose dismemberment creates the world, is also a creator in the Veda. But while Prajāpati creates the world through force of will, Puruṣa creates the world by becoming the sacrifice (in the double sense of victim and ritual) in *ṚV* 10.90:

1. Puruṣa has a thousand heads, a thousand eyes and a thousand feet. He pervaded the earth on all sides and extended beyond it the span of ten fingers.

2. This Puruṣa is all that has been and all that will ever be. He is the lord of immortality when he grows beyond everything by food.
3. Such is his greatness, but Puruṣa is greater even than this. All creatures are one quarter of him; three quarters are immortal in heaven.
4. With three quarters Puruṣa rose upward. One quarter of him is still here. From this he spread out to all directions, into that which eats and that which does not eat.
5. From him [the active female creative principle] Virāj was born, and from Virāj Puruṣa was born. As soon as he was born he spread eastward and westward over the earth.
6. When the gods prepared the sacrifice with Puruṣa as the offering, spring was the clarified butter, summer was the fuel and autumn was the oblation.
7. On the sacred *kuśa* grass they anointed Puruṣa, the sacrificial victim born at the beginning. With him the gods, the demigods and the sages all sacrificed.
8. From that great sacrifice of everything the dripping fat was gathered up. He [Puruṣa or Prajāpati] formed it into the creatures of the air and animals both wild and tame.
9. From that great sacrifice of everything were born the verses [of the *Ṛg Veda*] and the chants [of the *Sāma Veda*]. From it came the spells [of the *Atharva Veda*] and the formulae [of the *Yajur Veda*].
10. From it were horses born and all beasts with two rows of teeth. From it came cows, goats, and sheep.
11. When they divided Puruṣa how many portions did they make? What do they call his mouth and his arms? What do they call his thighs and feet?
12. His mouth became the Brahmin class. The Warrior class came from his arms. His thighs became the Producer class, and from his feet the Slave class was made.
13. The moon was born from his mind, and from his eye was born the sun. Indra and Agni were born from his mouth, and Vāyu the wind came from his vital breath.
14. From his navel came the mid-air. The sky was fashioned from his head. Earth came from his feet, and from his ear the regions of the sky. Thus the gods formed the worlds.

15. There were seven enclosing-sticks for him, and thrice seven fuel-sticks when the gods, offering sacrifice, bound Puruṣa as the sacrificial beast.
16. With the sacrifice the gods sacrificed to the sacrifice. These were the first ritual laws. These very powers reached the dome of the sky where dwell the demigods, the gods of old.[77]

Here we have the two stories of Prajāpati and Puruṣa. The former is an active creator god who exists as a separate personality alongside his creation, giving him the opportunity to interact with it and become the first sinner. The latter is a primordial giant who becomes creation itself through being sacrificed. Both figures are explicitly identified with the sacrificial ritual and the sacrificial victim, but it is only Prajāpati whom we can truly call a scapegoat, struck down by his angry children.

The scapegoat and the sacrifice are kept separate in the myths of Prajāpati and Puruṣa. This is a problem for Girard's theory, and in *Sacrifice* he conflates the figures of Prajāpati and Puruṣa in order to find in the incest of Prajāpati the pretext for the dismemberment of Puruṣa:[78]

> To show that sacrifice emerges from a scapegoat phenomenon, I would need a myth more robust than that of Purusha, who is not criminal enough for my taste. Neither the least little parricide nor the least little incest is attributed to him. The most spectacular feature of my demonstration hides itself the moment I need it.[[79]]
>
> Fortunately for me, there is something other than Purusha. There is a second founding myth of sacrifice in the Vedas, as I indicated a short while ago, and I shall turn to it now. The accusation we vainly seek in the *Hymn to Purusha* we shall find in the texts of the Brahmanas on Prajâpati, texts that are likely an amended and enriched reprise of the hymn....
>
> We must not see Prajâpati as a god *of* sacrifice, observes Sylvain Lévi. Such gods give us an impression of the divine and the sacrificial as two separate entities that join themselves for reasons that are fortuitous and alien to their respective essences. The union of the two is consubstantial and it is why Lévi calls Prajâpati *the sacrifice god*. I want to go even further in the same direction and call him *the god sacrifice*.[80]

In Girard's reading, Prajāpati, the scapegoat, and Puruṣa, the sacrifice, must be the same figure. He argues that we must see the myth of Prajāpati's incest and the sacrifice of Puruṣa as the same story told in two different ways. The *Śatapatha Brāhmaṇa* makes the same connection between Puruṣa and Prajāpati repeatedly and identifies Puruṣa-Prajāpati as the sacrificial altar in 6.1.1.5, lending some support to Girard's argument that Prajāpati's sin is a kind of supplement to the Puruṣa hymn. Girard continues:

> Why do the Brahmanas take up the word *prajâpati* rather than *purusha*? The two concepts are certainly close, but they are far from identical. That of the Brahmanas, probably the more recent, is more traditional than that which is in principle more ancient, and the tradition of the Brahmanas may well be the deliberate restoration of a crime that, because it is unanimously attributed to the god by his scandalized followers, justifies the primordial sacrifice.[81]

This tendency to supplement one story with elements of another, conflate figures from various myth complexes, and construct long concatenations of identifications are characteristics of a certain kind of hermeneutics that find their fullest expression in the Brāhmaṇas. It is perhaps because the Brāhmaṇas present a kind of theory of texts (ritual and liturgical texts) that they come to the same kind of conclusions as Girard and provoke the same kind of ire among the rank and file of historians of religion. But because of the many centuries over which they developed their system of thought, they may have also more fully explored some aspects of sacrifice that Girard has only passed over briefly. One example of this is the bifurcation of the victim into a transcendent salvific figure on the one hand and a banished figure, a *pharmakos* or *homo sacer*, on the other. This bifurcation begins in the Vedic tradition with Prajāpati and Puruṣa and continues when they give way to Indra and Viṣṇu. As the salvific incarnation of the god sacrifice, Viṣṇu takes over for Puruṣa as the pervasive spirit of the universe, identified with the sacrifice and with Dharma, the Sanskrit word that means law and justice (as in the German *recht*) as well as the physical order of the cosmos, and which I have translated, following Doniger, as "ritual laws" in *ṚV* 10.90.16. Indra, Viṣṇu's partner in the slaying of Vṛtra in the Vedas, suffers a different fate and becomes the exiled victim, a sinner like Prajāpati. In later Purāṇic myth, Indra becomes more and more of an outsider, a buffoon who is bested by the child Kṛṣṇa (an incarnation of Viṣṇu), cursed to be covered with vaginas, and falls from his station saddled with the guilt of his three great sins, which we will look at in the next chapter.

The identification of Viṣṇu with the sacrifice begins with the formula *yajña vai viṣṇuḥ* ("Viṣṇu is the sacrifice") in the Kauśītaki branch of the *Ṛg Veda*, where it appears as part of a ritual prescription in *Kauśītaki Brāhmaṇa* 4.2.11, 18.5.29, and 18.9.25.[82] The formula is repeated (again in a ritual context) in the *Aitareya Brāhmaṇa*, also belonging to the *Ṛg Veda*, and in the *Śatapatha Brāhmaṇa* of the White *Yajur Veda*.[83] The identification of Viṣṇu with the sacrifice,[84] and thereby with Puruṣa (the cosmic giant whose sacrificial dismemberment creates the universe), and thereby with Prajāpati (the creator god whose children kill him for committing incest with his daughter), and thereby with the Vedic sacrificer who benefits from the ritual is one of the many long and confusing chains of concatenations that provoked the ire of European Indologists in the nineteenth century. We can see this dense network of associations as a highly intellectualized variation of what Girard calls the "disequilibrium [that] facilitates sacrificial substitution," deliberately confusing the sacrificer with the victim and the sacrifice itself.

These Brāhmaṇic images of Viṣṇu also lay the groundwork for the vast corpus of Vaiṣṇava mythology built on the idea that Viṣṇu is the cosmic savior who incarnates himself in his various avatars to restore order, usually in the midst of a sacrificial crisis. The theology of the avatar is best summed up by this famous couplet from the *Bhagavad Gītā*: "Whenever the law (dharma) is in decline and disorder (*adharma*) prevails, I will create myself."[85] The two most popular avatars of Viṣṇu are the divine king Rāma, hero of the *Rāmāyaṇa* epic, and Kṛṣṇa, tales of whose youthful erotic escapades with the cowherd girls in the *Bhāgavata Purāṇa* surpass in popularity the stories of his role as a divine prince and the ultimate godhead in the *Mahābhārata*. As Rāma and as Kṛṣṇa, Viṣṇu takes form on Earth as a human being to win back the universe for the gods after it has been taken over by the demons. In the *Rāmāyaṇa*, Viṣṇu incarnates himself to defeat the otherwise invincible demon king Rāvaṇa. In the *Mahābhārata*, he comes to earth to destroy an evil generation of kings by instigating a genocidal war. But in many ways the avatar *par excellence* is not a mighty warrior prince like Rāma or Kṛṣṇa, but the dwarf Vāmana, whose myth is the most popular of the Brāhmaṇic stories of Viṣṇu.

The first association of Viṣṇu with a dwarf comes in the *Taittirīya Saṃhitā*, which says that one should sacrifice a dwarf animal to Viṣṇu. The prescription to offer a dwarf beast (*paśu*, the word that refers to a sacrificial animal) is rather puzzlingly connected to a version of the story of Indra slaying Vṛtra, presumably with the help of Viṣṇu, in which he pulls one thousand cows out of the dragon's belly, the first of which is humpbacked. At this point, Viṣṇu and the dwarf are still separate beings. Viṣṇu is the sacrificer (or the recipient of the sacrifice) and the dwarf (beast) is the victim.

The two figures are collapsed when the enigmatic three steps of Viṣṇu mentioned (but not elaborated upon) in the *Ṛg Veda* become the basis for the myth of the dwarf avatar, Vāmana, in the *Śatapatha Brāhmaṇa*. Since Viṣṇu is already associated with the sacrificial victim, the move from sacrificing a dwarf *to* Viṣṇu (or Viṣṇu sacrificing a dwarf) to sending Viṣṇu to the sacrifice *as* a dwarf is easily made. The myth begins, like the story of Indra coaxing Agni away from Vṛtra, in the wake of a demonic victory in the ongoing cosmic struggle. The demons are consecrating their victory over Indra with a sacrifice sponsored by their leader, Bali. According to the medieval *Skanda Purāṇa*, this sacrifice takes place at the transition between the Golden Age and the more degraded Age of the Trey, a liminal period called the Yugānta or the Turning of the Age, always associated in myth with monstrosity, undifferentiation, and cataclysmic violence—the signs of the sacrificial crisis.

In her analysis of all the variants of the Vāmana myth Deborah Soifer identifies three types of explanations for Bali's sovereignty at the beginning of the story. In the first type of explanation, Bali wins the universe as part of the ongoing struggle between the gods and the demons. The constant exchange of power between the gods and the demons in this type of myth also recalls Jan Heesterman's idea of the necessary exchange of goods through gifts and plunder in the classical Vedic economy. When the Aryans were still nomadic cattle raiders, their sacrificial system required the king (or chieftain) to alternate between the positions of *yajamāna*, a patron of the sacrifice bound by tradition to give away all his wealth in gifts to his guests, and *dīkṣita*, a consecrated warrior who rebuilds the treasury he has exhausted through conquest and raids, so that he can become a *yajamāna* again.[86] For reasons that will soon become clear, this oscillation of wealth and power is probably the core of the myth.

In the second type of explanation for Bali's sovereignty, a natural extension of the first and a common trope in the mythology of Viṣṇu, Bali has become so righteous by the proper performance of the ascetic practices that have displaced sacrifice that the god Brahmā is forced to answer his prayer for invincibility. In the later versions of the cosmic struggle, the gods and the demons constantly try to outdo each other in what we might call religiosity. As the tradition continues to develop their rivalry grows more and more mimetic, with the demons becoming less demonic and more godlike in the later stories. Every time the demons get the upper hand, it is because they have properly performed all of the necessary austerities, prayers, penances, devotions, and rituals called for in the Vedic worldview. A Vaiṣṇava myth that serves as a polemic against Buddhist heterodoxy illustrates this point. In the myth, Viṣṇu comes to earth in the form of the Buddha to preach false doctrines among the demons and thereby undermine the strength they gained through their orthodoxy. In other words, the demons are better than the gods and must be corrupted to restore the balance; the cosmic conflict between the gods and the demons, it seems, is truly beyond good and evil. It is worth noting that, as we observed earlier, the sacrificial struggle of the gods and the demons at first serves to create difference, defining the gods and the demons in opposition to one another. This begs the question of how, in later myth, the sacrifice seems to do the opposite, bringing the two sides closer and closer together. I will propose an answer that foreshadows my main argument: The Vedic sacrificial system is always-already in a state of collapse. The resemblance between the gods and the demons in later mythology, a clear sign of sacrifice's fading efficacy in ensuring social stability, signals the mythmakers' consciousness of this fact. It is not a coincidence that the gods and the demons have grown closer together in the period of the Purāṇas; the Vedic gods are being supplanted by Purāṇic gods like Viṣṇu and Śiva who offer novel forms of religiosity largely foreign to the Vedic system, though they arise directly out of its collapsing structures.

This point is well illustrated in the third type of explanation for Bali's sovereignty identified by Soifer: Bali has become sovereign over the universe through the intervention of his chaplain or *purohita* Śukra (to whom we will return in the next section). Śukra, a Brahmin of the great Bhārgava clan, knows the secret of the Viśvajīt sacrifice, which makes the sacrificer (Bali, in this case) "equal to Indra." But if he is equal to Indra by virtue of the ritual, then he is still inferior to Viṣṇu, who must come take form to stop him. In what Soifer describes as a "typical Purāṇic twist," many versions of the myth, including those found in the *Viṣṇudharmottara, Kūrma,* and *Skanda* purāṇas, describe Bali's reign as a righteous and illustrious one marked by generosity, prosperity, and security—all of the characteristics of the Golden Age of the world. Nevertheless, it has to end so that the gods can regain control of the sacrifice and sovereignty over the cosmos. To restore order, Viṣṇu is either born as a dwarf or born as himself and takes the form of a dwarf to visit Bali's sacrifice.

If Bali's reign is typically without the signs of a sacrificial crisis, we can take Viṣṇu's birth as a dwarf, albeit a Brahmin dwarf, as such a sign. *Skanda Purāṇa* 7.2.14–19 describes Viṣṇu's Vāmana incarnation in monstrous terms, with a big head, an oversized jaw, fat calves, a large belly, and a heart full of lust. It is this form that Vṣṇu takes to visit the sacrifice of Bali (usually identified as the elaborate Horse Sacrifice) often before the ritual has actually commenced. Like Don Corleone at his daughter's wedding in the opening scene of *The Godfather*, Bali is required to grant requests to all of his guests. And since Vāmana is a Brahmin, Bali is especially anxious to show generosity toward him (generosity toward Brahmins being the mark of a good king). It is at this point that the Vedic story of Viṣṇu winning the universe in three steps comes into the myth, for the diminutive Viṣṇu-Vāmana asks only for as much land as he can cover in three steps. But when Bali gives his assent, Viṣṇu assumes his Puruṣa-like cosmic giant form and covers the entire universe in three strides.

But the denouement of the myth is not as simple as a hubristic demon king paying the price for underestimating a god. As Soifer notes, there are a number of distinct versions of how the gods win the universe back from the demons. In the *Vāmana* and the *Skanda* purāṇas, Bali's son Bāṇa loudly protests Viṣṇu's treachery. In the *Bhāgavata* and *Brahmā* Purāṇas, Bali recognizes Vāmana as Viṣṇu and when the god has covered the whole universe in just two steps, the demon king offers his own head for the third step, a sign of the deepest devotion and humility.[87]

When he wins back the universe on behalf of the gods through his shape-shifting abilities, Viṣṇu is clearly usurping the role of the protean Indra.[88] The myth of Vāmana itself is a retelling of a story in the *Taittirīya Saṃhitā* in which the gods approach the demons, who rule the world, and ask for as much of the earth as Sālāvṛkī (Indra's werewolf form, to which we will return in the next chapter) can run around three times. The demons agree and Sālāvṛkī runs three times around the earth and wins it back for the gods.[89] Soifer notes that in twenty-eight of the thirty major variants of the Vāmana story, Viṣṇu is acting for Indra and restores the rule of the universe to him after winning it from Bali. It is clear here that the pair of Viṣṇu and Indra from Vedic mythology is breaking apart. Viṣṇu is controlling the sacrifice in the role of the Brahmin, the highest class in the ancient Indian social hierarchy, while Indra, along with the Kṣatriya class he represents, is relegated to a subordinate role, ruling the world on behalf of the Brahmins. The Kṣatriya rules the earth, but the Brahmin rules the sacrifice and in so doing rules the universe.

With the fate of Bali after Viṣṇu's three steps, we return to the question of the sacrificial crisis. Bali's reign may have been legitimate according to the rules of Dharma by virtue of his good and just actions. But in the *Matsya Purāṇa* (where, incidentally, Bali has already tried to offer him the entire universe *before* he takes his three steps), Viṣṇu exiles Bali into a realm full of hundreds of palaces, dancing girls, food, and other comforts, but binds him with the noose of Varuṇa (more on which in the next chapter) and makes him take an oath not to rise up against the Brahmins or gods again. Bali's reign is a mirror image of the way things ought to be. No matter how good a king a demon is, it is for Indra to reign in this universe and for the demons to reign in Hell. The fact that Bali's place of exile or "Hell" is described in the exact same terms as Heaven underlines the mimetic nature of the gods' and the demons' rivalry. At this point, they have become doubles. As the Vedic mythology of Indra gives way to the Purāṇic myths of Viṣṇu, the sacrificial struggle between the gods and the demons is as mechanistic and amoral as the swing of a pendulum.

The Gospels accomplish the unmasking of the sacrificial mechanism through the revelation of Christ's resurrection. The resurrection is a miracle because it reverses all expectations: a dead man walks, an executed criminal is clothed in the raiment of a divine king, and the stone rejected by the builders becomes the cornerstone. It is also, significantly, the fulfillment of a prophecy. We can see some similar elements in the apotheosis of Viṣṇu-Vāmana. His transition from misshapen dwarf to cosmic overlord is miraculous and it is also the precursor to the much more theologically significant moment in the

Bhagavad Gītā where Viṣṇu-Kṛṣṇa takes his universal form in the presence of Arjuna in the moments before the great sacrificial battle to reveal to him the new path of personal devotion that has superseded the sacrificial system. There is no prophecy in the Sanskrit tradition at this point, but the Vāmana myth functions as an exegesis if not a fulfillment of Viṣṇu's enigmatic three steps in the Veda.

Kṛtayugānta, "The End of the Golden Age": Revelations

The reader will have noticed by now (and hopefully with minimal annoyance) that my argument tends to wander afield, and so far it has taken us from the battlefields of eighteenth century colonial India to the mercantile exchanges of Paris to the world of Purāṇic mythology. This chapter's exploration of rivalries began with the dismissive attitude of Indologists toward the Brāhmaṇas and the parallels Girard sees between this antagonism and the contemporary attitude toward mimetic theory. For Girard, what links the Brāhmaṇas and mimetic theory is the fact that both see the mimetic nature of desire and explode the Enlightenment myth of rationality, which is bound to draw antagonism. But we have also seen that Girard is not actually analyzing the Brāhmaṇas, but one of the seminal texts of French Indology, Sylvain Lévi's *La doctrine du sacrifice dans les Brâhmanas*. Lévi's work, we have discovered, comes from a tradition of scholarship prone to take the side of the victims in the wake of France's humiliating defeat at the hands of the British in India. It also expresses a tension between universalism and particularism born from the author's political engagement in post-Dreyfus France. *La doctrine du sacrifice* and the ideas that inform it are also foundational to the sociological tradition to which Girard's theory (a "radicalized Durkheimianism") is an heir.[90] In many ways, *Sacrifice*, Girard's turn to Lévi, is mimetic theory's turn toward its own unexamined genealogy.

We have also begun to look closely at the rivalries of Sanskrit mythology that provide the grist for Lévi's mill, especially the ongoing mimetic rivalry of the gods and the demons, whose surface we have only scratched. We began by examining how Indra's divine kingship arises out of this ongoing cosmic struggle. We saw how the pair of Indra and Viṣṇu is analogous with

Prajāpati and Puruṣa in the Vedic literature. Then we watched Viṣṇu supplant Indra in the later Purāṇic literature as the embodiment of sacrifice as it transcends its boundaries, a movement exemplified by his transformation from a dwarf that recalls a sacrificial beast to a cosmic sovereign whose being is coterminous with the universe itself. The increasingly mimetic relationship between the gods and the demons has complicated the picture of sacrifice found in the earliest Vedic hymns. And, as will become more apparent later, the Brāhmaṇas with their near-obsessive tendency to draw connections and correlations has given us an exponentially more complex set of speculations on the meaning of sacrifice that anything Girard has ever examined before.

For Girard it seems the only way to truly uncover the sacrificial order is to show the innocence of the victim as the Gospels do. But does it not amount to the same thing to show that the victim and the perpetrators are arbitrary and interchangeable as is the case with the gods and the demons? It is a commonplace in literature for someone to learn the folly of scapegoating by walking a mile in the other's shoes, as in Mark Twain's *The Prince and the Pauper*[91] or John Howard Griffin's sociological-journalistic 1961 civil rights classic *Black Like Me*. Do the Sanskrit myths reveal the arbitrariness of the sacrifice and the contingency of social order in the same way? This will become an important question in the next chapter when we examine the relationships between kings and Brahmins in the literature and also continue exploring the genealogy of Girard's thought.

Priests and Kings, Oaths and Duels

The king should rise early in the morning, attend respectfully to learned priests who have grown old in the study of the triple learning, and abide by their advice.

—*The Laws of Manu* 7.37

Will no one rid me of this turbulent priest?

—King Henry II ordering the death of St. Thomas à Becket

In the last chapter, we examined the rivalries outside (European scholars vs. Brahmin authors, France vs. England, philology vs. sociology) and inside (gods vs. demons) of the Brāhmaṇa narrative as received and interpreted by Girard. Now we will examine a new rivalry: that of the royal and military Kṣatriya class and the priestly Brahmin class, along with the sacrificial institutions of the oath and the duel through which that rivalry is mediated. In order to understand the relationship between the two functions represented by Kṣatriyas and Brahmins in ancient India, we will employ the theories of Georges Dumézil—like Lévi, another French thinker whose influence on Girard has been underappreciated.

Dumézil's compelling argument about the tripartite structure that underlies Indo-European religion and society gives us a firmer grounding on which to do comparative work with Indian, Greek, Iranian, and Scandinavian cultures, but I am even more interested in his early and abandoned theory of the **bhlagh(s)-men*, the forgotten (or repressed) figure who serves as a sacrificial substitute for the king and who develops into the Brahmin (superior to the king) in the Vedic context. Even if the idea of the **bhlagh(s)-men* as ancestor of the Brahmin is too speculative, as Dumézil eventually thought it was, it still points toward an important facet of the Brahmin's identity and finds echoes in certain myths.

Examining the Kṣatriya-Brahmin rivalry in its human and divine iterations, I will propose that the Brahmin's mastery of speech and the Kṣatriya's mastery of force can be traced from the sacrificial enclosure all the way into the politico-legal structures that are the foundations of the ancient Indian worldview: the oath and the duel. To understand the implications of this genealogy, I will bring in the work of Italian philosopher Giorgio Agamben, specifically his writings on the anthropogenic power of the oath and the figure of the *homo sacer*. Using the medievalist Henry Charles Lea's 1866 work *The Duel and the Oath* as a starting point, I will argue that the duel and the oath both derive from an early stratum of Vedic ritual in which two sacrificers contended with one another instead of one sacrificer who enlisted a Brahmin priest to perform the ritual on his behalf. But, I will claim, when Brahmin ritualists abandoned the two-sacrificer model, they were left with the problem of integrating the now superfluous second sacrificer into the new ritual system. This second sacrificer, transformed into the always-already defeated party, is the basis for what I have identified as the Indian wolf-warrior cycle, visible in fragmentary references to groups of heterodox ascetics like the Vrātyas, in myths of sacred kingship, and in the story of Śunaḥśepa, the sacrificial victim who miraculously escapes his fate and whose story will conclude this chapter.

Mon semblable, mon frère!

The things Girard appreciates in Hubert and Mauss's *Sacrifice* essay are their argument that sacrifice is the origin of religion and their understanding of sacrifice as a "technique" (or perhaps a *techne*) visible in recognizable form in different cultures.[1] Girard gives the two sociologists a rather backhanded compliment in *Violence and the Sacred* when he marvels that "[their] failure to come to grips with the origin and function of sacrifice makes their accurate description of its operation even more remarkable."[2] We can now trace their line of inquiry into the violent heart of the sacred back to Mauss's encounter with Lévi and the Sanskrit tradition in 1895. But what we have not yet seen is that the work of Lévi and Mauss also has a critical intersection with another thinker who had a profound influence on the French structuralist tradition with which Girard is in constant conversation—Georges Dumézil.

Like Girard, Georges Dumézil was a "man of few ideas"[3] and, like Girard, he was sometimes accused of reading myths selectively to make them fit his theory.[4] The son of a classicist and a polyglot from childhood, Dumézil studied philology and the classics at the École Normale Supérieure, where he began his comparative work. His dissertation, *Le festin d'immortalité: Étude de mythologie comparée indo-européenne*, posited a connection between the Sanskrit *amṛta* and Greek *ambrosia* as two appellations for the Indo-European draught of immortality. At that time, Dumézil was also working closely with Mauss, to whom he later dedicated his 1948 book *Mitra-Varuna*. Henri Hubert was one of his examiners and, at the time of his thesis defense, questioned whether Dumézil had sufficient evidence to warrant his conclusions. Agreeing with Hubert, Dumézil's mentor, the linguist Antoine Meillet (another disciple of Durkheim) rejected the dissertation outright and sent him packing, first to Warsaw, then Istanbul, and finally Uppsala. Dumézil describes the setback:

> One of my teachers, who had originally encouraged me without gauging any more clearly than I had the difficulties involved, was aware, above all, of the uncertainties apparent in my first two essays, as well as sensitive to the criticisms that certain young and brilliant flamines did not fail to make of my Lupercalia. Was I going to compromise the prestige of the entire comparative method that was then establishing itself with such acclaim in the linguistic field by employing it in a lateral, clumsy, perhaps illegitimate way? Fortunately, at that very moment, others came to understand the scope and richness of the field, and, to put it simply, they rescued me: Sylvain Lévi, Marcel Mauss, and Marcel Granet were to be the guardian deities of this new discipline.[5]

During his exile, Dumézil's interest in Indo-European myth and language led to his research among the tribes of the Caucasus Mountains where he came into contact with an isolated group called the Ossetes, who were the sole descendants of the Alani, a medieval branch of the Scythians, and spoke a language related to the languages of Iran. Studying Ossetic mythology, Dumézil became very interested in a group of legendary people called the Narts who were divided into three great clans: the intelligent Alægatæ, the courageous Æxsærtægkatæ, and the wealthy Bor(i)atæ. He identified the clans as counterparts to the ancient Indian classes, or *varṇas*, of Brahmin, Kṣatriya, and Vaiśya and to the Roman trinity of Jupiter, Mars, and Quirinus. From this connection, Dumézil hypothesized that, before it split up and dispersed from Ireland to India, Indo-European society (or at least the Indo-European ideal of society) consisted of three functions: the priestly sovereign, the warrior, and the producer. Among the groups who spoke a language of the Indo-European family, including the Romans, the Norse, the Indians, and the Iranians, traces still remained in their myths and epics of this trifunctional model.

In 1933, Dumézil returned to France, where Lévi, an admirer and friend, secured him a position teaching Comparative Indo-European Mythology at the École Pratique des Hautes Études. Lévi also sent Dumézil to study ancient Chinese culture with the Durkheimian Sinologist and socialist activist Marcel Granet.[6] Along with the Chinese language, Dumézil picked up from Granet the missing piece of his "new comparative mythology," the Durkheimian notion of the "total social fact," in which "all kinds of institutions are given expression at one and the same time—religious, juridical and moral, which relate to both politics and the family; likewise economic ones. . . ."[7] Two years later, Dumézil published *Flamen-Brahman*, where, using the Sanskrit story of Śunaḥśepa as a prime example, he advanced the theory (which he later abandoned) that the Roman *flāmen diālis*, the Iranian *baresman*, and the Sanskrit Brahmin all corresponded to a Proto-Indo-European priestly figure called the **bhlagh(s)-men* whose role was to be a substitute sacrifice for the king. The same year, Dumézil's former teacher Meillet reversed his decision on his work and joined Lévi in nominating him for the position of Directeur d'Études.

Dumézil published *L'Idéologie des trois fonctions dans les épopées des peuples indo-européens*, the first part of his three-volume magnum opus *Mythe et épopée*, in 1968 while Girard was working on *Violence and the Sacred*.[8] In that work Girard mentions him briefly and makes use of Dumézil's analysis of the Roman Horatius myth.[9] The most sustained treatment of Dumézil in Girard's writings comes in chapter six of *The Scapegoat*, where he analyzes the Scandinavian myth of Baldr. Baldr, who has been granted invincibility against (almost) any attack by his mother Frigg, is being harmlessly assaulted by his compatriots the Ases in a game played in the public square. Frigg has made Baldr invincible by making all the gods, animals, and plants swear never to harm him. But the trickster god Loki learns that the young shoot of mistletoe was not held to the oath because it seemed to Frigg too small and puny to worry about. So Loki gives a sprig of mistletoe to Baldr's blind brother Hoehr, who then unknowingly kills him with it, turning the harmless game into the real death of Baldr. In Girard's analysis, Dumézil, despite having made a "masterly study" of Loki, misses the point of the myth:[10]

> It is easy to understand why the eminent scholar considers the game the Ases are playing astonishing. A little further on he will describe the game as both "spectacular" and "fake." He arouses our curiosity without satisfying it. . . . By suggesting that the game of the Ases is fake, G. Dumézil can be said to be speaking about the scene indirectly. It is clearly a question of collective violence.[11]

Despite this criticism Girard expresses a general admiration for Dumézil's scholarship in *Things Hidden since the Foundation of the World* and *The Scapegoat* and he never seems to include Dumézil (who was elected to the Académie Française in 1978 with the support of Claude Lévi-Strauss) in his attacks on structuralism.[12] But Girard has never evaluated the trifunctional thesis in print, instead concentrating on what he seems to consider Dumézil's generally perceptive readings of individual myths. In the next section, we will see what help Dumézil's trifunctional model may give to Girard's reading of myths, especially in the Indian context, asking the question raised by Dumézil's abandoned hypothesis of the sacrificial **bhlagh(s)-men*: Is the surrogate victim mechanism encoded into the deep structure of Indo-European myth and society?

Structure and *Skandalon*

On the first page of *Violence and the Sacred*, Girard addresses Hubert and Mauss's conception of the sacrificial victim, writing:

> Because the victim is sacred, it is criminal to kill him—but the victim is sacred because he is to be killed. Here is a circular line of reasoning that at a somewhat later date would be dignified by the sonorous term *ambivalence*. . . . When we speak of ambivalence, we are only pointing out a problem that remains to be solved.[13]

The circularity of Mauss and Hubert's argument in Girard's reading is a symptom of what he sees as the problem with all of Durkheimian sociology: a lack of concern for the victim; and it is ethically as well as methodologically troubling to him. All the theorists of sacrifice Girard argues against, from Bataille to Durkheim, have a blind spot when it comes to the sacrificial victim. Their picture of sacrifice is constructed from the point of view of the sacrificer or of the community benefiting from the sacrifice. Hubert and Mauss's theory leaves the victim in a loop of circular logic because the victim is not the center of the sacrifice and is therefore relegated to the realm of ambiguity (or ambivalence). What matter *why* the victim is to be killed?

As we have seen, the idea of the "total social fact" was the missing piece to Dumézil's trifunctional model. And it was after he came into contact with the Durkheimians but before he truly began to assimilate their sociological model into his work that he put forward the sacrificial **bhlagh(s)-men* hypothesis. On the sacrifice of Puruṣa (whom he identifies as a Brahmin) in the *Ṛg Veda*, he writes:

> It is possible that, for a long time in certain places, the legends existed in reality. Representing the mythic act of the creation of the world were periodic real, material acts that maintained the real world in its vigor and fecundity: human sacrifices. So in the spring and on other big occasions, an earthly Brahmin bled to make the universal sap rise in the world again and to restore the economic and political order of the world, like at the

> beginning a cosmic man, a "*Remède*," a celestial Brahmin, gave his substance and his life force to make up the matter of the world itself. What is more frequent in religions than these transpositions of earth to heaven, ritual to myth, periodical to primordial, seasonal to cosmogonic?[14]

If, like Dumézil, we take the Vedic sacrifice as a total social fact that presents itself as economic, juridical, moral, aesthetic, religious, mythological, and socio-morphological, it is tempting to consider that the story of Puruṣa may reflect an older tradition of sacrificing a Brahmin who gained his power by exploiting his sacred position as a sacrificial victim and substitute for the king, the possessor of economic and martial power. In the Mesoamerican world, the Aztec sacrificial rite of Toxcatl, in which a man representing the war god Tezcatlipoca is sacrificed at the end of a year, provides a model of just this kind of limited ritual power. Davíd Carrasco describes the ritual:

> Elaborate efforts were made to find the perfect deity impersonator for this festival. The captive warrior had to have a flawless body, musical talents and rhetorical skills. For a year prior to the sacrifice, he lived a privileged existence in the capital. He had eight servants, who ensured the he was splendidly arrayed and bejeweled, and four wives given to him during the last twenty days of his life. Just before the end of the sacrificial festival, we are told that he arrived at a "small temple called the Tlacochcalco . . . he ascended by himself, he went up of his own free will, to where he was to die. As he was taken up a step, as he passed one step, there he broke, he shattered his flute, his whistle" and was then swiftly sacrificed.[15]

The privilege of the Tezcatlipoca impersonator has an expiration date that comes when a priest takes a knife to him. But what if a sacrificial victim found a way to extend this yearlong period of privilege by finding a substitute (like the Doms among the Gōndi) or perhaps by giving up some of the perks of his position and extending them to the sacrificers? It is possible that at a later stage the Brahmins, who may have begun in very much the same position as this ersatz Tezcatlipoca, reversed the ritual to make themselves its controllers rather than its victims. This would explain how, in the classical *varṇa* system, the more vulnerable Brahmins somehow maneuvered themselves above kings in the social hierarchy.

Some more clues to this process can be found in the relationship between Indra and Viṣṇu we examined in the previous chapter. When we look at Viṣṇu's transformation into the Brahmin dwarf Vāmana in the context of the ritual surrounding the myth, we see that Viṣṇu takes the form of the sacrificial beast that he himself offers in the *Taittirīya Saṃhitā*. In the form of the victim—and a Brahmin victim at that—Viṣṇu wins the sacrifice and with it, the world, which he then turns over to Indra to rule. As a total social fact, the upshot of the Vāmana story is that at the economic level, the king is required to be ready to give all his wealth to Brahmins in return for the consecration of his reign; at the juridical level, the sacrificer-king is always-already bound to the sacrificing priest in obligation; at the moral level, the myth extols the generosity of a good king, even if he be a demon; at the aesthetic level, there is the idea of the large contained within the small that is common in myths that want to express the majesty of godhead; at the religious level, there is the birth of Vaiṣṇava devotionalism; at the mythological level, the royal god Indra rules at the pleasure of the Brahmin god Viṣṇu; at the socio-morphological level, the second function rules at the pleasure of the first.

Let us reexamine this myth as Girard might. Although it is embedded in the cosmic struggle between the gods and the demons, the Vāmana episode represents a moment in which the gods conquer the universe without resorting to violence. It is Viṣṇu's transcendent divinity (a function of his identification with the cosmic giant Puruṣa) and not his destructive power that wins the day for the gods. In short, the myth is about the mastery exercised by the Brahmin who has renounced violence. But this interpretation may rest on a too narrow definition of violence. The myth's denouement is, after all, the expulsion of Bali, which takes violent form in some variants and non-violent form in others.

At the core of the Vāmana myth, as we have seen, are another myth and a ritual: the Vedic myth of Viṣṇu's three steps and the ritual sacrifice of a dwarf beast. And in the Vāmana myth, the two become conflated and Viṣṇu becomes the dwarf who takes three steps at the sacrifice. From here it is not too much of a stretch to see Viṣṇu-Vāmana as the intended victim of the sacrifice. In the version from the *Brahmā Purāṇa*, Viṣṇu is identified as the Lord of the Sacrifice (Yajñeśa) and the Sacrificial Puruṣa (Yajñapuruṣa).[16] But he also comes to the sacrifice as a guest, which puts him under the protection of the sacrificer. Still, in Brāhmaṇic terms, Viṣṇu's transformation from dwarf to cosmic giant clearly marks him as a victim, since the correspondence between the sacrificial victim and the victim of the first cosmic sacrifice (Puruṣa) is the main correspondence on which all other Brāhmaṇic correspondences are based. The two appositive terms *yajñeśa* and *yajñapuruṣa* in the *Brahmā Purāṇa* are telling: Viṣṇu is both the victim (*puruṣa*) of the sacrifice and its lord (*īśa*).

At this point, we must remember that religion for Girard is "'always-already' interpretive" and look for yet another layer of meaning, because this apotheosis of the sacrificial victim is only background to what is really happening in the myth: the expulsion of Bali. And this expulsion is followed subtly by the voluntary self-expulsion of the hero of the myth, the Brahmin ascetic Viṣṇu-Vāmana, when he turns the polluting and violent business of kingship back over to Indra, having regained the world from the demons. To add to the confusion, it is Viṣṇu-Vāmana who bears the deformity that is the mark of the scapegoat, while Bali is the one who is expelled, but not for any of the usual criminal accusations; in fact, as we have seen, he is sometimes even presented as a model ruler. The recurring theme throughout this complicated myth cycle is the bifurcation of the victim, a theme that goes all the way back to Puruṣa and Prajāpati, if we trace it to its Vedic roots (see table 1).

What Girard wants to find in *Sacrifice* is "the crime that is not there" in the Puruṣa story. He finds it in the story of Prajāpati, where the bifurcation begins. As Vedic myth develops, the crime hides in the vast and ever-expanding system of differences that the myths create. In the next section, we will turn our attention to another divine pairing: Mitra and Varuṇa. For if Indra is the model of the "criminal god" so popular in the local traditions of India, then the paired gods Mitra and Varuṇa represent the prototype of the "law and order god" and, naturally, they also serve as Indra's rivals.

Indra, Mitra-Varuṇa, and the Magico-Sovereign Function

Mitra, whose name is cognate with the modern Hindi word for "friend," is the Vedic god of the contract. His name appears along with Indra's and Varuṇa's on Hittite cuneiform inscriptions discovered at Boğazkale in modern-day Turkey that date back to the fifteenth century B.C.E., identifying Mitra as

Table 1. Analogous Elements in the Rivalries of Puruṣa and Prajāpati and Viṣṇu and Indra

PURUṢA	PRAJĀPATI
Cosmic giant	Sovereign lord
Transcendent	Immanent
Blameless	Guilty of incest
Creates through self-giving	Creates through action

VIṢNU	INDRA
Cosmic giant	Sovereign god
Brahmin	Kṣatriya
Blameless	Guilty of three great sins
Wins the world for the gods by becoming a dwarf and taking three steps	Wins the world for the gods by becoming a wolf and making three circumambulations

part of a pre-Vedic class of Indo-European deities brought into India with the Aryan migration. In 1934, Dumézil was working on the myths and rituals associated with the Indo-European deity known as Ouranos in Greece, Uranus in Rome, and Varuṇa in India when Sylvain Lévi posed to him the question, "What about Mitra?"[17] After that Dumézil began to explore Mitra and Varuṇa's role as a divine pair of gods who represent, respectively, the contractual and the judicial forms of the magico-sovereign function, represented in India by the Brahmin class. Mitra and Varuṇa are often addressed as a cosmic pair in the *Ṛg Veda*, but we should also note that while Varuṇa is addressed alone in a good number of hymns, Mitra only has one Vedic hymn to himself. Dumézil's comparative analysis strongly suggests that for at least one group of Indo-Europeans, Mitra and Varuṇa were the apotheosis of the earthly pair of Brahmin and Kṣatriya-king. But in the Vedas, it is Indra who becomes the most distinctly kingly god while Agni, the deified sacrificial fire, becomes the priestly god—probably because it was the mobile cult of the fire sacrifice that dominated the Vedic ritual landscape. For whatever reason, Mitra is a very minor player in Vedic mythology and Varuṇa absorbs his contractual role along with his own judicial one.

The texts have various ways of understanding this symbiosis. The *Śatapatha Brāhmaṇa*, for example, conceives of Mitra and Varuṇa as the male and the female principles, a conception seconded by an analogy in the *Mahābhārata* that links Mitra to *puruṣa*, a term that refers to the male material principle in Yogic Sāṃkhya philosophy, and Varuṇa to *prakṛti*, the female spiritual principle.[18] In *Śatapatha Brāhmaṇa* 4.1.4, Mitra and Varuṇa are identified with paired elements of human consciousness: the *kratu* and the *dakṣa* ("formulator of desire" and "executor of desire"), and the *abhigantṛ* and the *kartṛ* ("the conceiver" and "the doer").[19] This passage is worth examining in detail because it is a kind of Rosetta Stone for understanding how the insights about mimetic desire Girard sees in the Brāhmaṇas are mapped onto a religio-political order. Purporting to explain why the sacrificer must offer a pressing of the *soma* to Mitra-Varuṇa, the passage is a remarkably complex and multi-layered bit of social and psychological theory.

> Mitra and Varuṇa are the *kratu* and the *dakṣa* of (the sacrificer) and thus they belong to his self (*adhyātma*). Whenever he desires in his mind (saying) "Perhaps this (should be) mine. I will do this," that is *kratu*. When that is accomplished, that is *dakṣa*. Mitra is the *kratu* and Varuṇa is the *dakṣa*. Mitra is the Brahmin class (or Brahmin nature) and Varuṇa is the Kṣatriya class (or Kṣatriya nature). The Brahmin class is the *abhigantṛ* and the Kṣatriya class is the *kartṛ*. In the beginning the Brahmin class and the Kṣatriya class were separate. Mitra, the Brahmin class, could stand in the law (*ṛte*) without Varuṇa, the Kṣatriya class. But Varuṇa could not stand without Mitra and whatever he did without Mitra's aid did not succeed. Varuṇa the Kṣatriya class called on Mitra the Brahmin class, saying, "Unite yourself to me! I will put you before me. Helped by you, I will be able to accomplish something!" Mitra said, "So be it!" And from that came the offering to Mitra and Varuṇa.[20]

The myth goes on to explain that while a Kṣatriya needs a Brahmin to function, a Brahmin does not need a Kṣatriya. The text then tells us why the priest must mix the *soma* offering to Mitra-Varuṇa with milk.

> This is the reason why he mixes it with milk. Once, [the god] Soma was none other than Vṛtra. When the gods slew Vṛtra, they said to Mitra, "You

> must slay him as well." But he was not pleased and said, "But I am everyone's friend (*mitra*). If I am no friend (*amitra*) I will become an enemy!" The gods answered, "Then we will exclude you from the sacrifice." At this Mitra said, "I will slay him too." After this all his cattle fled from him, saying, "He used to be a friend, but now he has become an enemy." Thus Mitra was left without cattle. So the gods mixed the *soma* with milk to replace Mitra's cattle. In the same way, the priest mixes the *soma* with milk to give him [Mitra or the sacrificer] cattle.[21]

This myth introduces a system of correlations that we must first understand before we proceed. The first level is myth$_1$, the now familiar story of the slaying of Vṛtra (here by all the gods together instead of by Indra or by Indra and Viṣṇu). The second level is myth$_2$, the cosmogonic understanding of myth indicated by the identification of Soma with Vṛtra. The third level is ritual$_1$, the mythic sacrifice from which the gods are threatening to exclude Mitra if he does not participate in killing Vṛtra. The fourth level is ritual$_2$, the actual human ritual that this verse is meant to explain (see table 2).

In the beginning Mitra is alone, "standing in the law" (or "standing firm") with his desires in his mind. Then Varuṇa, who finds himself unable to fulfill his own desires, enters into a symbiotic relationship with Mitra. Nothing yet indicates their relationship is a rivalrous one, but when the text equates the pair of Mitra-Varuṇa with Brahmin-Kṣatriya the rivalry is implicit. Varuṇa is unable to act without appropriating the desire of Mitra and their partnership becomes the template for both an Ego-Id model of the subject and a Brahmin-Kṣatriya model of dual sovereignty.

In the next stage, we find Mitra on the outside of a mob of gods who threaten him with expulsion if he does not join in their violent attack. When he does, Mitra becomes *amitra* ("no friend" or "without friends") until the gods restore what he has lost as a result of joining them. Mitra begins as a friend to all and ends as party to an obligatory contract sealed by the death of a sacrificial victim. For sharing in their crime and abandoning his status as the friend to all, the gods reward Mitra by replacing his cattle.

Mitra's transformation represents a transition from an idyllic undifferentiated state to an exclusionary and hierarchical social order. And as the god of the Brahmin class, Mitra's story represents the understanding of all Brahmins. Ideally, a Brahmin is, like Mitra, peaceful and a friend to all by

Table 2. Four Levels of Content in the Myth of the Lynching of Vṛtra

	SACRIFICER	OFFERING/VICTIM	PRIZE
Myth1	The gods	Vṛtra	Cattle and milk
Myth2	The gods	Soma	Creation
Ritual1	The gods	Soma	Sacrificial share
Ritual2	Sacrificer	*Soma* and milk	Immortality

nature. And it is because of his pacific purity that he has cattle-wealth that others must acquire by force. When society demands that the Brahmin participates in its violent system, as the gods do to Mitra, then he loses his purity and the friendship of the world and thus loses his wealth. As a result, society is now responsible for providing him with cattle-wealth for the gift of his presence. The first contract into which Mitra enters—the one that obligates the sacrificial priest to mix milk with his share of the *soma* (the blood of Vṛtra)—is not entered into voluntarily, but under duress at the moment in which the mob has focused on a single victim. The gods give him the choice to share in the guilt for killing Vṛtra or be forever excluded from the new life that Vṛtra's death provides. The pre-sacrificial society in which he is a friend to all is no longer an option once the founding murder has established the new order of sacrifice.

The Vedas most often ascribe the killing of Vṛtra to Indra, although the *Śatapatha Brāhmaṇa*'s version of the myth gets more to the point in terms of mimetic theory by making it a case of collective violence aimed at a single victim. It should not surprise us, then, that beginning with the Brāhmaṇas, the mythic tradition begins to saddle Indra with guilt. While the *Ṛg Veda* celebrates the killing of Vṛtra as a heroic act, the later tradition sees it as sinful. In the versions of the story in the *Mahābhārata* (first in 5.9–18 and then in 12.329.17–41) the sages have declared a pact of eternal friendship (*sakhya*) between Vṛtra and Indra. So after Indra breaks the pact and kills Vṛtra with the help of Viṣṇu he finds himself tormented by the guilt of breaking the divinely sanctioned peace and loses his throne.[22]

From the *Ṛg Veda* to the *Śatapatha Brāhmaṇa* the killing of Vṛtra undergoes a transformation. It begins as a duel between Indra and Vṛtra or Indra-Viṣṇu and Vṛtra. Then it becomes a collective murder in which Mitra is forced to participate, establishing the obligation to share with him not only the sacrifice but the milk that represents cattle-wealth. Later, it becomes one of Indra's three great sins. But the sin is not killing Vṛtra *per se*, but rather breaking the friendship pact laid on Indra by the sages (representing the magico-sovereign function). And as a sin against the pact, it is a sin against Mitra and Varuṇa, the sovereign gods of debt, obligation, and the oath, which brings us to the topic of the next section.

The Anthropogenic Oath

In *Superstition and Force*, his monumental 1866 study of law, culture, and religion in medieval Europe, autodidact historian Henry Charles Lea traces the development of torture, the ordeal, the oath, and the duel.[23] The oath and the duel respectively are the subjects of volumes one and two of the work, subtitled *The Wager of Law* and *The Wager of Battle*.[24] With this work, Lea became the first American scholar of medieval Europe of his generation to attain recognition on the continent. Working apart from any academic institution, Lea set his own ground rules: He would stick to primary sources as much as possible; he would attempt to focus on law as it was practiced and enforced rather than legal theory; and, recognizing the centrality of the Church in legal and political life, he would pay special heed to the ecclesiastical archive and canon law. As the work of a complete outsider, Lea's scholarship is of interest because its idiosyncratic (for the time) procedures helped the author escape becoming what the contemporary medievalist Edward Peters calls "one of those liberal nineteenth century anti-clerical historians whose works form as much a part of confessional as professional historiography."[25] No Sanskritist, Lea only briefly treats the legal traditions of ancient India along with Iran and Russia before launching into the history of the Anglo-Saxons. He problematically reproduces the nineteenth century trope of identifying an aboriginal Indian tradition under layers of Brahmin accretion, but his brief remarks on Sanskrit jurisprudence in the Indo-European context are still worth reading. Before treating the Indian material, Lea gives this definition of an oath:

> In its most simple form the oath is an invocation of some deity or supernatural power to grant or withhold his favor in accordance with the

> veracity of the swearer, but at all times men have sought to render this more impressive by *interposing material objects dear to the individual, which were understood to be pledges or victims for the divine wrath.*[26]

For Lea, the notion of sacrificial substitution (it is hard to see what he describes as anything else) does not belong to the oath proper but is a supplement to it, albeit a supplement that exists "at all times."[27]

Closely related to the oath and equally ubiquitous in the Indo-European world is the duel. In his conversations with Benoît Chantre in *Battling to the End*, Girard gives the archaic institution of the duel his first lengthy treatment.[28] Discussing Hegel's ideas on war, Girard says: "Dialectic is not first and foremost the reconciliation of humans with one another; it is simply the same thing as the *duel*, the struggle for recognition, and the 'opposing identities.'"[29] Countering what he sees as Hegelian thought's all too easy movement "from dialectic to reconciliation, from reciprocity to relationship," Girard embraces instead Prussian military theorist Carl von Clausewitz's insight that "*the oscillation of contradictory positions, which become equivalent, can very well go to extremes.*"[30]

Besides the kind of duel Girard and Clausewitz have in mind, the kind that tends toward the reciprocal and endless blood feud, there is another kind of duel: the judicial. Lea is careful to draw the distinction between what we commonly call a duel and the duel as judicial combat. "The object of the one," writes Lea, "was vengeance and reparation; the theory of the other was the discovery of truth and the impartial ministration of justice."[31] The duel calls down the vengeance of the deities, but gives them an opportunity to mete it out in single combat, either on the swearer, his opponent, or a chosen champion/victim. It is this kind of duel that concerns us for the moment.

Aside from stemming the spread of violence, both the oath and the judicial duel are tools for maintaining difference and averting the undifferentiation of the sacrificial crisis. In the case of ancient India, the texts make sure that the bonds into which oath-takers enter when they take their oaths correspond to their place in the social hierarchy. The *Mānavadharmaśāstra*, or "The Laws of Manu," is a *rechtsbuch* that dates to around 100 C.E., a period in which India was subject to Scythian, Bactrian, and Greek invasions from Central Asia and in which Buddhism was gaining state support. It is in part an ideological document meant to shore up post-Vedic social stratification and privileges in the face of cultural erosion, making it a text that overlaps Vedic and classical religion. The philologist and jurist Sir William Jones first translated the *Mānavadharmaśāstra* into English in 1797. Three years later, J. Christian Huttner translated Jones's English into German, and it was this translation that inspired Nietzsche to write, "The presupposition for a codification of this sort is the insight that the means of assuring authority for a *truth*, which has been won slowly and at considerable expense, are utterly different from the means needed to prove it."[32]

Ways of determining (or assuring authority for) the truth in Manu include the usual suspects of the ordeal, the oath, and the duel, all of which are significantly different (as are all of Manu's laws) depending on the social status of the person in question. In *Mānavadharmaśāstra* 8.113, the three functions of Indo-European society are required to swear by the thing that defines them: the Brahmin by the truth, the Kṣatriya by his weapons, and the Vaiśya by his "cows, grain, and gold." Members of the fourth class, the Śudras, whose impurity makes them ineligible to perform the sacrifice, are required to swear "by all the crimes." The next verse also provides the option of making the Śudra carry fire in his bare hands, be dunked underwater, or swear by the heads of his wife and children.

The Sanskrit word used in the *Mānavadharmaśāstra* for taking an oath is *śapati*. Like the English words "swear" and "oath," *śapati* and its nominal form *śapatha* mean both to vow something and to curse someone; they also denote the action of exorcising or conjuring a demon. There are several ways to use the word *śapati*. The first way—the verb followed by the conditional particle *yadi*—is a kind of deferred curse called down upon oneself should whatever comes after the *yadi* not be fulfilled, as in, "May lightning strike me dead if . . ." The second way, without the conditional *yadi*, requires a noun in the instrumental case to swear *by* and a noun in the dative case (and rarely in the accusative) to swear *to*. The third way is very like the second, but rather than swearing by an object, one swears by a name. Instead of being in the instrumental case, the object by which the oath is sworn is left in the nominative case and followed by the particle *iti*, which functions as a pair of quotation marks do in English. The example with which the great Sanskrit lexicographer Monier Monier-Williams demonstrates this usage is, appropriately, *Varuṇa iti*.

The difference between *swearing by Varuṇa*, punisher of oath breakers, and *swearing with the word "Varuṇa"* is not an insignificant one. In *The*

Sacrament of Language, a continuation of his work on the religio-juridical category of the *homo sacer*, Giorgio Agamben quotes Philo's exegesis of Deuteronomy in *Legum allegorae*: "Moses, too, let us observe, filled with wonder at the transcendency of the Uncreated, says 'And thou shalt swear by His Name' (Deut 6:13), not 'by Him. . . .'"[33] The name of Varuṇa is not sacred in the same way that the Tetragrammaton is in Hebrew, but the spoken name of a god has other significance in the Indian tradition: Calling on the gods by all their names is the way in which the priests summon them to be present at the sacrifice. Swearing with "Varuṇa" also affirms that the oath is a speech act.

Vrata is another Sanskrit word for "oath" that is usually translated with "vow." *Vrata* refers more specifically to religious vows such as the vow of celibacy that a high-caste male takes during the *brahmacarin* stage, the first phase of his life which he spends studying the Veda with a guru. A man in this stage, which is followed by the stages of householder, retiree, and renouncer, is said to be *vratasthita* ("engaged in religious observances"). The word also refers to the religious practice common among goddess worshippers in modern India in which the devotee will promise to undergo a penance or perform a service if her prayers are answered.[34]

Agamben connects the oath to the rite of consecration or *sacramentum*, concluding that the oath is not a way to derive the force of law from religion, but rather a constitutive act in and of itself.[35] Agamben writes: "[The] magico-religious sphere does not logically preexist the oath, but it is the oath, as originary performative experience of the word, that can explain religion (and law, which is deeply connected to it)."[36] He then addresses the issue of anthropogenesis, demonstrating that continental philosophy has not yet completely abandoned the big questions. Anthropogenesis—or, as Girard would say, hominization—is the mysterious alchemical process by which a species of bipedal primates is transmuted into humanity. For Girard, it is the moment after the spontaneous primal murder in which human culture is born as the symbolic realm of myth, ritual, and prohibition. Agamben, working from Claude Lévi-Strauss's idea that the sacred is the function of the "fundamental inadequation between signifier and signified,"[37] comes to a conclusion that resonates with Girard's, despite its structuralist bent. For Agamben, the moment of hominization or anthropogenesis is contained in the oath, when humans bind themselves to language as their constitutive potentiality. "Something like a human language was in fact only able to be produced," he writes, "at the moment in which the living being, who found itself co-originarily exposed to the possibility of both truth and lie, committed itself to respond with its life for its words, to testify in the first person for them."[38]

But Agamben resists a purely cognitive model of this transformation, arguing against the scientists whose professional prejudice leads them to act "as if the becoming human of man were solely a question of intelligence and brain size and not also one of *ethos*, as if intelligence and language did not also and above all pose problems of an ethical and political order."[39] While Girard insists that this ethical and political order is based on the lynching of an innocent victim, Agamben's argument is somewhat closer to Hegel's master-slave dialectic: The birth of the sacred and human history is simultaneously a division between life and language and a decision to bind the two together. "In order for something like an oath to be able to take place," argues Agamben, "it is necessary, in fact, to be able above all to distinguish, and to articulate together in some way, life and language, actions and words."[40]

Agamben argues that the anthropogenic oath is the moment at which the speaking animal discovers itself speaking and is exposed to the possibility of truth and falsehood, and oath can be "a blessing if the word is full, if there is correspondence between the signifier and the signified" or "a curse if the word is empty, if there remains, between the semiotic and the semantic, a void and a gap."[41] Tying this idea to religion, Agamben speaks of the "double possibility inscribed in *logos*," which he sees enshrined in Christianity (although he is clearly speaking of the Heraclitean *logos* and not Girard's Johannine *logos*).

> Religion and law technicalize this anthropogenic experience of the word in the oath and the curse as historical institutions, separating and opposing point by point truth and lie, true name and false name, efficacious formula and incorrect formula. That which was "badly said" became in this way a curse in the technical sense, and fidelity to the word became an obsessive and scrupulous concern with appropriate formulas and ceremonies, that is, *religio* and *ius*. The performative experience of the word is constituted and isolated in a "sacrament of language" and this latter in a "sacrament of power." The "force of law" that supports human societies, the idea of linguistic enunciations that stably obligate living beings, that can be observed and transgressed, derive from this attempt to nail down the originary

> performative force of the anthropogenic experience, and are, in this sense, an epiphenomenon of the oath and the malediction that accompanied it.[42]

It is on the question of the well-spoken oath and the badly spoken curse that Agamben brings us back to the Veda. As Jan Heesterman has convincingly argued, the development of Vedic ritual is a process of displacing violent death from the sacrificial arena and replacing it with rules and regulations. Heesterman maintains that "sacrifice generally turns on the act of violence, on death, by which its opposite, life, may be won," but that by the time of the classical sacrificial ritual "violent death was replaced . . . by the non-violent ritual error, to be avoided or expiated in a 'technical' way."[43] In other words, Vedic sacrifice is the site on which violence is displaced by truth; saying the words properly becomes the focus of the ritual as violence is moved farther and farther away. The primacy of the binding power of words completely effaces the threat of violence that was once central to the sacrifice.

Just as Girard argues that, in the process that began with the advent of Christianity, the sacrifice on which culture is founded has lost its efficacy, bringing the walls down around it, Agamben argues that the oath is similarly bereft of its binding power, and with similar consequences:

> [Humanity] finds itself today before a disjunction, or, at least, a loosening of the bond that, by means of the oath, united the living being to its language. On the one hand, there is the living being, more and more reduced to a purely biological reality and to bare life. On the other hand, there is the speaking being, artificially divided from the former, through a multiplicity of technico-mediatic apparatuses, in an experience of the word that grows ever more vain, for which it is impossible to be responsible and in which anything like a political experience becomes more and more precarious. When the ethical—and not simply cognitive—connection that unites words, things, and human actions is broken this in fact promotes a spectacular and unprecedented proliferation of vain words on the one hand and, on the other, of legislative apparatuses that seek obstinately to legislate on every aspect of that life on which they no longer seem to have any hold. The age of the eclipse of the oath is also the age of blasphemy, in which the name of God breaks away from its living connection with language and can only be uttered "in vain."[44]

The accounts of Girard and Agamben have some important similarities that are worth noting in this discussion of Vedic myth and ritual. Both see at the foundation of culture an archaic institution at an advanced stage of decay. Both also see an ethical or political and not just a cognitive component to the mechanism of anthropogenesis or hominization. Both see the system built on either the oath (for Agamben) or the foundational murder (for Girard) responding to its imminent demise with violent but ineffectual countermeasures. Although the two models are obviously irreconcilable, traces of both Girard's foundational sacrifice as well as Agamben's anthropogenic oath are visible in Vedic ritual. We have already discussed the Girardian elements present in myths of the Vedic sacrifice, but we can see also traces of the oath in the element of sacred speech and the insistence on the part of the Vedic tradition that participants in the sacrifice strictly adhere to the ritual script: Brahmin ritualists are above all concerned with the correct recitation of the words of the ritual and the ritual texts are full of expiatory verses to be recited after someone misspeaks or utters a "malediction." On the other side of the coin, there is the idea of the vow, although it takes on much greater significance in the epic literature, where heroes bound by oaths bring themselves and their houses to ruin. The Agambenian model of sacred speech, comprising the duality of the oath and the curse, is as present in Vedic ritual as is the Girardian model of sacrifice. But we can also say that one seems to precede the other, as we examine Heesterman's argument that this oath-form of the ritual is an innovation laid on top of an older pre-classical agonistic form of Vedic sacrifice that is based not on the oath, but on the duel, as we shall see in the next section.

The Duel

The second volume of Lea's work, *The Wager of Battle*, is a treatment of the duel. In understanding the duel, Lea returns again to the triangle of the oath in which a swearer swears to another while a vengeful deity holds the swearer to the truth. *The Wager of Battle* begins with the pronouncement that "[there] is a natural tendency in the human mind to cast the burden of its doubts upon a higher power and to relieve itself from the effort of decision by seeking in the unknown the solution of its difficulties."[45] As much as it does in the oath, the sacrificial logic also inheres in the duel, which medieval scholastics traced back to the "duel" between Cain and Abel, a sacrificial *mise-en-scène* if ever there was one.[46] The problem with this line of thought is the fact that in the duel between Cain and Abel, the winner is expelled and cursed rather than exonerated by God. For Girard, the story of Cain and Abel is the story of mimetic doubles, their rivalry, and the murder that becomes the foundation of the community. But, he argues, unlike other such myths (like that of Romulus and Remus), the Biblical narrative takes the side of the victim, who is Abel.[47]

When Girard first talks about the duel in *Violence and the Sacred* it is in the context of the "oscillations" of conflict that are common to both Greek classical drama and sacrificial ritual. In the Sanskrit tradition we can find this back and forth movement in the verbal contest, which, in its most obscene and overtly sexualized form, is written into the script of the most elaborate of all the Vedic rites, the Horse Sacrifice. And the alternating victories and defeats experienced by the warriors competing for *kudos* in the Homeric epics find an echo in the main theme in the mythic war of the gods and the demons. In both these cases, one ritual and the other mythic, the reversals are non-dialectical in that they end without any teleological resolution or sublation. But this is not so in the legal traditions of the oath and the duel, which end with the vindication of the truth of one party after its being subjected to the threat of destruction. At the end of the judicial duel or in the taking of the oath, the truth is created when the threat or exercise of violence eliminates one of the two possibilities that existed at the beginning of the process (i.e., truth or falsehood).

The judicial duel or combat, like the oath, produces a truth. But how does it relate to the other type of duel, the type used to repay an injury or an insult? Judicial combat and the agonistic duel have a complicated relationship. Both of them belong to a religio-judicial system whose function is to contain conflict.[48] But the purpose of a duel is to settle disputes between two parties without calling in a third, while judicial combat necessitates a triangle composed of the two disputants and a deity to grant victory to the party in the right. The judicial duel, like the oath, breaks up a pair of combatants by introducing a third (divine) figure to be the arbiter of justice, a role to which Varuṇa is especially suited since he observes everything at all times. As Sukumari Battacharji nicely puts it, "[When] two persons conversed, he was the invisible third."[49]

In medieval Europe, the institution of judicial combat began to experience a kind of crisis when it became polluted through contact with the undisguised sacrificial combat of the gladiatorial arena. Lea lays the blame partly at the feet of clerics like the twelfth century French cardinal Pierre de Fontaines, who began translating the Latin *arenarius* and *athleta* with the French *champion*, no doubt because of the etymological association with the late Latin *campio*, from *campus*, or "field." Consequently as the word *champion* entered the French language in the thirteenth century, champions by dint of association came to have the same kind of outsider status as gladiators, actors, and prostitutes had in Rome.

> By the thirteenth century, the occupation of champion had thus become infamous. Its professors were classed with the vilest criminals, and with the unhappy females who exposed their charms for sale, as the champion did his skills and courage. They were held incapable of appearing as witnesses, and the extraordinary anomaly was exhibited of seeking to learn the truth in affairs of the highest moment by a solemn appeal to God, through the instrumentality of those who were already considered as convicts of the worst kind, or who, by the very act, were branded with infamy if successful in justifying innocence, and if defeated were mutilated or hanged.[50]

In Germany in the thirteenth and fourteenth centuries, champions and their children were also barred from inheriting property. But in Italy, champions were raised in status rather than denigrated and laws were passed preventing criminals from becoming champions and preventing champions from being classed as criminals for practicing their profession. At this point, the champions begin to look very like what Agamben calls the *homo sacer*, made sacred by their participation in the violence of the judicial duel.

Agamben may put the oath at the origin of language and humanity, but using mimetic theory it is not hard to imagine how the oath might derive from the duel. The duel begins with two opposing parties, mimetic rivals, as Girard would have it. But a third is added when the duel enters the realm of ritual and law: Instead of two opposing parties, there is a party of the truth and a party of the lie and a deity is invoked to intervene and grant victory to the party of the truth. But in the oath, this triangle becomes a duality again when the opposing combatants are collapsed into one figure, who may either be telling the truth or telling a lie, and that one figure is then opposed to the deity, who holds him to his word with the threat of violence.

Heesterman argues that an agonistic, two-sacrificer model of Vedic sacrifice preceded the classical one-sacrificer model and if he is right, then the transition between them parallels the transition from duel to oath. In the earlier agonistic model two sacrificers compete with one another in the same enclosure for the goods of the sacrifice: wealth and life. Heesterman finds ample evidence for this earlier form in the ritual itself (e.g., the fact that two of the three sacrificial fires are kindled with the sacrificer's own fire drill while the third, the *dakśiṇāgni*, is lit with the flame from another fire, presumably the opposing sacrificer's in the earlier ritual). The agonistic sacrificial model, based on the duel, is perfectly suited for the cyclical Aryan cattle-raiding economy: A successful sacrificer would be obligated to distribute his wealth in the form of gifts to all the attendees at his sacrifice; leaving his treasuries depleted and requiring him to enter into another sacrificial contest to replenish them. But as the Brahmin officiants' status became more dependent on ritual purity they began to systematically exclude the uncontrollable element of contest from the sacrifice. And with the element of contest went the second sacrificer. Eventually the rivalry gave way to ritual and the violence gave way to an obsessive fidelity to words of the rite and all that was left was a single sacrificer bound to the officiating Brahmin priest. But traces of the earlier duel-sacrifice are visible in the myths of the gods and the demons, and especially in the magical rivalry between their priestly representatives.

Uśanas Kāvya, the Devil's Advocate[51]

In a later chapter, we will examine the figure of the Indo-Iranian Kavi (poet-magician) and its relationship to the Greek *pharmakos*. But at this point, enmeshed as we are in the rivalry of the gods and the demons, we will only concern ourselves with one particular Kavi, Kāvya Uśanas, also called Śukra, the *purohita* or chaplain of the demons in their war against the gods. His counterpart on the side of the gods is Bṛhaspati, but Śukra and Bṛhaspati are not exactly equals; only Śukra, a priest of the Bhārgava Brahmin clan, holds the closely guarded secret of restoring life to the dead, a spell called the *mṛtasaṃjīvinīvidyā* ("the knowledge of giving life to the dead"). This spell is crucial in the battle between the gods and the demons presented in *Mahābhārata* 1.71, which clearly portrays an agonistic model of the sacrifice:

> A great feud arose between the gods and the demons over the sovereignty of the universe and every creature in it, moving and standing. To insure victory, the gods selected Angiras's son, the ascetic [Bṛhaspati] as their sacrificial priest while the [demons] chose Uśanas Kāvya. These two Brahmins were long-time bitter rivals. The gods killed the demons who had gathered for the battle, but Uśanas drew on the power of his knowledge to bring them back to life and they rose again to make war on the gods. The demons in turn cut down the gods in the heat of battle but the wise Bṛhaspati could not resurrect them because he did not have the Mṛtasaṃjīvinī Vidyā possessed by Uśanas. The gods became desperate.[52]

Uśanas's resurrection spell has tipped the balance of the rivalry and so the gods decide to level the playing field again. To this end, they send the handsome youth Kaca, who also happens to be Bṛhaspati's son, to Śukra (Kāvya Uśanas) so that he can be accepted as a student and learn the secret of reviving the dead. The gods have the expectation that Śukra will consent to become Kaca's guru, but to make sure they instruct the son to seduce Śukra's beloved daughter as well. Somewhat surprisingly, Śukra happily agrees to take his rival's son as a pupil and, less surprisingly, his daughter Devayānī does indeed fall in love with the youth.[53]

Eventually the demons get wind of the fact that Bṛhaspati's son is learning at the feet of their preceptor and are rightly suspicious. So when the demons catch Kaca alone tending his guru's cows in the forest they murder him on the spot. To make sure that Śukra cannot resurrect him, the demons cut Kaca's corpse up into pieces and feed them to jackals. Nevertheless, when Devayānī deduces what has happened after the cows come back alone, Śukra is able to bring Kaca back to life using his spell. Some time later, the demons fall upon Kaca again when he is alone in the forest gathering flowers. This time they burn his corpse until nothing is left but ashes. Then they put the ashes in wine and give it to Śukra, who unknowingly drinks down all that is left of his pupil. Devayānī guesses that the demons have murdered Kaca a second time and begs her father, who is by this time beginning to get angry with the demons himself, to bring him back again. But when Śukra begins to use the spell, he hears Kaca's voice from inside his stomach, warning him of what has happened and what will happen if Śukra resurrects the ashes he has swallowed. The demons have conspired to have Kaca end up in Śukra's stomach so that the Brahmin cannot use the resurrection spell without himself being torn apart and killed in the process. Devayānī is distraught at the prospect of having to choose between losing her father or the man she loves, but Śukra comes up with a solution. He teaches the resurrection spell to Kaca while the latter is still in his stomach, then uses it to bring Kaca back. When Kaca comes back to life, he bursts out of his guru's side, killing him. But since Kaca knows the resurrection spell he is able to bring Śukra back to life, in the process restoring the demon's most powerful weapon and missing an opportunity to insure that the gods and only the gods possess the secret of *mṛtasaṃjīvinīvidyā*. Once brought back to life, Śukra blames the wine more than the demons for what has happened and proclaims that "Starting today, any Brahmin foolish enough to drink wine will be condemned for his folly in this world and the next as a Brahmin-slayer and a man without dharma."[54]

At first, Devayānī is beside herself with joy to have her beloved back. But her happiness turns sour when Kaca explains to her that he must now go back to the gods and, more than that, after being "born" from Śukra's belly, he considers Devayānī his sister and any romantic involvement between them would be incest. Enraged, Devayānī curses Kaca, saying, "If you reject me, despite my pleas, in favor of Duty, Power and Pleasure,[55] then your knowledge of magic will fail you, Kaca!"[56]

Devayānī's curse of Kaca is of a recognizable type to those familiar with the epic: A man expends enormous effort or time (in Kaca's case, it took a thousand years to acquire the *mṛtasaṃjīvinīvidyā*) to gain a magic weapon, only to have it taken away through the vengeful proclamation of someone to whom he has done a seemingly minor wrong. The classic example is the story of the Kaurava hero Karṇa (whom we will treat at length in the next chapter), who becomes a pupil to the Brahmin warrior Paraśurāma, sworn enemy of all Kṣatriyas, in order to learn the secret of a magic missile capable of destroying his mimetic rival Arjuna. Karṇa, who was abandoned as a newborn and raised by a family of the Sūta caste, is a Kṣatriya by birth (although he doesn't know it) and Paraśurāma takes him on as a student with the understanding that he is the Sūta he says he is. One day when Paraśurāma is taking a nap with his head in his pupil's lap, a demonic insect bores its way through Karṇa's thigh. Karṇa bears the excruciating pain without moving a muscle so that his guru's sleep will not be interrupted. But when Paraśurāma wakes up and sees Karṇa's wound, he concludes that only a Kṣatriya could bear that much pain without moving or crying out. In his anger, Paraśurāma gives Karṇa the magic knowledge he promised, but then curses him to forget it when he needs it most. In Karṇa's case, the curse spells his death on the battlefield.

But in the story of Kaca, the result of Devayānī's curse is never revealed. In his analysis of the myth Dumézil takes this to mean that the point of the Kaca story is simply to restore the perfect (and fearful) symmetry between the warring gods and demons.[57] Indeed, the events of the story have no effect on the balance of power; Kaca never reappears in the epic and the gods never attempt to use the *mṛtasaṃjīvinīvidyā* he has gone to so much trouble to obtain. After Kaca leaves Śukra and Devayānī, the narrative quickly moves on to a new conflict, this one between Devayānī and Śarmiṣṭhā, the daughter of Vṛṣaparvan, king of the demons. With the arms race between the gods and the demons at a point of equilibrium, a new but familiar rivalry springs up inside the demon camp: the rivalry of Brahmins and kings, this time played out through their daughters.

The story of Devayānī and Śarmiṣṭhā is an even more elegant demonstration of mimetic desire and its relation to violence. Devayānī and Śarmiṣṭhā are bathing together when the rather lecherous Indra takes form as a wind and picks up the girls' dresses lying on the riverbank, mixing them up. When the girls get out of the water, Devayānī mistakenly picks up Śarmiṣṭhā's dress and puts it on. Śarmiṣṭhā becomes furious and begins to abuse the Brahmin's daughter, saying, "Your father stands humbly below my father, even if he is lying or sitting, and praises and flatters him incessantly. You are the daughter of a man who must praise, flatter, and hold out his hand. I am the daughter of man who *is* flattered and gives but does not receive! Beggar girl! You are unarmed and abandoned, and you tremble before me with my armed strength. Go find your equal, because you are certainly not mine!"[58]

Having humiliated the Brahmin's daughter, Śarmiṣṭhā takes her dress back and throws Devayānī down a well. Fortunately, a passing prince comes upon the well and helps Devayānī climb out. The girl immediately goes to her father Śukra and tells him all that has happened, relating Śarmiṣṭhā's cutting insults word for word. She then tells him that she can no longer live in the land of the king whose daughter has so dishonored her. Śukra reassures her that, despite what Śarmiṣṭhā says, a Brahmin is more powerful than any king could ever be. At his daughter's insistence, Śukra then goes to Śarmiṣṭhā's father and demands that he apologize and then send his daughter to be Devayānī's slave for life. Knowing that without Śukra on their side, the balance of power will shift toward the gods, the king of the demons gives away his daughter as a slave to keep the peace with his priest.

By all indications, when Devayānī puts on Śarmiṣṭhā's dress at the beginning of the episode, it is by mistake and not because of some acquisitive mimesis. Nevertheless, the result is the same: a spreading conflict that threatens to engulf the entire community of demons if a victim is not offered up as appeasement. It is worth noting that the incident begins as the result of the actions of Indra, who mixes up the dresses knowing full well that he will be striking at the heart of the demons' solidarity. With that in mind, in the next section we will return once again to the figure of Indra, this time examining him in connection with one of the most opaque myth fragments in the Vedic corpus.

The Wolf-Warrior Cycle

As Bṛhaspati and Śukra respectively fulfill the role of the priestly, or magico-sovereign, function on the side of gods and the demons, Indra and Vṛṣaparvan fulfill the martial function. In the last chapter, we looked at the relationship of Indra and Viṣṇu and the parallels between the story of Viṣṇu winning back the universe for the gods in the form of the dwarf Vāmana and the story of Indra winning back the universe in the form of the Sālāvṛkī or werewolf. In Sanskrit, the word for "wolf" is *vṛka* (from the Vedic *vṛkṇa*, "to tear").[59] It is the second element in the mysterious compound form *sālāvṛkī* or *sālāvṛkeya*, which Albrecht Weber translates as "werewolf" and David Gordon White renders "house-wolf"[60] but Stephanie Jamison in her interpretation of the myth in *The Ravenous Hyenas and the Wounded Sun* argues we should read as "mother hyena" (for *sālāvṛkī*) and "young hyena" (for *sālāvṛkeya*).[61] Perhaps, in light of what we will soon see about Indra's role, it should also make us recall Shakespeare's "universal wolf" of appetite, which, "So doubly seconded with will and power / Must make perforce an universal prey /And last eat up himself."[62] In the following sections, we will look closely at some myths, folk tales, and ritual elements that point to the existence of a wolf-warrior cult that stands as the unassimilated remainder left after the transition from the archaic agonistic two-sacrificer ritual to the classical sanitized one-sacrificer ritual.

Indra-Sālāvṛkī and the Yatis

We will begin with a myth that, fragmentary as it is, may have a lot to tell us about the early agonistic (or perhaps "duel-istic") form of Vedic sacrifice: the myth of Indra and the Yatis. In its simplest form, the story of Indra and the Yatis can be summarized with this line from the *Maitrāyaṇī Saṃhitā* of the Black *Yajur Veda*: "Indra handed over the Yatis to the Sālāvṛkeyas."[63] The earliest texts do not condemn Indra's actions, except insofar as they interrupt the ritual, but by the time of the more developed mythology of the *Aitareya Brāhmaṇa*, his killing of the Yatis has become identified as one of his three great sins.[64]

The Yatis themselves are usually identified as heterodox ascetics, black magicians, and outlaws. But in her reading, Jamison rejects this and argues for identifying the Yatis as Vedic priests. "The myth not only provides evidence that the Yatis were ritual priests," she writes, "but makes it dramatically clear that the Yatis were beset by beasts while performing a ritual. Their violent death seems all the more shocking because it interrupts and profanes the ritual and desecrates the ritual ground."[65] Later versions of the myth have a few of the Yatis surviving or turning into plants or ritual implements after they are devoured, and thereby becoming part of the sacrificial ritual.[66]

The story of Indra and the Yatis does not appear in the *Ṛg Veda*, but references to the Yatis themselves do. Of the three occurrences of Yati in the plural, two of them, *ṚV* 8.6.18 and *ṚV* 8.3.9, associate the mysterious group with none other than the Bhṛgus, the rather unconventional Brahmin clan to whom Śukra (from our previous story) belongs, leading Jamison to conclude that "the Vedic Yatis are completely parallel to the Bhṛgus, performing the usual cultic services of praise . . . and receiving the gods', particularly Indra's, aid in return."[67] The *Ṛg Veda* also connects both the Yatis and the Bhṛgus to wild dogs, specifically in the context of ritual purity. But while the Yatis become victims of the wolfish Sālāvṛkeyas, the Bhṛgus seem to have a different relationship with the canine family; in *ṚV* 9.101.13, the author advises the sacrificer to drive the greedy dog away just as the Bhṛgus chased away a creature referred to as "Makha."[68]

In his programmatic essay "The Bare Facts of Ritual," J. Z. Smith takes a quote from Franz Kafka's "Reflections on Sin, Hope and the True Way" to illustrate the role of coincidence in ritual:

> Leopards break into the temple and drink the sacrificial chalices dry; this occurs repeatedly, again and again: finally it can be reckoned on beforehand and becomes part of the ceremony.[69]

Jamison's interpretation of the story of Indra and the Yatis is remarkably similar to Kafka's fragment, except that in the case of the Vedic myth that she is reading, not only must the intruding wild animals be absorbed into the ritual system, there must also be some blood expiation:

> The Yatis, far from being enemies or victims of Indra, are his righteously sacrificing devotees. When Indra delivers them to the hyenas, he is not committing a callous act of violence, but is acting benevolently toward both the Yatis and the Hyenas and furthering the proper functioning of both cosmos (macrocosm) and ritual (microcosm). . . . The Yatis, on the one hand, "deserve" their death because of certain ritual flaws committed when under attack. On the other hand, in death they fulfill their ritual objectives. These objectives are various, but they all center around the portion of the ritual known as the Uttaravedi. It is in the vicinity of the Uttaravedi that animal sacrifices are performed, and the animal-sacrificing Yatis, by a sort of ritual symmetry, become sacrifices to animals. The Uttaravedi is also used in the Varuṇapraghāsa ceremony and its associated rain-making rituals, and the plants into which the Yatis are transformed are precisely those used to bring rain that ensures life on earth.[70]

MBh 13.94.5 presents another Indra myth that is easily interpreted as another version of the story of the Yatis. In it, Indra comes to earth as a beggar named Śunaḥsakha ("Friend of Dogs") in order to slay the sorceress Yātudhānī, whose name, like that of the Yatis, comes from the root √*yā* ("to go") and carries the double meaning of "wanderer" and "sorcerer." In the struggle of Indra and Yatis, both sides take on liminal roles, Indra as a werewolf and the Yatis as migrant magicians. However, Indra's role as the Sālāvṛkī, the "house-wolf" (which may mean "domesticated wolf"), seems to belong more to the realm of the civilized while the wandering Yatis seem more connected to the forest. It is also tempting to connect the Yatis with the mysterious wandering ascetic, also called a Yati, who confronts an Adhvaryu priest during a sacrifice and denounces his violence in *MBh* 14.28 (one of the Hindu texts often cited in favor of ethical vegetarianism). Tamar Reich argues that this Yati could be either a *nāstika*-type reviler (more on which in the next chapter) who acts as the opponent in the verbal sacrificial contest or a representative of Buddhism, Jainism, or some other contemporary heterodox sect renouncing animal sacrifice in favor of non-violence.[71] Complementing this fragmentary myth of Indra and the Yatis, there also exists a tradition that tells what I would argue is the same story told from the point of view of the wolves, the Vrātya cycle, which is crucial to understanding the story of Indra and the Yatis.

The Vrātya's Oath

Anyone familiar with scholarship on Indo-European religion has probably come across the *Männerbund*, a group of young oath-bound warriors who fight in real or ritual battles in a state of self-induced frenzy that is sometimes described as an actual transformation into savage beasts. They are strongly associated with a ritual performed in midwinter, around Christmastime, an association that survived into European folklore as the belief that to be born on Christmas Day was to be born a werewolf.[72] Commonly cited examples are the West African leopard men, the berserker warriors of Scandinavia, the were-tigers of Sumatra, and, in Indian mythology, the Maruts, whom we saw being led by Indra in the story of Indra's kingship described by Sylvain Lévi in chapter one.[73] They are, as David Gordon White has called them, the "Dog-men" of Indo-European myth, living at the edge of civilization and humanity.[74] Dogs have a generally unfavorable reputation in the Vedic tradition, a reputation that often attaches to the men associated with them. Likewise in the Christian folk tradition dating at least to the fourth century Church Father John Chrysostom, as Kenneth Stow has demonstrated, it is Jews who are regarded as the "dogs" who despoil the loaf that represents both the Eucharist and the Christian community, an accusation that mirrors the one in *ṚV* 9.101.1 to keep the dog away from the sacrifice lest he despoil it.[75]

In the Indian tradition, the ancient Vrātyas are another group that fits the pattern of the canine *Männerbund*. The Vrātyas are a martial band of priests often referred to as "dogs" who conducted their violent sacrifices deep in the wilderness in the dead of winter and who kept the sacrificial gift for themselves. They are, like the divine war band the Maruts, both priests and warriors. Furthering the comparison, the *Baudhāyana Śrauta Sutra* even describes the leader of the Vrātyas as "Indra-like" and the group as "Marut-like."[76] In the period from mid-January to mid-March known as Śiśira (nearly identical, as White points out, to the name of the divine hound Sīsara),[77] the Vrātyas hold a sacrifice called a Sattra that lasts sixty-one days (the period of a dog's gestation) in which they slaughter humans or cows (or cows in the place of humans) in order to bring back the sun and end the midwinter famine. The Vrātyas' Sattra sacrifice is also famously subject to the unwanted and often disastrous presence of dogs. One of the most well known Sattras in Sanskrit literature, the one that serves as the frame story of the *Mahābhārata*, is cursed to fail (i.e., remain uncompleted) by the divine she-dog Saramā when the sacrificer's brothers unjustly beat one of her pups after accusing him of despoiling the sacrifice.

In an earlier stratum of the ritual literature, the Vrātyas are identified with the figure of the Dīkṣita, the sacrificer who remains impure to the point of untouchability until his ritual bath at the end of the sacrifice. But unlike the Dīkṣita, the Vrātya does not employ a Brahmin priest to remove his impurity so that he can return to the social order. This absence of the official Brahmin-approved means of re-sanctification has led some scholars to the view their central rite, called the Vrātyastoma, as a ritual designed to purify the Vrātyas and allow them to reenter the Brahminical fold, perhaps after they have entered impure countries as warrior bands. Bruce Sullivan gives this description of the ritual:

> To obtain the cattle for this sacrifice, the Vrātya raided their enemies or rivals and rustled the cattle. Another Vedic text, *Baudhāyana Śrauta Sūtra* (18.26), mentions that sons of Kuru brahmins set out on a Vrātya expedition against the neighboring Pañcāla, and when asked their identity they

> replied that they were the Maruts (sons of Rudra who accompany Indra on his martial exploits as a warrior band). They rustled cattle to perform their distinctive ritual practice, a sixty-one-day animal sacrifice known as the Vrātyastoma that would provide them religious transcendence. At the center of it was the Mahāvrata rite, which entailed the drinking of alcohol, dancing, and music, especially singing, and an obscene and reviling dialogue between a man and woman whose ritual copulation was the rite's climax, so to speak. The woman is described as a puṃścalī, a prostitute. In the tradition of the Vrātya as known in Vedic literature, then, we find brahmins stealing the cattle of others for their own religious benefit. That they were defying conventional behavioral norms seems evident from the later tradition's attitude toward the Vrātya: they were understood as non-Āryan by Manu (2.39), for example.[78]

As Sullivan notes, at first glance the Vrātyas appear from the sources to have been a distinct group from Brahmins. But in Jan Heesterman's important and influential reevaluation of the Vrātyas in 1962, he argues convincingly that the rites of the Vrātyas were in fact once a central part of the ancient Vedic sacrifice, a part that the Brahmin priests marginalized as they demonized (or "canin-ized") the Vrātyas themselves. The exclusion of the Vrātyas and their rites, according to Heesterman, was a result of a dramatic shift in thinking that set the pure ritual universe and its Brahmin guardians against the impure profane world.[79] Maintaining the purity of the ritual meant rendering it non-violent and part of eliminating violence is eliminating contest. In contest there is the element of defeat, with the obligation of retaliation it places on the defeated party. According to Heesterman's theory, the period in the development of Vedic ritual to which the Vrātyas and their practices belong precedes the period of Brahminical revision and thus still retains the element of the sacrificial contest. So what role might the Vrātyas have played in this as yet unsanitized rite? Accounts of the Vrātyas and myths that reflect the Vrātya ritual model all portray them as a defeated party in the sacrificial contest. As such, they pose the threat of retaliation, which is obligatory in the much riskier earlier ritual cycle with its endless rounds of primitive accumulation and ruinous expenditure, but excluded in its classical form. Of the early form of Vedic sacrifice, Heesterman writes:

> Sacrifice turns on the manipulation of the sacred. However, the sacred is ambiguous and unpredictable, dispensing both life and death. It was this ambiguity that was acted out by the contenders in the sacrificial contest. But this also meant that the outcome could never be definitive. The triumphant sacrificer had to be prepared to be challenged in his turn, at the next outbreak of the war and raiding season. The archaic world of sacrifice was broken in its very centre.[80]

This situation, in which outcomes were not predetermined and which necessitated that one of the sacrificers must lose, was a dangerous one for Brahmin ritualists as well as for the sacrificers themselves. After all, Brahmins who had promised their clients ritual success must have had a lot to answer for when the sacrificer that employed them was defeated. It makes sense then that they would have wanted to "fix" the contest to make success a guarantee, and maintaining purity would have been something over which they could exercise absolute control. And if the promised health, wealth, and male progeny did not immediately follow ritual success, they could always explain that karma sometimes works on the *longue durée*. The Brahmins, therefore, had every reason to expel the violent contest that was once the broken center of Vedic ritual and make it into a heretical relic of the past. We get some notion of this from chapter seventeen of the *Pañcaviṃśa Brāhmaṇa*:

17.1.1. Thus the gods went to the Heavenly Realm, and the demigods (*daivā*) were exiled to live the life of Vrātyas. They went to the place from which the gods departed for the Heavenly Realm but they did not find the praise hymn (*stoma*) or the incantation hymn (*chanda*) through which they could overtake them. Then the gods said to the Maruts: "Deliver to them the praise hymn and the incantation hymn by which they may reach us." They gave to the Maruts the sixteen-part praise hymn, which is secretly the *anuṣṭubh* meter.[81] Thus, they reached them.

17.1.2. Those who lead the Vrātya life are forsaken and destitute because they do not practice the study of the Veda, nor do they farm or trade. By the sixteen-verse praise hymn this can be attained.

17.1.3. This is a praise hymn of the Maruts. The lesser incantation hymns also belong to the Maruts.

17.1.4. He (the priest) adds the verse in three-measure meter to the beginning and puts the verse in two-measure meter in its place. In this way he makes them flourish by their form.

17.1.5. The incantation hymn that begins with "O Indra, fond of praise" [*ṚV* 8.98.7] is uneven (*viṣama*). Likewise, the Vrātya life is uneven. Thus he makes them all even (*sama*).

17.1.6. With these verses the hymn of Dyutāna is chanted.

17.1.7. Dyutāna the Marut was (the Vrātyas') chief (*gṛhapati*). They performed this praise hymn and all of them succeeded. Thus there is this hymn for success.

17.1.8. If they were to perform the conclusion explicitly (*niruktaṃ*), the chief alone would succeed and he would keep the others from success. Because they perform it implicitly (*aniruktaṃ*), he firmly establishes all of them in success and welfare.

17.1.9. Those who take food from impure people, who call impure speech pure, who strike the guiltless with a stick, who use the speech of the initiated even though they are uninitiated, their guilt can be removed by the sixteen-versed praise hymn. Here are the four sixteen-versed praise hymns by which they are freed from their guilt.

17.1.10. The hymn that begins, "The god who bestows wealth" must be used for the Agniṣṭoma hymn. He establishes them among the gods.

17.1.11. But they say also: "It should be offered with the *satobṛhatī* verse that begins, 'The greatest of those who prosper has shown himself.'" A Vrātya band is uneven in the same way. He makes all of them equally great (*sato bṛhataḥ*).[82]

17.1.12. About this others say: "The *satobṛhatī* meter is unsteady and tremulous. (The Agniṣṭoma hymn) must therefore be performed with the hymn that begins: 'The god who bestows wealth.'"

17.1.13. Firmly established on the other hand is the *bṛhatī* verse with its repeating verse-quarters. He undertakes a verse-quarter again (like?) the child longing for its mother.[83]

17.1.14. A turban, a goad, a bow without arrow, an easterner's rough chariot, a garment with black fringes, one white and one black goatskin, a silver ornament worn on a necklace, all that is paraphernalia of the chief.

17.1.15. The other (Vrātyas) have tunics with red borders and corded fringes, with strings at each side; each of them has a pair of shoes and doubly-joined goat's hides.[84]

17.1.16. This is the booty of the Vrātyas. On whom they bestow it, they purify (or wipe off) themselves (*mṛjānā*).

17.1.17. Each of them brings their chief thirty-three cows, for thirty-three devotees of the god had come (through this Vrātyastoma) to success. So this rite serves for attaining success.

17.2.1. Now for the Vrātyastoma with six sixteen-versed hymns. This rite should be performed by those who lead the Vrātya's life because they are base and reviled.

17.2.2. One after another, those who lead the Vrātya's life because they are base and reviled are seized by sinfulness (*pāpmāna*). Therefore there are six sixteen-versed hymns by which they are delivered from sinfulness.

17.2.3. Because the Agniṣṭoma hymn has twenty-one verses, the twenty-one versed hymn is a firm support, and so they are firmly supported even in the middle of the sacrifice.

17.2.4. It is a rite accompanied by verses of praise. The verses are sacrificial beasts. It is the sacrificial beasts that lead the lowest to supremacy. By means of the sacrificial beasts he leads them to supremacy.

17.3.1. Now for the Vrātyastoma with two sixteen-versed hymns. This should be performed by those who lead the Vrātya's life because they are the last-born.

17.3.2. Those who lead the Vrātya's life because they are the last-born are forsaken and destitute. Because the purifying (*pavamāna*) hymns are nine-versed and the nine-versed hymn is the forefront (*mukha*) of the hymns he leads them to the forefront of the sacrifice.

17.3.3. Because there are two sixteen-versed hymns, they are delivered by them from their sinfulness.

17.3.4. Because the Agniṣṭoma hymn has twenty-one verses, the twenty-one-versed stoma is a firm support, and so they are firmly supported even at the end of the sacrifice.

17.4.1. Now for the hymn for those whose penises are flaccid. This should be performed by those who lead the Vrātya's life because they are the oldest.

17.4.2. They ascend from peak to peak so the hymns ascend to keep from falling down.

17.4.3. Indeed this was formerly performed by those whose penises were flaccid. Their chief was Kuṣītaka, son of Samaśravas. Luśākapi, son of Khargala, cursed them, saying: "They have broken their vows and have applied two smaller hymns." Because of that, none of the descendants of Kuśītaka amounts to much, for they have fallen off from the sacrifice.[85]

Much of this text is obscure even to luminaries like Willem Caland, on whose 1931 English translation (only marginally less incomprehensible to the average reader than the Sanskrit original) I have based my own. Nevertheless I will do my best here to make sense of it. In 17.1.1 we see a group of demigods or perhaps followers of the gods, who have been inexplicably left behind after the gods have gone to Heaven. But the gods, although they have exiled these demigods to live the Vrātya life, have not forgotten them and supplied them with a hymn or chant that will allow them to follow. The next verse, 17.1.2, addresses the question of what a Vrātya is and seems to suggest that those who live the life of a Vrātya are outcasts from Vedic society. Perhaps significantly, the text tells us they do not study the Vedas (the province of Brahmins) or farm or trade (the province of the Vaiṣya). It does not, however, tell us that they do not fight (the province of the Kṣatriyas). While S. N. Biswas takes this to mean that the Vrātyas have become impure because they traveled abroad to make war,[86] Heesterman argues that the *Pañcaviṃśa Brāhmaṇa* portrays the Vrātyas existing "betwixt and between" Brahmin and Vaiṣya or Brahmin and Kṣatriya, just as the initiated sacrificer is no longer of Earth but not yet of Heaven.[87] They seem to be missing some crucial part of themselves that can only be amended ritually. To underline this need for ritual reconstruction, parallel images of incomplete people and incomplete or unsymmetrical verses, both in need of repair, reappear in 17.1.5 and 17.1.11.[88]

17.1.3 identifies the chant given to the Vrātyas as the Marut chant, strengthening the connection between the two groups. Verses 17.1.4–6 describe the way in which the priest rearranges the verses of a Ṛg Vedic chant in order to make it metrically regular and therefore ritually effective (the *raison d'etre* of the *Sāma Veda*, on which the *Pañcaviṃśa Brāhmaṇa* is a commentary). To make it "even," along with the Indra hymn *ṚV* 8.98, the priest also chants the hymn ascribed to Dyutāna (*ṚV* 8.85), the Vedic sage and Vrātya chief (which the text clearly means with the word *gṛhapati*) who is also a Marut. Dyutāna's hymn is dedicated to Indra, but it specifically portrays the god as the leader of a well-armed band of thirty-six Maruts. The name Dyutāna means "bright or shining" but looks very much like the word *dyūta*, which refers to gambling, dice-playing, and the stakes of a dicing match, all closely tied to the Vrātyas, as we shall soon see. And in the discussion of explicit versus implicit chanting in 17.1.8 we see that secrecy, or at least a certain amount of discretion, is the key to the Vrātyas' success.

Verse 17.1.9 begins by describing the Vrātyas as "swallowing poison," which according to Heesterman, "usually refers to the accepting of food and presents from, and the officiating at sacrifices of, unqualified patrons."[89] They also swallow poison,[90] or harm themselves, through their behavior: hitting people with sticks, taking food[91] from the wrong people, using wrong speech (which may refer to the obscene chants that are part of the Vedic ritual) and saying the words of a Dīkṣita without being a Dīkṣita. Other than hitting people with sticks, all of these sins seem to suggest a heterodox ritual.

17.1.14–15 describes the trappings of the Vrātyas and their chief (black clothes, goatskins, silver chains), which are also associated elsewhere with the Maruts. The phrase "booty of the Vrātyas" (*vrātyadhanaṃ*) in 17.1.16 refers to the idea that whomever receives the accouterments of the Vrātya also receives a burden of impurity or guilt. *Dhana*, which I have translated as "booty," has the sense of both "prize" and "prey," and opposes the Vrātya's lugubrious lot to the goods claimed by the victorious sacrificer. This verse in particular points clearly to the scapegoat nature of the Vrātya while the next verse calls our attention to another element of Vrātya heterodoxy: the fact that the Vrātyas give their payment of the cows to their own chief and not to a Vedic Brahmin (as payment for ritual services rendered), circumventing the sacrificial economy.

As this passage indicates, the Vrātyas bear many of the marks of the scapegoat in that they are defiled and accursed, and they literally bear the sins of others as their lot. But the Vrātyas could not be excluded completely without leaving a lacuna in the Brahminical ritual structure, and the Vedic system cannot abide a void. Therefore, it always follows exclusion with an attempt at systematic completion. Heesterman argues that the Brahminical image of the Vrātya, especially the one found in book fifteen of the *Atharva Veda*, which celebrates the Vrātya's rites, is an attempt on the part of late Vedic Brahmin authors to synthesize all known sacrificial ritual into a hierarchical system that only includes the Vrātya rituals as lesser and superseded practices.

Even after being expelled from the sacrificial system, the Vrātyas remained tied to it as the outsiders who constitute the boundaries of ritual purity by standing beyond them. The Brahmin authors do not seem to know quite what to do with the Vrātyas. One solution, described in the *Āpastambha Śrauta Sūtra*, is to treat the Vrātya as a guest (*atithi*), which is to say, with ambivalence—and here we are not speaking in circularities when we use the term. In the next section we will examine one more group of canine outsiders, this time from Europe—who also served as scapegoats for the mainstream religious tradition—and try to draw some conclusions.

The Good Walkers Seen from the East

Carlo Ginzburg based *The Night Battles*, his famous study of the shamanistic agrarian peasant cult called the Benandanti, or "Good Walkers," on judicial records found in the Archiepiscopal Archives of the Northern Italian town of Undine. What Ginzburg found was a set of trial transcripts in which inquisitors sought to demonstrate that the Benandanti were heretics. The inquisitors' questions and the Benandantis' answers were reported verbatim according to the practice of the court. And in these records Ginzburg is convinced that he has found a relatively undistorted picture of the Benandanti in their attempts to describe themselves to the inquisitors, steadfastly maintaining their innocence of heresy and resisting all attempts to lump their practices in with the blasphemous Sabbat of the witches, whom they actually believed themselves to be fighting against in the name of Christ during their night battles. Ginzburg gives this picture of the group as it emerges from the trial records: "[The] benandanti constituted . . . a true and proper sect, *organized in military fashion about a leader* and *linked by a bond of secrecy* . . ."[92] This description has some suggestive similarities with the Vrātyas, Maruts, and other *Männerbund*-type groups. The fact that nearly all of the Benandanti had been born with a caul points to a certain amount of organization in that members of the group had the wherewithal to seek out and convert those with common birth circumstances. The stated purpose of the Benandanti was to fight, in some kind of a trance or dream-state, on behalf of God and their agrarian community against evil witches who tried to destroy the harvest. Ginzburg is ambiguous about the possible connection of the reported (dream) battles between good Benandanti and evil witches and the European myth of the Wild Hunt of Wotan in which disembodied spirits chase down evil female spirits or witches. He concludes that the Benandanti sect in seventeenth century Friuli represents a confluence of Slavic, Germanic, and Middle Eastern folklore and their practice is an amalgam of the cult of the dead and the cult of fertility. Their ritual battles occur during the changes of the seasons, and the stakes for which the Benandanti and their enemies contend are above all the produce and fertility of the fields. Using the testimony of an unrepentant defendant from a late seventeenth century Livonian werewolf trial, Ginzburg argues for a real rather than an analogical connection between the seasonal battles of the Benandanti against the witches and an ancient belief attested in Germany and Russia that werewolves are the "Hounds of God," descending into Hell three times a year to rescue the crops from the demonic witches who have stolen them.[93] The persistence of this belief in the mind of one accused werewolf attests to an older and more complex lycanthropic tradition only partially subsumed by Church doctrine. And with their connection to werewolves, oaths of secrecy, and participation in a battle for the community's survival during the dead of winter, the Benandanti bear a strong resemblance to the Vrātyas as they appear in the Vedic literature.

When we look at the story of the Sālavṛkeyas and the Yatis alongside what we know about the Vrātyas and their European analogues the Benandanti, the contours of an Indo-European wolf-warrior myth and ritual complex begins to take shape. Behind the battles of the Sālavṛkeyas against the Yatis and the Benandanti against the witches we can see a struggle between two groups of priests and sorcerers, one of which is closely associated with wolves or wild dogs and which is led by a lycanthropic form of the god Indra or one of his counterparts. The story of the Yatis presents a picture of the (temporarily) victorious wolf-warriors, but ultimately the battle is as undecidable and unending as the struggle between the two Vedic sacrificers in the pre-classical ritual cycle or the war of the gods and the demons in the Brāhmaṇas. But all this changes when religious elites begin to subsume the old model under a new one and the wolf-warrior faction finds itself on the wrong side of history.

At this point, it will be useful to return to the work of Giorgio Agamben. Building on the work of the classicist Rodolphe Jhering and the philological researches of the Grimm brothers, Agamben posits a connection between four figures of Indo-European law and folklore who live on the margins of human society: the werewolf; the Germanic *friedlos* or "man without peace;" the *homo sacer*, the banished man of ancient Roman law who can be killed with impunity but not sacrificed; and the bandit.[94] Agamben leaves out a fifth figure that belongs in this liminal company, the ascetic who retires to the forest to pursue liberation and who is classed, as Gregory Schopen has argued, along with criminals and spies and regarded as the "idiot fringe" in classical India.[95] As outsiders connected specifically to the violent and antinomian elements of the sacrifice, the Vrātyas and related groups absorb all the impurity that Brahmin ritualists exclude from the sacrificial enclosure. They inhabit the liminal space of the archaic sacred.[96] The Vrātyas and their Indo-European counterparts may well have represented the defeated party in the sacrificial battle (which is another way of saying "the sacrificial victims"). But while the official doctrines of the Brahmins and the Church may have scapegoated them, the heterodox or folk tradition preserves the memory of their innocence, or at least, in the Indian case, the fact that they were once part of the system and not its opponents. In a later chapter, we will see how these outsider figures continue to haunt the Indian sacrificial landscape. But first, we turn to another liminal figure from Sanskrit myth—the king.

Sacred Kingship in Sanskrit Myth

The foundations of classical India, according to Heesterman, can be found in the archaic sacrificial contest and the priestly domestication of its original violence. South Asia in the period of the Vedas was home to both the nomadic pastoralists who brought the Vedas in from Central Asia and semi-settled agriculturalists who were indigenous or belonged to an earlier wave of migration. The Indian state came about through the conflict of these two groups, sacralized in the agonistic sacrifice, in which a ceremonial cattle raid represented the king's subjugation of his land.[97] While the roving warrior bands had great need to channel their violence outward lest it tear apart their groups, which depended on cohesion for survival, agricultural settlements were more tolerant of conflict. Although internal strife still presented a serious problem for the agriculturalists, the network of ties and mutual obligations that had arisen among them was able to contain conflict for a longer period.[98] Warrior chiefs were kings in search of a kingdom to rule and profit from, while the semi-settled world was a kingdom, looking not necessarily for a king, but for an arbiter and protector.

This situation is reflected in the myth of the wicked first king Vena and his righteous son Pṛthu. Along with kingship, the Vena-Pṛthu myth also deals with the sacrifice and the cow, which went from an animal to be herded and slaughtered in the Vedic period to an animal to be protected and milked in the classical period. And like the Vrātyas who kept the sacrificial gift to themselves, Vena earns his sacrificial death by ordering that all offerings be made to him alone. The *Ṛg Veda* mentions Pṛthu in 8.9.10, 10.94.14, and 10.148.5, only saying that he is the son of Vena without attributing good or evil qualities to either him or his father. One other fragment that appears in 10.123, among other places, refers to Vena as one who has "'impelled' the calves of the speckled cow who is the earth, whose white udder [probably a reference to the moon] yields Soma as milk for the gods."[99] The action of "milking the earth," which is such an important theme in later mythology, appears here in a neutral form without any indication of being either a crime of exploitation or a heroic conquest.

In the version from *Atharva Veda* 8.10.22–29, the outlines of the myth begin to take shape. Here, the familiar celestial menagerie of gods, ancestors, demons, and other supernatural beings joins Vena in milking the earth. When he takes his turn at milking, Vena brings forth cultivation and grain, developments allowing for the transition from a nomadic to an agricultural lifestyle. But in the *Mahābhārata*, Vena and Pṛthu are sharply distinct and Pṛthu is exclusively responsible for milking the earth. And Vena is no longer the father of Pṛthu, but the evil king who precedes Pṛthu's righteous reign. Vena is an easily identifiable scapegoat figure. His crimes bring about a sacrificial crisis and his collective murder remains utterly undisguised in the myth. He confuses people with *paśus*, a word that refers to a domesticated sacrificial beast, and begins to strangle them while he is still just a child. The *Bṛhaddharma Purāṇa* describes the evils of Vena's reign in terms of miscegenation:

> When Vena left the path of dharma, all classes and all castes became mixed for when the sages told him that mixing castes led to hell, he announced his intention to cause them to intermarry thoroughly. The atheist Vena caused Brahmins to beget sons in Kṣatriyas, Kṣatriyas in Vaiśyas, and so forth. . . .[100]

In the version from chapter fourteen of the *Bhāgavata Purāṇa* Vena completes the destruction of Dharma by demanding, among other things, to receive the gifts of the sacrifice. The resulting famine forces the sages to band together and kill him, subsequently creating an heir by "churning" or burning his corpse. The Brahmins begin to feel the terrible consequences of murdering a king (even a bad king) when the social order disintegrates even further, with thieves plundering the people and the Brahmins unable to stop them.[101] After learning that "seeing the fault" (*tad-doṣa-darśinaḥ*) isn't enough to keep the world in line, the Brahmins return to the preserved corpse of their victim and bring forth an ugly black dwarf named Niṣāda ("Sit-Down"), so named because the Brahmins tell him to "sit down" and stay out of the way so they can then bring forth the king Pṛthu to restore order, proclaiming him to be Viṣṇu himself. From the evil king Vena's collective murder, indeed directly from his corpse, comes both the outcaste figure of Niṣāda[102] and the "good son" Pṛthu who undoes all the evil his father has wrought by reasserting the hierarchy of class, or *varṇa*.[103]

Heesterman sees the Vena story as indicative of the uneasy alliance between Brahmin and king and between the forces of spiritual power and temporal authority:

> Ideal kingship is thus duly brought about through sacrifice. However, as soon as Pṛthu has been produced, he confesses his utter ignorance of *dharma* and prays the brahmin seers to guide him at every step. This may be a pious ideal but it is not a solution. Between Vena, who arrogates all power and authority only to fall victim to his own sacrality, and Pṛthu, *rite* ["properly"] produced in sacrifice but pitifully lacking in both power and authority, the unresolved conundrum remains suspended. There can only be compromise and accommodation but no definitive solution. The void between the enchanted world of sacrality and the disenchanted realm of transcendence can not be firmly bridged.[104]

Like the figure of the Vrātya, the king, as represented by Vena and Pṛthu, can neither be totally exorcised from the system nor fully assimilated to it. Instead he maintains a necessary but liminal role, regarded with caution by the Brahmin ritualists. In the next section, we will examine one of the Brahmins' strategies for keeping the power of the ruling class under control, specifically the binding power of the oath held by what Dumézil calls the "Varuṇic" Brahmins.

Indra, Soma, and Mitra-Varuṇa

Girard makes much of the god Soma in *Sacrifice*, identifying the offering of the *soma* plant as the point at which the Brāhmaṇas reveal the sacrificial mechanism. As evidence of the text's "revealing genius, probably involuntary but all the more striking if so" and its "full and complete revelation of the real function of sacrifice,"[105] Girard takes a passage quoted by Lévi from *Śatapatha Brāhmaṇa* 3.9.4.17:

> When he is about to crush the Soma with the pressing-stone, let him have in his mind of someone he hates, thinking "With this I strike So-and-so, not you!" Whoever kills a human Brahmin is guilty. How much more so for one who strikes Soma, for Soma is a god. But they do kill him when they press him. They kill him with the stone, and he rises from that place and lives. Therefore no guilt is incurred. But if he has no one to hate, he may even think of a blade of grass, and he will incur no guilt.[106]

For Girard, this passage is evidence that the Brahmin ritualists know that the real function of sacrifice is to purify violence. By casually suggesting that the sacrificer channel his anger toward an enemy into the crushing of the *soma* plant, the text reveals that they know what they do. While real violence will result in reprisals and escalate into a spreading conflagration of destruction, sacred violence within the ritual enclosure will bring no reprisals and keep the community's peace intact.

As we saw in the *Śatapatha Brāhmaṇa*, the gods compel Mitra to join them in killing Vṛtra by threatening to exclude him from the sacrifice, the curse to which the Vrātyas are subject. As a result of taking part in the violence, Mitra then loses his status as the "friend to all" and becomes Amitra. This originary exclusion of the Brahmin deity is then followed by a ritual pact on the part of the gods to replace the cows Mitra has lost along with his "friend" status with gifts of milk to go with every *soma* offering. In *Taittirīya Saṃhitā* 6.1.11, Soma, Varuṇa, and Mitra are linked once again in what looks like a typically opaque set of connections and substitutions. First the text instructs the sacrificer to purchase the *soma* with a milch cow, so that "he makes the *soma* worth a cow, the sacrificer worth a cow, the Adhvaryu worth a cow, and he does not drag down the greatness of the cow." Immediately after the ritual purchase of the *soma*, the text connects the sacred draught to Varuṇa, the violent enforcer of obligations. Then the text requires the priest to ritually transmute it into a substance of non-violence, connecting it with Mitra, the friend to all and guardian of the peace. The passage reads:

> The *soma*, when bought and tied up, is connected with Varuna. He says, for the purpose of peace, "Come as Mitra [or "as a friend"] to us, creating firm friendships." He says, "Enter the right thigh of Indra." The gods placed the *soma* that they purchased in the right thigh of Indra; now the sacrificer is Indra. That is why he says this.[107]

In this passage, Indra (with Soma now in his right thigh) stands in for the sacrificer, just as Soma, the Adhvaryu priest, and the cow do in the previous verse. We also get the threefold identification of Soma, Mitra, and Varuṇa. This elaborate chain of equivalences and substitutions ends in the identification of Indra-Soma in the heavenly realm with the sacrificer in the enclosure. Reading a text like this, one begins to have sympathy for the nineteenth-century Indologists who dismissed the Brāhmaṇas as incomprehensible nonsense. But before we jump to their conclusion, we may yet be able to shed light on some of this obscurity by turning at last to the story of Śunaḥśepa.

Cutting Varuṇa's Noose

The reader might recall from chapter one that the story of Śunaḥśepa, or "Dog-penis," is the myth that served as one of the primary sources for the Anglican vicar Joseph Townsend's 1816 account of "Hindoo" sacrifice as well as the Indological speculations of Moritz Winternitz, Max Müller, and H. H. Wilson about the existence of human sacrifice in ancient times.[108] The story of Śunaḥśepa, first recorded in full in *Aitareya Brāhmaṇa* 7.13–18, is recited ritually at the Rājasuya, or Royal Consecration Sacrifice, to remove any guilt or evil from the consecrated king. It is also, as David Shulman notes, a close parallel to the Biblical Aqedah, or the Binding of Isaac.[109]

The story, as told in the *Aiṭareya Brāhmaṇa*, begins when King Hariścandra takes the advice of the sage Nārada, who has told him that a man gains eternal life when he is reborn through his son, and prays to Varuṇa for a male child, promising, more than a little counter-productively, to sacrifice him to Varuṇa after the boy is born. Soon after the birth of his son, named Rohita, Hariścandra begins to put off his sacrifice with a series of excuses. After a time, Rohita grows into adulthood and Varuṇa loses his patience, demanding the sacrifice at once. Accepting what he must do, Hariścandra goes to his son and explains that he must be sacrificed to Varuṇa. But Rohita, unlike the biblical Isaac and having no desire to be the guest of honor at a Puruṣamedha, grabs his bow and runs into the forest. His vow broken by his son's actions, Hariścandra is seized in the "Noose of Varuṇa" as his stomach becomes painfully distended from edema (dropsy). Hearing of his father's affliction, Rohita starts out for home. But before he reaches Hariścandra, Indra, disguised as a wandering beggar, stops Rohita and advises him to forsake his father and save himself. Indra's argument makes sense: If his father is willing to sacrifice his son to save himself, why should Rohita be any different?

A year later, Rohita tries to go home again and is once more stopped by Indra and sent back into the forest. This goes on every year for five years until the sixth year, when Rohita finds in the forest a poor Brahmin family with three sons. Rohita sees an opportunity to save himself and his father and offers to buy one of the boys to act as his sacrificial substitute. The father, Ajīgarta, will not let go of his eldest son and heir and the mother is too attached to her youngest son, but both parents agree that they are willing to part with their middle son, Śunaḥśepa, for a hundred cows. Pleased that he has found a way to save his own life and free his father from Varuṇa's punishment for oath breakers, Rohita finally returns home with Śunaḥśepa in tow. Since a Brahmin is naturally worth more than a Kṣatriya, Varuṇa accepts the substitution. And the sacrifice of Śunaḥśepa serves a dual purpose: Not only does Varuṇa accept the offering of Śunaḥśepa as repayment of Hariścandra's obligation to him, the god also shows Hariścandra the consecration ritual so that he can sanctify his kingship with Śunaḥśepa as the "human sacrificial beast" (*puruśaḥ paśum*).[110] Officiating at the rite is an illustrious company of Vedic sages—Viśvāmitra as the Hotṛ, Jamadagni as the Adhvaryu, Vasiṣṭha as the Brahmin, and Ayāsya as the Udgātṛ. But when there is no one to bind Śunaḥśepa to the sacrificial post, the unfortunate Brahmin's greedy father steps forward and offers to bind his son for a hundred more cows and even proposes to do the killing himself for another hundred. When he sees that his own father is willing not only to tie him up, but also to wield the knife, it finally dawns on Śunaḥśepa that he really will be killed "as though he were not human" (*amānuṣam iva*).[111] In despair, the doomed victim cries out to the gods, reciting *Ṛg Veda* 1.24–30. As the verse leaves his mouth, Śunaḥśepa's bonds melt away at the same time as the king's distended stomach is cured. In uttering the proper verse, Śunaḥśepa has "finished" the sacrifice without his blood being spilled.

The gathered sages are amazed at Śunaḥśepa's ritual perspicacity and beg the boy to instruct them on the rest of the rite. When Śunaḥśepa's father sees what has happened and the way the sages are praising the boy, he realizes he has underestimated the value of his middle son and tries to reclaim him. But Śunaḥśepa refuses to go back to his greedy father, complaining that not even a lowborn Śudra would sacrifice his own son. Viśvāmitra then offers to adopt Śunaḥśepa as his son, renaming him Devarata ("Given from God," the Sanskrit equivalent of the Biblical name Jonathan), but the Brahmin boy sees a problem in this. Viśvāmitra is technically a Kṣatriya who has become a Brahmin through his austerities and piety (as we will see in the next section), not a Brahmin by birth. So, perhaps to sweeten the deal, Viśvāmitra adds that he will make Śunaḥśepa his eldest son and place him before the hundred other sons he already has. Śunaḥśepa agrees, but the older fifty of Viśvāmitra's sons complain about the unfairness of this new development and the loss of their birthright. As a result, Viśvāmitra curses them to lose caste and inherit the least desirable lands of the earth. The younger fifty sons, who quickly line up behind their new older brother Śunaḥśepa, he blesses in turn with promises of cattle and heroic sons of their own.

In the story of Śunaḥśepa, we see a mythologization of the ritual we examined in the last section (*Taittirīya Saṃhitā* 6.1.11). Both the ritual and the Śunaḥśepa myth begin with the sacrificial victim—the *soma* plant in the ritual, the prince Rohita in the myth—bound in obligation to Varuṇa. The ritual continues with the priest calling on Mitra to bring peace instead of Varuṇa's iron law of retribution. In the myth, this short invocation is expanded into an episode in which one victim (Śunaḥśepa) is purchased as substitute for another, just as the *soma* is purchased as the substitute for the sacrificer in the ritual. But then Mitra steps in in the form of Viśvāmitra (significantly, the name Viśvāmitra means "Friend to All" just as Mitra is a friend to all before the gods force him to join their lynch mob in the *Śatapatha Brāhmaṇa*) to claim the victim from Varuṇa. The last phase of the ritual, in which the sacrificer becomes Indra with Soma in his thigh, is conceived in the myth as the moment when the Kṣatriya-Brahmin Viśvāmitra adopts Śunaḥśepa as his son. In the end of the story, as Shulman notes, "Śunaḥśepa achieves the best of both worlds, Kṣatriya leadership and divine knowledge (*daiva vede*) proper to the Brahmin."[112]

We should also mark the role of Indra himself in the myth, stepping in to save the son from his father (and Varuṇa) five times. Although he disappears after the substitute is found, Indra is clearly the opponent of Varuṇa in this story. Shulman goes on to describe the role of Varuṇa's noose in this myth as the bondage of the sacrificial system, marked by a cycle of fathers sacrificing their sons in order to obtain the fruits of the sacrifice: eternal life through progeny in the case of the Kṣatriya Hariścandra, and cattle in the case of the Brahmin Ajīgarta. Shulman writes:

> This is the universal law that underlies Varuṇa's part in this transaction: the god gives and takes lives; the procreative father produces offspring that reproduce his own self, only after promising to perform the lethal sacrifice; the two poles of life and death, creation and violent destruction, are completely interdependent, and human beings are caught between them. A person lives out his life in the brief respite granted the sacrificial victim (a respite won by the father, who will nevertheless eventually revert to his unhappy role as sacrificer). In this sense, this *aqedah*-like scenario has less to do with the god *per se*, a willful being hungry for the child, than with a divine structure or process built into the world as Vedic man perceives it.[113]

We can also see in the Śunaḥśepa myth a shadow of the Indo-European **bhlagh(s)-men*, the Brahmin sacrificial substitute for the king. If Dumézil is right about this hypothetical figure's connection to the Brahmin class, then who better to understand that "a person lives out his life in the brief respite granted the sacrificial victim" than the Brahmins, who have turned what was once a brief period of sacrality before becoming sacrificial victims into an unquestionable position of privilege and authority?

Although this element fades in later variants from the *Rāmāyaṇa* and the Purāṇas, the story of Śunaḥśepa is by far the most radical critique of sacrifice in the Sanskrit tradition. It proclaims the innocence of the victim and the greed of those who would keep the sacrificial system in place, while at the same time acknowledging that the survival of the community is only guaranteed by sacrificial repetition. But if Śunaḥśepa had simply refused to be the substitute for Rohita then there would be nothing anti-sacrificial about the myth. It is his *refusal to return to his father's world* that is the true anti-sacrificial moment. As Shulman notes of Śunaḥśepa:

> He, and he alone, breaks through the constraining limits of sacrificial causality, operating in its most literal and brutal mode. His father, surely the worst of the three [fathers, i.e., Hariścandra, Ajīgarta, and Viśvāmitra] pictured here, perfectly exemplifies the notion of deadly paternal aggression at work within the sacrificial system. Ajīgarta is a monstrous image of the violent father, knife raised above his son's head; but he is clearly part of the same world as Hariścandra and no less bound by its inner laws. Śunaḥśepa, on the other hand, escapes death by invoking the gods in Vedic verses. . . . Language, the sacred text, the knowledge that it represents—all of these, in the right hands, offer a way out of the trap that has held Hariścandra and Rohita captive. Śunaḥśepa has this redeeming knowledge. . . . There is no going back into the nightmare of repetition and replication from which Śunaḥśepa has just escaped. He will not recapitulate his father's career; he moves forward, away from the cyclical violence that consumes the victim, that identifies fathers with their sons.[114]

As the method of Śunaḥśepa's escape demonstrates, Varuṇa's noose is fastened not with a Gordian knot that one must cut, but with a riddle that one with the proper knowledge can unravel.

There is also something very anti-sacrificial about the actions of the Viśvāmitra, the Kṣatriya-Brahmin hybrid and "Friend to All" whose being hearkens back to the pre-sacrificial state hinted at in the story of Vṛtra's lynching. When Viśvāmitra causes the "last to become first" and raises the lowly "Dog-penis" into the "Gift of God," adopting him as his own heir, he gives his sons a choice: They can accept the boy who was to be sacrificed but who saved himself—Oedipus-like, with his own wits—as their elder brother, or they can fall to the state of Śunaḥśepa's base Brahmin father. In other words, as the Gospels have it:

> He who loves his brother abides in the light, and in it there is no cause for stumbling. But he who hates his brother is in the darkness and walks in the darkness, and does not know where he is going, because the darkness has blinded his eyes.[115]

In Girard's interpretation of Christianity, Christ's understanding of the sacrificial order comes from the fact that he embodies the Johannine *logos*, which he distinguishes from the Greek *logos*. But what is the source of Śunaḥśepa's knowledge? Shulman's answer to this question is as elegant as it is provocative: Śunaḥśepa embodies the "middle"; he is the middle son, the "medium" of exchange, the heir to the mediating figure of the Kṣatriya-Brahmin Viśvāmitra. As such, Śunaḥśepa is, according to the speculative philosophy born of the Vedic ritual system, the connection or *bandhu* between one element of a concatenation and another. Because he stands in this place between, Śunaḥśepa "knows and is the sacrifice that activates unseen connections; and in the Vedic system, it is precisely this form of reflective consciousness that, by internalizing the entire process in the knowing self, permits transcendence of its inherent evil and violence."[116] Śunaḥśepa, the "Dog-penis," is the embodiment of everything excluded from the sacrificial enclosure; he is the impure canine Vrātya priest, the Brahmin tainted by violence, the unacceptable offering. Viśvāmitra's fifty elder sons say as much when they complain in the *Rāmāyaṇa*'s version of the story that accepting Śunaḥśepa as their older brother would be like eating dog meat.[117] But as the excluded, he is also the void left by that exclusion. And it is the generative void at the heart of sacrifice, according to Heesterman, "that provided the open space for inquiry and debate, faith and unbelief, bondage and release, submission and protest—in short, for the never-ending gamble of freedom."[118]

For the story of Śunaḥśepa to be a true unmasking of the sacrificial system according to Girard, there must be some charge against him of which he is not guilty. At first glance, it seems that Śunaḥśepa is chosen as a victim more or less at random; he happens to be a Brahmin (and therefore worth more than a Kṣatriya) whose parents are willing to give him up. But it is in his rather unlikely name, "Dog-penis," that we see the hidden accusation. His name identifies Śunaḥśepa as the Dog-man, the scapegoat figure found throughout the Indo-European world in various forms. We have seen the earliest form in the Vedic Vrātyas: the sacrificial priests excluded from the ritual and identified as black magicians and outlaws. In medieval India, it is the Kāpālika, the Śaiva ascetic belonging to a lost sect that we only know through disparaging accounts claiming that they undermined the caste hierarchy and practiced human sacrifice and cannibalism.[119] In Central Europe, it is the shape-changing magician calling himself the Benandanti or "Good Walker" but called "witch" by the Inquisition. The story of Śunaḥśepa has the same status Girard claims for the story of Joseph in the Hebrew Bible, an interpretation rather than a myth. To get a better idea of what this means, we need to widen our view to include the myth-cycle of which the story of Śunaḥśepa is a part, the mimetic rivalry of Viśvāmitra and Vasiṣṭha.

The Dueling Logō *of Viśvāmitra and Vasiṣṭha*

Like the Christian story that leads from Mt. Moriah to Calgary, the story of Śunaḥśepa is also a story of fathers and sons. First Śunaḥśepa's father rejects him and is prepared to bind him to the sacrificial post and drive a knife into him. Then when his father tries to get him back, it is Śunaḥśepa's turn to reject him and accept a new father:

> [Śunaḥśepa's father] Ajīgarta Sauyavasi said [to Śunaḥśepa], "This great evil deed I committed pains me. I would make amends to you for it. Please accept a thousand cows." Śunaḥśepa replied, "He who has committed one evil would commit another. You have not abandoned your low-class ways. What you have done cannot be amended and restored." At the mention of the word "restored," Viśvāmitra joined the conversation, saying, "[Ajīgarta] was truly horrific as he stood there with knife in hand, ready to butcher you. Do not be his son, come be my son instead!"[120]

David Gordon White sees the Śunaḥśepa episode as part of the larger Viśvāmitra-Vasiṣṭha cycle, noting that in later variants it is on the advice of Vasiṣṭha and not Nārada that King Hariścandra makes his bargain with Varuṇa.[121] With this in mind, we can see the pattern of a struggle in the Śunaḥśepa story. On one side, we have the binding sovereignty and ritualism of Varuṇa and Vasiṣṭha, guardians of the sacrificial order and representatives of the Brahmin class. On the other side we have the excluded remnants of the pre-sacrificial order, Indra and Viśvāmitra, the representatives of the martial class who step in to disrupt the sacrifice. White argues that in the rivalry of Viśvāmitra and Vasiṣṭha we see a reflection of the transition from Vedic ritualism favorable to Brahmins to the post-Vedic religious forms of renunciation and devotionalism, both more favorable to the martial Kṣatriyas:

> The mythology of the upstart Viśvāmitra may be seen in this light as a riposte by the priestly caste to a princely power play against its authority. This changing relationship between the two elements of the Hindu power elite is also reflected in the mythology of the Vedic and Hindu gods. Here we see a gradual replacement of Varuṇa, the Vedic god who represents magical and contractual priestly authority, by Indra, the royal god of military might: in later mythology, Viśvāmitra becomes a double of the *kṣatriya* Indra and Vasiṣṭha a double of his father, the brahmin Varuṇa. And, as had been the case with Vedic Indra, so it comes to pass with Viśvāmitra: after losing many battles against the brahmin orthodoxy, embodied by Varuṇa and Vasiṣṭha respectively, in the end Viśvāmitra and his iconoclastic ethic (of *nivṛtti* over *pravṛtti*, of renunciation over conventional Vedic sacrificial activity) win the war.[122]

The rivalry of Viśvāmitra and Vasiṣṭha is undoubtedly the most famous and recognizable mimetic rivalry in Indian myth. In the earliest versions of the cycle, found in the *Ṛg Veda* and the *Taittirīya Saṃhitā*, Viśvāmitra and Vasiṣṭha are competing sacrificers outdoing each other with ritual acuity, but Viśvāmitra is associated with a non-Vedic tribe. In the *Jaiminīya Brāhmaṇa* the rivalry escalates into violence as Vasiṣṭha's son kills the sons of Viśvāmitra, and in the later *Devībhagavāta Purāṇa*, the two Ṛṣis have turned into vultures and are causing the entire universe to disintegrate with their rivalry.[123] In post-Vedic myths Vasiṣṭha is a trueborn Brahmin, but his rival Viśvāmitra is born a Kṣatriya and rises to the rank of Brahmin over the course of his rivalry with Vasiṣṭha. The beginning of their mutual enmity is described in *Mahābhārata* 1.165.1–44, when Prince Viśvāmitra is hunting in the forest and comes upon the ashram of the Brahmin Vasiṣṭha. Vasiṣṭha offers the prince hospitality and, using his magic wishing cow, produces a great feast. Viśvāmitra is impressed and offers to trade anything, including his kingdom, for the cow. Vasiṣṭha refuses on the grounds that he needs the cow to produce the dairy products like milk and clarified butter that are necessary to perform his sacrificial duties. Viśvāmitra grows angry and tries to take the cow by force. Vasiṣṭha himself refuses to lift a hand against the prince, but when Viśvāmitra's men take the cow's calf, she becomes enraged and from her anus, using dung and urine, she produces armies of foreign warriors to drive back Viśvāmitra's hosts (though without killing any of them). After he is dealt a humiliating defeat by a cow's rear end and waste products, Viśvāmitra abandons his Kṣatriya-hood, saying, "A curse on the power of the Kṣatriya. Brahmin power is truly power."

So Viśvāmitra devotes his life to austerities, penance, and asceticism with the aim of becoming as great a Brahmin Ṛṣi, or Brahmārṣi, as Vasiṣṭha is. Technically speaking, the Royal Sage or Rājārṣi is the highest rank to which a Kṣatriya-born man can rise, but the noteworthy thing about Viśvāmitra is that he breaks the rules and becomes one of the Brahmārṣi, much to the consternation of Vasiṣṭha. In other words, the rivalry of Viśvāmitra and Vasiṣṭha leads to the two becoming more and more alike. On this phenomenon of mimetic doubling Girard writes:

> Beyond a certain threshold of frustration, those in conflict are no longer content with the objects themselves over which they are fighting. Mutually exasperated by the live obstacle, the scandal, that each is henceforth for the other, they become mimetic *doubles* and forget the object of their quarrel; they turn against each other with rage in their hearts. From now on each sets upon the other as a mimetic rival. . . .[124]

Vasiṣṭha and Viśvāmitra's rivalry begins with Viśvāmitra's acquisitive desire for the cow belonging to Vasiṣṭha, which is soon supplanted by his desire to be a Brahmin exactly like Vasiṣṭha, a desire he paradoxically fulfills by the renunciation of desire itself—ascesis.

Set against the background of Vasiṣṭha and Viśvāmitra's rivalry, the salvation of Śunaḥśepa takes on greater significance. It is, in a way, the destruction of the rivalry. When Viśvāmitra first accepts Śunaḥśepa the Dog-penis as his teacher, then makes him his heir and renames him Devarāta the Gift of God, he is acknowledging the significance of the miraculous rescue he has just seen: That which is excluded from the sacrifice is in fact identical with the connection, the *bandhu*, that allows Vedic sacrificial science to transcend itself. As we have seen, the Vedic sacrifice begins as a kind of unending ritual contest, which gives way to a bounded and heavily ritualized form of sacrifice from which not only violence and contest are excluded, but also a now obsolete type of ritualist identified with the Vrātya and other liminal lycanthropic figures. This excluded figure, exemplified by Śunaḥśepa, comes back to haunt the sacrifice as its undoing. We will return in chapter four to this very significant connection between the *bandhu*, Śunaḥśepa, and the Indian *homo sacer*.

Tretayugānta, "The End of the Age of the Trey": The Two Forms of Sacrifice

In this chapter, we added another figure to Girard's intellectual genealogy: Georges Dumézil. After examining Dumézil's theory of a trifunctional paradigm underlying Indo-European social organization, we turned to his discarded hypothesis about the archaic role of the Brahmin as a sacrificial substitute for the king. Next we used Dumézil's insights to interpret the figure of Mitra, forced by the gods to participate in the lynching of Vṛtra in order to obtain a share in the sacrifice. We concluded that the myth of Mitra interprets sacrifice as the repetition of a primal lynching through which bonds of shared bloodguilt replace the idyllic egalitarianism of the pre-sacrificial world. We then turned to Giorgio Agamben's conception of the oath, and used Girard's and Agamben's work to demonstrate how the institution of the oath derives from the classical single-sacrificer model while the duel derives from the archaic two-sacrificer model that is repressed in the classical system.

As evidence for the preexistence of the two-sacrificer model, we looked at the figure of Uśanas Kāvya, the high priest of the demons, and his role in the ongoing battle between the gods and the demons. Finally, beginning with Carlo Ginzburg's analysis of the European Benandanti, we read the myths of Indra and the Yatis, Viśvāmitra and Vasiṣṭha, Śunaḥśepa, and the Vrātyas, uncovering in them the shadowy presence of a figure that embodies the self-deconstructive potential of the sacrifice. In the next chapter, we will continue to follow this figure as it appears in different forms, turning our attention to the great epic of India, the *Mahābhārata*, which will prove to be the most fertile subject for mimetic theory in the entire body of Hindu mythology.

Epic Variations on a Mimetic Theme

Śamit[ar], mfn. one who keeps his mind calm, Rāj.; *(°tṛi)*, m. a killer, slaughterer, cutter up (of a slaughtered victim), preparer, dresser, R[ig] V[eda].; Br[āhmaṇas].; M[ahā]Bh[ārata].

—Monier Monier-Williams. *Sanskrit-English Dictionary*

Mighty Ghaṭotkaca will be the *śamitar* when this overnight sacrifice is spun out, O Strong-armed Hero.

—*Mahābhārata* 5.139.43

May you have no *śamitar* among your relatives.

—*Āśvalāyana Śrauta Sūtra* 3.3.1

The three epigraphs that begin this chapter give three different perspectives on the figure of the *śamitar*, or *śamitṛ*, a ritual counterpart to mythical outsider figures like the Vrātya or Śunaḥśepa. The *śamitar* is not a priest, but a low-class ritual technician who works outside of the sacrificial arena, smothering or strangling the victim and then cooking its carcass on a fire that is also separate from the other sacrificial fires. There is a story in *MBh* 1.189 in which Death serves as the *śamitar* in the sacrifice of the gods, with the result that no one dies while he is so employed, as in the 1934 film *Death Takes a Holiday*. As long as Death is busy with the sacrificial victim, it would seem, other members of the community need not fear him coming for them.

The double meaning of the euphemism *śamitar* ("appeaser" or "pacifier") is suggestive, but not surprising. The *śamitar* brings peace to the animal by killing it quickly and also brings peace and appeasement to the community through his role in the sacrificial ritual. The epic hero Karṇa's pronouncement that Ghaṭotkaca will be the *śamitar* in the sacrifice of battle that is the climax of the *Mahābhārata* gives the role to an appropriately liminal figure. Ghaṭotkaca, which means something like "Jughead" or "Bald Pot," is the hybrid offspring of the Rabelaisian hero Bhīma and the ogress Hiḍimbī. But the benediction in the *Āśvalāyana Śrauta Sūtra* makes it clear that a *śamitar* is not a person to whom one would wish to be connected. In other words, the attitude reflected in the text toward *śamitars* and what they do is like that of contemporary suburban communities toward landfills: "Not in my backyard."

In this chapter, we will continue our exploration of outsider figures from the previous chapter, this time focused on the epic *Mahābhārata*. First we will look at the text itself, its plot, the narrative devices it employs, and the scholarly arguments surrounding it. Then I will argue for the existence of three non-Girardian "critiques" of sacrifice in the epic, Śaiva, Vaiṣṇava, and existential, all of which operate in relation to the outsider figure we have been following. The Śaiva critique is presented in the myth of Dakṣa and the disastrous consequences of his failure to invite the god Śiva, who is also his son-in-law, to his sacrifice. We will see the Vaiṣṇava critique in the story of the Śaiva king Jarāsaṃdha, who plans to rule the world by sacrificing all the other kings. The existential critique, a sort of dialectical overcoming of the tension between the Śaiva and Vaiṣṇava critiques, is found in the peculiar heroism (or anti-heroism) of Karṇa. Along the way, we will look at the myth of the churning of the ocean and examine the Hindu idea of *dveṣabhakti* and the connection Girard sees between tragedy and sacrifice.

The Textual Battlefield of the *Mahābhārata*

There is no piece of Sanskrit literature more suited to a Girardian reading than the *Mahābhārata*, a massive epic of 100,000 couplets that chronicles the dynastic rivalry of two groups of warring cousins—the Pāṇḍavas and the Kauravas—as it escalates into a cataclysmic world-engulfing war that climaxes with the destructive apotheosis of the incarnate god Kṛṣṇa. Composed roughly between 400 B.C.E. and 400 C.E., the *Mahābhārata* is an encyclopedic text that says of itself, "What is not here is nowhere else."[1] In *Sacrifice* Girard describes the *Mahābhārata* as "an absolutely astonishing and exemplary book from the viewpoint of my theory, because everything functions sacrificially."[2] And Girard is not the first to notice this fact. Writing on the Horse Sacrifice that takes place near the end of the epic after the war is over, Tamar Reich argues that this episode, along with the many, many other "interpolated" episodes that take the reader out of the main narrative, is not the mere result of centuries of accretion in an orally transmitted text. Recognizing a common theme that evidences the inner coherence of the epic, Reich concludes that "[the] only thing all these materials seem to have in common is some kind of association with the notion of sacrifice, though they vary quite radically in their understanding of the term."[3] She goes on to write:

> I contend that they constitute part of an ongoing cultural debate about the meaning of a central trope in the *Mahābhārata*, the comparison of the bloody war of the Bhāratas to a huge sacrifice. The [Horse Sacrifice episode], like much of the *Mahābhārata* text, is a result of a textual expansion process motivated by various agents' desire to insert their own position on what for them is an already given text of canonical importance. Thus, the *Mahābhārata* textual tradition is a case of the sedimentation of debate.... Here we have the whole range of debate, from hidden to fully explicit, and historical layers are notoriously difficult to separate....[4]

In Reich's argument, she makes a reference to Gananath Obeyesekere's very useful discussion in *The Work of Culture* of myth as a kind of record of a community's competing understandings of various symbolic forms, a theory of myth that stands quite apart from Girard's. For Girard interpreting myths is a process of demystification with the aim of uncovering their violent foundations. The life a myth takes on after it becomes a myth, with its patterns of what Obeyesekere calls associations, interpretations, and debates seems never to have interested him. But neither has he ever denied the complexity of myth transmission and transformation. It is also worth noting than none of the myths Girard has ever treated have demonstrated the kind of inner tensions and coexisting divergent viewpoints that are so clearly in evidence in the *Mahābhārata*. The *Mahābhārata* is explicitly "about" sacrifice, but it is also ambivalent about what sacrifice is or should be. In *The Scapegoat*, Girard acknowledges that a myth undergoes many transformations as it is perpetuated but seems to think this beside the point:

> We can identify the commemoration in mythology of those violent acts that are so successful that they force their perpetrators to reenact them. This memory inevitably develops as it is transmitted from generation to generation, but instead of rediscovering the secret of the distortion it loses it over and over again, each time burying it a little deeper. As religion and cultures are formed and perpetuated, the violence is hidden. The discovery of their secret would provide what must be called a *scientific* solution to man's greatest enigma, the nature and origins of religion.[5]

This is precisely the kind of claim that would draw howls of derision from most *Mahābhārata* scholars. For Reich, Obeyesekere, and others, the quest for the origins of religion is one that has been rightly abandoned, not only for its quixotic nature but because of the many distortions that it has wrought. It does not help Girard that he titles the chapter in *The Scapegoat* from which this quote is taken "The Science of Myth," the very phrase popularized in the nineteenth century by the widely disparaged F. Max Müller. But Girard has heard all this before and is singularly unperturbed:

> It is important not to confuse the reciprocal and ritualized extermination of "methodologies" with the totality of actual intelligence. This drama is no more distracting than storms at sea; they roll over the surface but leave the depths untouched. The more we become disturbed, the more real our agitation appears while the invisible escapes us. The pseudo-demystifiers

> can destroy each other without really weakening the critical principle which is the source for them all but which becomes less accurate. Recent doctrines have all evolved from one single process of decoding, the oldest to be invented in the Western world and the only truly lasting process . . . the decoding of representations of persecution.[6]

Here we have it: "*Ah! qu'en termes galants, ces choses-là sont mises!*" But Girard says something here that relates directly to my central argument when he claims that "the decoding of representations of persecution" is "the oldest to be invented in the Western world." Mimetic theory and all other hermeneutics of suspicion, from psychoanalysis to Marxism to deconstruction, are only possible for Girard in the post-Christian context. It is worth remembering here that the word "deconstruction," which Girard finds especially execrable, came to Derrida from Martin Luther through Heidegger. John D. Caputo gives us the genealogy of the term:

> Heidegger identified two . . . *pre*philosophical sources as particularly important to his project: the early Christian experience of time and the ethical experience of the Greek *polis*. To be sure, access to these "revolutionary" experiences could be gained only by means of the most traditional texts, the New Testament and the Nicomachean Ethics. Accordingly, such texts could not be approached by conventional academic reconstructions but required a new, more radical method Heidegger called "*Destruktion*." A "destruction" does not destroy but breaks through to the originary factical experiences from which the text arises, the term having been suggested to him by Luther's notion of a *destructio* through the crust of scholasticism to the life of the New Testament.[7]

If one reads no further than this, deconstruction does not look too dissimilar from Girard's "decoding." But the point to be made here is that the demystification that constitutes the ocean on which Girard finds his ship tossed by the angry storms of intellectual fashions is the product of an engagement with the Bible and a certain conception of canon and scripture that we do not find in India. Girard never claims that this "decoding" is universal. But he does claim that mimesis is. Does it not make sense, then, that in India, where we would expect to find all the cultural products of mimetic desire—including originary violence, myth, ritual, and prohibition—we could also expect to find a *different* way of decoding them? Following this expectation, I would argue that we need to keep our eyes open for a different approach to reading the *Mahābhārata*, which I will attempt to uncover in this chapter.

It would be only too easy to write an entire book on the mimetic themes of the *Mahābhārata*, but in the interest of keeping this work from becoming an epic in its own right, I will limit myself to four especially salient aspects of the text. First we will look briefly at the central rivalry (what else?) between the Pāṇḍavas and the Kauravas, its escalation to the climactic battle at Kurukṣetra, and its aftermath. Next we will examine the stories of two failed sacrificers: Dakṣa, the father-in-law of the god Śiva, and Jarāsaṃdha, the would-be Universal Monarch. Then we will turn to the epic's outer frame story for one of the most well-known myths about the war of the gods and the demons, the story of the churning of the ocean of milk to obtain the elixir of immortality. Finally, we will conclude with a longer look at the story of the figure we might call the "tragic villain" of the epic, the Kaurava hero Karṇa.

"Escalation to Extremes:" From the Dicing Match to Kurukṣetra

Arguing for the confluence in classical India of potlatch traditions from the non-Indo-European cultural substrate and the Indo-European traditions brought in with the Veda, Marcel Mauss writes the following about the *Mahābhārata* in *The Gift*:

> The Mahabharata is the story of a tremendous [*gigantesque*] potlatch—there is a game of dice between the Kauravas and the Pandavas, and a military festival, while Draupadi, sister and polyandrous wife of the Pandavas, chooses husbands. Repetitions of the same cycle of legends are met with in the finest parts of the epics. . . . But the whole is disfigured by its literary and theological style.[8]

Mauss, like many other European scholars of his era, seeks to uncover in the epic a "core" that has been surrounded and penetrated by innumerable subplots, back stories, digressions, and interpretative overlays of various theological, political, and philosophical stripes. This approach obscures the profound conceptual unity of the text especially when one pays attention to its sacrificial themes. Mauss comes very close to this unified thematic structure when he lays out the ritual elements of the text: the festival, the dice game, and the contests at Draupadī's bride-choice or *svayaṃvara*. It will be useful at this point to give a very brief summary of the main plot of the epic, which contains elements of the war between the gods and the demons and Dumézil's trifunctional Indo-European paradigm.

Following a succession crisis in the Bhārata dynasty, the demons see their opportunity to control the earth and take birth in the human realm as Kṣatriyas. When the goddess Earth complains to them of being oppressed by the demons, Viṣṇu and other gods intervene to rescue her. Two groups of cousins are born into the Bhārata lineage (The Lunar Dynasty), each with its own succession claims: the five sons of King Pāṇḍu, known as the Pāṇḍavas, and the hundred sons of Pāṇḍu's blind older brother Dhṛtarāṣṭra, called the Kauravas. Pāṇḍu has been cursed by a sage to die if he touches his wives, so due to his forced celibacy his sons are born with the help of divine surrogate fathers. The Pāṇḍavas—Yudhiṣṭhira, Arjuna, Bhīma, and the twins Nakula and Sahadeva—are in reality the sons of the gods Dharma (the deified cosmic and moral order), Indra, Vāyu (the wind), and the Aśvin twins (horse gods), respectively. According to Dumézil (and Stig Wikander before him), the Pāṇḍavas and their divine fathers represent the three functions of Indo-European society: Dharma and Yudhiṣṭhira represent the magico-sovereign function (Brahmins); Vāyu and Bhīma and Indra and Arjuna represent the martial function (Kṣatriyas); and the Aśvins and Nakula and Sahadeva represent the economic function (Vaiśya).[9] Their hundred cousins the Kauravas, conversely, are incarnations of Rākṣasas (lesser demons or "goblins") except for the eldest, Duryodhana, who is an incarnation of the demon Kali, the spirit of the Kali Yuga.

After both sets of cousins are born, Pāṇḍu, finally succumbing to temptation, sleeps with one of his wives and dies immediately, leaving the orphaned Pāṇḍavas to be raised in the court of Dhṛtarāṣṭra. During their youth the two groups of cousins develop an instant rivalry with each other and begin to form outside alliances in preparation for the inevitable war between them. It is at this point that the itinerant warrior Karṇa, whose story we will examine in detail below, enters the picture as the Kauravas' staunchest and most powerful ally against the Pāṇḍavas. After Karṇa has joined the Kauravas, Duryodhana makes a move to eliminate his rivals by attempting to burn the Pāṇḍavas alive in a very flammable guesthouse he had built especially for them. But the five heroes guess what their cousin is up to, and escape by substituting five other bodies for their own and going into hiding until they reappear publicly at the *svayaṃvara* or bride-choice of the princess Draupadī. Seeing the need for friends to protect themselves from the treachery of the Kauravas, the Pāṇḍavas gain some even more powerful allies through their common marriage (an anomalous instance of polyandry in the Sanskrit epics) with Draupadī, herself an incarnation of Śrī, goddess of prosperity and good fortune. Draupadī's brother Dhṛṣṭadyumna, who will lead the Pāṇḍava army, is the incarnation of the Vedic fire deity Agni. It is also at their wedding that the Pāṇḍavas first meet the figure that will guarantee their victory absolutely, the prince Kṛṣṇa, their mother's brother's son and the incarnation of Viṣṇu, the supreme god.

For a brief period after the wedding, the cousins divide the kingdom, with the Kauravas retaining the ancestral throne at Hāstinapura and the Pāṇḍavas building a new palace at Indraprastha with the help of the divine architect Māya. When Yudhiṣṭhira performs a Rājasūya sacrifice that confers universal sovereignty on the sacrificer (already an insult to Duryodhana), the tensions increase. Duryodhana attends the sacrifice as a guest, where he finds himself humiliated in front of the entire court as a result of the *trompe-l'œil* the Pāṇḍavas had built into their palace. The floor is fitted with sheets of crystal made to look like pools of water, and when Duryodhana walks over them, he lifts his robes to keep them out of the water only to find that he is walking on dry floor. Wrongly assuming that the next "pool" is another illusion, he walks headlong into it and falls in the water, causing all the kings in attendance to erupt into laughter and Duryodhana to seethe with murderous rage.

With the help of his uncle, the crafty Śakuni, Duryodhana hatches a plan for revenge. Knowing that Yudhiṣṭhira's one weakness is gambling, he invites the Pāṇḍavas to a dice match at his palace. To the shock and horror of his brothers, Yudhiṣṭhira loses round after round, as Duryodhana continually raises the stakes so that the eldest Pāṇḍava loses his wealth, his armies, and his lands, before finally gambling away his brothers, himself, and their wife Draupadī, all of whom are now the slaves of the Kauravas. Gleeful with victory, Duryodhana then orders his brother Duḥśāsana to drag Draupadī into the assembly hall so that everyone can see the newest member of his harem. When she protests, Karṇa commands Duḥśāsana to disrobe her, but he is unable to do so because Kṛṣṇa, unseen, has miraculously made Draupadī's sari infinitely long so that no matter how much is pulled off, more cloth remains to cover her. At this point, Dhṛtarāṣṭra steps in and forgives Yudhiṣṭhira's debt on his disappointed son's behalf, returning everything he had lost. But, to his brothers' and Draupadī's even greater shock and horror, Yudhiṣṭhira no sooner regains all his losses than he accepts Duryodhana's offer of a rematch. In the second gambling match the Pāṇḍavas lose again, and this time Dhṛtarāṣṭra cannot help them. As a consequence, the Pāṇḍavas and Draupadī are exiled for thirteen years with the condition that the last year must be spent incognito, without being discovered by the Kauravas, if they are to get back their kingdom.

The Pāṇḍavas spend the first twelve years of exile in pilgrimage and penance as well as gathering powerful magical weapons to use against the Kauravas when the inevitable war occurs. In the thirteenth year the Pāṇḍavas hide out in the court of a minor king, where they adopt ingenious disguises and escape detection. But when the thirteen years are over Duryodhana refuses to honor his bargain and return the Pāṇḍavas' half of the kingdom, preferring to risk it all in war than see his father's kingdom split apart. The battle lines drawn, the Pāṇḍavas turn to Kṛṣṇa, who serves as their ambassador to the Kauravas, to make a final attempt to avoid bloodshed. But this fails and Kṛṣṇa, who has sworn not to fight but only to drive Arjuna's chariot, joins the side of the Pāṇḍavas while sending his armies to fight for the Kauravas.

Just before the first day's battle, Arjuna has a sudden doubt about fighting the Kauravas, who are his cousins and in whose army many of his beloved gurus and friends are serving. To remind Arjuna of his duty, Kṛṣṇa delivers the famous *Bhagavad Gītā*, the "Song of the Lord," convincing Arjuna of his obligation to fight and revealing his own identity as Viṣṇu, the Cosmic Destroyer. The eighteen-day war on the plain of Kurukṣetra (an ancient sacrificial terrain consecrated in a previous age by the Brahmin warrior Paraśurāma's bloody twenty-one-fold extermination of the Kṣatriya class)[10] then follows, in which all the divine and demonic forces converge in a massive battle that is described in explicitly sacrificial terms. When he leads the Pāṇḍavas to victory, Pyrrhic though it may be, Kṛṣṇa completes the mission for which he became incarnate, relieving Earth's burden of demons and restoring the balance of Dharma.

But even after the Pāṇḍava victory, there is more violence to come when Aśvatthāman, the son of the slain Kaurava general Drona, comes upon Duryodhana, who is dying on the ground after being struck down by Bhīma in a duel, and vows to make one last raid on the Pāṇḍavas and exterminate their line completely. That night, when the remnant of the Pāṇḍava army is sleeping, Aśvatthāman descends on the camp and murders every last man in his sleep, including Draupadī's sons, father, and brother, leaving only the five Pāṇḍava brothers and Draupadī alive. This is the last straw for Yudhiṣṭhira, who announces that after the heartbreak of the fratricidal war of succession, he no longer desires kingship, but only wants to renounce the world and become a wandering ascetic. Kṛṣṇa talks Yudhiṣṭhira out of this drastic step and convinces him instead to perform a Horse Sacrifice to sanctify his rule.

Blaming Kṛṣṇa for the war, the Kauravas' bereaved mother curses his clan, the Yādavas, dooming them to kill each other in a drunken mace battle, while Kṛṣṇa himself dies (or returns to Heaven) when a hunter mistakes the heel of his foot for a deer's ear and shoots him with an arrow. The Pāṇḍavas, having reigned justly and righteously for a good amount of time, decide when they come to the end of their lives to make the pilgrimage to Heaven in their physical bodies, which their semi-divine status allows. But, one by one, four of the five brothers and Draupadī fall off the mountain path to Heaven as a result of some iniquity committed during their lifetimes that disqualifies them from entering the abode of the gods. Only Yudhiṣṭhira and a dog that has been following him throughout his journey are able to make it all the way to Heaven. But when he gets there and finds out that no dogs are allowed, Yudhiṣṭhira prepares to turn back around and leave rather than enter Heaven and abandon the dog that has followed him so faithfully. At this, the dog takes his true form as Dharma, Yudhiṣṭhira's divine father, and announces that he has passed the last test and is welcome to enter Heaven. But when Yudhiṣṭhira arrives, he is shocked to see not his brothers and wife, but the Kauravas feasting and drinking. When he asks where his family is, the gods inform him that they are in Hell. Bemused and bewildered, Yudhiṣṭhira descends into Hell, a dark and disgusting place filled with the stench of putrefaction and the miserable screams of the damned. Nevertheless, Yudhiṣṭhira vows to forsake his place in Heaven and stay with his family to offer them what comfort he can. Dharma then reappears and announces that *this* has been the final test and sends Yudhiṣṭhira to the real Heaven to join his wife and brothers.

Two Failed Sacrificers: The Śaiva and the Vaiṣṇava Critiques

What appears above is a brutally truncated telling of the epic, and I will bring out some of the details I have skipped over later in this chapter, which will be devoted to discussions of some of the *Mahābhārata*'s many mimetic myths, including the stories of Dakṣa, Jarāsaṃdha, Karṇa, and the churning of the ocean. In the course of this discussion, we will encounter three different models of sacrificial critique. The first two are marked by characteristics associated with two of the great post-Vedic sects and the third is unique but shares much with certain elements of twentieth century Western philosophy. First is what I call the "Śaiva critique," derived from the figure of the lycanthropic *homo sacer* examined in the last chapter and represented by the story of Dakṣa. Next we will look at what I have termed the "Vaiṣṇava critique," consisting of an unmasking of the arbitrary, ludic nature of the sacrifice and the interchangeability of persecutors and victims and represented by the story of Jarāsaṃdha. And later we will get to the "existential critique," represented by the story of Karṇa, in which an individual refuses to be part of either the crowd or its victims, but makes the heroic choice to testify with his life for a new regime of truth.

Dakṣa's Insult

The story of Dakṣa's sacrifice is a paradigmatic Śaiva myth in the same way that the story of Vamana the dwarf is a paradigmatic Vaiṣṇava myth. Each narrative reflects the defining characteristics of its divine protagonist: Viṣṇu's nature is to pervade and transform, to hide the limitless inside the limited, and to "play" on earth to provide his devotees with the chance to share in his divine presence while Śiva's nature is to encompass the extremes of asceticism and eroticism and represent the sometimes terrifying figure of the outsider. Along with embodying Śiva's essential nature, Dakṣa's sacrifice also represents a return of the repressed, in which the exorcised agonistic element of the Vedic sacrifice comes back with a vengeance to unleash its destruction. Śiva is like a psychoanalyst of the Vedic fire sacrifice, making it recall to consciousness the psychic trauma of its past.

The story appears several times in the epic, but the one we will treat here is from *MBh* 12.274, which is narrated after the war when the Kaurava general Bhīṣma lies dying on a bed of arrows and delivers a lengthy deathbed disquisition on Dharma to the gathered Pāṇḍavas. In the preceding chapters, Bhīṣma has told a version of the story of Indra slaying Vṛtra, in which Vṛtra is first weakened by a "fever" produced by Śiva to make him vulnerable to Indra's attack. After hearing this story, Yudhiṣṭhira tells Bhīṣma that he now wants to hear about the origin of this mysterious fever, which brings us to the story of Dakṣa's sacrifice.

Dakṣa, one of the Prajāpatis (demiurges) decides to hold a great Horse Sacrifice, to which he invites all the gods except for Śiva. The sage Dadhīci,[11] who has been watching the divine procession on its way to Dakṣa's house, grows angry that Śiva is not invited to the sacrifice. Unable to convince Dakṣa of the dire consequences this oversight will bring, he uses his yogic vision to see what is happening at the home of Śiva, where he perceives that the god's wife is enraged by this slight to her husband's honor and is telling him so. Spurred into action by his wife's words, Śiva creates a flaming many-armed demon called Vīrabhadra and sends it to Dakṣa's sacrificial enclosure. On arrival, Vīrabhadra and the terrifying army that emanate from his pores begin to wreak havoc, extinguishing the sacrificial fires with blood, tearing the sacrificial stakes out of the ground, and generally destroying the sacrificial enclosure. Terrified, Dakṣa begs for mercy from Vīrabhadra and asks for Śiva's grace to make it so that, even though the sacrifice has been destroyed, he may still gain the merit of performing it. Śiva, as the lord of the sacrifice, agrees.

There are many variants of the story of Dakṣa's sacrifice. In some, Śiva's wife Pārvatī burns herself up on the sacrificial fire in rage and humiliation, prompting Śiva's violent retribution on Dakṣa. In others, Śiva decapitates Dakṣa and replaces his head with the head of a goat. The myth is rich in sexual and sectarian themes. It tells the story of how the outsider god Śiva came to have a share of the Vedic sacrifice, which is to say, how the Śaiva sect was grafted onto the Brahminical tradition. It also has strong incestuous overtones. Dakṣa, as a prajāpati, is forced to commit incest because he is the father of all beings. But more than this, some versions of the myth play up Dakṣa's personal distaste for Śiva and his belief that this dreadlocked yogi is not good enough for his daughter, whom he invites to the sacrifice while making a point of leaving Śiva off the guest list.

This myth also parallels two important Vedic myths: the myth of Prajāpati's incest, which Girard treats in *Sacrifice*, and the fragmentary myth of Indra and the Yatis. On Prajāpati's incest, Girard writes:

> The Brahmanas charge Prajâpati with the very crime whose absence from the *Hymn to Purusha* I find so regrettable from a theoretical point of view, a crime ready-made to justify a lynching in the eyes of an archaic or backward mob: incest. Like Oedipus, like all divinities, Prajâpati's crime is not without extenuating circumstances, but they are not the same as those of Sophocles' hero. The god cannot become sexually active without making himself guilty of incest, since he is the father of all creatures without exception. When he makes love to the goddess Aurore [Uṣas in the Sanskrit], his daughter, all the other creatures are scandalized and decide—unanimously, of course—to put him to death. It is the unanimity of the first lynching. The collective dimension is here, but the execution of the sentence is entrusted to a single god, the most cruel and sinister of Vedic gods, Rudra.[12]

In retelling the story of Rudra (or Śiva, as he is known in the later literature) piercing Prajāpati's groin with his arrow, I cannot hope to do better than Roberto Calasso, whose reading of the myth interprets the act as the birth of the transcendental signifier and the externalization of desire, so I will borrow his words:

> When Rudra let fly his arrow at Prajāpati, who spurted his seed toward [his daughter] Uṣas [Dawn], this first of all actions likewise split apart. Even in the instant itself, even in that first instant, nothing would ever be *one alone*. As Prajāpati spread his seed in the void, the arrow opened a wound in his groin, a rift that looked forward to all other rifts. Through that metallic point, the barely created world penetrated he who had created it. It turned

> against the Father, injected its poison into him. To the fullness that turned impulsively outward corresponded a tiny void that was forming within that fullness.
>
> Time entered upon the scene between the surfacing of the intention and the act that followed it. As long as there is only mind, intention is action. But, as soon as there is something outside mind, Time slips in between intention and act. And then one escapes forever from the mental universe that is still open, like an open wound, in Prajāpati's groin.
>
> Why did anything happen? Rudra, the obscure Archer, was guardian of the fullness that lacks nothing. But the fullness burned. And burning, it conceived the excitement of there being something it did lack, something on which to throw itself. Burning can easily generate hallucination. One begins to think that all does not lie within one's own fire, but that something exists outside, that an outside exists somewhere over there. A white substance, the best to burn. One day they would call it *soma*. And that becomes the object of desire, that cold, external, intoxicating being whom the fire has yet to scorch.
>
> Fullness had to be wounded, a breach of dispossession opened. Later that breach would be encircled, closed, albeit slowly, by the same power that had produced it, the same power from which it was born—Time, he who demanded but a single idol for his celebration: the arrow. In the compact surface of existence, that breach, that void, amounted to no more than a tiny crack, no broader than a grain of barley, like the wound that Rudra's arrow opened in Prajāpati's groin and that was never to close. But the idea that in some future time that tattered edge of bleeding flesh might close was enough to suggest the possibility of a higher level of fullness, something in respect to which the fullness of the beginning seemed crude and stifled. It didn't matter whether that fullness turned out to be—as indeed it would be—unattainable. Its flickering image blotted out any desire to return to the earlier fullness.[13]

Calasso's reading of the myth, with its imagery of the irruption of time between intention and action, recalls the story from the *Śatapatha Brāhmaṇa* that we examined in the last chapter, in which the paired gods Mitra and Varuṇa are identified with the *kratu* ("who formulates desire") and the *dakṣa* ("who executes desire"). And in the variant of the Dakṣa myth found in the

Skanda Purāṇa, Śiva castrates a figure called Kratu, here identified with the sacrifice itself, instead of beheading Dakṣa.[14]

In other versions of the myth, which parallel Vedic stories of Rudra's intrusion into the sacrificial ground, the conflict begins when Śiva comes to Dakṣa's sacrifice all in black and demands everything he sees, embodying the Vrātya ascetic and the defeated sacrificial party returning for revenge. In this myth Śiva is also a hunter like Indra, stalking the sacrifice as it tries to flee, providing further evidence for connecting this myth with the oath-bound war band, modeled as it is after a hunting party. And in the version of the myth found in the *Aitareya Brāhmaṇa, Jaiminīya Brāhmaṇa*, and the *Maitrāyaṇī Saṃhitā*, the gods create Rudra out of the worst parts of themselves (but refuse to name him) and then compel him to punish Prajāpati in exchange for dominion over the beasts, so that none of them will have to take on the guilt of attacking their father.

In this myth we have a clear scapegoat (especially in the cases where Śiva decapitates him and replaces his head with that of a goat) in the figure Dakṣa-Prajāpati. Just as his own mother tears Pentheus apart in *The Bacchae* as a result of his refusal to give Dionysus his due, so his daughter destroys Dakṣa for his failure to honor Śiva (who is also a member of his family just as Dionysus is a member of Pentheus's) at his sacrifice. And more than that, Dakṣa is unequivocally guilty of committing incest, a classic accusation against the scapegoat. But alongside this recognizable scapegoat figure, we also have the figure of the lycanthropic *homo sacer* in the form of Śiva, whose appearance is that of a Vrātya ascetic and whose frenzied attack on the sacrifice at the head of a troop of ghosts and goblins bears a striking resemblance to the Vedic myth of Indra and the Yatis.

Āpaddharma *as a State of Exception*

I have said that the myth of Dakṣa's sacrifice is the paradigmatic Śaiva myth. It is also a powerful iteration of the Śaiva critique of sacrifice, in which the expelled party from the archaic two-sacrificer system returns to haunt, and indeed to destroy, the classical ritual model with its single sovereign sacrificer. The power of a sovereign, Carl Schmitt and Giorgio Agamben tell us, is founded on his ability to decide the state of exception, in which the sovereign takes the opportunity to suspend and transcend law in order to eliminate a threat to its stability. This concept appears in the *Mahābhārata* as the subject of Bhīṣma's deathbed lecture on *āpaddharma*, "the dharma of emergency."

Āpaddharma is for times of distress like natural disasters, which can occur at any time. Outside the epic, we have some historical examples of *āpaddharma*. Hartmut Scharfe connects the *āpaddharma* clause to reports that the ninth and eleventh century Kashmiri kings Śaṇkaravarman and Harṣa stole property from temples when their treasuries ran low.[15] And for instances of translating an ancient ideal into a modern idiom, we need look no farther than a recent Indian newspaper article. As the depth of the global financial crisis became clear in 2008, Gurchuran Das wrote an op-ed piece for *The Times of India* titled "Changing Rules of Dharma." Drawing on the concept of *āpaddharma*, Das called for the Indian government to cut interest rates and recapitalize failing banks. Taking a cue from Bhīṣma (by way of Keynes), he argued, "The Mahabharata points out that rules of dharma change in times of crisis when one is forced to observe apad-dharma. Paradoxically, defending capitalism requires state intervention."[16]

In the epic, *āpaddharma* is appropriately signaled by the presence of the *homo sacer*, the wolfish outlaw.[17] The Sālavṛkeyas, the Vrātyas, and the Bhṛgus, who all belong to what White calls the "dog-man tradition," exist in the state of exception that Agamben describes, using Thomas Hobbes's phrase, as the place where "man becomes wolf to man." There are many animals in the stories Bhīṣma uses to illustrate *āpaddharma*, but the wolf appears in three very significant instances. First, *MBh* 12.132.9 describes a wicked man who has lost his power and wasted away so that the whole world fears him "like a wolf." Next, *MBh* 12.140.27 describes a situation very much like Hobbes's lycanthropic state of nature, instructing kings to keep their subjects in line lest they devour each other "like wolves." Finally there is the cryptic verse 12.132.2, which reads, "This is dharma, this is *adharma* ('not-dharma'); it is just like the track (or the step) of a wolf (*adharmo dharma iti etad / etad yathā vṛkapadaṃ tathā*)."

For Agamben, the Weimar-era writings of Schmitt have rightly predicted the situation that has prevailed in Europe and America since the terrorist attacks of 2001, where the state no longer has to abide either by its own or by international laws, but is free to exercise power at will under the guise of the War on Terror. Schmitt has revealed the lawlessness behind the law and it cannot easily be hidden again. In light of this, Agamben concludes his essay *State of Exception* by asking, "what does it mean to act politically?"[18] If we substitute the word "dharmically" for "politically," then Agamben's question becomes a restatement of the central problem for the heroes and the authors of the *Mahābhārata*. Referring to the concept as it appears in the roughly contemporary legal text *The Laws of Manu*, Doniger argues that *āpaddharma* is evidence that "the entire elaborate system [of laws] that Manu has created is acknowledged to be one that does not work when one is faced with an emergency—emergencies being the stuff that human life, and certainly human law, is made [of]."[19]

The state of exception that is *āpaddharma* pervades the *Mahābhārata*, from the Pāṇḍavas' polyandrous marriage to Draupadī to the fratricidal war between the Pāṇḍavas and the Kauravas. And these rampant exceptions to the dictates of dharma coincide with the epic's shift away from Vedic religion toward the new devotionalism associated with Kṛṣṇa, Viṣṇu, and Śiva. Schmitt argues that "the exception in jurisprudence is analogous to the miracle in theology,"[20] and, significantly, it is after Kṛṣṇa shows himself to Arjuna in his terrible cosmic form that he gives the Pāṇḍava hero instructions to ignore conventional rules of combat and ties of kinship and to become an extension of the divine sovereign. This idea of subsuming one's own personal karma into the divine plan of a personal god then becomes the Vaiṣṇava politico-theological paradigm for all action in the Kali Yuga, the Dark Age initiated by the events of the epic; after the *Gītā* and the *Mahābhārata* war, *āpaddharma* effectively becomes just plain "dharma" and the state of exception becomes the rule. But rather than any specific negation or subtraction of dharmic rules, *āpaddharma* represents, to quote Doniger, a "counter-structure [that] indicates the system was designed for those who disobeyed it."[21] And in the Śaiva critique of sacrifice, it is the counter-structure to Vedic ritualism, embodied in the *homo sacer*, that is made manifest and brought back to spoil the party.

Jarāsaṃdha's Crime[22]

Between the wedding of the Pāṇḍavas to Draupadī and Duryodhana's humiliation at court in Indraprastha, Yudhiṣṭhira consults Kṛṣṇa about performing the Royal Consecration Sacrifice to establish his supremacy over all kings. Kṛṣṇa agrees that Yudhiṣṭhira is worthy to undertake the rite and assume the title of Universal Monarch, but then warns of a serious complication.

There is in Magadha, explains Kṛṣṇa, a king called Jarāsaṃdha, who was born in two living halves from the two twin wives of King Bṛhadratha, each having eaten half of an enchanted mango. The women were horrified and left their monstrous offspring at a crossroads to die of exposure. But an ogress named Jarā discovered the two half-children and bound them together so that she could more easily carry them home to devour them. But when they were joined, the two become one perfectly formed boy. The ogress recognized the child as royalty and presented him to the king as his son, who then gave the child the name Jarāsaṃdha, "Joined by Jarā." Upon his prodigious birth a great Ṛṣi predicted that he would one day become a Universal Monarch and would behold Śiva. Now, this Jarāsaṃdha, together with his general Śiśupāla (whom we will discuss in the next chapter), has become a de facto (without completing the royal consecration) Universal Monarch by defeating every king who would oppose him. In his hubris, he has even assumed Kṛṣṇa's own title of Vasudeva. Kṛṣṇa also explains that Jarāsaṃdha has been imprisoning the rival kings he has conquered in his dungeons. And, according to Kṛṣṇa, once he has conquered and captured the fourteen remaining rival kings, he is planning to offer them to Śiva in sacrifice. Kṛṣṇa then tells Yudhiṣṭhira that he must kill Jarāsaṃdha and set free the kings he has imprisoned before he performs the ritual.

As van Buitenen notes, it is Kṛṣṇa alone who makes claims about Jarāsaṃdha's evil nature and his intention to sacrifice the kings he has captured, and the very fact that Kṛṣṇa, Bhīma, and Arjuna are able to enter his court (uninvited) dressed as *snātaka*s (Brahmin students who have completed their education and are ready to begin their lives as householders) points to the "evil" king's very righteous treatment of Brahmins.[23] But after Jarāsaṃdha receives the three ersatz Brahmins into his court he quickly begins to suspect that these men, whose muscled arms bear the scars of bowstrings, may not be what they appear. Confirming his suspicions, the trio announces that they have come, not for an audience with Jarāsaṃdha, but to do battle with him. Jarāsaṃdha protests that he has done nothing to warrant this hostility, at which point Kṛṣṇa delivers the following speech:

> You, O King, have destroyed the Kṣatriyas who inhabit this land. You have incurred this atrocious guilt and yet you think yourself innocent? Greatest of the lords of men, how could a king attack blameless kings? And

> now, having imprisoned those kings, you plan to sacrifice them to [Śiva]! The evil you have done affects us, Son of Bṛhadratha, because we follow Dharma and are able to enforce it. No one has ever witnessed the seizing of men for sacrifice,[24] so how can you wish to sacrifice kings to the God [Śiva]? You are a Kṣatriya yourself, but you designate other Kṣatriyas as sacrificial beasts! What other man's mind is as twisted as yours?[25]

Jarāsaṃdha, still admitting to no wrongdoing, agrees to a duel with Bhīma and, as will happen again in the epic, Kṛṣṇa talks the bellicose Pāṇḍava into striking when his opponent has passed out from exhaustion. Using this unsporting tactic, Bhīma kills Jarāsaṃdha after two weeks of ceaseless battle. The heroes then set free all the captured kings, who promise to support Yudhiṣṭhira's claim to the throne, and return to the Pāṇḍava capital at Indraprastha.

The Jarāsaṃdha episode exemplifies what I am calling the Vaiṣṇava critique of sacrifice. While the Śaiva critique of sacrifice, represented in the story of Dakṣa, derives from the archaic two-sacrificer system and the expelled figure of the *homo sacer* left over after the transition to the one-sacrificer model, the Vaiṣṇava critique operates differently. Although the movement from two opposing sacrificers to one is reflected in the story of Jarāsaṃdha's monstrous double birth, this is not the main thrust of the critique. When Kṛṣṇa and Yudhiṣṭhira foil the rival king's purported plot to rule the world by sacrificing all its kings, they do it so that they can do precisely the same thing. While the Śaiva critique focuses on the repressed violence and exclusion of the ritual, the Vaiṣṇava critique illuminates the arbitrary nature of the subject-positions within the ritual structure: the sacrificer can just as easily become a victim. Kṛṣṇa's half-hearted condemnation of Jarāsaṃdha's violence is belied by his subsequent instructions to Bhīma to kill his rival by whatever means necessary. Although the story of Jarāsaṃdha bears some of the marks of a scapegoat narrative, it also sufficiently muddies the waters about his guilt to leave much room for doubt as to who is telling the truth. After reading the episode, the reader is left with a not entirely anachronistic sense that this has all been a witch-hunt, calculated to unite the rest of the kings behind Yudhiṣṭhira and eliminate all potential rivals. In the last analysis Jarāsaṃdha looks much more like an expedient victim than a dangerous monster.

The Vaiṣṇava critique is a mirror image of the Śaiva critique. While the Śaiva critique operates from the position of the excluded, the Vaiṣṇava critique operates instead out of the sacrifice's own structuring principles. Kṛṣṇa is condemning one form of human sacrifice while setting the stage for another, far bloodier one, namely the battle at Kurukṣetra. Kṛṣṇa's horror at the idea of sacrificing kings to obtain universal sovereignty must be feigned. In actuality he simply does not want the wrong king to be doing the sacrificing. Jarāsaṃdha bears the marks of the scapegoat: He was exposed at birth like Oedipus, but brought back through the action of an ogress who accidentally joins his two halves while trying to eat him. He is also accused of plotting a terrible crime, namely regicide, and is clearly a Śaiva figure. Van Buitenen notes that the length of his duel with Bhīma (thirteen days) also mirrors the length of the Pāṇḍavas' coming exile (thirteen years) and that, after Jarāsaṃdha is dead, Kṛṣṇa, Arjuna, and Bhīma mount the defeated king's chariot, an action that he connects to the archaic two-sacrificer model in which one sacrificer battled the other on his chariot.[26]

Why does Kṛṣṇa so loudly decry Jarāsaṃdha's planned human sacrifice? The answer is in the larger plan Kṛṣṇa is enacting in the epic. In the *Bhagavad Gītā*, Kṛṣṇa establishes himself as the supreme deity, superseding all previous revelations and providing, with himself as an object of devotion, a new universal religion unconnected with any previous Vedic system or school. The only way to usher in this new order is with a sacrifice of battle that destroys many more kings than Jarāsaṃdha was holding in captivity and even ends with the immolation of the Pāṇḍava line at the hands of the Śaiva figure Aśvatthāman (who is exiled in the manner of Cain after his night raid on the Pāṇḍava camp). But at the bloody end of the war Kṛṣṇa, displaying an ability previously only exercised by the Bhṛgus, resurrects the dead embryo who is the future of the Pāṇḍava dynasty and demonstrates his power over and above the sacrifice. In orchestrating the sacrifice and establishing himself as master of life and death, the two poles of the sacrificial ritual, Kṛṣṇa empties the sacrifice of its transcendent power and takes that power upon himself. But his is not a divine wrath that serves as a mask for human violence; Kṛṣṇa's divine wrath and human violence are one and the same and their victims are revealed as mere expedients. Kṛṣṇa condemns Jarāsaṃdha's plan to sacrifice a hundred kings as sinful, knowing full well that he himself is bringing about the extinction of very nearly every king on earth. The Vaiṣṇava critique of sacrifice, like the Gospels, makes possible a true escalation to extremes that make sacrifice both more violent and less effective, leading to the ultimate failure of the *Mahābhārata*'s sacrificial war. And we must call it a failure, since it marks the beginning of what the text itself calls the most degraded of all ages, when all distinctions will be blurred, the Vedas will be forgotten, ritual will lose its efficacy, and the world will fall into a decay that culminates in the great cosmic dissolution called the *mahāpralaya*.

We have now seen the Śaiva critique of sacrifice, which comes from the *homo sacer* that has been expelled to ensure the stability of the sacrificial order, and the Vaiṣṇava critique of sacrifice, which understands the arbitrary and illusory nature of the sacrifice and uses this knowledge to manipulate it. Now we will return the never-ending struggle of the gods and the demons, this time in the context of the epic. In the next section, we will examine what is one of the most paradigmatic stories of the rivalry: the churning of the ocean.

Ugraśravas Tells the Story of the Churning of the Ocean

The *Mahābhārata* epic is told within a series of frame stories.[27] The main story is recited by the traveling bard Ugraśravas[28] at a twelve-year sacrifice being performed by Śaunaka (another Bhṛgu, like Śukra the high priest of the demons or Karṇa's Kṣatriya-hating preceptor Paraśurāma) as he remembered hearing it recited by the Brahmin Vaiśampāyana at the anomalous snake sacrifice of King Janamejaya. Vaiśampāyana in turn has heard it from the Vedic Ṛṣi Vyāsa, who is generally regarded as the epic's "author." The story of the churning of the ocean occurs as part of the outer frame, a prelude before Ugraśravas begins to recite the epic proper. Śaunaka asks to hear the origin of the divine horse Uccaiḥśravas, who has come up as part of another story. Uccaiḥśravas, along with other divine animals like the wishing cow Kāmadhenu, is a product of the churning of the ocean. Which brings us to the story.

The episode begins with a description of the fabulous Mount Meru, the home of the gods, where they have assembled to hatch a plan to obtain the *amṛta*, the elixir of life. The *amṛta* is contained in the ocean and can only be obtained by churning it like a tub of raw dairy product. The only tools capable of churning the ocean are Mount Mandara (another celestial mountain), which will serve as the churning rod, the giant tortoise Akūpāra to hold it up, and the cosmic snake Ananta ("Endless") to drive the motion of the churning rod.[29] And the gods alone are not capable of doing the deed, so they have to enlist the help of the demons to pull from the other side of the snake. The image presented here is something like a gigantic tug-of-war with the gods pulling Ananta's tail and the demons pulling his head, whipping up the ocean into froth. On its surface, this story doesn't look especially sacrificial, but the text's description of the deed makes its sacrificial nature clear:

> And as [Ananta] was forcefully pulled up and down by the gods, blasts of fire and smoke belched forth from his mouth. The clouds of smoke became massive storm clouds with flashing lightning and rained down on the gods, who were weakening with heat and fatigue. From the mountaintop rained showers of flowers, and garlands fell down among the gods and the demons. Then, as the gods and the demons were churning the ocean with Mount Mandara, a mighty roar came from it like thunder rumbling in the clouds. All the creatures that live in the depths were being crushed by the giant mountain and went to their deaths by the hundreds in the salty ocean. The mountain also drove all the sea creatures, like the ones who dwell in underwater abysses, to their destruction. While Mount Mandara was being driven back and forth, large trees crashed into one another and fell down from the peak along with the birds nesting in them. The friction of the trees started one wildfire after another, making the mountain blaze like a black monsoon cloud lit up by lightning. The flames drove out elephants and lions, burning them up, and all creatures of many kinds met their deaths. Then Indra the king of the gods flooded the fire that was raging everywhere with a downpour of rain from the clouds. The many juices of the herbs and saps from the trees flowed into the ocean, and with the milk of these juices that had the power of the draught of immortality and the exudation of molten gold [from the mountain], the gods obtained deathlessness.[30]

The deathlessness of the gods, seemingly, has been bought with the death of a multitude of creatures. The environmental devastation described in the myth finds its echo in the burning of Khāṇḍava Forest (which we will examine below) as well as in the *Mahābhārata* war itself. The epic often conflates environmental catastrophe, especially fires and storms, with human violence, just as Girard argues that the Book of Revelation is doing when he writes in *Battling to the End*, "[Violence] is today unleashed on the entire planet, causing what apocalyptic texts announced: confusion between the disasters caused by nature and the disasters caused by men, a confusion of the natural and the artificial."[31] And the violence does not end with burning mountains and roiling seas. As the gods and the demons continue to churn, the ocean soon turns to milk and cream begins to rise to the top, along with the sun, the moon, the aforementioned cosmic animals, the goddess Śrī (later to be incarnated as Draupadī), and the magic chest-jewel of Viṣṇu. Finally, the goddess Dhanvantari, bearing a white gourd filled with the *amṛta*, rises out of the ocean and the short-lived truce between the gods and demons comes to an abrupt end. When the demons see Dhanvantari bearing the *amṛta*, they scream out, "It is mine!" and take hold of it. But Viṣṇu quickly takes the form of a beautiful woman and seduces the demons into handing it over. As soon as they do, the gods attack and a bloody battle ensues in which the demons are slaughtered wholesale and their remnants driven under the ocean. One demon, Rahu, manages to get close enough to the *amṛta* to take a swallow, but Viṣṇu chops off his head before it passes through his throat, leaving Rahu as an immortal but disembodied head who periodically swallows the sun and moon, causing solar and lunar eclipses.

In the myth of the churning of the ocean, we have the pre-classical agonistic sacrificial model laid bare. The sacrifice requires two sides to complete it, just as the churning requires a party on either side of the rope. The prize of the sacrificial contest is life, just as the churning of the ocean yields the elixir of immortality. In the sacrificial contest, only one side can win, just as in the churning of the ocean, only the gods or the demons can possess the elixir. There is also a strong element of the sacrificial crisis: The churning/ritual begins with the gods and the demons more or less undifferentiated. The fact that the myth is clearly cosmogonic suggests that the figure before the churning called Viṣṇu is not Viṣṇu as we know him. After all, his emblematic chest jewel has not yet been created. Neither do the gods yet have on their side Śrī (also created in the churning), the goddess who brings victory to whichever side she joins. The gods as victorious masters of life, death, and the sacrifice are only constituted through the creation and ingestion of the *amṛta*. Viṣṇu's sexual temptation of the demons also has an air of rampant mimeticism: In the time of undifferentiation when the objects of desire are in flux, Viṣṇu transforms the desire of the demons for the *amṛta* into a sexual desire by introducing himself as a new prize to be won.

The myth of the churning of the ocean is one of the many "interpretive" myths throughout the *Mahābhārata*, providing a key to understanding the nature of the battle at the center of the epic. The two violent conflagrations are meant to be read as parallel, but instead of sea creatures and forest animals sacrificed for the immortality of the gods, the epic's main storyline has the entire Kṣatriya class offered up as a battlefield sacrifice to restore dharma. The complexity of the *Mahābhārata* lies in the fact that it gives those victims a profound awareness of the drama in which they are caught up and a voice with which to protest. And not all of them provide tacit approval for the sacrificial system by accepting their fate as it is handed to them by the gods. One such protesting victim is Karṇa, the unknown sixth Pāṇḍava, who keeps his identity secret and takes up arms against his brothers in the most compelling storyline in the entire *Mahābhārata*. What remains of this chapter is devoted to his story and using it as a lens to reread the epic.

Karma and *Katharma*: The Tragic Sibling Rivalry of Karṇa and Arjuna

In 2001 I was in the Ṛṣi-ridden town of Rishikesh (literally, "Ṛṣi's Hair") in the foothills of the Himalayas when one of my companions asked a nearby dreadlocked *bhang*-smoking ascetic why he chose to beg on the streets in a loincloth rather than work in a shop. The ascetic answered without hesitation, "*Mera karam hai*," which means, "It is my *karam*," *karam* being the Hindi form of the Sanskrit word *karma*. In this case, the Ṛṣi of Rishikesh was using the term *karma*, usually taken to mean "action," to denote dharma, in the sense of "duty," an easy enough transposition to make since one fulfills one's dharma through one's karma. That is to say, dharma is nothing but a meaningless abstraction until it is put into action, which is one of the central themes of the *Mahābhārata*. And it is more than possible to be bound by conflicting duties such that to act on one duty would cause one to be in violation of another duty, which is also one of the central themes of the *Mahābhārata*.

Of all the characters in the epic, there are none who enact the contradictions of duty and action and evoke tragic pity and horror in doing so more than Karṇa, abandoned at birth and fated to fight against and die at the hands of his own brother. As the true eldest Pāṇḍava, Karṇa is born when Kuntī (the future wife of Pāṇḍu), still a young girl, unthinkingly tries out the mantra she has been given that allows her to conceive children with the gods. When the sun god Sūrya, answering her call, comes down and hands her a baby with golden armor and earrings attached to his body, the young and unmarried Kuntī is horrified and sets the child in a box and floats him down the river, where he is found and raised by Adhiratha, a member of the Sūta (charioteer) class. Karṇa grows up thinking that he is a Sūta (albeit a Sūta equipped with magic golden armor) and does not meet his brothers until years later when he wanders into the kingdom of Dhṛtarāṣṭra at the time when the Pāṇḍavas and Kauravas are being raised together and trained in kingship and the martial arts. Almost at first sight, Karṇa quickly forms a strong bond with his brothers' rival Duryodhana and a mutual hatred with Arjuna.

When Karṇa arrives at court in the first book of the epic, he is just in time to see the great warrior Arjuna dazzling crowds at a tournament by spectacularly displaying his skill with bow, club, sword, and mace. As usual, the envious Kaurava prince Duryodhana is seething with rage as he watches the world shine on his cousin and so he is elated when the impressively built Karṇa strides in and announces to Arjuna, "Whatever feat you have done, I will do it better in front of all these people. Do not be so taken with yourself."[32] Before he has even finished issuing his challenge, the crowd abandons their erstwhile hero Arjuna and unanimously sides with Karṇa, "rising as one like a pitcher heaved from the well (*yantra utkṣipta iva kṣipram uttasthau sarvato janaḥ*)," causing Arjuna to experience shame (*hrī*) and anger (*krodha*).[33]

And things get even worse for Arjuna when, true to his word, Karṇa quickly matches him feat for spectacular feat, prompting Duryodhana to offer the new arrival the hospitality of his kingdom. Karṇa expresses his wish for the eternal friendship of Duryodhana (which is music to the Kaurava's ears) and then challenges Arjuna to a duel. Arjuna gladly accepts and vows to kill Karṇa, cursing him for a trespasser. Drona, the guru of the Pāṇḍavas and Kauravas alike, authorizes the duel and the audience prepares to watch the world's greatest warrior take on this newcomer who has proved to be his equal. But as the two evenly matched foes take their places across from one another in the arena, another of Drona's pupils reminds everyone that it is proper before a duel for both parties to identify their lineage.

"At this," the text tells us, "Karṇa hung his head in shame, and his face faded like a lotus showered by the rains."[34] Karṇa knows he has no noble lineage to claim and thus no right to a duel with someone so far above his station. But Duryodhana quickly steps in on behalf of his new friend and offers to make him a king then and there, summoning some Brahmins to perform the consecration ritual and bestowing upon Karṇa the kingdom of Anga. Seeing his adopted son elevated to kingship, Adhiratha, the elderly Sūta who raised Karṇa from infancy, comes into the arena to embrace him, eliciting mocking laughter from the Pāṇḍavas and this insult from Bhīma: "Son of a Sūta! You have no right to die in a fight with Arjuna! Better you should stick with the horsewhip that suits your kind. Churl! You have no more right to enjoy the kingdom of Anga than a dog has to eat the offering cake by the sacrificial fire!"[35]

Duryodhana responds to Bhīma's taunt with a few lines about the mysterious origins of Kṣatriyas and rivers, followed by the argument that his golden armor and earrings are obvious markers of Karṇa's royal status and some words to the effect that anyone who opposes Karṇa opposes him as well. But by the time he is finished with his speech, the sun is setting and the duel is called off (or rather, as we shall see, postponed). As Karṇa exits the arena with Duryodhana, the crowd is split, some calling out, "Hail Arjuna!," others, "Karṇa!," or, "Duryodhana!"[36]

The bitter and entirely unprovoked enmity between Karṇa and the Pāṇḍavas is so intractable that when his mother reveals to him his true identity as a long-lost Pāṇḍava before the great battle, Karṇa refuses to leave the side of Duryodhana, who took him in as a brother, to ally himself with the family that abandoned him, even with the knowledge that doing so would save his life.[37] The rivalry between Karṇa and Arjuna specifically is also unmistakably mimetic. The challenge that Karṇa presents is precisely his *equality* with Arjuna, as is represented by his ability to imitate Arjuna's feats of skill and the way in which he wins over Arjuna's admirers so quickly in the arena. After he enters the main narrative, Karṇa, in the space of one chapter, goes from being a stranger, to being the rival of Arjuna, to being one of the

Kauravas and therefore a rival of all the Pāṇḍavas. But Bhīma will not let him forget his (false) humble origins, comparing him to the lowly dog that steals the sacrificial cake (echoes of the Vrātyas and the Sālavṛkeyas).

Karṇa's rivalry with Arjuna intensifies at the *svayaṃvara* of Draupadī. This event, hosted by her father King Drupada, brings all the eligible princes in the land together to compete for the hand of the princess. And because it takes place when the Pāṇḍavas are in hiding after Duryodhana's (successful, for all he knows) attempt to burn them alive, everyone, Karṇa included, believes them to be dead and no one expects to have to compete with them. Although *svayaṃvara* literally means "self-choice," all of Draupadī's suitors must complete a task before they can be part of her pool of potential husbands: Every man must string an enormous bow and use it to hit a bull's-eye on a distant target. While all the other suitors fail even to string the bow, the mighty Karṇa does so with ease, notches his arrow, and hits the target dead on. But the proud Kṣatriya Draupadī, instead of applauding his skill, sneers, "I will not choose a Sūta."[38] Karṇa's humiliation is further compounded when Arjuna, disguised as a Brahmin, completes the same task and wins Draupadī's approval, despite being (at least to Draupadī's knowledge) no more a Kṣatriya than Karṇa is.

Karṇa is not the only one angered at Draupadī's choice of the ersatz Brahmin. Like the suitors that surround Penelope in the *Odyssey*, the suitors at the *svayaṃvara* have the potential to turn into a dangerous mob and they begin to do just that after Draupadī spurns them in favor of a wandering priest. Furious at their treatment, the assembled kings decide to throw King Drupada and his daughter on the fire and then take care of the interloping Brahmin and his friends. But the disguised Pāṇḍavas soon prove more than a match for the resentful suitors and the mob violence gives way to two duels, one between Karṇa and Arjuna, and the other between Śalya (another Kaurava brother) and Bhīma. The fighting ends when Karṇa, suspicious but still unaware of Arjuna's true identity, withdraws in deference to the superior power of a Brahmin over that of a Kṣatriya, as in the duel of Viśvāmitra and Vasiṣṭha.[39]

Ritual and Tragedy

In his discussion of Aristotle's concept of *katharsis* and the *katharma* (the figure who is responsible for the *katharsis*) in *Violence and the Sacred*, Girard connects tragedy to ritual killing, making *katharsis* another link in his chain of substitutions that leads from the founding murder to civilization:

> Once upon a time a temple and an altar on which the victim was sacrificed were substituted for the original act of collective violence; now there is an amphitheatre and a stage on which the fate of the *katharma*, played by an actor, will purge the spectators of their passions and provoke a new *katharsis*, both individual and collective.[40]

For Girard, Aristotle is unambiguously talking about sacrifice in his discussion of *katharsis*, whether or not the philosopher is aware of the ritual use of that term (i.e., "the mysterious benefits that accrue to the community upon the death of a human *katharma* or *pharmakos*"), already archaic at the time of his writing.[41] In *Poetics* Aristotle is "discretely vague" about exactly what kind of emotions *katharsis* is meant to purge, but for Girard it is clear enough that he is explaining how tragedy functions to protect the community from its own violence:

> Aristotle's [*Poetics*] is something of a manual for sacrificial practices, for the qualities that make a "good" tragic hero are precisely those required of a sacrificial victim. If the latter is to polarize and purge the emotions of the community, he must at once resemble the members of the community and differ from them; he must be at once insider and outsider, both "double" and incarnation of the "sacred difference." He must be neither wholly good nor wholly bad. A certain degree of goodness is required in the tragic hero in order to establish sympathy between him and the audience; yet a certain degree of weakness, a "tragic flaw" is needed, to neutralize the goodness and permit the audience to tolerate the hero's downfall and death.[42]

With relation to the society in the epic itself, Karṇa seems to fit the description of the Aristotelian tragic hero perfectly. He is like the Pāṇḍavas in that he is a great warrior, half-divine, possessed of all the cardinal virtues, and the heir to the throne of Dhṛtarāṣṭra. But he is also very unlike them. He is unlike them physically in that he was born with golden armor and earrings attached to his body, unlike them socially in that he was abandoned by his mother as an infant and raised by a family of the lowly Sūta caste, and unlike them politically in that he is sworn to the Kaurava cause. And as the perfect *katharma* and sacrificial victim, Karṇa also has an awareness of what he is participating in. Before the battle begins, Karṇa has foreknowledge of his fate and the outcome of the war and counts his own impending defeat in the duel with his archenemy Arjuna, as well as Duryodhana's defeat in his duel with Bhīma, as part of the great sacrifice to come. When refusing the final offer made by Kṛṣṇa (at his mother Kuntī's tearful insistence) to be united with his true brothers the Pāṇḍavas before it is too late, Karṇa delivers the following remarkable speech on the sacrificial nature of the coming war:

> Duryodhana the Dhārtarāṣtra will hold a grand sacrifice of war. Of this sacrifice, you shall be the witness, [Kṛṣṇa], and you shall be the Adhvaryu priest at the ritual. [Arjuna] the Terrifier with the monkey standard stands girt as the Hotṛ priest; [his bow] Gāṇḍiva will be the ladle; the bravery of heroes the sacrificial butter. The *aindra, pāśupata, brāhma* and *sthūṇākarṇa* missiles will be the spells employed by the Left-handed Archer [Arjuna]. Saubhadra, taking after, if not overtaking, his father in prowess will suit perfectly as the Grāvastut priest. Mighty Bhīma, the tiger of men who finishes an army of elephants with his roar of battle, will be the Udgātar and the Prastotar priest. Yudhiṣṭhira, the eternal king whose spirit is dharma, well versed in oblations and recitations, will act as Brahmin. The sounds of the drums, the blowing of conchs, and the piercing roars of the lions will be the *subrahmaṇyā* invocation. Madri's two glorious and valorous sons Nakula and Sahadeva will fill the position of the Śamitar priest. The clean chariot spears with their spotted staffs will be the sacrificial poles at this sacrifice, [Kṛṣṇa]. The arrows, hollow reeds, iron shafts, and piles of calf-teeth will be the soma jars, and the bows will be the soma strainers. Swords will be the potsherds, skulls the *puroḍāśa* cakes, and blood will be the oblation at this sacrifice, Kṛṣṇa. The spears and gleaming maces will be the kindling and the enclosing sticks; the students of Drona and Kṛpa Śāradata will be the spectators. The arrows fired by the great warriors, [Arjuna] the Gāṇḍiva bowman, Drona, and the son of Drona will be the pillows. Sātyaki will act as the Pratiprasthātar; [Duryodhana] will be the sacrificer, with his great army as his wife. Mighty Ghaṭotkaca will be the Śamitar when this overnight sacrifice is spun out, O Strong-armed Hero. Majestic Dhṛṣṭadyumna, who was born from the fire,[43] will

> be the sacrificial fee when the fire ritual takes place. I regret those insults I heaped on the Pāṇḍavas to please Duryodhana [but] when you see me cut down by the Left-handed Archer [Arjuna], that will be the re-piling of the fire of their sacrifice. When [Bhīma], roaring like a beast, drinks the blood of Duḥśāsana,[44] that will be the *soma* draught. When the two Pāñcālyas bring down Drona and Bhīṣma, that will be the conclusion of the sacrifice, [Kṛṣṇa]. When the mighty [Bhīma] kills Duryodhana, then the sacrifice will be over. The weeping of those gathered daughters-in-law and granddaughters-in-law, whose masters, sons, and protectors have all been slain, along with the mourning of Gāndhārī at the sacrificial site now overrun with dogs, vultures, and sea hawks, will be the final bath of the sacrifice, [Kṛṣṇa].[45]

The long and complex litany of sacrificial implements, participants, and actions in this speech needs to be clarified. Karṇa mentions seven types of priests as well as the Śamitar and the sacrificer or Dīkṣita and identifies each with a character from the epic (see table 3). Some of these identifications are more superficial than others. Bhīma seems to be the Udgātar because of his loud voice and Satyākī and Saubhadra's assisting roles seem to come from the fact that they are related to Kṛṣṇa and Arjuna. But the roles of Adhvaryu, Śamitar, and Dīkṣita are highly significant. As the Adhvaryu, Kṛṣṇa organizes every aspect of the sacrificial battle and, later in the epic, he is present at the five sacrificial killings predicted by Karṇa—Drona's, Bhīṣma's, Duhśasana's, Duryodhana's, and his own. We should also note here that this sacrifice ends with the death and defeat of the sacrificer, pointing again to the archaic two-sacrificer model.

The actual death of Karṇa himself beats anything out of Sophocles for ironic tragedy and pathos. Karṇa finally meets Arjuna and his charioteer Kṛṣṇa on the Kurukṣetra on day seventeen of the eighteen-day battle. The lengthy indecisive fighting between Arjuna and Karṇa proves that the two warriors are indeed equally matched. Karṇa's best chance to kill Arjuna (if he has a chance at all) comes when he fires the snake arrow, an arrow that is actually a snake named Aśvasena, who is one of the few survivors of the burning of the Khāṇḍava forest.

The Khāṇḍava forest fire, described in *MBh* 1.19, is another massacre perpetrated by Arjuna and Kṛṣṇa (publicly revealed at this time to be the

Table 3. Figures from the Epic and Their Analogues in the Sacrifice

ROLE	DESCRIPTION	CHARACTER
Dīkṣita	The consecrated sacrificer, considered impure for the duration of the ritual	Duryodhana
Adhvaryu	Offering priest in charge of measuring enclosure, building altar, bringing implements, etc.	Kṛṣṇa
Hotar	Reciter of hymns and invocations	Arjuna
Grāvastut	Assistant to the Hotar who sings the praises of the *soma*-pressing stones	Arjuna's son Saubhadra A.K.A. Abhimanyu
Udgātar	Priest of the *Sāma Veda* responsible for chanting hymns in proper meter	Bhīma
Prastotar	Assistant to the Udgātar who chants the opening invocation	Bhīma
Brahmin[*]	Overseer of entire ritual and responsible for correcting mistakes in words or actions	Yudhiṣṭhira
Śamitar	"The Appeaser," the one who kills the sacrificial animal	Bhīma's son Ghaṭotkaca / Nakula and Sahadeva
Pratiprasthātar	Assistant to the Adhvaryu	Sātyakī, kinsman of Kṛṣṇa

*This is a more specific ritual sense of the term.

incarnations of the proto-Vaiṣṇava gods Nara and Nārāyaṇā, cultic precursors to Viṣṇu) that foreshadows the battle at Kurukṣetra while also recalling the churning of the ocean. In this story, Agni, the deified sacrificial fire, comes to Arjuna and Kṛṣṇa in the form of a Brahmin and asks for food. When they assent, the Brahmin takes on his true form and reveals that the food he wants is the entire Khāṇḍava forest, home of the snake king Takṣaka. He has not been able to consume it because Indra, as a friend of Takṣaka, protects the forest by sending down rain whenever it starts to burn. To feed the insatiable Agni, Arjuna and Kṛṣṇa set fire to the forest, ward off Indra's rain with arrows, and kill any creature that tries to escape. Aśvasena, Takṣaka's son, is one of the few to get out alive and swears revenge on Arjuna.

So when Aśvasena sees that Karṇa is dueling with Arjuna, he takes the form of an arrow and slips unnoticed inside Karṇa's quiver. When Karṇa fires him, Aśvasena changes himself into a fiery poison missile and flies straight toward Arjuna's head, but he only manages to knock off the Pāṇḍava's crown because Kṛṣṇa uses his divine power to magically lower the earth beneath Arjuna's chariot. Infuriated, Aśvasena slithers back to Karṇa and asks to be fired again, but Karṇa refuses. Thus, the perfect opportunity for a survivor of another sacrificial massacre to take his revenge on Arjuna and Kṛṣṇa comes to naught and the duel continues.

Karṇa's moment of truth comes when one of the several curses placed on his head causes his chariot wheel to become stuck in the mud. He calls for a halt to the fighting so that he can get out and free the wheel. But as he struggles to right his chariot a cloud passes over the sun, severing the connection with his divine father (Sūrya, the sun god) that had always sustained him. Simultaneously, he also succumbs to Paraśurāma's curse and forgets the spell that could save his life.[46] Desperate, Karṇa pleads with Arjuna to respect the rules of combat and not to attack an unarmed enemy. Arjuna is inclined to lay down his bow, but Kṛṣṇa is insistent and unmoved, delivering a litany of Karṇa's evil deeds to extinguish any spark of pity in Arjuna's heart and exhorting him to do the deed. Arjuna obeys, and when barrages of arrows fail to kill Karṇa, Kṛṣṇa orders Arjuna to decapitate the warrior with a razor-tipped missile, causing his head to fly off his trunk and setting Karṇa's spirit free from his body, whence it rises up to the sun in a blaze of glory.[47]

"The Worst of Good Men"

So far we have been examining the strikingly mimetic aspects of the Karṇa-Arjuna rivalry, but there are also some equally striking non-mimetic or anti-mimetic elements to consider in Karṇa's peculiar heroism, which prompts Kṛṣṇa to call him after his death "the worst of good (or truthful) men (*satpuruṣādhamaḥ*)."[48] Karṇa is as doomed and stubborn as is the Kaurava general Bhīṣma, whose oath of celibacy is the main cause of the succession crisis in the Bhārata line.[49] But while Bhīṣma is caught up in the internal contradictions of Dharma, Karṇa has risen above in a moment of heroic authenticity. Karṇa knows himself to be a Kṣatriya, but not because he is a Kṣatriya through the lineage of his mother with whom he has no connection.

Instead, he is a Kṣatriya because he has been made one through the generosity of Duryodhana, whom he loves and who loves him in return. When he "lies" to Paraśurāma and identifies himself as a Sūta, Karṇa is only repeating the taunts of Draupadī and Bhīma, to whom he is indeed a Sūta. And when Kuntī and Kṛṣṇa offer him the chance to join the Pāṇḍavas and become the victorious "Kṣatriya" that is his birth identity, he refuses and chooses to remain the doomed Kṣatriya he became when he bound himself to Duryodhana. It is as if Karṇa is saying to Kṛṣṇa and the Pāṇḍavas, "I am a Kṣatriya, but not for the reasons you think."

Aditya Adarkar correctly points out that Karṇa departs from the cross-cultural heroic paradigm identified by Otto Rank[50] in that he refuses the crown and glory of the hero, choosing to remain in opposition to Arjuna instead of truly imitating him by becoming a Pāṇḍava. Adarkar argues:

> By rejecting power and fame, Karṇa provides another angle altogether on development: Karṇa is a character who 'develops' not by rejecting a previous identity but by clinging to it. That is, he does not change but remains fixed. This contrasts with a western notion of individualism which centers on the ability of the self to evolve, to reform itself, that assumes that individuals are truly free only if they are able to 'become' whatever they want to be.[51]

With this in mind, is it not possible to see Karṇa's two refusals to save his life and become a Pāṇḍava as something akin to Jesus's refusal of Satan's offer of universal kingship?[52] Along these same lines, can we not also read Karṇa's denunciations of Kṛṣṇa as the architect of the war as a parallel to Girard's insight that Satan (for Girard, a code name for the mimetic principle, thus, "The Accuser") is "the concealed director-producer of the Passion"?[53] And what do we make of Karṇa's refusal to be like his models (to whom he is also a model), choosing only to imitate and reflect his divine father Sūrya, both with his shining armor and his steadfast dependability? Is it not another version of the non-mimetic love for his father that Jesus models and that is revealed at his baptism in Matthew 3:17? Karṇa must, after all, be doing something right or his soul would not return to the sun in such a publicly spectacular fashion upon his glorious death on the battlefield. Consider these passages from the epic describing Karṇa's death and apotheosis:

> The Earth was drenched with the blood of men, horses, and elephants, deep red like the planet Mars; it was as if she were a prostitute, decked out in crimson robes and gold purified by fire. At that terrible moment of resplendent beauty, oh King, the Kauravas, their bodies marred with blood, perceived all this and could no longer stand there, resolving to depart this world for the realm of the gods. Grieving at the death of Karṇa, they called out, "Oh, Karṇa! Alas, Karṇa!" Hastily they set out for their camp, seeing the sun who makes the day take on a sanguine hue. Karṇa was lying slain on the ground, still shining like the bright-rayed sun pierced with sharp gold-tipped and feathered arrows loosed from the Gāṇḍiva bow and dyed in his blood. And before he went down into the western ocean to bathe, Father Sun, always compassionate to his devotees, touched Karṇa's blood-spattered body with his reddish rays.[54]

These passages, filled with lengthy metaphors of blazing splendor and fiery destruction, are clear enough in their depiction of the "reflective" relationship of Karṇa and the sun: The sun turns blood-red as it sets to reflect Karṇa's bloody corpse; Karṇa's body is described in ways that recall a sunset, with red and gold rays emanating from it in the form of Arjuna's arrows; and the death of Karṇa is the setting of the sun for the Kauravas.

For another perspective on Karṇa's character, we can look to one of Girard's early, pre-*Violence and the Sacred* essays, 1964's "Racine, Poet of Glory." The essay is a study of the seventeenth century French dramatist Jean-Baptiste Racine, whose work exemplifies the dominant aesthetics of Parisian culture under Louis XIV. Analyzing Racine's ability to reinvigorate the mediating power of metaphor, specifically the metaphor of "glory," Girard writes, "Racinian glory is radiance; it is the dazzling light that is reflected in the faces turned toward a glorious being."[55] Girard is referring especially to the titular Jewish queen Berenice's desire for the Roman emperor Titus in Racine's *Bérénice*, and to Eriphyle's desire for the hero Achilles in *Iphigénie*, but he extends this discussion to the idea of sovereignty, as it is constituted in poetry, myth, ritual, and politics. Using an as yet unnamed concept that is a clear precursor to the idea of "pseudonarcissism"[56] to reinterpret what Hegel (and more so, Kojève) calls the "master/slave dialectic," Girard argues that the Hegelian-Kojèvian model "is based on a systematic confusion between relations of power and desire." And anticipating his later work, he goes on to argue that "the ultimate consequence of the contradictions that define glory [is that] the world that it engenders can tend only toward self-destruction."[57]

In an appendix to *Sacred Violence* Hamerton-Kelly expands on the critique, arguing for the primacy of desire over power. For Hamerton-Kelly (and Girard), the weakness of Hegel's (and Kojève's) thought is that enslaving (as opposed to killing) the Other is a form of dialectical overcoming, which is "itself a form of sacrificial order, subsequent to the discovery of the sacrificial mechanism."[58] Without the mediation of the surrogate victim, conflict in early proto-human communities is to the death, not to submission. Therefore, before there can be a master and a slave, there must first be a surrogate victim.

So, without the master/slave dialectic, how then does Girard explain Racine's work, which is riddled with images of mastery, slavery, servitude, and submission (as is, for that matter, the Kṛṣṇaite love poetry that is heir to the *Mahābhārata*'s devotional tradition)? Girard argues that Racine's work, as the quintessential literature of seventeenth century *préciosité*, "dematerializes" the concrete historical power relations from which it arises by transmuting them into the rhetoric of glory, while at the same time it also "imbues [that rhetoric] with the *spirit* of violence that is the defining feature of the world of subtle aggression engendered by glory."[59] Racine's preoccupation with the violent excess of pagan Rome stems out of the necessity to turn to pre-Christian sacrificial societies in order to critique the diffused violence that inhabited the social world of seventeenth century France. This diffused violence and the threat it poses is, for Girard, "the first fallout from modern individualism,"[60] represented by the Cartesian subject.

But is it possible to speak of (what appears to be) a "pre-modern individualism," at least in nascent form, in the character of Karṇa? Adarkar sees in Karṇa a new kind of subjectivity outside of the cosmico-social one constituted by Kṛṣṇa in the *Mahābhārata*, in which duty and devotion are fused. Refuting Western assumptions about the "fatalism" of the epic and Indian religions in general, he argues that Karṇa's decision to determine his own identity or *svabhāva* is an exercise of existential freedom that still falls within the dharmic framework as *ātmatuṣṭi*, or "conscience."

For Girard, Karṇa's "fatalism" might be more akin to Jesus's moment of truth in the Garden of Gethsemane when he decides to die and expose the sacrificial system rather than be a part of it. But unlike Jesus, Karṇa does not want to destroy the sacrificial system, although his conflation of the war with sacrifice in *MBh* 5.129.29b-54 reveals that he knows the nature of the war and is choosing to be one of its victims rather than its beneficiary (significantly, Karṇa *does not include himself* in his list of sacrificial technicians, even though he is to be one of the generals of the Kaurava forces). Neither is Karṇa's rejection of Kṛṣṇa's offer to join the Pāṇḍavas a rebellious Miltonian "reign in Hell" moment, rejecting Kṛṣṇa's condescension in favor of glorious defeat. Indeed, in some ways he is acting more like a double agent *for* Kṛṣṇa than a rebel opposing him. In *MBh* 5.129.35 Karṇa tells Kṛṣṇa not to let anyone else know his true identity as the eldest Pāṇḍava because if the dharma-minded Yudhiṣṭhira knew the truth, he would give the crown to him, and he in turn would be obligated to give it to his liege lord Duryodhana, whom Karṇa knows full well is unfit to rule the kingdom.[61]

A few lines from T. S. Eliot's 1940 poem "East Coker," which describes the poet's return to the place of his ancestry in preparation for death, may shed some light on Karṇa's dilemma:

> And the conversation rises and slowly fades into silence
> And you see behind every face the mental emptiness deepen
> Leaving only the growing terror of nothing to think about;
> Or when, under ether, the mind is conscious but conscious of nothing—
> I said to my soul, be still, and wait without hope
> For hope would be hope for the wrong thing; wait without love,
> For love would be love of the wrong thing; there is yet faith
> But the faith and the love and the hope are all in the waiting.
> Wait without thought, for you are not ready for thought:
> So the darkness shall be the light, and the stillness the dancing.[62]

The last lines, "the darkness shall be the light, and the stillness the dancing," seem to echo *Paradise Lost*'s, "Evil, be thou my Good" (4.110), undercutting the distinction I have made between the Miltonian Satan and Karṇa, but while Milton's Satan makes his choice out of pride, Karṇa has a different motivation. As Adarkar puts it:

> In making the choice to stay on the side of the Kauravas, Karṇa is not merely resigning himself to losing the war—although that seems inevitable

> to him—and achieving glory in heaven. Neither is he merely resigning himself to being killed by Arjuna, although, in a way, that also is inevitable since Kṛṣṇa is Arjuna's protector. Karṇa resigns himself to those facts, but then—in a movement based only on an absurd faith in himself—he believes that he will still defeat Arjuna in battle here on this earth. Karṇa chooses to act with a horizon of possibility that contains, paradoxically, only impossibilities. Karṇa can do so because of the fierce loyalty with which he clings to the *dharmic reality* of his loyal human relationships: Karṇa is steadfast in having faith in a dharma that makes sense (and will reward him) here, in this life.[63]

In Adarkar's analysis, Karṇa has no fear of death or defeat (none of the epic heroes fear either of these, seemingly) but only what he calls, following Paul Tillich, an "anxiety of meaninglessness," or in Eliot's terms, "the growing terror of nothing to think about." While courage, which Karṇa has in spades, can help us face fear, anxiety is a different matter. It can only be overcome by existential choice or the grace of God (in this case, Kṛṣṇa). Accepting Kṛṣṇa's offer to make him king and avert the war would be to sacrifice the Pāṇḍavas and thus prop up the sacrificial system by feeding it more victims. But it would also give Karṇa's life meaning in making him the hero who assumes his true identity in the Rankian hero mold, which is also the mold of Kṛṣṇa, who does just that in his own myth cycle.[64]

Karṇa's life would also have meaning if he were to fulfill his role as a sacrificial victim, for, as Girard points out, the Aristotelian tragic hero is also the perfect victim, like Oedipus.[65] But he even eludes this second characterization by dint of his paradoxical "faith in a dharma that makes sense (and will reward him) here, in this life." In short, Karṇa does not hope for victory because that would be hope for the wrong thing (i.e., the kingship of Duryodhana). He does not love because to love would be the wrong thing, be it Kuntī, the mother who abandoned him or Duryodhana, the brother who adopted him (and whom he could save by taking the Pāṇḍava crown). So he chooses the waiting without thought that is faith.

Karṇa is not choosing suicide, which is against dharma, but a life made meaningful through death. As Bruce Sullivan has pointed out, in the epic "[s]elf-willed death, whether threatened or performed, is a literary device or narrative strategy that assists the text in conveying emotional and spiritual messages to its audience."[66] Karṇa's decision to go into battle is indivisible from his decision (which recalls Śunaḥśepa's transformation from sacrificial victim to the gift of the gods and Viśvāmitra's adopted son) to be and to abide by the code of the Kṣatriya he *chooses* to be rather than the Kṣatriya he was *born* to be. And that makes all the difference. He is not rejecting dharma, much less creating a mirror image of dharma like the shadow ethos of the Miltonian Satan. While Milton's Satan (especially in his Byronic guise) is a hero to the Romantic champions of individualism, Karṇa is a hero of universalism. As the mathematically minded Alain Badiou puts it in his eighth theorem in *Saint Paul: The Foundation of Universalism*:

> Where the imperative of his own continuation is concerned, the subject supports himself through the fact that the taking-place of the truth constituting him is universal and thereby effectively concerns him. There is singularity only in so far as there is universality. Failing that, there is, outside of truth, only particularity.[67]

Through his own unique paradoxical choice, Karṇa is simultaneously constituting dharma and universalizing it.

Dveṣabhakti: *The Devotion of the Enemy*

This analysis of Karṇa's choice brings us back to the existential ethics that have long informed Girard's work. In the last section I have argued that Karṇa's story seems, on the surface, like a mere refusal or a romantic gesture of individualism, but actually turns out to be an affirmation of the universal. I will further clarify what I mean by this by comparing Karṇa's battlefield apotheosis with that of another hero-villain from the Sanskrit epics: Rāvaṇa, the ten-headed demon[68] slain by Rāma, the hero of the *Rāmāyaṇa*.[69] The Rāvaṇa story's theme of *dveṣabhakti*, I will argue, serves to partially demythologize the trope of sacred rivalry.

Rāma, the rightful prince of Ayodhya and the seventh avatar of Viṣṇu, is married to the beautiful princess Sītā, whom he has won in a *svayaṃvara* much like Draupadī's. But because of the jealousy of one his father's wives, Rāma has been banished into the forest, where he lives as a hermit with Sītā and his brother Lakṣmaṇa. One day, the demoness Śūrpaṇakhā, sister of Rāvaṇa, is traveling in the forest when her eyes fall upon Rāma and she is instantly smitten with him. She throws herself at Rāma, but he is disgusted by her appearance and is fully devoted to his wife Sītā. Instead of casting her out completely, Rāma decides to play a joke at her expense and that of his brother, telling Śūrpaṇakhā that Lakṣmaṇa might be more amenable to her advances than he is. But Lakṣmaṇa, of course, is just as repulsed and rains down a litany of abuses and insults on her. When Śūrpaṇakhā flies into a rage and tries to attack Sītā, who is standing nearby, Rāma orders Lakṣmaṇa to grab her and cut off her nose and ears.[70]

The disfigured Śūrpaṇakhā runs away and enlists the help of some of Rāvaṇa's best soldiers to avenge her, but Rāma and Lakṣmaṇa easily rout them in battle. Still seeking revenge, Śūrpaṇakhā goes directly to her brother Rāvaṇa, the mighty ten-headed demon king of Lanka, and tells him what has happened. In the course of her narration, she happens to describe the beauty of Sītā, causing Rāvaṇa to fall in love with her sight unseen. Thus begins the turning point of the epic, when Rāvaṇa disguises himself as a Brahmin and kidnaps Sītā, taking her back to Lanka and prompting Rāma to go on a quest to regain his wife and destroy Rāvaṇa.

Rāma and Rāvaṇa's war over Sītā not only recalls the story of Paris, Menelaus, and Helen in the *Iliad* (a comparison Wendy Doniger has fruitfully explored in *Splitting the Difference*), it is also yet another instantiation of the endless war that rages throughout the Brāhmaṇas between the gods and the demons over an indivisible object. But this particular rivalry is interpreted in the later literature in the light of *bhakti*, or devotional theology, and when Rāvaṇa finally goes down to defeat in battle, his soul ascends to Heaven in a shining light because he has been a great devotee of Rāma, practicing *dveṣabhakti*, the devotion of hatred. Simply having Rāma occupy his mind for so many years has filled him with the divine grace.

In the epic, Rāvaṇa's desire is ostensibly for Sītā, kindled through the mere description of her beauty, but the theological interpretation gets closer to a mimetic insight into the nature of rivalry. The point of Viṣṇu's incarnation as Rāma is to destroy Rāvaṇa, a demon whose power has grown to rival that of the gods. Sītā's abduction is just a way of making that happen. But the rivalry is not a one-way street. Rāvaṇa is as drawn to his destroyer as he is to

Sītā. As these verses from Vālmīki's Sanskrit version of the epic illustrate, it is not merely Śūrpaṇakhā's description of Sītā that enthralls Rāvaṇa, but her description of Rāma:

> Seeing Śūrpaṇakhā speaking bitter words against [Rāma] in the presence of his ministers, Rāvaṇa became infuriated and asked her, "Who is Rāma? How brave is he? What about his form and his heroism? And why did he enter the impenetrable Daṇḍaka forest? What is the weapon that Rāma used to kill so many demons in war, killing even Dūṣaṇa and Triśiras, and the invincible Khara? Oh, lady of bewitching limbs, who disfigured you? Tell me that!"
>
> When the king of demons asked her in this way, the demoness Śūrpaṇakhā, in a fit of fury, began to describe Rāma precisely:
>
> "Daśaratha's son Rāma possesses keen eyes and mighty arms, but has sack-cloth and deer skin for his clothes. Still he resembles the god of love. Drawing a golden-tipped bow that gleams like Indra's, he showers down glowing iron arrows that are like poisonous serpents. On the field of battle, he moved with such speed that it was impossible to perceive when and how he drew his deadly arrows from his quiver, or how he notched them or fired them from his bow. All I could see was that great army being annihilated with a downpour of arrows, like a crop of grain devastated by a hailstorm of Indra. Thus a lone soldier with his deadly arrows exterminated fourteen thousand demons with terrible might, including Dūṣaṇa, and Khara, within one and half hours.
>
> Daṇḍaka is a safe place again for the sages, who are accorded protection. High-minded Rāma, who has cut off my nose and ears and humiliated me, somehow leaves only me out [of his campaign]. Maybe it is because he is hesitant to slaughter a woman, being such a law-minded soul.
>
> Rāma's brother Lakṣmaṇa is a highly resplendent man equal in bravery to his brother, of whom he is a follower, a comrade, and a devotee, such a stouthearted one is he. That Lakṣmaṇa is impetuous, invincible in battle, victorious, valiant, wise, strong, and always at Rāma's side.
>
> Rāma's righteous wife, with almond-shaped eyes and a face as round as the moon, always takes delight in the happiness of her dear husband. She is glorious in her beauty, with long straight hair, and shapely nose and thighs. She shines like a goddess in the woods, like the goddess Śrī in human form.

> Her complexion is like polished gold, her nails are rosy and pointed. With her rounded hips and slim waist, she is the daughter of the king of Videha, and known as Sītā.
>
> I have never seen anyone with such beauty, neither goddess, nor nymph, nor sprite, nor fairy, nor any woman on the face of earth! Whoever marries Sītā and feels her arms around him lives higher than Indra himself. She is a highly gracious lady, praiseworthy in the shape of her body, without compare in her looks. She will be the perfect wife for you, and you will be the perfect husband for her.
>
> Oh, mighty-shouldered hero, but when I tried to bring back this lovely-faced, big-bosomed, callipygian woman to be your wife, that cruel Lakṣmaṇa disfigured me. You too will become a slave at the arrows of the god of love when you see Sītā with her face glowing like the full moon. So if you have a mind to make her your wife, and if you want success, now is the time to put your best foot forward. Do the demons a favor, Rāvaṇa, by killing Rāma who dwells in that hermitage. If you kill Rāma and Lakṣmaṇa with your sharp arrows, you can then happily enjoy the widow Sītā as much as you like. Oh, demon king Rāvaṇa, if my advice pleases you, make this idea a reality! Don't overthink it! Oh, great and powerful king of the demons, remember your power and kidnap that lovely-limbed Sītā to make her your wife. Remember that Rāma with his straight-shooting arrows destroyed the demons stationed at Janasthāna, even Dūṣaṇa and Khara. You must do something!"[71]

Śūrpaṇakhā's exhortations awaken Rāvaṇa to his proper relationship to his rival Rāma and his part in the drama about to unfold, so he quickly commits the crime of rape and in so doing takes on one of the stereotyped accusations against the scapegoat. As soon as the hero appears, Rāvaṇa quickly becomes a villain, which he does not seem to have been before. Other than the rape of Sītā (which is a "rape" in the sense of "abduction" rather than a sexual assault, because he does not touch Sītā while she is in his palace) Rāvaṇa's life is generally regarded as good and righteous. Indeed he would have to be good and righteous to become as powerful as he is, since right makes might in the Indian mythical cosmos.

While Karṇa keenly perceives the sacrificial nature of the battle in the *Mahābhārata*, everyone in the *Rāmāyaṇa* seems, for the most part, to be completely caught up in the *līla*, or "play," to such an extent that Rāma himself forgets his own identity as Viṣṇu. And in true Girardian form, once the fighting is done and order is restored in the form of the idyllic Rāmrāj—described as a new Golden Age of peace, prosperity, and everyone staying in his proper place (the opposite of the dreaded Kali Yuga)—the ostensible object of Rāma and Rāvaṇa's rivalry quickly becomes immaterial. After Rāma defeats Rāvaṇa, he promptly exiles the wife he has just spent years fighting to get back because she has been alone in another man's house and is no longer pure.

But if we read the rivalry of Rāma and Rāvaṇa as yet another instantiation of the rivalry between the gods and the demons, we must also take note of the shift from mythological to theological (or psychological) thinking in the Vaiṣṇava interpretation of the *Rāmāyaṇa* and the reimagining of cosmic order necessitated by his shift. *Dveṣabhakti*, although left out of most mainstream lists of devotional typology, such as the *Bhaktirasāmṛtasindhu* of the sixteenth century Bengali poet and theologian Rūpa Gosvāmin, has a powerful and persistent presence in the stories of Karṇa and Rāvaṇa (and Śiśupāla, as we shall soon see). Is *dveṣabhakti* some variety of what Bernard Schweizer identifies as "misotheism" in the writings of British authors Rebecca West, Phillip Pullman, and Algernon Swinburne?[72] Does it serve to mediate rivalry by making it a form of *bhakti* in which the object or image to which one is devoted is a pathway to the Absolute? With these questions in mind, we will compare the stories of Karṇa and Rāvaṇa and try to determine what role mythology and "anti-mythology" might have to play in these paradoxical encounters.

The Apotheoses of Karṇa and Rāvaṇa

Rāvaṇa's apotheosis, like Karṇa's, takes place on the field of battle following a lengthy duel with a Viṣṇu-figure who is the epic's hero. In the Sanskrit version of the *Rāmāyaṇa*, Rāvaṇa's defeat simply ends with Rāvaṇa falling dead after being struck through the heart by Rāma's arrow. But other traditions have him ascending to Heaven as a result of his devotion to Rāma. Still others have it that Rāvaṇa, being the wisest and most learned of the demons, only abducted Sītā so that he could receive the grace of a death at the hands of Rāma. In the *Viṣṇu Purāṇa*, Kṛṣṇa's monstrous enemy Śiśupāla (whom we will discuss in the next chapter) is said to be a reincarnation of Rāvaṇa come back to earth to receive another cleansing death from Viṣṇu.

Like some other mythic Hindu anti-heroes, Rāvaṇa also has a cult of worshippers in India and his temples can be found in Andhra Pradesh, Rajasthan, and Uttar Pradesh, among other places. In the South, he is seen as a kind of culture hero, representing Dravidian South India's last stand against the Aryan invaders from the North.[73] In his 1929 book *Tamil Literature* M. S. Purnalingam Pillai defends Rāvaṇa's behavior toward Rāma's wife, arguing that he "took away Sita according to the Tamilian mode of warfare, had her in the Asoka woods companioned by his own niece, and would not touch her unless she consented."[74]

While his nature is more transparent than most of the mythic figures Girard examines, Rāvaṇa fits the mold of the scapegoat perfectly. He is a king, he is monstrous, he commits an unforgivable crime, he dies at the hands of the hero so that the blissfully perfect community of the Rāmrāj can be founded, and he is elevated to a god. The profoundly mimetic nature of his character is also reflected in his kidnapping of Sītā and his rivalry with Rāma, both of which are elements clearly derived from the Brāhmaṇic wars of the gods and the demons. Karṇa, although he is in much the same position as Rāvaṇa in terms of the great cosmic struggle, is a very different figure. He refuses to become a Pāṇḍava, choosing his own *svābhava*. And he does not go willingly to his death for the greater good of balancing the universe, but instead goes into battle with the paradoxical hope that he can overcome the inevitable. And lastly, unlike Rāvaṇa, he is presented in terms that are strikingly human. Arguably, he is the most human character in the epic, and it is his humanity that resists mythologization and marks him as a clear-eyed witness to the true nature of the war.

Dvāparayugānta, "The End of the Age of the Deuce": Three Critiques of Sacrifice

In this chapter, we have examined the Śaiva critique of sacrifice in the story of Dakṣa, the Vaiṣṇava critique in the story of Jarāsaṃdha, and the existential critique of sacrifice in the story of Karṇa. All three operate in relation to the outsider figure: the Śaiva critique tells the story of the expelled party returning to destroy the sacrifice; the Vaiṣṇava critique equates human and divine violence, restoring the element of unpredictability to the world of ritual; and the existential critique makes of the outsider a kind of paradoxical hero, participating in his own demise without submitting to it. We also looked at the story of the churning of the ocean and the connection it makes between rivalry, sacrifice, and deathlessness. In the next chapter, we will continue our discussion of the *Mahābhārata* while also returning to Vedic ritual, the story of Śunaḥśepa, and the lycanthropic *homo sacer*. As we have seen so far, a close reading of Hindu mythology through the lens of mimetic theory gives us a far richer understanding of the Indian texts and their relationship to other Indo-European materials while also illuminating the connections between Girard's work and those of thinkers as varied as T. S. Eliot and Jan Heesterman. In the penultimate chapter, we will go still farther afield into the realms of Norse mythology and contemporary continental philosophy.

Meaning: The Secret Heart of the Sacred

A man sets out to discover a treasure he believes is hidden under a stone; he turns over stone after stone but finds nothing. He grows tired of such futile undertaking but the treasure is too precious for him to give up. So he begins to look for a stone which is too heavy to lift—he places all his hopes in that stone and he will waste all his remaining strength on it.

—René Girard, *Deceit, Desire and the Novel*

Rabbi Bunam used to tell young men who came to him for the first time the story of Rabbi Eizik, son of Rabbi Yekel of Cracow.

After many years of great poverty which had never shaken his faith in God, he dreamed someone bade him look for a treasure in Prague, under the bridge which leads to the king's palace. When the dream recurred a third time, Rabbi Eizik prepared for the journey and set out for Prague. But the bridge was guarded day and night and he did not dare to start digging. Nevertheless he went to the bridge every morning and kept walking around it until evening. Finally the captain of the guard, who had been watching him, asked in a kindly way whether he was looking for something or waiting for somebody. Rabbi Eizik told him of the dream which had brought him here from a faraway country.

> The captain laughed: "And so to please the dream, you poor fellow wore out your shoes to come here! As for having faith in dreams, if I had had it, I should have had to get going when a dream once told me to go to Cracow and dig for treasure under the stove in the room of a Jew—Eizik, son of Yekel, that was the name! Eizik, son of Yekel! I can just imagine what it would be like, how I should have to try every house over there where one half of the Jews are named Eizik and the other half Yekel!" And he laughed again. Rabbi Eizik bowed, traveled home, dug up the treasure from under the stove, and built the House of Prayer which is called "Reb Eizik Reb Yekel's Shul."
>
> —Martin Buber, "The Treasure," *Tales of the Hasidim: The Later Masters*

Games, Riddles, and Rituals

Citing Roger Caillois's *Les jeux et les hommes*, Girard identifies the four types of games listed by Caillois with the four stages of ritual (see table 4). First are the games of imitation, corresponding to the advent of acquisitive mimesis, when humans begin to learn by imitating and their imitation gives rise to conflict as models become rivals. Second are the games of competition, corresponding to the struggle of the mimetic doubles, when the mimetic rivalries have intensified to the point that rivals become enemy twins, like Viśvāmitra and Vasiṣṭha. Third come the games of vertigo, corresponding to the sacrificial crisis in which all distinctions are swallowed up in the widening conflict. And finally are the games of chance, corresponding to the spontaneous selection of the sacrificial victim. In the Vedic ritual, these four stages are represented by the enigmatic disputation called the *brahmodya*, the ceremonial chariot race and cattle raid, the ingestion of *soma*, and the dicing match.

We can observe other types of animals mimicking each other, competing with each other, and spinning themselves into a state of frenzy (like a dog chasing his tail, for instance); it is games of chance alone that are unique to humans. For Girard, the game of chance is an iteration of the primary symbolic process, the process used to pick the victim: the selection of one from many.

Girard argues that this first differentiation, which engenders the possibility of language, is born in "sacred terror." The primal horde that has killed

Table 4. Corresponding Elements of Games, the Surrogate Victim Cycle, and Vedic Ritual

CAILLOIS'S GAMES	GIRARD'S STAGES	ELEMENTS OF VEDIC RITUAL
Games of imitation	Acquisitive mimesis	*Brahmodya*
Games of competition	Struggle of rivals	Chariot race, cattle raid
Games of vertigo	Sacrificial crisis	*Soma* drinking
Games of chance	Victim selection	Dicing match

its first victim to bring peace and unanimity does so again and again when the crisis of mimetic rivalry reaches its peak. As the killing is repeated, it begins to take on a recognizable shape and rhythm. And whether they are actually linked to the killing or not (consider Kafka's thirsty leopards in the temple), the elements that accompany it (howls of rage from the mob, cries of terror from the victim) soon become associated with the peace bought by the victim's death. It is at this phase that something besides another victim—such as the spot where the killing happens or the implement with which it is done—can represent the victim. And that is why Girard calls the victim the "transcendental signifier."

When Girard calls the victim the transcendental signifier, he is referring to a system of signification that does not arise from a Lévi-Straussian binary opposition. This kind of dichotomy, Girard thinks, is "purely synchronic and static" and thus it cannot account for the beginning of the system, which is exactly what he wants to do.[1] Instead he argues that the first order of signification is not based on binary distinctions at all:

> There is a simpler model that is uniquely dynamic and genetic—but also completely ignored. This is the model of the exception that is still in the process of emerging, the single trait that stands out against a confused mass of still unsorted multiplicity. It is the model of drawing lots, of the short straw. . . .[2]

Girard notes that this kind of symbolic system is frequently associated with ritual and with games of chance, both of which are intimately bound up together in Vedic sacrifice. It also calls to mind the sacrifices of Puruṣa (and Śiśupāla, as we shall soon see), where undifferentiated monstrosity is violently transformed into order. We can see this model reflected in the "state of exception" at the heart of the political theology of Carl Schmitt and in Giorgio Agamben's work on the *homo sacer*. Bertrand Russell well illustrates the contradictions inherent in this kind of system of exclusion and differentiation with a famous paradox in which one imagines a set of all sets that are not members of themselves, which would be a set that appears to be a member of itself if and only if it is not a member of itself; or, as he illustrates it, in a town where the barber shaves only those men who do not shave themselves, who shaves the barber?[3] In ritual, Girard sees this kind of contradiction in the sacred king who is both outside the community and at its very center. When classes and distinctions become confused, as they always must in a system founded on paradox, the sacrificial crisis occurs.

In his analysis of the dicing game associated with the Vrātyas (which actually seems to have been played with nuts or round tokens that do not necessarily resemble the cubical objects we have in mind when we think of "dice"), Harry Falk argues for identifying it as a version of the shortest straw victim selection technique described by Girard. If Falk is right then the dice match that plays such an important role in Vedic ritual as well as epic and Śaiva mythology could only select a loser and never a winner.[4]

At this point in my argument, we are approaching what I see as a crucial intersection between mimetic theory and ancient Indian thought. Don Handelman and David Shulman's discussion of the ritual meaning of the dice game points us in the right direction:

> Movement in the course of play, which might even seem random, sooner or later becomes a burdensome imbalance or excess, in which a remnant—the last nut or token—can no longer be resumed or contained. A stubbornly resistant piece of inner reality remains excluded—or extruded—this being the conclusive sign of its owner's defeat.[5]

The always incomplete nature of the Vedic sacrifice and the persistent idea that the sacrificial remainder has the power to destroy is a reversal of the sentiment expressed in Psalm 118:22 ("The stone the builders rejected has become the cornerstone"); instead of the stone the builders rejected becoming the cornerstone, it becomes the stone that smashes apart the glass house of Vedic ritual. As many Śaiva myths (most notably the myth of Dakṣa, in which the outsider god Śiva comes to destroy the sacrifice of his father-in-law after he is left off the guest list) demonstrate, the expelled party—the loser—can very often come back and wreak havoc on the community founded on its expulsion. But at the same time, this excluded remnant is also seen as a sign of the sacrifice's generative power. The *Śatapatha Brāhmaṇa* holds that the part of the sacrifice that remains "incomplete" (*nyūna*) is the part that is "generative" (*prajanana*).[6]

Although they seemed, by the time of the *Śatapatha Brāhmaṇa*, to accept the impossibility of performing the sacrifice perfectly, the Vedic Brahmins also strove to eliminate the aleatory element from ritual altogether and to make sure that the world of the sacrifice was as certain as the world outside the sacrifice was uncertain, that death was as impossible in the sacrificial enclosure as it was inevitable in the real world. In the process, the science of sacrifice, which gives birth to astronomy, mathematics, and philosophy in India, binds all types of knowledge to a denial of the violence done to the sacrificial victim. But the story is more complex than that, because the sacrificial victim, the **bhlagh(s)men-kavi-pharmakos*, is always present as the excluded middle, signifying the secret knowledge of the sacrifice as well as the one who possesses that knowledge—the solver of riddles like Oedipus and Śunaḥśepa.

Writing on ritual and riddle, Handelman argues that the logic of riddles rests on the same paradox of confusion between class and members that Russell formulates. But the riddle only has the *appearance* of a paradox because there is a solution to the riddle—a solution that would be a logical impossibility were it not on a higher level of abstraction.[7] This logical process of abstraction has an analogue in the Girardian primal scene. When the violence of the crowd is spontaneously directed against the surrogate victim in the founding murder, we see the literal abstraction, in the sense of "taking out," that comes along with the victim taking on the role of the transcendental signifier and opening up the possibility of "abstract thinking." The Vedic dice game described above by Handelman and Shulman seems to present another parallel, where the random movement of play tends toward a state of imbalance that can only be rectified by the expulsion of one.

In the rituals subsequent to the foundational murder that allow the community to "continue life under the sign of the reconciliatory victim,"[8] the process of spontaneous and literal abstraction is replaced by a selection mechanism containing elements of both Russell's paradox and the sacrificial crisis. As myth begins to obscure the violence in which it originates, the ritual and the riddle work in parallel: the ritual works to defuse the violence that would destroy the community be channeling it into sacred violence and the riddle works to defuse the contradictions that would destroy the system by channeling them into false paradoxes that can be solved on a higher level of abstraction. This latter process, continued in ever more nuanced iterations, also describes the earliest phase of the philosophical traditions rooted in Vedic hermeneutics, the moment in which Girard sees the Indian sacrificial tradition beginning to transcend itself.

Fooling Brahmins

In *Jokes and Their Relation to the Unconscious* Freud makes this observation: "In the joke, the wording is given and the technique is disguised. In the riddle, the reverse takes place: the technique is given and the wording has to be guessed."[9] The Sanskrit tradition also makes such a distinction on the levels of language and technique. Dharmadāsa's thirteenth century poetical treatise the *Vidagdhamukhamaṇḍana* defines the riddle or *prahelikā* with this couplet: "That is *prahelikā* in which both an inner and an outer meaning are expressed, making one meaning visible by disguising the real meaning."[10] And in classical Sanskrit drama, both the sacred riddle and the profane joke are embodied in the figure of a Brahmin clown called the *vidūṣaka* who speaks his riddles in Sanskrit during the ritual preliminaries but tells his jokes in vernacular speech during the play itself.[11]

As in the Oedipal myth, where the hero must answer the riddle of the Sphinx or be torn apart by her, the Sanskrit riddle is closely tied to the violent and agonistic institutions of the duel, the contest, and the sacrifice.[12] The relationship between ritual and riddle is evident in the Vedic tradition. In enigmatic terms, the notoriously obscure "Riddle of the Sacrifice," the first hymn of the first book of the *Ṛg Veda*, makes a direct connection between the ritual being performed and the paradigmatic sacrifice it purports to repeat. In Doniger's translation, the verse reads: "Those that are in the future say they are in the past; those that are in the past say they are in the future. The things that you and Indra did, Soma, still pull the axle pole of space as though yoked to it."[13] Stephanie Jamison suggests that verses like this one may have been composed at a stage in the ritual's development where improvisation was still a possibility and Brahmin priests challenged each other to verbal contests called *brahmodyas* in which they were "[challenged] both in formulating a metaphorical representation of a cosmic or mystical truth, and in recognizing the homologies involved in the representation, that is, in solving the riddle."[14]

It is from the riddling disputation of the *brahmodya* that we get the figure of the *nāstika*, or "nay-sayer," later identified with heterodox teachers like Buddhists and Jains, but originally simply the ritual verbal opponent of the *āstika* or "yea-sayer." Originally the *āstika* and the *nāstika* were more like two high school debate teams assigned to affirmative and negative positions. But unlike a debate, the *brahmodya* requires each party not to refute the other's argument with rebuttal, but to out-riddle the other. Heesterman describes the rules of riddling:

> The question of the challenger is couched in terms of a well-turned enigma to which his opponent should react, not with a clear-cut, unambiguous solution, but with an equally enigmatic rejoinder, till one of the parties is reduced to silence or till the strongest, well aware of his strength, enforces silence by withdrawing.[15]

Since either the winner or the loser can end by withdrawing into silence, even the outcome of the *brahmodya* is enigmatic. It is easy to imagine a situation in which the Brahmin who believes himself to have won withdraws into silence while the Brahmin he supposes he has beaten silently gloats over having riddled the other into submission. As the ritual becomes more formalized, the risk of defeat is removed from this part of the proceedings and replaced with a carefully scripted set of questions and answers between priests and sacrificer in which the sacrificer names his mythical counterpart in the accounts of divine sacrifice. Still later, the entire lengthy disputation is collapsed into the moment of silence that would have marked the end of the *brahmodya*, but now stands as a synecdoche representing the *brahmodya* in its entirety. In the history of the *brahmodya* Heesterman traces the pacification of the agonistic sacrifice "from contest, involving the formulation and enacting of the antithetical relation, to rigorously fixed liturgy and identificatory statement, to the final internalization of the whole procedure by the single, unopposed sacrificer."[16] Hegel himself could not have formulated a neater dialectic.

One place where this verbal dueling is not formalized and left in its open-ended form is in the explicitly sexual exchange between the priests and the wives after the sacrificer's chief wife has (feigned?) sexual intercourse with the dead sacrificial horse. But if the sexual aspects somehow eluded being orchestrated and minimized by the Brahmin ritualists, the spectacle of violence did not, and the absence of violence became the answer to the ultimate riddle.

Heesterman convincingly argues that the fate of the *brahmodya* is indicative of the Brahmin ritualists' strategy of removing all traces of killing from the sacrificial ritual, supplanting the sacrificial contest with the single-sacrificer model, and replacing violence with the ritual mistake, which, unlike real violence, can be undone by reciting a few expiatory verses, called *prāyaścitti*. In an article on the subject of ritual mistakes, Axel Michaels lists some of the common things that can go wrong (and be corrected) in Vedic ritual, including a polluted fire, an incorrectly recited verse, or spilled milk, which could turn the sacrificer into a leper if not followed by a *prāyaścitti*.[17] At least in the case of Vedic ritual, it seems that there *is* some use in crying over spilled milk, as long as the crying includes the proper Sanskrit verse.

Examining the Vedic substitution of ritual mistakes for violence against a sacrificial rival is useful for clearing up some misunderstandings of Girard's theory. John Milbank has critiqued Girard's insistence on the connection between rivalry and scapegoating, arguing:

> [Scapegoating] does not seem to be quite as widespread a phenomenon as Girard allows. Nor, when it occurs, does it always seem [connected to] the suppression of rivalry, but rather with the bearing away of many different impurities, many of a simply ritual variety.[18]

But as Heesterman has shown us, ritual impurity, at least in the Vedic case, is itself a displacement of rivalry. The elimination of the *brahmodya* is at least partially an attempt to bring the mimetic doubling of the *nāstika* and the *āstika* under control by expelling the *nāstika*.[19] But like the sacrificial killing post, which remains safely outside the enclosure, the *nāstika* slips away surreptitiously from the ritual grounds and returns to haunt it in the form of the Buddhist, the Jain, and other figures who seek to pull the rug out from under the sacrificial system.

Rolling the Bones and Cooking the Books

The stage of ritual Girard calls "delirium" involves the orgiastic and ecstatic elements that accomplish the replication of the primal horde's chaos and the forgetting of the founding murder in order to invest its repetition with sacred power. Long before Kant found it necessary to deny knowledge to make room for faith, the architects of ritual found it necessary to efface knowledge through willful forgetting in order to raise the edifice of religion. In Girard's understanding of religion, myth is a palimpsest written over a murder mystery, the traces of which are still visible where the writing is thin, but only to the scrupulous outside observer. Girard writes in *Job: The Victim of His People*: "Ritual thought can never fully grasp its own origin."[20] Before the Christian revelation that signals its destruction, ritual is a closed system with no ability to get outside of itself, according to Girard. But this does not mean that the sacrificial mechanism is an enclosed perpetual motion machine impervious to change and decay. The second chapter of *Violence and the Sacred* is dedicated to the idea of the sacrificial crisis in which sacrifice has broken down and begins to multiply violent conflicts instead of defusing them. Girard sees this crisis at work in Euripides's *Heracles* and Sophocles's *The Women of Trachis*. He is clear on the point that the failure of a sacrificial system is something categorically different from its revelation, which occurs only in the Gospels. He describes what keeps a sacrificial crisis from getting outside of the sacrificial system as "some sort of braking mechanism, an automatic control that goes into effect before everything is destroyed."[21] He goes on to identify this "automatic control" that recreates the sacrificial economy from the ruins of the old one as the surrogate victim mechanism, the generative form of scapegoating that produces all myth and ritual. The only thing that stands against this relentlessly self-reproducing principle of ritual is Christianity.

Heesterman takes up the question of ritual and Christianity in *The Broken World of Sacrifice* and comes to a conclusion that is both similar to and distinct from Girard's, and worth examining in detail:

> It was ritual that brought about the definitive collapse of the world of sacrifice. This proposition may seem overly provocative and bound to create misunderstanding. After all, sacrifice is a privileged occasion for

> elaborate and highly profiled ritual, and it seems all but impossible to distinguish between sacrifice and its ritual. Who says *sacrifice* says *ritual.*[22]

Heesterman's claim that ritual spelled the end of Vedic sacrifice in India is part of his argument against rival Vedic scholar Frits Staal's theory of the "meaninglessness of ritual." Staal's theory, put forth in *Rules without Meaning*, compares Vedic mantras to birdsong and explains the static nature of the Vedic sacrifice by its lack of semantic content or referents in the world outside of ritual. Heesterman objects that this explanation tells us nothing about the relationship between sacrifice and ritual, which is what concerns him. To understand this relationship he attempts a kind of limited morphogenetic theory to explain the way that in the Indian context "sacrifice was changed—not by an 'organic' process of accretion or erosion, but purposefully and fundamentally [into] a closed, unchanging and meaningless structure, a separate realm cut off from the lived-in world."[23] This purposeful transformation, which amounts to the exclusion of contest from a sacrificial ritual that originally had contest at its center, gives birth to the multiple contradictions and aporias that inhabit the Vedic literature. Phenomenologically speaking, it is the challenge of the ritualist to create an unchanging structure out of the building blocks of lived experience—contingent phenomena such as gestures, speech acts, and social relationships. To transmute a conglomerate of these phenomena into an unchanging structure it is necessary to eliminate anything like contingency. Where the early forms of sacrifice had been founded on "the enigmatic relationship of life and death enacted in the contest," the later, more heavily ritualized forms have at their center "the mutual exclusion of irredeemably contradictory parts."[24]

There is perhaps a good reason why the French Indologist Charles Malamoud titled his book on Vedic sacrifice *Cooking the World*. In English the phrase "cook the books" can mean not only to make a soup out of the collected works of Charles Dickens, but also to alter a company's account books to show profit where there is really loss (as the Enron corporation did throughout the 1990s). In Sanskrit, Hindi, and Anglo-Indian slang the word for "perfect" is *pakka*, which literally means "cooked," "ripened," or "matured." We might also recall Claude Lévi-Strauss's formulation of the distinction between nature and culture as the difference between the raw and the cooked. In its "raw" form, sacrifice is based on the contingency of the contest. But after it has been "cooked" by the Brahmins into ritual, sacrifice becomes a comfortingly predictable (and bloodless) affair. But, as Heesterman reminds us, "Who says *sacrifice* says *ritual*." Sacrifice and ritual are always-already one. In Heesterman's conception of the innate difference-in-identity (nicely summed up in the Sanskrit philosophical-theological mouthful *svābhāvikabedhābedha*) of sacrifice and ritual, we have something like the paradox Jean-Pierre Dupuy presents in "Totalization and Misrecognition," namely how "the totality . . . engenders itself in the very moment in which it is actualized."[25]

To put the paradox in terms of Girard's reading of the Gospel, if the Logos of Jesus is expelled to protect the sacrificial system, does that not mean that the expellers already "know what they do" before it has been revealed to them, making Jesus's revelation no revelation at all? Or to put it in terms of the myth we discussed in the second chapter, how can the Brahmins learn the ritual from Śunaḥśepa when they are already nearly finished performing it? Or to put it in Vedic philosophical terms, what was the model and what was the copy and what was the connection between them?[26] Dupuy's reading of Girard solves this paradox as it applies to mimetic desire with the introduction of "pseudo-narcissism," in which one's autonomy as an "interdividual" comes from desiring the other's desire for oneself (think of two mirrors facing each other).

"[The] illusion of self-sufficiency," Dupuy argues, "is therefore *produced by the very thing that it produces*: the fascinated gaze of the Others."[27] The pseudo-narcissistic interdividual thinks that she has what others want because of the way they look at her. But the others are looking at her only because she acts as if she has something they want. Desire only desires itself. Thus (at the generative level, at least) there are no true objects of desire, only subjects of desire. In Girardian terms, the true non-mimetic subject is only possible in the coming of the Kingdom of God, that is the Kingdom of a New Kind of God. But we cannot be rid of (the Old) God, thought Nietzsche . . .

". . . because we still have faith in grammar"

This structuring paradox of desire is also present in the Vedic hymns, in which the paradigmatic first sacrifice is performed according to an already-existing script. One famous verse reflecting this paradox occurs in two significant hymns in the *Ṛg Veda*. The verse reads: "With the sacrifice the gods sacrificed to the sacrifice. These were the first ritual laws (*Yajñena yajñam ayajanta devās tāni dharmāṇi parathamāni āsana*)." The word *yajña*, or "sacrifice," occurs three times: first as a noun in the instrumental (*yajñena*, or "with the sacrifice"), then in the accusative (*yajñam*, or "the sacrifice") and then in the verbal form (*ayajanta*, or "they sacrificed"). This grammatical trinity, besides being an instance of what Kimberly Patton calls "divine reflexivity,"[28] creates a paradoxical picture of sacrifice in which it is simultaneously an action, the instrument through which the action is accomplished, and the direct object of that action. The verse first appears in *ṚV* 1.164.50, the obscure *Asya Vamāsya* hymn, and then again in the later *ṚV* 10.90.10, "The Hymn of Puruṣa." We will look at each occurrence of the verse in turn, beginning with *ṚV* 1.164.

The *Asya Vamāsya*, also known as the "Riddle of the Sacrifice," has been a perennial topic for Vedicists since it was first introduced to the Western world in 1875 by the German Orientalist Martin Haug. Haug identifies the "Riddle of the Sacrifice" as a collection of riddling verses from the ritual verbal contest or *brahmodya* that is part of the more elaborate sacrifices. Since it is a type of anthology and not a cohesive whole, Haug argues, it is useless to try and understand it as such, although other scholars have tried to read it that way. The hymn's ritual uses are detailed in other parts of the Vedic corpus. The *Aitareya Āraṇyaka* prescribes that it be recited in the twelve-day Mahāvrata ritual connected to the Vrātyas we looked at in the last chapter. Both the *Laws of Manu* (2.251) and the *Ṛgvidhāna* of Śaunaka command a Brahmin who has stolen gold to recite it as expiation.[29] And two of its most well-known verses, 34 and 35, are part of the script for the *brahmodya* performed as part of the Horse Sacrifice. Those verses, read as question and response, are as follows:

34. I ask you about the farthest end of the earth; I ask where is the navel of the world; I ask about the seed of the potent stallion; I ask about the final abode of speech.
35. This altar is the farthest end of the earth; this sacrifice is the navel of the world; this *soma* is the seed of the potent stallion; this Brahmin here is the final abode of speech.[30]

In a 2000 article, Jan E. M. Houben revisits *ṚV* 1.164 and argues against Haug, identifying the hymn not as a compendium of Vedic riddles but as a cohesive text tied to the Pravargya ritual described in the commentarial tradition of the *Yajur Veda*.[31] The Pravargya is an offering of hot milk or *gharma* made during the performance of an elaborate *soma* sacrifice to the Aśvins, the twin horse gods. The name of the ritual means "to be placed on" and refers to the ritual vessel in which the milk is heated and the construction, use, and disposal of it are the main parts of the rite.

A solemn Vedic sacrifice requires priests representing the schools proceeding from each of the four Vedas to participate. Typically there is a Hotṛ priest of the *Ṛg Veda*, an Adhvaryu of the *Yajur Veda*, an Udgātṛ of the *Sāma Veda*, and a Brahmin of the *Atharva Veda*. It is the Adhvaryu priest whose special responsibility is the *pravargya*. He is required to ritually construct the pot from clay, heat it on the sacrificial fire, milk the cow into the heated vessel, producing a hiss and cloud of steam, and make the offering of the hot milk.[32] Before its performance the sacrificer memorizes the verses of the Pravargya in another ceremony called the "Intermediate Initiation" (Avāntaradikśita). Other than the fact that the former is learned during the latter, Houben argues for a further connection between the Pravargya and the Avāntaradikśita by noting the parallel processes undergone by the sacrificer during the Avāntaradikśita and the *pravargya* pot during the Pravargya rite. The sacrificer is sent outside the village to memorize his verses, while the pot is prepared out of sight; the sacrificer is blindfolded, while the pot is wrapped in an antelope's skin; the sacrificer cannot lie down, while the pot is suspended in a sling; the sacrificer receives inspiration, while the pot receives "life"; the sacrificer chants the verses, while the heated pot makes a bubbling and hissing sound when milk is poured into it.[33]

In Vedic ritual, the sacrificial implements often take on mythical lives of their own and the clay pot used in the Pravargya is no exception. The pot is alternately called *gharma* ("heat," after the offering it contains), *pravargya* (after the ritual and the action it names), *mahavīra* ("great hero"), *samraj* ("great king"), and, significantly, the "head of Makha," to which we will return later.[34] The myth connected with the Pravargya ritual is found, among other places, in the *Śatapatha Brāhmaṇa*. It contains allusions to the story of Indra beheading Makha in *ṚV* 10.171.2 and the beheading and then re-heading (with a horse's head) of Dadhyañc, two popular variants of the "beheaded sacrifice" motif. In his introduction to the fifth volume of the *Śatapatha Brāhmaṇa*, Julius Eggeling interprets the Pravargya complex, which he finds to be much too solemn and complicated for such a simple (and even optional, according to the texts) rite within the *soma* sacrifice:

> As the sun is the head of the universe—or, in figurative language, the head of Prajāpati, the world-man—so its earthly, and earthen, counterpart, the Mahâvîra pot, is the head of Vish*n*u, the sacrificial man, and the Sacrificer; and this ceremony is thus performed in order to complete the universe and sacrifice, as well as the divine body of the Sacrificer, by supplying them with their head, their crowning-piece, so to speak; and to imbue them with the divine essence of life and light.[35]

Eggeling concludes that the *pravargya* pot represents the sun and imbues the sacrificer with the sun's power. But the power of the sun would be too much for a man who has not partaken of the ritual beverage *soma*. And it is for this reason that the Pravargya is optional; it is performed before the actual pressing of the *soma* plant, so a sacrificer who is undergoing his first *soma* ritual (i.e., one who has never partaken of the *soma* before) would not be able to safely perform it and would therefore skip the rite completely. But if the sacrificer *has* ingested *soma* before, he can perform the preliminary Pravargya, and it will not matter that he has not drunk the *soma* in *this* particular ritual, since having quaffed the *soma* once is enough to fortify one to share in the power of the sun anytime thereafter.

The ritual can end either with the pot and implements being arranged in the shape of the sun or in the shape of a man; according to the text the *pravargya* pot is the head of the sacrifice, reunited with the cosmic body through the ritual. Heesterman sees this element of the Pravargya as clear evidence that the ritual is "closely related to the rites of the brick altar with which it shares the proceedings of fetching the clay, the manufacture of a fired clay pot and the concern with the 'head of the sacrifice' (real ones under the brick altar, an imaginary one represented by the *mahāvīra* pot of the Pravargya)."[36] From the same evidence, Houben concludes that the Pravargya and thus the "Riddle of the Sacrifice" are evidence of the way in which the ritual structure of Vedic sacrifice, whose "open-ended elements . . . invited elaboration and speculation, and, hence, unavoidably also diversification,"[37] functioned as a kind of philosophical forum or laboratory for a speculative philosophy:

> As in ancient Greece, philosophy developed in dialogue with the mythologemes of a sacred tradition. But there it was the written transmission of ideas which enabled subsequent thinkers to deal with similar problems and make progress in certain directions. In ancient India, where writing came into use for transmitting philosophical thought at a later date than in Greece . . . it was initially the ritually stabilized transmission of ideas which enabled successive thinkers to do the same.[38]

We have seen that the "Riddle of the Sacrifice" and the Pravargya ritual to which it is connected show us a trail leading back to the very literally foundational sacrifice signified by the heads under the altar while its riddling proto-philosophical elements simultaneously point the way up and out into the giddy heights of post-Vedic mysticism. Which trail are we to follow? In *Sacrifice*, Girard explains that "[mimetic] theory is a kind of radicalized Durkheimianism that, far from moving in the direction of the rite, that is to say, its effacement of violence, seeks instead to return to the violence and quite deliberately takes the myth the wrong way."[39] In the case of Vedic myth, this strategy is further complicated by the many red herrings one finds along the way. Both the Pravargya rite and the "Riddle of the Sacrifice" are practically shouting and waving their arms as they gesture toward the mythical and primordial sacrifice of Puruṣa. But in a more subtle and secretive way, continued through the guru-to-pupil transmissions of the esoteric tradition, they are also calling our attention to the victims whose heads are hidden under the foundation of the altar (later, the temple) and the violence to which they were subject.

How to Keep Your Head

In the endless contests between the gods and the demons, Girard notes, "there is always an object that both groups want to secure exclusive possession of. It is often something as enormous, splendid, fantastic as the imagined antagonists themselves."[40] As Dupuy's theory of pseudo-narcissism suggests, this object is an illusion produced by mutually arising desire. In a great number of Sanskrit myths, that splendid object is identified as "the head of the sacrifice." Heesterman explains:

> In the *Ṛg Veda* the head in expressions like the head of the universe, the head of the bull, or the head of the cow appears to indicate an invisible and mysterious place where the essence, especially of Agni and Soma, is hidden. The head, then, is associated with or contains a treasure or secret that is the essence of the universe. Everything depends upon obtaining the head, and the gods have to contend for its possession.[41]

The head of the sacrifice becomes an important mythological trope in Vedic and classical literature, but it is also the subject of a riddle, or what Heesterman calls an aporia at the center of the ritual: The sacrifice calls for severed heads but also forbids the severing of heads. The fragmentary *Vādhūla Brāhmaṇa*[42] or *Vādhūla Anvākhyāna* (sometimes called the *Vādhūla Sūtra*)[43] tells a story in which a king of the famous Kuru clan obtains the secret *Paśuśīrṣa Vidyā*, "the knowledge of the victim's head." Heesterman argues that the esoteric knowledge of the *Paśuśīrṣa Vidyā* is "the riddle contained in the structure of the ritual, the urge to encompass the world from which it has broken away . . . in its most pregnant form."[44] In order for the sacrifice to work, a human head must be buried along with four animal heads underneath the first layer of bricks used to form the altar. And since everything used in the sacrifice must be properly consecrated, the heads must be obtained ritually. But this presents a problem because Vedic sacrifice does not call for decapitation. What then is the source of these heads?

Here the mythical texts and the ritual texts (the śrauta sūtras) are in sharp disagreement. The myths of the head of the sacrifice strongly suggest the presence of a victim whose decapitation provides a temporary peace in the struggles between the gods and the demons. One especially suggestive myth is found in *Taittirīya Saṃhitā* 2.5.1.1. The story concerns Viśvarūpa, a figure that stands in between the gods and the demons, acting as a chaplain to the gods but a kinsman to the demons and promising each side to give them the sacrificial share reserved for the other. With his three heads, Viśvarūpa consumes the *soma*, the *sūrā* (another, probably alcoholic, intoxicating drink), and the sacrificial cakes, leading Indra to fear that Viśvarūpa will become the new Indra.[45] Accordingly, Indra decapitates Viśvarūpa, saddling himself with the sin of brahminicide and causing the demon's father Tvaṣṭṛ to become angry and cast his *soma* into the fire, thereby creating Indra's new rival, Vṛtra. If the mythmakers saw this story as an explanation of *Paśuśīrṣa Vidyā*, then clearly the head must come from a defeated sacrificial, not to say mimetic, rival.

But the ritual texts must eliminate the sacrificial contest and the rival and find another way to obtain these heads that preserves the integrity of the single-sacrificer model. The *Kātyāyana Śrauta Sūtra* (16.1.18) makes no bones about the need for a human sacrifice (along with the sacrifice of a goat, a ram, a horse, and a bull) to obtain the heads of the five sacrificeable animals (humans are animals too, in this case) that are buried beneath the altar.[46] To get around the fact that Vedic sacrifice does not include cutting off a victim's head, the text simply adds that in this case, the victim should be decapitated after it is smothered. The *Śatapatha Brāhmaṇa* (6.2.1.39) says that this is no longer practiced and that one need only sacrifice a goat. The most painstaking of the Vedic ritualists, Baudhāyana, saves the Vedic ritual from pollution while not leaving out the heads by instructing the sacrificer to also perform, outside the enclosure, a separate, agonistic ritual complete with dicing to obtain the five necessary heads, which one of the officiants will then come and pick up.[47] The *Mānava Śrauta Sūtra* (6.1.2.23) offers still another solution, claiming that the human head must be the head of a Vaiṣya killed by lightning (Indra's weapon) or an arrow, which can be obtained by conquering an enemy on the battlefield. Here, the sacrificial struggle is expelled from the Brahmin's enclosure and relegated to the realm of war, the business of the Kṣatriya.[48]

We can conceive of the secret of the *Paśuśīrṣa Vidyā* in a number of ways other than the simple knowledge of the heads beneath the altar. Heesterman points to the myths of Namuci, Dadhyañc, Makha, and Viśvarūpa (all of whom are decapitated by Indra), which the tradition presents as illustrations of the secret of the *Paśuśīrṣa Vidyā*, arguing that in each case the head "is associated with and contains a treasure or secret that is the essence of the universe."[49] He continues: "Without belonging unequivocally to the asuras, the rivals of the gods—[the heads] seem to be intermediary figures between the two parties of devas and asuras, in a position to grant favor to either of them—[the asuras] try to withhold the treasure from Indra and the devas."[50] The *Paśuśīrṣa Vidyā*, then, is the knowledge that, despite the absence of a rival in the classical Vedic ritual, sacrifice is always a contest, and moreover a contest with no winner or loser that can only repeat itself ad infinitum.

Although it is never made explicit, there also seems to be a connection between the *Paśuśīrṣa Vidyā* and the other piece of secret knowledge that the gods are always trying to keep from the demons in their endless arms race, the *mṛtasaṃjīvinīvidyā*, the resurrection spell possessed by the Bhṛgus. In the story of the Aśvins, Dadhyañc, and Cyavana (one of the paradigmatic "head of the sacrifice myths," which we will discuss below), the secret possessed by the Aśvins, Heesterman notes, "seems also to involve the knowledge of severing and restoring the head," and what is this but another type of resurrection spell?[51] The connection between the *Paśuśīrṣa Vidyā* and the *mṛtasaṃjīvinīvidyā* is evident in the famous story of the Bhṛgu sage Jamadagni and his wife Reṇukā, whom he orders his son Paraśurāma to decapitate.[52] After the deed is done, Jamadagni rewards Paraśurāma's willingness to commit matricide by restoring her head and bringing her back to life as only a Bhṛgu can. In the case of the *Paśuśīrṣa Vidyā*, we have a ritual aporia that comes close to a deconstruction of the sacrifice; in a sense, it is analogous to the "things hidden since the foundation of the world" that Jesus promises to reveal to his disciples in Matthew 13:35.

As Heesterman notes, the Vedic ritualists not only exclude violence from the sacrificial enclosure, stipulating that the victim must be killed outside of its confines, they also exclude the language of killing, substituting the euphemisms *saṃjñapayati*, "to cause to consent," and *ālabhate*, a middle-voice verb meaning "to take hold of."[53] The head of the sacrifice presents a problem for this sanitized version of the ritual. In myth, stories of the head of the sacrifice are connected with the figure of the horse-headed Dadhyañc (more on whom below) and the canine figure of Makha, while the figure of Prajāpati represents the single sacrificer, the answer to the riddle, the victim, sponsor, and officiant in one. The heads under the altar, like the eponymous telltale heart beating in the chest of the victim concealed beneath his murderer's floorboards in Poe's story, attests to the violent relations that lie hidden beneath the surface of the bloodless single-sacrificer model of classical ritual.

"Creation *avant la lettre*"

The "Hymn of Puruṣa" in *ṚV* 10.90 is one of the latest hymns added to the *Ṛg Veda*, as indicated by its references to already existing *Ṛg*, *Yajur*, and *Sāma* Vedas (the *Atharva Veda* is later still) and the four-tier social hierarchy of Brahmin, Kṣatriya, Vaiṣya, and Śūdra that developed in the very late Vedic period. The hymn repeats the *yajñena-yajñam-ayajanta* verse ("With the sacrifice the gods sacrificed to the sacrifice") from "The Riddle of the Sacrifice," but this time the word *yajña* is identified not just with the ritual but also with the sacrificial victim, who is altogether absent in the other hymn. In this repetition of the enigma of sacrifice we do have a victim, but it is not the victim whose head is under the altar. It is the victim transformed into a god. Giving her gloss of the passage, Doniger notes:

> The meaning is that Puruṣa was both the victim that the gods sacrificed and the divinity to whom the sacrifice was dedicated; that is, he was both the subject and object of the sacrifice. Through a typical Vedic paradox, the sacrifice itself creates the sacrifice.[54]

In this hymn, straightforward compared to "The Riddle of the Sacrifice," the cosmic giant Puruṣa truly becomes the transcendental signifier when the gods take him apart to create the world and his dismemberment serves as the origin of the subject-object distinction. The paradox we examined earlier remains, but now it is accompanied by a spectacularly violent display that completely effaces any traces of a real victim. The Puruṣa hymn presents a new paradox in which the presence of a divine victim hides a real victim. In his treatment of the hymn, Girard writes:

> Purusha suggests something like a double of reality as a whole; he is a creation *avant la lettre*, containing the multitude of beings in a form that remains poorly differentiated. It is from this still formless form that the universe will emerge, by virtue of the first sacrifice. . . . The fact that all the sacrificers preexist the first, original creation is not explained any more than their number, which is, by all evidence, great.[55]

Girard sees in the mysteriously assembled group of gods and sages at the sacrifice of Puruṣa another instance of the murderous mob, retroactively transformed into "sacrificers" by the repetition of their spontaneous lynching.

Heesterman is the Indologist who has the most sympathy for Girard's work, responding to the arguments made in *Violence and the Sacred* and Walter Burkert's *Homo Necans* with the pronouncement that "[faced] with such closely argued and consequential studies, which in Girard's case even purports to a total anthropology of civilization, it is hard to dismiss summarily the concept of sacrifice as a product of yesterday's scholarly imagination."[56] As we have seen, Heesterman draws a distinction between sacrifice and ritual in a way that is analogous to Girard's distinction between the founding murder and the repetition that elevates it into sacrifice. And like Girard, Heesterman turns to the crucifixion in order to explain the paradox.

> [We] should be careful in identifying sacrifice with its ritual. There is at least one documented case of a sacrifice *without* sacrificial ritual—the Crucifixion. In actual fact it was not a sacrifice at all, but a judicial execution and an ignominious one at that. Yet, for all we know, it came almost immediately to be recognized as a sacrifice. It was even seen as the ultimate sacrifice, instituting an entirely new, eschatological order.[57]

For Girard, the crucifixion is a non-sacrificial event and a revelation of the sacrificial mechanism that was set into motion by the founding murder. For Heesterman, it is a judicial execution brought into the sacrificial economy after the fact. Girard is in agreement with Heesterman, though, in that he sees that the Christian community did not comprehend the revelation of the crucifixion and re-mythologized it by embedding it in the narrative of "Christus Victor"[58] and what Girard calls "sacrificial" Christianity.[59]

Heesterman posits a space or interval between the execution of Jesus of Nazareth and the crucifixion of Christ where ritual in the form of the communal commemorative meal and narrative in the form of atonement theology transform the death of Jesus into a sacrifice. Girard too, despite his unequivocally non-sacrificial interpretation of the crucifixion, sees Christianity as a concealment mechanism or a "ritualization" as Heesterman would have it. For all of his recent defenses of the Catholic Church and Benedict XVI, following Girard's theory one would have to see Christianity as a giant mistake, a religion founded on the event that was meant to destroy religion. Early in his work, Girard even suggests reading theology in the same way we read myths: "Instead of rejecting the theological basis [of sacrifice] outright, qua abstraction (which is the same, in effect, as passively accepting it), let us expose its assumptions to critical examination."[60]

Like Girard, Heesterman sees sacrifice, especially Vedic sacrifice, as a mechanism for controlling and channeling violence that if left unchecked would engulf the community. But Vedic sacrifice, rather than an unconscious mechanism, is a deliberately strategic practice designed and performed by a priestly class who, unlike the mob that crucified Jesus, know exactly what they do. Comparing sacrifice in the Vedas to sacrifice in the Christian tradition, Heesterman writes:

> On the face of it there is hardly any common ground with the history of the Christian liturgy—valorization of a unique sacrifice on the one hand, breaking the self-perpetuating cycle of sacrifice on the other—but in both cases the development is set off by a catastrophic sacrifice that ritual is called on to counteract and lead into beneficial channels.[61]

The terms that Heesterman uses—the "inner conflict" of tradition, the "broken world" of sacrifice, the "conundrum" of the king's authority—reflect his vision of Vedic sacrifice as an institution in a state of collapse from its very inception, but somehow able to survive longer than it has any right to through the ingenious machinations of ritual. Ultimately Heesterman's conception of sacrifice is firmly grounded in the "mediation" school of thought exemplified in the work of Mauss. But his idea of how sacrifice sustains itself is related to Girard's theory of myth: Just as Girard sees the role of myth as the elimination of all traces of violence from its account of the founding murder, Heesterman sees the main purpose of the elaborations of Vedic sacrifice as the "elimination of death and catastrophe from the ritual."[62]

For Girard, the revelation of the Gospel makes it increasingly difficult for myth to keep the sacrificial system intact by blinding its participants. For Heesterman, it was the emergence of the new concepts of dharma and *ahiṃsa*, or "non-violence," out of the Vedic sacrificial system itself during the "Axial Age" between 800 and 200 B.C.E. that spelled its collapse. But

Heesterman's argument that the Brahmin ritualists sought to exclude contest from the sacrifice is only a partial explanation. Along with contest, they eliminated one of the two sacrificial contestants. In so doing, they removed what they rightly perceived as the true danger—a defeated enemy who can return to take vengeance and thereby set off an escalating feud of mimetic violence. In the much remarked-upon story of Śunaḥśepa, the Brāhmaṇas reveal the expelled figure and identify him with the key to understanding the sacrifice and through it, the world. Like the Vrātyas, Indra, Śiva, and the other lycanthropic figures we have identified so far,[63] Śunaḥśepa is an avatar of the Indo-European **bhlagh(s)-men* who lives out his life between his consecration and his sacrificial immolation. Śunaḥśepa is Puruṣa, identified by Dumézil as the "*Remède*." But he can also be a poison.

Finding the *Pharmakos*

In his 1973 essay on Shakespeare, structuralism, and Northrop Frye, Girard introduces Jacques Derrida's investigation of the *pharmakos* as a line of inquiry that parallels his own:

> The generative effect [of the single victim mechanism], which remains for the most part hidden in [Frye's] *Anatomy of Criticism* is more fully uncovered in the work of Jacques Derrida, notably in . . . *La Pharmacie de Platon.* Derrida shows, quite convincingly, I believe, that, in the text of Plato, the difference between Socrates and the Sophists results from an arbitrary expulsion of the latter, invisible to both the author and the reader because it is effected through an unconsciously systematic use of certain semantic ambiguities. The pivotal word, lo and behold, is the word *pharmakos* itself and its cognates, notably *pharmakon* which means good and bad drug, medicine and poison. The drug can work either way, just like violence itself which is poison but may become its own cure through the single-victim effect and the ritual reenactments of that effect.[64]

In archaic Greek religion, the *pharmakos* was a human victim chosen because of a physical deformity or ugliness and ritually expelled from the city either as part of a calendrical festival or during a period of crisis.[65] In *Violence and the Sacred*, Girard compares the *pharmakos* to the figure of Oedipus, as we saw in our discussion of Karṇa as a tragic hero.[66] In *Victim of the Muses*, Todd M. Compton argues that the ritual of the *pharmakos* is deeply connected to a different literary genre, namely poetry, not just in Greek society, but in the wider Indo-European world. Compton argues that the *pharmakos* "provides an essential foundation for the study of the legendary lives of the Greek poets . . . [especially] Aesop, Hipponax and Tyrtaeus."[67] He also connects the *pharmakos* to the werewolf and the very wolfish figure of Starkarðr, the Danish hero-poet-magician described in the thirteenth century Scandinavian *Gautrekssaga* as having an "ugly muzzle, long snout, wolf-grey hair and hanging paws, rough neck and rugged hide."[68] In the next two sections, we will look briefly at Starkarðr and then turn to the figure Dumézil identifies as his Indian counterpart, Śiśupāla.

Starkarðr the Poet-Warrior

Starkarðr is named after his grandfather, a misshapen four-armed giant who abducts and impregnates a human woman before Thor (the Norse counterpart of Indra) slays him and rescues her. Later the woman gives birth to the giant's son, a normal human male named Storvirkr, who later becomes the father of the hero Starkarðr. But when Starkarðr is just a boy, the king Haraldr kills his father and takes him into his household to raise alongside his own son, Vikar. After they have grown as close as brothers, Vikar and Starkarðr are separated when yet another king kills Haraldr and takes Vikar as hostage, leaving Starkarðr to be raised by one of his vassals. But when Vikar and Starkarðr are grown, they join forces again to win back Vikar's father's realm. Trouble befalls them once more when the winds die in the middle of a raiding expedition and leave Vikar, Starkarðr, and their fleet stranded on an island. After consulting an oracle, the men learn that only a human sacrifice to Odin can bring the winds back. They all draw straws and are horrified when the lot falls to King Vikar, prompting the men to delay the rite until some loophole can be found.

Later that night, a stranger wakes up Starkarðr and summons him to a council of the gods, where the stranger reveals himself as Odin and informs Starkarðr that he must be the one to sacrifice his friend. Odin goes on to say that if he does this, not only will the winds return, but Starkarðr himself will receive divine power and Vikar will be reborn in glory in the realm of the gods. At this point Thor, the slayer of Starkarðr's giant namesake and grandfather, rises to curse Starkarðr. What follows is a duel-like exchange of curses and blessings in which Thor curses Starkarðr and Odin mitigates each curse.

> Thor, taking the floor immediately, declares that he cannot bear good will toward a young man whose grandfather was a giant whom he had had to kill and whose grandmother, in her girlhood, had preferred this giant to him—to him, Thor, the "Thor of the Æsir"! Concluding, he imposes a first fate, a bad one: "Starkarðr will have no children." Odin formulates a compensation: "Starkarðr will have three human life spans." But Thor rejoins: "He will commit a villainy, a *niðingsverk,* in each." And the duel continues: "He will always," says Odin, "have the best arms and the best raiments." "He will have," says Thor, "neither land nor real property." Odin: "He will have fine furnishings." Thor: "He will never feel he has enough." Odin: "He will have success and victory in every combat." Thor: "He will receive a grave wound in every combat." Odin: "He will have the gift of poetry and improvisation." Thor: "He will forget all he has composed." Odin: "He will appeal to the well-born and the great." Thor: "He will be despised by the common folk."[69]

The next day, Starkarðr convinces Vikar's men to hold a "mock sacrifice" in which Vikar stands on a stump and places loosely around his neck a calf's intestine looped around a low branch not high enough to hang a man by.[70] Starkarðr then pokes a flimsy reed at the king and says, "I give thee to Odin." At this moment the calf's intestine becomes a rope and tightens around the king's neck while the branch begins to pull him in the air and the reed become a spear that pierces his body, killing him.[71]

Śiśupāla against the Gods

Dumézil connects Starkarðr to the Indian epic figure Śiśupāla, whose story is recounted in *MBh* 2.33–42, shortly after the story of the human-sacrificing king Jarāsaṃdha and just before the ill-fated dicing match that costs the Pāṇḍavas their kingdom. Śiśupāla is a scion of the Cedi dynasty, born "braying like an ass" with a monstrous four-armed and three-eyed form. To understand the meaning of this portentous birth, Śiśupāla's parents consult the household priest and ministers. But suddenly a disembodied voice addresses the father, "King, he is born as your son, illustrious and powerful, so do not fear him, but watch over him carefully. You are not to be his death and his time to die has not yet come. His death, the one who will slay him with a sword, has already been born."

The voice, judging by its speech, has assumed that Śiśupāla's father intends to kill the infant and warns him against it. But the queen bears her son a mother's love rather than a father's enmity and begs the voice to tell her who will be responsible for the child's death. The voice answers, "The one on whose lap he sits when he loses his extra arms and eye, that one will be his death." After this pronouncement, all of the kings of the earth begin arriving at the Cedis' capital to see the four-armed, three-eyed infant. One day, Kṛṣṇa comes to pay his respects and when the queen places Śiśupāla on his lap, the boy's extra arms fall off and his third eye disappears into his forehead. Realizing what this means, the queen falls to her knees and begs Kṛṣṇa to spare her son's life. Knowing that Kṛṣṇa is a righteous prince and would not harm an innocent man, the queen also understands that Śiśupāla will have to commit some sin to bring about his own death at the hands of Kṛṣṇa, so she makes him promise to pardon Śiśupāla for one hundred capital crimes.

A year later, during the portion of Yudhiṣṭhira's Royal Consecration Sacrifice in which the sacrificing king dispenses gifts to his guests, Śiśupāla comes to the Pāṇḍava court along with royalty from all over northern India, including Kṛṣṇa, who is after all a prince of the Yādava line. But when Yudhiṣṭhira gives Kṛṣṇa the guest gift of the highest honor, Śiśupāla flies into a rage. He accuses the Pāṇḍavas of playing favorites, awarding the highest honor to Kṛṣṇa over all the other guests more deserving by dint of their age, the size of their kingdoms, or their role as gurus. After a rejoinder from Bhīṣma, who makes the case that Kṛṣṇa is the supreme godhead (which everyone in the epic seems to forget from time to time), the highest honor falls to Kṛṣṇa over Śiśupāla's objections.

Fuming over his humiliation and what he sees as the favoritism of the Pāṇḍavas, Śiśupāla waits until the guest gift ceremony is done and then conspires with the other kings present at the sacrifice to disrupt the ritual and attack the Pāṇḍavas. This mounting hostility of the guests does not go unnoticed by Yudhiṣṭhira, and the king confers with Bhīṣma.[72] Bhīṣma tells Yudhiṣṭhira not to worry and makes a speech that is worth quoting in full:

> Do not be afraid, tiger of the Kuru clan. Can a dog kill a lion? This is an auspicious (*śiva*) and well-trodden (*sunapīta*) path, which I have chosen before. These kings of the earth are banding together and barking like a pack of dogs surrounding a sleeping lion; they are standing in front of the sleeping lion of the Vṛṣṇis [Kṛṣṇa] and barking like dogs in front of a lion. And as long as [Kṛṣṇa] remains sleeping, that man-lion king of the Cedis Śiśupāla makes lions of them of all. Oh best of kings, that fool Śiśupāla seems like he wants to lead all those kings to a man straight to the throne of Yama [Death]. Surely [Kṛṣṇa] is ready to take away the glory of Śiśupāla, oh Bharata. His judgment has gone astray, the king of the Cedis' judgment and that of all the other kings, son of Kuntī. Fortunate are you, oh sensible prince! Whomever [Kṛṣṇa] wishes to take, his senses become deranged like those of the Cedi king. [Kṛṣṇa] is the beginning and the end of the fourfold creation upon the triple world, Yudhiṣṭhira![73]

In his speech reassuring Yudhiṣṭhira, Bhīṣma makes some noteworthy comments. First he implies to Yudhiṣṭhira that this conspiracy against Kṛṣṇa is just a farce, a well-traveled path that Śiśupāla is walking, one that may well run parallel to *la route antique des hommes pervers*. Then he compares Śiśupāla and his allies to a pack of dogs surrounding the lion that is Kṛṣṇa. And finally, he strongly suggests that Kṛṣṇa is behind this whole masquerade, implanting madness in the mind of Śiśupāla in order to take away his glory (*tejas*). The Girardian elements are all here: A lynch mob is forming and acting on impulse they mistakenly believe to be their own, but in this case the intended victim is manipulating them every step of the way.

But Bhīṣma's speech is not an aside to Yudhiṣṭhira, unheard by the rest of the company, like the ones Homeric heroes are so fond of making. Śiśupāla, who has been with them the entire time, responds with insults and threats, listing all the misdeeds of Bhīṣma and Kṛṣṇa, including the treachery they so lately used to kill the human-sacrificing king Jarāsaṃdha. After hearing his words, Yudhiṣṭhira's brother Bhīma is possessed by a fury, and has to be restrained from attacking Śiśupāla by Bhīṣma, who then explains the latter's monstrous birth and destiny to die by Kṛṣṇa's hand. Again, Bhīṣma's words here are significant:

> It is not the Cedi king's own idea to challenge [Kṛṣṇa]. Surely it was the decision of the lord of the world, Kṛṣṇa himself. Unless he were possessed by the gods, no king on earth would dare insult me like this defiler of his clan has, oh Bhīma. He must be an inseparable member of the body of [Kṛṣṇa], Oh prince of the strong arms, and [Kṛṣṇa] wants to get it back. That is why the evil-minded Cedi king roars as fierce as a lion, paying no heed to any of us.[74]

It is clear, at least to Bhīṣma, that Śiśupāla's doomed desire to fight Kṛṣṇa is coming from outside him and is part of the god's cosmic play. But even announcing this fact in front of everyone does nothing to give anyone pause, least of all Śiśupāla himself, who responds by praising the prowess and nobility of the Kaurava warriors and insults Bhīṣma by saying that he lives at the mere pleasure of the more powerful kings who surround him, just as the *bhūlinga* bird, who feeds on the morsels of flesh stuck in the jaws of a lion, lives at the pleasure of the lion who allows her to do it.

This provokes a response in Bhīṣma, who fires back, "So I live at the pleasure of the kings? These kings whom I count as no better than straw (*tṛṇa*)?" The war of words now spreads to the wider assembly that Bhīṣma has just disparaged and someone shouts, "This evil and insolent old Bhīṣma is not worthy of our forgiveness. Let the angry kings band together and kill him properly, like a beast of sacrifice! Or else burn him in a fire of straw!" After telling the kings in no uncertain terms just how much their threats scare him (very little), Bhīṣma calls on them to stop their talk and to challenge Kṛṣṇa to a duel, saying, "Whoever's spirit is eager for death, let him challenge Kṛṣṇa the Mādhava, wielder of bow and mace, to a duel until he is struck down and enters the body of this god!" Śiśupāla readily agrees and proclaims that he will now kill Kṛṣṇa and then lay waste to all the Pāṇḍavas who stood by and allowed him to take the supreme gift over all those who were more deserving. At this Kṛṣṇa enumerates to the assembly all the crimes of Śiśupāla, which presumably total one hundred, the number he promised Śiśupāla's mother he would forgive. He also mocks Śiśupāla for unsuccessfully attempting to win the hand of Kṛṣṇa's wife Rukminī, but having no more success in getting her than a Śūdra would have in hearing a Vedic recitation. Śiśupāla makes one last jab at Kṛṣṇa, taunting him for admitting that he came second to Rukminī, but doesn't get much further because Kṛṣṇa throws his discus and cuts off his speech along with his head.

This remarkable story raises some important questions about the classical Hindu understanding of sacrifice and divinity. First there is the issue of Śiśupāla's monstrous birth. The text is clear that Śiśupāla's form is to be regarded as monstrous, but significantly, he closely resembles the iconography of the high gods, especially Śiva, who is often pictured with four arms and three eyes (the third eye being the mark of yogic power). Why then, is Śiśupāla's form considered so abominable? Is it because he represents a monstrous double of the gods, all of whom are present in the form of kings at Yudhiṣṭhira's coronation? This explanation is consistent with Dumézil's interpretation of the myth as representing a conflict between Kṛṣṇa-Viṣṇu and Rudra-Śiva. Dumézil notes that Śiśupāla's four-armed, three-eyed appearance, his name (Śiśa is a Vedic epithet of Rudra), and his affinity with the human-sacrificing king and Śiva devotee Jarāsaṃdha all mark him as a profoundly Śaiva figure, concluding:

> Śiśupāla is, as solidly by nature as he is ephemerally in form, a hero "on the side of Rudra-Śiva. . . ." And this is of great interest because the one who delivers him from his superfluous arms and eye, and with whom he will nonetheless remain to the end in a state of violent hostility, is Kṛṣṇa-Viṣṇu, a god of a completely different sort. In more than one regard the "opposite" of Rudra-Śiva, he will even be, in the Hindu trinity, his polar partner. Śiśupāla is thus found, from his earliest youth, in contradictory relationships with the two great gods.[75]

The epic consistently comes down on the side of those who hold Kṛṣṇa-Viṣṇu as the highest manifestation of divinity, so it is no surprise that the struggle between the two figures ends with Rudra-Śiva being absorbed into Kṛṣṇa-Viṣṇu, revealing that he is nothing but another aspect of the supreme god. Kṛṣṇa and Śiśupāla are in a kind of violent dialectic. Their first meeting turns the Śaiva monster into a human and sets him loose to wreak havoc on humanity for a bounded period of time, while the second meeting resolves the two opposites into a higher synthesis, accomplished through Kṛṣṇa's destruction and absorption of Śiśupāla.

This myth demonstrates an awareness of the figure of Śiva the outcast behind the ever-expanding transcendent god Prajāpati-Viṣṇu. In Śaiva mythology, it is a Prajāpati (Dakśa) who attempts to exclude Śiva from the sacrifice. In the story of Śiśupāla, Kṛṣṇa-Viṣṇu destroys the Śaiva hero at the sacrifice and absorbs him into his transcendent self. All these mythic and ritual patterns conform to a movement away from violent contest toward a new form of priest-centered sacrifice, based on the exclusion (or attempted exclusion) of this figure of the defeated party. In the next section, I will examine yet another incarnation of this figure, the Kavi, and its connection to the Greek *pharmakos*.

Pharmakos and Kavi: The Vaiṣṇava Critique, Part Two

The Vedic word "Kavi" refers to a priest who is also a seer and an initiate in the esoteric philosophy, as in *ṚV* 10.129.4: "Kavis seeking with wisdom in their hearts found the bond of the existent in the non-existent (*Sato bandhumasati niravindan hṛdi pratīṣyākavayo manīṣā*)." The Kavi also has a deep connection to the sacrificial priesthood. The word is related to the Greek terms *koiēs* ("a priest of Samothrace")[76] and *thuo-skoos* ("the priest who inspects the burnt offering") and is still more closely related to the identical term *kavi* in the ancient Iranian *Zend Avesta*. Jarrod Whitaker also points out the Kavi's connection to the Vedic cattle raider, arguing that the term extends from poet-priests to "sacrificers and chieftains, who should know hidden, secret, and true things in ritual performances."[77]

According to the Aryan migration hypothesis, the Iranian people and the Vedic people were part of the same group that came across Central Asia and only split apart when the Vedic people came into India around 1500 B.C.E. For this reason scholars are especially interested in differences between Indian and Iranian sources from around that period, since they allow us to construct an Indo-Iranian past that has not yet passed into what Dumézil calls "ultrahistory." It is of great interest then that in the Iranian materials the word *kavi* is used to refer to three different groups: a class of priests, a class of rulers opposed to the reforms of Zoroaster, and the royal dynasty of whom Zoroaster's patron Viśtāpa is the last. Comparing them with other priest-kings like the Lamas of Tibet and the Si Singa-mangaradja of the Sumatran Bataks, Indologist Jan Gonda concludes that the *kavi*s of ancient Iran may represent a similar class of sacral sovereigns:

> To conclude: it may be true that the institutions and ideas of Iranian kingship—which have been of paramount importance in the history of the Ancient Near East and have not failed to influence also the European conceptions of kingship—are to the historian of religions especially valuable because they offer a very unambiguous example of sacral kingship among Indo-European peoples.[78]

Along with a pre-Vedic sacral kingship (or at least a sacral chieftaincy), whose traces remain in the sense of *kavi*, there is another sense connected to poetic transmission, as in *kāvya*, the word used to describe high poetry in the classical tradition. For a better understanding, we can look at the fourteenth and fifteenth century Sanskrit critic Mallinātha's *Ghaṇṭāpatha*, a commentary on Bhāravi's sixth century epic poem *Kirātārjunīyah*. In his notes on the text, J. A. F. Roodbergen affirms that the word *kāvya*, known to the second century B.C.E. grammarian Pāṇini to refer to "a descendent of [a figure named] Kavi" and "the work of a *kavi*," has by this time come to have the sense of a special kind of descriptive activity.[79] The philologist Joseph Twadell Shipley connects *kavi* to the name of Laocoön, the Trojan priest of Apollo killed by snakes sent by the gods for his attempts to keep the Greek wooden horse out of the city, as well as the word *kudos*, a term Girard makes much of in his treatment of the Homeric texts in *Violence and the Sacred*.[80] It seems that the word *kavi* and the related term *kāvya* index a nexus of Indo-European ideas relating sacred kingship to sacrifice and to poetry.

Let us now return to Dumézil's speculative description of the actual sacrifice of a Brahmin or **bhlagh(s)-men* that provides the model for the sacrifice of Puruṣa:

> So in the spring and on other big occasions, an earthly Brahmin bled to make the universal sap rise in the world again and to restore the economic and political order of the world, like at the beginning a celestial man—a *remède*, a celestial Brahmin—gave his substance and his life force to make up the matter of the world itself.[81]

Dumézil uses the word *remède* to describe the sacrificial victim, conjuring up images of the *pharmakos* and the Kavi, whose sacred kingship derives from his status as a poison and a cure and whose contradictory nature is exemplified in the stories of Kāvya Uśanās (Śukra) that we examined in the previous chapter.

In contemporary Sri Lanka, we can see what may be a survival of the sort of Kavi embodied by Kāvya Uśanās in the deadly form of black magic called *vas kavi*, practiced by certain Buddhist monks despite religious injunctions against its use. The practice involves the recitation of certain esoteric mantras or verses. On the monks who practice this brand of sorcery, Gananath Obeyesekere remarks, "Psychologically viewed, these people are pathological murderers, and I suspect that some of them may actually administer poisons disguised as charms."[82] In the Sinhalese *vas kavi*, we see a literalization of the archaic Greek *pharmakon*, understood by Derrida as the "poisoned gift."

Kavi comes to mean "poet" in the classical age, but in the *Ṛg Veda* the term seems to refer to some sort of magico-sovereign "fashioner" akin to Varuṇa. "In short," writes Dumézil, "if the kavi has a patron among the sovereign gods, it is less Mitra, who is closer to the sacrificing priests, than Varuṇa, whom [*ṚV*] 5.13.1 calls the *divaḥ kaviḥ*, 'the kavi of heaven.'"[83] Beyond the technical and ritual specialization of the priests trained to perform the sacrifice, the Kavi has the power to create through language. And in the case of Kāvya Uśanās, this power is also conceived as the power to resurrect the dead. Just as *pharmakon* has the double meaning of both poison and antidote in the Greek as well as close associations with the sacrificial victim and with poetry, so the Kavi in the Vedic context represents the poet and the sacred sovereign with the power to both kill and resurrect.

Both the Scandinavian Starkarðr and Śiśupāla also have deep connections to improvisational poetry. In the case of Starkarðr, as Compton notes, "[The] link between poet and warrior is not obscure, for Starkarðr is an aggressive satirist. His verbal attack often accompanies physical attack."[84] Śiśupāla, while not as obviously poet-like, is still notable for his ability to hurl insults at Bhīṣma and Kṛṣṇa. In fact, given that their argument occurs in the context of the sacrificial ritual, the disputation between Bhīṣma and Śiśupāla can be seen as a very real form of the ritualized insults that are part of the *brahmodya* in the scripted Vedic rite. This brings us to another meaning of the term *kavi* argued by H. D. Velankar, namely the *kavi* as "god or man . . .

[who] can unravel the intricacies of an enigma, the central task of what he believes is the Vedic word contest."[85]

For Dumézil, the stories of Starkarðr and Śiśupāla both reflect a conflict between the priestly first function and the royal second function, represented respectively by Odin and Thor[86] in the Starkarðr myth and Viṣṇu and Śiva (increasingly taking over for Indra in the post-Vedic materials) in the Śiśupāla myth.[87] He notes that the three *niðingsverk* predicted by Thor correspond to the model of the "sins of the sovereign" (attributed to Indra in the previous chapter), one against each of the three Indo-European functions. Starkarðr is cursed to commit one sin in each of the three lifetimes granted to him and doomed to be reviled by the people; Śiśupāla is allowed one hundred mortal sins before Kṛṣṇa comes and takes his life. In each case, an unnaturally long lifespan is granted to the victim that will terminate because of some evil that he himself has committed. It is not hard to see in both of these myths the figure of the **bhlagh(s)-men* and the length of time granted to the sacrificial victim between his consecration and immolation.

By far the most remarkable thing about the Śiśupāla myth is that Bhīṣma takes every opportunity to reveal to everyone present the true nature of the struggle between Kṛṣṇa and Śiśupāla, but no one will listen. He compares the crowd to dogs around a sleeping lion. He points out that Kṛṣṇa has clearly driven Śiśupāla insane with rage to provoke a fight and reclaim the part of himself (the Śaiva part) that is trapped in Śiśupāla by killing him. Bhīṣma, famous throughout the epic for his great wisdom as well as his inflexible adherence to the "terrible vow" that gives him his name, seems to believe what he is seeing is no more real than a shadow play, but Śiśupāla and the angry mob he leads are locked into the illusion. When Śiśupāla says that Bhīṣma is like the bird the lion allows to pick the flesh from in between his teeth, but which will die the moment the lion decides to snap his jaws shut, he is accurately describing the moment at hand; Bhīṣma is surrounded by an overwhelming host of warriors who have suddenly become hostile toward him and his kin and could close in on them at any moment. But Bhīṣma is only amused by this, seeing the crowd as pawns in a game that only he is able to perceive, and tells them so. At that moment, the mob turns on Bhīṣma and demands that he be sacrificed. Knowing that he is not destined to be the victim of this violence, Bhīṣma then predicts what is about to happen, namely that Kṛṣṇa will slay Śiśupāla and absorb his *tejas*.

What we see in this story is a repeat of the Vaiṣṇava critique. It is a revelation of the sacrificial mechanism that is profoundly different from what Girard says is the meaning of the cross, namely the innocence of the victim, but it is a revelation nonetheless. Rather than the innocence of the victim (though that is basically what Bhīṣma is saying when he says that Kṛṣṇa is controlling Śiśupāla's actions), Bhīṣma's words reveal the illusory nature of the conflicts that are taking place at Yudhiṣṭhira's sacrifice. His pointing out that Kṛṣṇa, who is the destroyer in the *Mahābhārata*, is in control of what is happening (rather than Śiśupāla) foreshadows what Kṛṣṇa will tell Arjuna about the entire *Mahābhārata* war in the *Bhagavad Gītā*,[88] and the doomed and intransigent figure of Śiśupāla foreshadows both Karṇa and Duryodhana. In this episode of the epic, the rivalries that have been ritualized in the Vedic sacrifice are brought back to life, only to be revealed as no more real than the scripted ritual. It is also noteworthy that the word used for the court in which all this takes place is *sabhā*, whose earlier meaning is the clearing in the woods where the Vrātyas practiced their sacrifices.[89]

Girard might say that this reading only reinforces his theory that myth is always working to conceal the violence behind human institutions and that portraying a real killing as part of a predestined cosmic plan is only another way to cover it up. But if we look closer, we can see that there is a kind of revelation here, not the revelation of a literal foundational lynching, but an unmasking of the forces that govern that kind of spontaneous single-victim mob violence. Like a pre-classical Vedic sacrificer of the type Heesterman hypothesizes, Yudhiṣṭhira is putting his life at risk when he enters the ritual space. He invites his enemies to attend in large numbers, putting himself at their mercy. These gathered enemies then contest with each other for a prize, which he awards to Kṛṣṇa, putting himself at risk again, this time from the *ressentiment* of the losers. The anger of the mob, personified by the Dionysiac figure of Śiśupāla, is free-floating at first, attaching now to Bhīṣma, now to Kṛṣṇa, until it finally rebounds on Śiśupāla himself. The Śaivic forces of destruction are in evidence in Śiśupāla's monstrous-divine birth. Once born into the world, the violence Śiśupāla embodies must be allowed to run its course, so Kṛṣṇa gives him a limit to how much death and destruction he can engender (one hundred crimes), knowing that at the end of this time, he will absorb Śiśupāla's violence, and that of the crowd for which he speaks, back into himself. None of this, of course, destroys the sacrificial institution in the same way that Girard says the Gospels do, but it does relativize it as yet another system and not a transcendent reality. By the time of the *Mahābhārata*, the path of karma (represented by the performance of sacrifice) and the path of knowledge (represented by an understanding of the esoteric nature of sacrifice) are considered roughly equal, but both are subordinate to the path of devotion.[90]

Śiśupāla is guilty of the crimes for which he is killed, but the text gives us the distinct impression that he had no choice in the matter, that his guilt is more structural than moral. One thing is worth noting though: although the increasingly violent rage of the crowd does directly precede the death of Śiśupāla, it never attaches to him as it does to Bhīṣma. The same is the case for Vikar in story of Starkarðr: the crowd is panicked, but they do not latch onto Vikar as a victim. In both cases, it is the gods working through humans (Bhīṣma, Starkarðr) initiated into their mysteries that determine the identity of the victim. True demystification of the surrogate victim mechanism for Girard would proclaim the victim's innocence. In a kind of partial demystification, these stories elevate the selection of sacrificial victims from ritual technique to yet another form of religion subordinate to the realm of transcendent dharma associated with the god Viṣṇu. This rhetorical move is entirely in line with the doctrinal thrust of the *Mahābhārata*, a fusion of the Kṛṣṇaite Viṣṇu-Nārāyaṇa cult with the Vedic sacrificial system.[91] But this appropriation opens up a gap in the sacrificial system; Kṛṣṇa's duel with the doomed Śiśupāla is a kind of miniature hierophany that not only reveals Kṛṣṇa's divinity but also functions as a kind of exploration of theodicy. As Hiltebeitel notes, "[It] is easy to see how for many of [the epic's] characters which grow on our sympathies . . . even Śiśupāla and, on some strong occasions, Draupadī—the *Mahābhārata* is an argument with God."[92] Unlike the silent Puruṣa in the *Ṛg Veda*, the victims of the *Mahābhārata* get a chance to talk back.

Cyavana Visits Plato's Pharmacy: The *Śatapatha Brāhmaṇa*

The Bhṛgu sage Cyavana is the brother of Śukra, the high priest of the demons, and like his brother he is well known for opposing the gods, especially Indra. Stories of Cyavana predate those of Śukra, appearing first in the

Ṛg Veda, then later in the *Śatapatha Brāhmaṇa*, the *Jaiminīya Brāhmaṇa*, and the *Mahābhārata*. The most famous story about Cyavana contains many elements of the sacrificial crisis and specifically Plato's myth of the *pharmakon*, with the twin horse gods the Aśvins in the place of the Egyptian Thoth. Like Thoth, the Aśvins are considered to be the inventors of medicine and the physicians to the gods, the administrators of the *pharmakeia*. But, in keeping with the outsider status of the *pharmakos*, physicians, like actors and wandering beggars, are considered ritually impure and excluded from the sacrifice. Their type of knowledge may have its uses, but it has no place in the Brahmin's sanitized ritual enclosure. In the Dumézilian scheme, the Aśvin twins, like the Dioscuri of Greek mythology, are associated with the third function, represented in the social hierarchy by the Vaiṣya class and thus not part of the constant rivalry between Brahmins and Kṣatriyas. It is through the intervention of the sage Cyavana that they finally get a share of the sacrificial *soma*.

In *ŚB* 4.1.5, Cyavana is left behind on earth after the rest of the Bhṛgus (or the Angirases, the text is unsure to what Brahmin clan he belongs) have gone to Heaven. We do not know why they left him behind, but it may have been that he was too old to travel. The text does describe Cyavana as a very old man, using the phrase "decrepit and witch-like" (*jīrṇi* and *kṛtyārūpa*) three times. Some time later, when the king Śaryāta and his raiding party[93] settle near where the aged Cyavana is meditating, Śaryāta's sons stumble upon the "decrepit and witch-like" Cyavana and pelt him with stones and clods of earth. Enraged over his stoning, Cyavana lays a curse of discord on Śaryāta's house, making father fight with son and brother fight with brother. Searching for the cause of this spontaneous outbreak of intra-familial violence, Śaryāta gathers his cowherds together to see if they have seen anything unusual in the vicinity. They report to him the incident in which his sons had thrown rocks at a "decrepit and witch-like" old man and Śaryāta realizes immediately who the man is and what must be done. Bringing his daughter Sukanyā with him, Śaryāta goes to where Cyavana is and supplicates him, saying, "Namaste, sage. I have unknowingly offended you and I am giving you my daughter Sukanyā to atone for it. Now please let peace return my family." Then he leaves his daughter with the sage and returns to his people and orders them to break camp and be on their way, determined not to harm Cyavana again.

Later, after Cyavana has taken Sukanyā as his wife, the Aśvin twins come across the princess in their wanderings and, seeing how young and beautiful she is, try to talk her into abandoning her marriage to the "decrepit and witch-like" Brahmin and running off with them. Sukanyā refuses, saying that she will stay with the man to whom her father has given her. But Cyavana has seen his wife's conversation with the Aśvins from afar and goes to Sukanyā to find out what the twin gods were telling her. After Sukanyā relates their conversation and the Aśvins' taunt, Cyavana says to her: "If the Aśvins come again to seduce you, tell them they are in no position to disparage me because they are neither quite perfect (*susarva*) nor complete (*samṛddha*). When they ask what you mean, say, 'I will tell you after you have made my husband young again.'"

The Aśvins return some time later and Sukanyā follows her husband's instructions, telling them they are neither quite perfect nor complete. The Aśvins are taken aback at the implication that they are flawed in some way, so they agree to restore her husband's youth to find out what she means. In order to attain whatever age he desires, the Aśvins tell Cyavana, he should submerge himself in a nearby pool and then come out again. After he does what the Aśvins have said and emerges from the pool as a handsome youth, Cyavana keeps his promise and tells the Aśvins why they are not complete or perfect. "The gods," he tells them, "are performing a sacrifice at the Field of the Kurus and they have not invited you. Therefore you are neither complete nor perfect."

The Aśvins set out for the Field of the Kurus, where they arrive in time for the first pressing of the *soma* and the chanting of the *bahiṣpavamāna* invocation. The Aśvins demand that the gods let them in. But the gods refuse, saying, "We will not invite you in. You have been wandering too much and too closely among men, healing them." The Aśvins then reply, "You are sacrificing with a headless sacrifice!" "How is it headless?" ask the gods. "We will tell you," the Aśvins answer, "after you invite us to the sacrifice." The gods then invite them in and give them a share of the *soma*, which is why there is a *soma* cup dedicated to the Aśvins directly following the recitation of the *bahiṣpavamāna* during the great pressing of the *soma*. The Aśvins, the text explains, are the "head" of the sacrifice that was missing.

The story of Cyavana's rejuvenation, ostensibly an explanation for why an offering to the Aśvins occurs during the ritual, amounts to a series of three parallel stories of expulsion: first of Cyavana, then of Sukanyā, then of the Aśvins. The first expulsion occurs when Cyavana's clan mysteriously abandons the "decrepit and witch-like" old man. When the sons of Śaryāta attack the sage, they bring on a sacrificial crisis in which the blurring of distinctions leads to violence among the members of Śaryāta's clan. In mythic fashion, the blame for the rampant violence and chaos is laid at the feet of an offended god (or sage in this case). To allay the crisis, Śaryāta brings about the second expulsion, that of Sukanyā. Like Agamemnon, Śaryāta offers his daughter to the offended deity and peace returns. But the story does not end there. It continues with the arrival of the divine twins, who learn from Cyavana that they too have been expelled from the sacrifice of the gods because of their impure profession of medicine. But in this last case, Cyavana returns them to make the sacrifice complete again.

The Brahmin clan expels Cyavana, who bears the marks of the scapegoat, for some unknown reason. Śaryāta expels Sukanyā because his family has offended Cyavana. And the gods expel the Aśvins for mixing with mortals and healing them. In each case, the expelled figure becomes the center of the next connected myth: Cyavana is at the center of Sukanyā's story, and Sukanyā is at the center of the Aśvins' story. In structuralist fashion, this myth cycle is a machine for resolving differences: humans and gods, family and non-family, kings and sages. But for Girard, negotiating differences only accounts for a little of the work of myth. He insists that "[the] issue that structuralism will never be able to work out . . . is the reciprocal dependence between the differential principle and the undifferentiated symmetries in the relationship between doubles, the 'zero degree' of structure."[94] The problem of doubles is not an issue in the story of Cyavana found in the *Śatapatha Brāhmaṇa*, but it takes center stage in another variant of the myth, which we will examine in the next section and which takes us down to the "zero level" of structure.

Throwing the First Stone: Cyavana in the Jaiminīya Brāhmaṇa

The version of the Cyavana story from *JB* 3.121–128 is the same basic story but contains changes that make it more coherent. In this version, Cyavana (definitely a Bhṛgu now) instructs his sons to leave him behind on earth so that he can use his powers to make himself young again and get a beautiful young wife. And instead of being pelted with rocks, he is smeared with mud and feces to the point of unrecognizability, which informs his curse on Śaryāta that his kin will no longer recognize each other and begin to fight one another. Also, it is Sukanyā herself, not her brothers, who offends Cyavana, prompting the sage to actively demand her for his wife, rather than passively accepting her as a peace offering. And neither does Śaryāta give her up willingly. In fact, he tells Sukanyā to run back to the palace as soon as she gets the chance, since the old man will be too weak and feeble to give chase. And when she does try to escape, Cyavana frightens her by summoning a huge black snake and this fright, not any sense of loyalty, is why she is so unwilling to run away with the Aśvins. So in this version of the myth, Sukanyā is not a scapegoat expelled to protect her clan from the danger caused by her brothers' crimes. Instead her marriage to the ancient sage is doubly justified in a way that covers up two of the myth's three expulsions: the Bhṛgus do not expel Cyavana, he stays behind to find a wife; and Śaryāta does not expel Sukanyā, she earns her marriage to Cyavana through her own guilt.

But immediately following the sanitized myth in which no innocent is unjustly expelled or attacked, the myth recreates the sacrificial crisis through an act of doubling. To make him young and get an answer from him as to why they are not perfect, the Aśvins throw Cyavana into the water (this time the sacred Sarasvatī River). And when they do, the two gods go in as well and all three come out as identical handsome young men; Cyavana becomes a double of the Aśvins, who are already doubles of each other. But Sukanyā has no trouble picking out her husband because Cyavana has given her a previously agreed-upon signal so that she can recognize him.

Yet another double enters the myth in the explanation of how Cyavana wins the Aśvins an oblation at the sacrifice. Building on the cryptic reference to the headless sacrifice in the Vedic text, the *Jaiminīya* has Cyavana send the Aśvins not to the sacrificial enclosure of the gods at the Field of the Kurus, but to see Dadhyañc, the horse-headed (as the Aśvins often are) sage of the Atharva clan and possessor of the secret of the sacrifice, namely how the sacrifice is made whole after the head is cut off.[95] He tells them that Indra has threatened to behead him if he reveals this secret but the Aśvins promise to replace his head if Indra cuts it off, so he reveals the secret, bringing down the wrath of Indra. But after Indra beheads Dadhyañc, the Aśvins replace his horse-head, enacting the secret of the sacrifice that he has just given them. This notion that there is a "secret" of the sacrifice and that it has something to do with decapitation is prevalent in the Brāhmaṇas and its violent revelation here points to the scandalous nature of sacrifice, which is removed from the first half of the myth.

The Demon of Drunkenness: Cyavana in the Mahābhārata

The *Mahābhārata*'s version of the Cyavana story, told in *MBh* 3.121–125, reapportions innocence and guilt among the victims according to a different formula and places the focus squarely on the identification of ritual delirium with sacrificial crisis. This time, no one pelts Cyavana with rocks or smears him with feces. Instead, like many sages (notably Vālmīki, the legendary inventor of *kāvya*) he has meditated in one spot so long that an anthill has grown up around him. Sukanyā comes upon the hill and pokes a stick at what she thinks is an insect but is actually Cyavana's eye peeping at the beautiful maiden through a hole in the anthill. Enraged at this genuinely unintentional injury, Cyavana curses Śaryāta's men (transformed into an army from an anachronistic band of nomads) to become constipated rather than to begin fighting each other. And when Śaryāta hears his daughter's story and guesses the cause of the trouble, he propitiates Cyavana and gladly gives him his daughter's hand when the sage asks for it.

When the Aśvins arrive on the scene, they are just in time to see Sukanyā naked as she emerges from her bath at the river and they try to seduce her away from her aged husband, whom they disparagingly describe as *gatādhvan*, which means "one who has traveled his road" and Robert Goldman suggests we should render "over the hill;"[96] the "witch-like" image is gone completely, along with the violence. As in the *Jaiminīya Brāhmaṇa*, the Aśvins enter the fountain of youth along with Cyavana and all come out looking the same, but Sukanyā is somehow able to recognize her husband even without a signal. To celebrate his restored youth, Cyavana offers to sacrifice for his father-in-law. And here the nearly forgotten original purpose of the story finally emerges when Cyavana offers a cup of *soma* to the Aśvin twins, only to have Indra interrupt the sacrifice with an objection. "It is my opinion that the Aśvins are not worthy of *soma*," he argues. "These physicians are not worthy of the sacrifice offered to the Gods."

Cyavana replies that the Aśvins are as much gods as Indra is and, more than that, they have just restored his youth to him. But Indra is unmoved, demanding, "How can these two be worthy of *soma*? They are physicians and servants. They change their forms at will. And they wander in the world of mortals!" Finally he threatens to hurl his thunderbolt weapon at Cyavana if he dares to offer *soma* to the Aśvins. Like a good Bhṛgu sage, Cyavana is unimpressed by threats from the gods and calmly makes the *soma* offering in defiance of Indra's wrath. Angered at his impertinence, Indra starts to hurl the thunderbolt but Cyavana paralyzes his arm with a spell before he can let it fly. Next Cyavana conjures up a demon called Mada ("Intoxication") with arms like mountains, eyes like the sun and moon, and four fangs in his enormous mouth, each a thousand leagues long. As Mada starts coming for Indra, the king of the gods becomes petrified with fear and agrees to share the *soma* with the Aśvins if only Cyavana will call off his demon. Cyavana agrees and destroys Mada, dispersing his demonic essence among the four great vices: hunting, gambling, liquor, and women.

We can see plainly in Mada the monstrous double and in his name, "Intoxication," the signs of the sacrificial crisis. The fact that the epic has Cyavana redirecting this power into hunting, gambling, liquor, and women also shows real perspicacity on the part of the mythmakers. Hunting and gambling are the royal vices, both connected to the downfall of many a mythical king (and probably a few historical ones) and both are ritualized elements of the sacrifice. Liquor, a literal intoxicant, is a sacrificial offering in several Vedic rites, including the Royal Consecration Sacrifice. Women, in this case, represent the sexualized figure of the woman, present in the sacrifice as the sacrificer's wife, hidden behind a screen so as not to pollute the ritual. All four of the repositories of Mada are ambivalent, necessary to ritually reproduce the delirium of the original sacrificial crisis but also having the power to corrupt the sacrificer if misused.

Table 5 compares the three Cyavana stories from the *Śatapatha Brāhmaṇa*, the *Jaiminīya Brāhmaṇa*, and the *Mahābhārata* in terms of the three expulsions that occur in each narrative. The "guilt" of the Aśvins remains consistent, since the crime of which they are accused is endemic to their nature. But Sukanyā goes from being blameless, to being cruel, to being unwittingly guilty of poking Cyavana's eye. The expulsion of Cyavana himself remains mysterious, but we will look more closely at it in the next section.

Table 5. The Three Expulsions in Three Variants of the Cyavana Narrative

	EXPULSION	CRIME	EXPULSION	CRIME	EXPULSION	CRIME
ŚB	Cyavana	Being "witch-like"	Sukanyā	None	Aśvins	Mixing with mortals
JB	Cyavana	None	Sukanyā	Attacking Cyavana	Aśvins/ Dadhyañc	None/revealing secret of sacrifice
MBh	Cyavana	None	Sukanyā	Accidentally attacking Cyavana	Aśvins	Shape-shifting, mixing with mortals

The Kṛtyā as Monstrous Double

Let us now return to the *Śatapatha Brāhmaṇa*. The phrase used to describe Cyavana's physical appearance when he becomes the victim of spontaneous violence is *jīrṇiḥ kṛtyārūpa*, which I have translated as "decrepit and witch-like." The last term, *kṛtyārūpa*, Eggeling translates as "phantom-like" in the *Śatapatha Brāhmaṇa*. And in his Sanskrit dictionary, Monier Monier-Williams renders it as "appearing like a phantom." But I think they miss the point by describing the sage in ghostly terms, giving the sense that he is translucent or ephemeral in some way. The precise term *kṛtyārūpa* is richly evocative of yet another transformation of the *pharmakon*, connected with the power of female sexuality and the Kavi; literally, *kṛtyārūpa* means "having the form of a Kṛtyā," which is a kind of witch or sorceress specifically connected in *ṚV* 10.85 ("The Marriage of Sūryā" a hymn still recited in part at traditional Hindu weddings) to the blood that stains the bride's gown on the night of her defloration. Verses 28–30 describe the danger presented by the blood:

28. The purple and red appears, a Kṛtyā; the stain is imprinted [on the gown]. The wife's family prospers and her husband is bound in the bonds.
29. Throw away the gown, and distribute money to the priests. [The stained

gown] becomes a Kṛtyā walking on two feet and, like the wife, it draws close to the husband.

30. The [husband's] body becomes ugly and pale if the husband covers his penis with his wife's robe out of his evil desire.

The Kṛtyā is a double of the wife created when she loses her virginity. It can be absorbed safely into her new family if the bloody gown is disposed of and the officiating priests are paid off, but will become a kind of succubus if not dealt with properly.

A few verses later, the hymn returns to the bloody gown:

34. [The gown] burns, it bites, and it has claws, as dangerous as poison to eat. Only the priest who knows the Sūryā hymn can receive the bridal gown.

35. Butchering, carving, and dividing it into pieces, behold the forms of Sūryā, which only the priest can purify.

These verses are connected to a wedding ceremony, one of the most innocuous rituals imaginable (in most cases). Their clear evocation of sacrificial violence speaks in favor of Girard's insistence upon violence as the basis for "the unity of all rites." In verse 28, we have the appearance of blood and the husband is placed in bonds. The text uses the word *bandha*, which is the same word used for the fetters that bind the victim to the sacrificial post and is also closely related to *bandhu*, the word used for the esoteric connections that are the objects of study for initiates into the mystical traditions. Verse 29 gives us an either/or scenario: either destroy the gown and pay the priests or it becomes a monstrous double of the wife that imitates her desire for her husband. And verse 30 tells us that if the husband should reciprocate and succumb to evil desires by penetrating the gown sexually, the Kṛtyā will possess him and make him deformed and pale. In verse 34, the Kṛtyā takes a demonic and dangerous form that only a priest who knows this verse can handle.[97] The final verse has the priest cutting up the Kṛtyā, using the words *āśasana*, *viśasana*, and *adhivikartana* ("cutting," "dissecting," and "carving into pieces," the last applied especially to an animal carcass), thereby making it clear that the gown has gone from being a monstrous double to a sacrificial victim. Just as Girard describes the way in which the phenomenon of possession, which is fairly common among members of South Indian goddess cults, "can appear as sickness, cure, or both at once,"[98] the hymn tells us that the Kṛtyā can either bring good fortune to the husband and his family or become this monstrous double, which requires a sacrificial solution.

Returning to the myth of Cyavana, I would suggest that the use of the phrase *kṛtyārūpa* is meant to conjure up images not only of a wasted and wizened man (like the cursed husband in the hymn described above) but also a dangerous and powerful *pharmakon* capable of bringing either death or wealth to the house of Śaryāta. The Kṛtyā is described as being like a poison and the word the text uses for "poison" is *viṣa*, which has the sense of an "actively pernicious" poison. In "Plato's Pharmacy," Derrida uncovers these elements in the mythology of the Egyptian deity Thoth, the "god-doctor-pharmacist-magician" who is a healer to the gods as well as an accomplice of the demons (in his case, led by the chaotic god Set), responsible for medicine, magic, and writing. Derrida writes:

> As a substitute capable of doubling for the king, the father, the sun, and the word, distinguished from these only by dint of representing, repeating, and masquerading, Thoth was naturally also capable of totally supplanting them and appropriating all their attributes. He is added as the essential attribute of what he is added to, and from which almost nothing distinguishes him. He differs from speech or divine light only as the revealer from the revealed. Barely.[99]

In Derrida's description of Thoth and in the stories of Cyavana we have been examining, we get a more complex picture of the figure we have seen in so many guises: the Kavi-*pharmakos-*bhlagh(s)-men-homo sacer*. The story of Cyavana's rejuvenation gives us two images of this figure, both with pronounced protean characteristics: the Aśvins (itinerant healers and shape-shifters excluded from the sacrifice) and Cyavana (the poisonous "decrepit and witch-like" old man abandoned by his clan and the innocent victim of spontaneous mob violence). But this does not yet get to the poetic nature of the Kavi. Echoing Louis Renou, Stephanie Jamison describes the Vedic Kavi as "both a sage and a poet, someone specializing both in the interpretation of verbal enigmas and the composition of complex and enigmatic verbal products."[100] This poetic aspect is one we have yet to uncover.

In the stories we have examined so far, we have explored a number of different avatars of the banished figure whose presence shapes Indian myth and ritual from the Vedic period onward. We have seen its traces in the lycanthropic Vrātya, the poet-magician called the Kavi, and specific figures like Cyavana and Śunaḥśepa. We have also seen in the fragmentary myths of opposing groups like the Yatis and the Sālavṛkeyas and the archaic two-sacrificer model something that resembles the *pharmakon* and the *pharmakos* in Greek ritual, used by Derrida to mount a critique of logocentrism. In the following section, we will follow Derrida's move in "Plato's Pharmacy" and go from the mythical *pharmakos* to the *logos* in order to understand how the Hindu tradition creates its own unique epistemology of the victim.

The Broken *Bandh-a/u*: Śunaḥśepa Unbound[101]

As we have seen, the term *kavi* denotes not only a poet and master of riddles and sacred speech, but also a deadly form of black magic. In Ireland, the far western reaches of the Indo-European world (where the word *ārya* is retained in the place-name Éire, or Airlann in Ulster-Scots), there is a folk etymology for *fili* ("poet") that traces it to the words *fi* ("satire" or "poison") and *li* ("praise"), encapsulating the two poles of the poet's power.[102] Derrida sees the same set of contradictory meanings in the "poisoned gift" of writing, and in "Plato's Pharmacy" he describes the Trinitarian relation of the *logos*, the speaking Father, and the *pharmakon* of writing in terms that could as easily describe the story of Śunaḥśepa:

> *Logos* is a son, then, a son that would be destroyed in his *very presence* without the present *attendance* of his father. His father who answers. His father who speaks for him and answers for him. Without his father, he would be nothing but, in fact, writing.... The specificity of writing would thus be intimately bound to the absence of the father. Such an absence can of course exist along very diverse modalities, distinctly or confusedly, successively or simultaneously: to have lost one's father, through natural or violent death, through random violence or patricide; and then to solicit the aid and attendance, possible or impossible, of the paternal presence, to solicit it directly or to claim to be getting along without it, etc.[103]

As A. K. Ramanujan has noted, the "Indian Oedipus" presents an inversion of the Greek Oedipal model in that the aggression is directed from the father toward the son.[104] Following this pattern, the Indic *pharmakos* is represented by the myth of Śunaḥśepa, where violence is directed toward the son, reversing the patricide that Derrida sees in Plato. Unlike Oedipus, Śunaḥśepa loses his father through the father's violence, not his own. But a reversal is not a displacement, and Śunaḥśepa still ends up as an orphan with the need for a new father figure. Of course, the poisoned gift in "Plato's Pharmacy" is writing, which came much later to India than to Greece. And even after they developed a system of writing for use in matters of trade and government, the Indians did not commit the Vedas to writing until more than 2000 years after their composition, although some of the Upaniṣads may have been written down a few centuries earlier. And just as King Thamus's dire prediction about the deleterious effects of writing in the *Phaedrus* would suggest, the written Vedic tradition retains less than the pupil-to-student oral transmission.[105]

Derrida gives us this elegant account of the misery of the *logos* committed to writing:

> This misery is ambiguous: it is the distress of the orphan, of course, who needs not only an attending presence but also a presence that will attend to its needs; but in pitying the orphan, one also makes an accusation against him, along with writing, for claiming to do away with the father, for achieving emancipation with complacent self sufficiency. From the position of the holder of the scepter, the desire of writing is indicated, designated, and denounced as a desire for orphanhood and patricidal subversion.[106]

Looking back at the story of Śunaḥśepa, we see the roles reversed between father and son again. Śunaḥśepa is an orphan, but he does not stand accused of patricide. Instead he does the accusing, condemning his father's greed, and above all, the sacrificial system that would allow him to be murdered "as though he were not human" (*amānuṣam iva*).

Śunaḥśepa's story is about memory and speech. The boy's "memory" of the proper Vedic verse and then the act of speaking it are what truly set him free from his sacrificial Varuṇic bonds. He then transmits the verse to the surrounding Brahmins, who memorize it but do not write it down; writing is altogether absent. But if the myth is not about writing and speech, it is definitely about *logos*. And what can we call the spectacular and spontaneous Vedic recitation by which the forest-born Śunaḥśepa saves his life if not an instance of the Platonic anamnesis? But to properly connect the Śunaḥśepa myth with the violent origins of Western philosophy uncovered by Derrida we must return to Girard's reading of the essay in 1972, the year both *Violence and the Sacred* and "Plato's Pharmacy" were first published in French. Relating Derrida's essay to the significance of the *pharmakos* as a true sacrificial victim, Girard writes:

> Derrida's analysis demonstrates in a striking fashion a certain arbitrary violence of the philosophic process as it occurs in Plato, through the mediation of a word that is indeed appropriate since it really designates an earlier, more brutal variant of the same arbitrary violence. The long line of sacrificial forms, each derived from the other, contains no "right" form from the point of view of philosophy, sociology, or psychoanalysis. But it does contain one genuine, unique event whose essence is invariably betrayed, to one degree or another, by all the translations and metaphoric derivations that Western thought has produced.[107]

Western thought is marked by the betrayal of a unique and scandalous event: the violent expulsion or destruction of a surrogate victim. But I have been arguing that the Sanskrit tradition, exemplified in the story of Śunaḥśepa, offers something different. In India, the link between arbitrary collective violence and the deepest structure of the "original mechanism of the symbolic process" is not lost, but retained in an esoteric tradition. And now that we have seen the connection between the *kavi* and the *pharmakos* as sacrificial victims and sources of sacred speech, we will see how the Indian idea of the *kavi* impacts the development of poetics and philosophy.

Sacrificed in Language: From Kavi *to* Kāvya

Indian poetics, like the much maligned but none the less perspicacious theory of myth as "disease of language" put forth by Max Müller, is based on the way in which language functions at the level of phonetics and grammar. As Edwin Gerow explains it:

> Poetics is (in India) a development of an interest in certain kinds of expressive devices that are grounded in language. Some devices are specifically linked to the Sanskrit language (metrics, prosody, alliteration, etc.)—what the poeticians will term *śabdālaṃkāra*; others—the *arthālaṃkāra*, as the simile of [the grammarians] Yāska and Pāṇini—are not specific to the language as sound, but concern rather the expressive content of that language (while not being any the less determined grammatically, syntactically: the comparative compounds of Pāṇini).[108]

In one Sanskrit myth, the birth of the genre of *kāvya* is itself mimetic. It is told in the story of Vālmīki, the legendary author of the *Rāmāyaṇa* and the first poet. While in the forest, Vālmīki hears a pair of birds singing and is appreciating the beauty of their song when a hunter kills the male bird with his arrow. Overcome with anguish (*śoka*) at the sight, Vālmīki spontaneously composes a couplet (*śloka*) to curse the hunter: "Oh hunter! Because you killed that pair of birds enraptured with love, you will never find a resting place (if you wander) for all of eternity!"[109] In this tradition, the purpose of the first and paradigmatic poetic utterance is to place on the hunter a curse of restlessness like the one placed on the Wandering Jew or the Flying Dutchman. The episode, called the *Krauñcavadha*, or the "Killing of the Songbird," appears at the beginning of the *Rāmāyaṇa*, where the origins of the epic itself are recounted.

In his remarkably thorough study of this episode, Charles Vaudeville has made some observations that are worth comment. First, Vaudeville makes the connection between the *krauñca* bird and the *krauñca* tone, associated in Vedic "sonic theology" with the demons but also with the high priest of the gods, Bṛhaspati. It is through the latter connection that we get the episode in the sixth book of the *Mahābhārata* in which the Pāṇḍavas draw up their army into the bird-shaped *krauñca* formation, originally conceived by Bṛhaspati to aid the gods in their war against the demons. Vaudeville also notes that "it is likely that a 'Kruñca-like song' or 'tone' was already associated with the idea of 'desire, longing' for a second (= for a mate?)."[110] And in the *Skanda Purāṇa* Krauñca is a demon cursed to become a mountain by the sage Agastya.

From the *Krauñcavadha* episode of the *Rāmāyaṇa* and from the Vedic and classical connotations of the word, we can see that this *krauñca* whose death marks the spontaneous beginning of *kāvya* is at once associated with desire, death, the curse and exile placed on a killer, and the relationship between humans and animals. The poetic language in which Vālmīki will go on to recite the *Rāmayāṇa* begins as a linguistic surrogate for the avian victim of a hunter's arrow, cursing the hunter to become a wandering exile of the Cain-Alcmaeon type. Like the archaic Greek rituals whose roots Walter Burkert traces to Neolithic hunting bands in *Homo Necans*, the *Krauñca-vadha* story has poetry growing out of the spontaneous reaction to watching an animal being killed.

Pūrva Mīmāṃsā and the Language of Sacrifice

In the *namaskriyā* or opening supplication of the *Raghuvaṃśa*, Kālidāsa's *kāvya* version of the *Rāmāyaṇa* story, the author expresses his dedication to Śiva and his consort Pārvatī with a verse that provides a window into the classical Indian understanding of signification: "I pray to the parents of the world, Pārvatī and Śiva, who are connected like speech and meaning, [to grant me] the knowledge of speech and meaning. (*Vāgarthau iva saṃpṛktau vāgarthau pratipattaye jagataḥ pitarua vande pārvatīparameśvarau.*)" Giuliano Boccali notes that Kālidāsa, considered the paragon of poesy in Sanskrit literature, deliberately breaks the rules by his repetition of *vāgarthau* (*vāc*, or "speech" plus *artha*, or "meaning"), a *dvandva* compound used to name two terms in a relationship like "rest and relaxation" or "law and order." Boccali argues that the twice-told *vāgarthau* in this *namaskriyā* (of which this verse is the earliest example in Sanskrit literature) is a synonym for the more commonly used *śabdārthau*, or "word and meaning," a term commonly used in the Vedic hermeneutical tradition of Pūrva Mīmāṃsā.[111] Jaimini, the chief exponent of Pūrva Mīmāṃsā, in his third century B.C.E. treatise, the *Pūrva Mīmāṃsā Sutra*, explicates the term in this formulation regarding the language of the Veda: "The connection between a word and its meaning is *autpattika* (a word that means 'inherent' and 'eternal' in this context). (*Autpattikas tu śabdasyārthena saṃbandha.*)"[112]

Śālika Nātha Miśra, a student of Jaimini, argues that words do not always refer to objective truths because not all speakers are reliable. We can infer the truth of words based on our knowledge or judgment of the speaker's reliability. How then, he asks, can we ascertain the reliability of the Veda, which has no speaker because it is *apauruṣeya* or impersonally originant? To answer this question, Śālika uses the master's dictum that "revelation's teaching is inerrant, though its object be imperceptible" to argue against those who would doubt the infallible authority of the Vedas. Because they speak of things that are supranormal and not accessible to men except through revelation, the Vedas have no author whose reliability we need to judge nor is there any author that could rival their authority in such matters.[113] The entire Pūrva Mīmāṃsā position depends upon the infallibility of the Vedas and the eternal and uncreated relationship between word (*śabda*)[114] and meaning (*artha*) outside of spoken language. The poet Kālidāsa and the proponents of Pūrva Mīmāṃsā, using, respectively, poetic-theological and logical-formal conventions, remove the structure of the sign from human discourse.

For Kālidāsa, the relation between signifier and signified is as mystical and eternal as the relation between Śiva and Pārvatī, identified in Yogic philosophy as Puruṣa (the male-physical principle) and Prakṛti (the female-spiritual principle).[115] In this light, the *Krauñcavadha* episode takes on new meaning. After seeing the matched pair of male and female *krauñca* birds separated by violence, Vālmīki enters into a new kind of language that unites the similarly separated pair of word and meaning in such a way that they will remain inseparable. The violent rupture of the *Krauñcavadha* is what we might call an "event," giving birth to a new kind of representation, exemplified by *kāvya*.

Meaninglessness and Arthavattva*; or, Speculative Realism c. 200 B.C.E.*

Because their approach is geared toward codifying rules for the proper way to carry out the rituals described in the Vedas, Jaimini and the other proponents of Pūrva Mīmāṃsā see the *artha* in *śabdārtha* in the sense of "purpose" more than "meaning." Focused on recovering the true purpose behind the ritual commandments of the Veda, Pūrva Mīmāṃsā is a theory of sacrifice as much as it is a school of hermeneutics. Seeking to counter Buddhist arguments against the sacrificial system and the social hierarchy constructed upon it, Jaimini adopts Buddhism's rigorous analysis of all forms of knowledge, but adds the sole exception of the Veda. While Buddhist thought ultimately leads to the teaching of the "emptiness" of all the Vedic concepts, Pūrva Mīmāṃsā instead constructs, as Francis X. Clooney puts it, "a very sophisticated understanding of language as a reality which pre-exists its speakers and structures the world according to values not anthropocentric in any individual, 'person-oriented' sense."[116]

But Jaimini's system is not a naïve literalism. It is better compared, in its rejection of Buddhist "mind-only" ontology and Upaniṣadic Gnosticism, to the recent philosophical movement known as "Speculative Realism."[117] Like Quentin Meillassoux and other Speculative Realists, Jaimini seeks to apprehend a reality that is not merely a "correlate" of human thought like Kant's world of phenomena or the illusory world of the Buddhists. But unlike Meillassoux and company, he uses linguistic science to ground his apprehension of the real, granting Vedic language the same privileged status (as an "archaeological" rather than an "architectural" construction) that some Speculative Realists, following Badiou, give to transfinite mathematics.[118] This comparison is even more apt when we consider that Georg Cantor, the nineteenth century mathematician who developed the set theory of which they are so enamored, believed that God himself had revealed it to him.[119] For Jaimini, the Vedas constitute the same kind of revelation, not mystical, but formal and logical. He rejects what will be of great concern to subsequent generations of philosophers, namely the esoteric meaning of the Veda, insisting on the ordinariness of Vedic language.[120] Just as Meillassoux holds that the mathematical (apart from the finite world of mathematical statements made by humans) *is* the possible, Jaimini holds that the Vedic *śabda* is the inexhaustible real.[121]

Speculative Realism and Pūrva Mīmāṃsā also share the goal of establishing a reality that exists apart from, before, and without need of humanity, as the name Pūrva Mīmāṃsā suggests when we take it as "Investigation of the Prior." In *After Finitude*, Meillassoux argues that the main problem for Kant-inspired "correlationism" is comprehending "the ancestral," which Jaimini might call the *pūrva*, the universe before the advent of life or any being to perceive or conceive of it.[122] But for Meillassoux this is more than just a restatement of the Zen koan about the tree falling in the forest when no one is listening, it is the central problem of philosophy:

> Our question was the following: what are the conditions under which an ancestral statement remains meaningful? But as we have seen, this question

> harbours another one, which is more originary, and which delivers its veritable import, to wit: *how are we to conceive of the empirical sciences' capacity to yield knowledge of the ancestral realm?* For what is at stake here, under the cover of ancestrality, is the nature of scientific discourse, and more particularly of what characterizes this discourse, i.e. its *mathematical* form. Thus our question becomes: how is mathematical discourse able to describe a world where humanity is absent; a world crammed with things and events that are not the correlates of any manifestation; a world that is not the correlate of a relation to the world? This is the enigma which we must confront: *mathematics' ability to discourse about the great outdoors; to discourse about a past where both humanity and life are absent.*[123]

Similarly, Jaimini is intent on removing humanity from the center of the world. Neither sacrifice nor the Vedas exist "for us." As Clooney points out, this pre-Copernican rejection of anthropocentrism leads Jaimini to a kind of "non-supernatural transcendence" in which the sacrificer experiences a kind of selflessness, not in the renunciation of desire, but in the realization that his desire for this or that object is subsidiary to his desire for Heaven, conceived of as Being.[124] Neither does this decentering replace the human with the transcendent or some kind of archaic god that demands sacrifice. Jaimini's system, as Clooney argues, "relieves the sacrificial theorist of the burden of either defending or purifying the I-thou transaction of a greedy self and a potent deity."[125]

In her article, "Language of Sacrifice," anthropologist Veena Das elaborates the Pūrva Mīmāṃsā theory of sacrifice and the place of language in it. Das argues that what distinguishes Pūrva Mīmāṃsā from classical Western anthropology (represented by Hubert and Mauss, Evans-Pritchard, and Turner) is the primacy of desire instead of purification in their respective conceptions of sacrifice:

> At the risk of some oversimplification, it may be stated that anthropological discourse on sacrifice assumes that the sacrificator is a bearer of pollution, sin or guilt and the sacrificial cult provides the means for cleansing the person or the social body of these moral stains. Further, the immolation of the victim becomes the central moment of the sacrifice since it constitutes the renunciation of a significant object by the sacrificator to

> bring about a sudden and violent cleansing of sin, the separation of that which has been wrongly united, and a release of powerful forces. . . . In contrast to these views, the Pūrva Mīmāṃsā school elaborates a structure in which *it is not the sin but the desire of the sacrificator* which is taken as fundamental.[126]

Jaimini well understands desire and its place at the heart of the sacrificial world. In removing metaphysics and mysticism from his rigorous system of thought, he concludes with an explanation of sacrifice that complements Girard's. For Jaimini, the sacrifice is where one submits one's inherent desire for the fullness of Being to the impersonal and indifferent laws of the universe. He also understands the place of sacrificial violence and expulsion at the heart of the social order, calling the sacrifice the "womb of *Ṛta* ("order")."[127]

The word *ṛta*, though basically synonymous with dharma, is worth examining further. Described by William K. Mahoney as "the hidden structure on which the divine, physical, and moral worlds are founded, through which they are inextricably connected, and by which they are sustained," *Ṛta* is cognate not only with the English words "rite" and "ritual" but with "art" and "harmony."[128] Because he recognizes that the act of sacrifice is the beginning of the world as we know it, Jaimini, like Giorgio Agamben, sees the inherent and eternal bond of word and meaning as constitutive of human life. Das explains:

> Since human existence would be impossible but for the existence of language, it is in the eternality of the Word that we have to seek the principle of dharma. This is why the centrality of sacrifice in the constitution of dharma derives not from the fact that it is good for men or that it is good for gods, but from the fact that there is a Vedic command that asks men to sacrifice.[129]

For Jaimini, the most important of all the commands in the Vedas is this one (given in the optative, not the imperative mood): "Let him who desires Heaven sacrifice (*Svarga kāmaḥ yajeta*)."

Unlike the philosophical speculation in the Upaniṣads, which displaces the actual practice of the sacrifice and introduces an internalized sacrifice in the form of asceticism and meditation, Pūrva Mīmāṃsā seeks to keep the ritual system in place while at the same time understanding its meaning beyond the mere rules of its performance. As Clooney suggests:

> [Just] as Jaimini recognized human desire and the human search for meaning, but refused to structure the sacrifice in an anthropocentric or personalist fashion, the participation of God in the sacrifice—the "revelatory" re-constitution of temporal reality itself as utterly transcendent—could be understood to replace focus on the personhood of God, life of God "in himself," or even personal (human) relationship with God. Theology and anthropology would then be seen as two parts of a single fuller reflection on the sacred, as God and human beings participate in a sacred event not reducible to either: both are *śeṣa* ["remainder"].[130]

Here are what I believe to be the points of Pūrva Mīmāṃsā salient to the discussion at hand: First, the ritual injunctions contained in the Vedas represent an inexhaustible real that preexists and does not necessitate speech or action, either human or divine. Second, it is the nature of human beings to desire. Third, Vedic ritual gives them the means to attain the things they desire. Fourth, the proper execution of the Vedic ritual commands sublimates one's individual desire to a selfless desire for Heaven (i.e., plenitude of Being), whether one is conscious of it or not.

This formulation is a far cry from dismantling the ritual apparatus, but it is startling in its insistence on separating ritual from myth and metaphysics. Admittedly Jaimini avoids any discussion of violence at a time when one of the major issues in the critique of sacrifice was precisely the opposition to its violence, which makes his "demystification" a necessarily limited one. What remains is that Jaimini sees in ritual the means to recover one's true desire, not the desire for objects, but the pure desire for Being, Girard's "metaphysical desire." It is important to note that other schools of Indian thought that explicitly rejected sacrifice quickly reinstated it in the inverted forms of asceticism or Gnosticism. And Jaimini's new Vedic orthodoxy did not survive in its "Speculative Realist" form for very long either before it was "theologized" by his followers with the addition of the *apūrva*, the transcendent heavenly realm in which sacrificial action bears fruit, a concept antithetical to Jaimini's insistence that the sacrifice always ends in ashes, nothing more.

Mahāpralaya, "The Great Dissolution": Ashes and Cinders

We began this chapter with an examination of the role of riddles, games, and disputation in the Vedic sacrifice, finding connections in the classical ritual model to Girard's idea of the random selection of the victim as the primary mode of signification. We also compared Girard's theory with the debate about the "meaninglessness of sacrifice" in Indological circles, examining the work of Frits Staal and Jan Heesterman. Moving on to specific instances of riddles in ritual, we examined the *Asya Vamāsya* hymn and the insoluble paradox of the severed heads buried underneath the sacrificial altar. Then, following Girard's argument for seeing the victim as the transcendental signifier, we revisited the sacrifice of Puruṣa and began to draw connections between the figures of the Brahmin, the hypothetical **bhlagh(s)-men* of Dumézil, the Kavi, the Greek *pharmakos*, and Indo-European scapegoat-poets like Śiśupāla and Starkarðr, reading them all as avatars of the *homo sacer* figure who has been our constant companion throughout this book. Adding yet another figure to this growing list, we looked at three stories of the Bhārgava Brahmin Cyavana and made a tentative linguistic connection between him and the witch-like figure of the Kṛtyā, who embodies both a pernicious poison and a monstrous double of the wife in Vedic marriage rites. In the next section, we returned to the figure of Śunaḥśepa from chapter three, this time in the context of the *logos* and its relation to writing and speech as theorized in Derrida's essay, "Plato's Pharmacy." Reading Śunaḥśepa, whom we have already identified with the figure of Oedipus and the *homo sacer*, as the embodiment of the *logos*, we made the connection between the poet or Kavi and the language of poetry. We also saw how the myth of the invention of poetry from the *Rāmāyaṇa* connects poetic speech to a curse, an exile, and the violent separation of male and female. Finally, looking more closely at the question of language, we compared Sanskritic theories of language and sacrifice with those of contemporary philosophers, paying special attention to the way they decenter the human.

To conclude, we will return to the meaning or the meaninglessness of sacrifice. One could argue that asking about "the meaning of sacrifice" is as categorically mistaken a question as Wittgenstein thought "the meaning of life" was. So perhaps instead we should ask about the *artha* of sacrifice. When we do, we can begin to see a meaning indeed. It is somewhat unexpected that, with all of the elements in Sanskrit mythology that point toward some kind of revelation of the scapegoat mechanism, Jaimini comes to an entirely different conclusion about what is going on in the sacrificial arena. Girard might ascribe this fact to humanity's capacity to deny its own violence in the face of all evidence. But there is more to the story than that. In debunking the myths of divine violence and human agency, positing the existence of metaphysical desire, and espousing his rather dim view of humanity's ability to understand itself or transcend its baser nature, Jaimini is mounting a systematic critique of sacrifice that predates the Gospels by several centuries. And even if he concludes (as de Maistre will in nineteenth century France) by affirming its necessity, neither does he completely rule out its contingency. The sacrificial system would exist with or without us and by that logic we are separable from it and vice versa. As Heesterman has argued, sacrifice in the Vedic context is not meaningless. But its meaning is void: specifically, the void between Brahmin and sacrificer produced by the rupture of the old cyclical sacrificial order. "[It] was precisely this void," he writes, "that provided the open space for inquiry and debate, faith and unbelief, bondage and release, submission and protest—in short, for the never-ending *gamble* of freedom."[131] In the next and final chapter, we will reach some conclusions and attempt to answer some of the questions that have arisen in our exploration of the relationship between mimetic theory and Hindu mythology.

Yajñānta: The End of Sacrifice

I've burned my own house down; the torch is in my hand.
Now I'll burn down the house of anyone who wants to follow me.

—Kabir

Love is not consolation. It is light.

—Simone Weil, *Gravity and Grace*

Summary of Arguments

This book began with two aims. The first was to ascertain whether and to what extent Girard's mimetic theory and his idea of the sacrificial origin of religion and culture could enrich our understanding of Hinduism. The second was to see what kind of corrections or nuances the Hindu tradition could offer to Girard's theory of religion. In the introduction I laid out Girard's thesis, with special attention to the role of the victim as the "transcendental signifier." Then I listed and countered some specific ideological and methodological concerns about using mimetic theory to interpret Hindu materials, defending Girard against charges of ethnocentrism with the caveat that we must beware of turning Girard's theory into a sacred cow. To refute Girard's unsupported claim about the sanctity that every religion but Christianity enjoys in the contemporary discipline of religious studies, I led us into a brief digression exploring the current political climate threatening the academic freedom of those who would study Hinduism in a critical way. The introduction concluded with a discussion of the cases for and against believing in the reality of human sacrifice in India. I did not express an opinion of my own in this controversy, but I will do so now. It seems to me unjustified to rule out the existence of human sacrifice in India and relegate it to the realm of the purely metaphorical in light of the significance that human sacrifice has in the Sanskritic imagination.

The second chapter, "Rivalries," focused, as the title would indicate, on the conflicts that provide the background for Sylvain Lévi's *La doctrine du sacrifice dans les Brâhmanas*, the work to which *Sacrifice* is both a commentary and a response. I began by examining the ire that the Brāhmaṇas elicited among early Indologists with their endless "theological twaddle." I then moved on to the Anglo-French rivalry that informed the unique character of French Indology and from there to Lévi's central argument and its place in the development of French sociology, especially the work of Durkheim and Mauss, to whom Girard is so deeply indebted. Then I turned my attention to the rivalries inside the text, specifically those between the gods and the demons, between Indra and Vṛtra, and between Indra and Viṣṇu.

The third chapter, "Priests and Kings, Oaths and Duels," began like the previous chapter, by reconstructing a genealogy of Girardian thought, this time examining the continuities and discontinuities between mimetic theory and the work of Georges Dumézil, using Dumézil's model of the trifunctional paradigm to gain new insights into the Indra-Viṣṇu rivalry introduced in the second chapter. I argued that the myth of the Mitra, who is forced to participate in the lynching of Vṛtra in order to obtain a share in the sacrifice, represents a Girardian primal scene while also illustrating Dumézil's idea of the division of spiritual and temporal authority between the priestly and royal classes in Indo-European ideology. I then compared Girard's thinking with that of the Italian philosopher Giorgio Agamben, arguing that the institutions of the oath and the duel not only derive their structure from the sacrificial logic of substitution and exclusion, they also represent two competing models of sacrifice in ancient India: the classical single-sacrificer model and the archaic two-sacrificer model, respectively. To elucidate the two-sacrificer model, I looked at the mythology of Uśanas Kāvya (also known as Śukra) the high priest of the demons, and the mythic arms race in which the gods try to restore the balance of power by obtaining the secret resurrection spell that only he possesses. Finally, I used my readings of the myths of Indra and the Yatis, Viśvāmitra and Vasiṣṭha, Śunaḥśepa, the Vrātyas, and Carlo Ginzburg's analysis of the Benandanti to argue for the shadowy presence of a figure that embodies the self-deconstructive potential of the sacrifice. This figure, the Sanskrit Dīkṣita (or perhaps Ādidīkṣita, "The First Dīkṣita"), is a lycanthrope, a *homo sacer*, identified with the defeated party in the archaic two-sacrificer system and the dread state of undifferentiation in which man is wolf to man that sacrifice desperately tries to keep at bay. It is in uncovering and analyzing references to this figure that we find the Indian alternative to the Isaiahan "suffering servant" and can begin to understand the unique content of the Hindu sacrificial system's self-critique.

The fourth chapter, "Epic Variations on a Mimetic Theme," was devoted to the textual goldmine that is the *Mahābhārata* epic. After a brief discussion of the polyvocality of this text, which may allow it to escape inclusion in Girard's category of myth by preserving the voice of the victims alongside those of the victors, I laid out, in the briefest possible form, the outline of the narrative from the early episodes of the Pāṇḍava-Kaurava rivalry to its bloody *dénouement* on the Kurukṣetra battlefield. Next I analyzed the myths of two failed sacrificers, each of which presents a variety of the Hindu critique of sacrifice, which I have designated "Śaiva" and "Vaiṣṇava." The first myth, demonstrating the Śaiva critique, was that of Dakṣa, the demiurge whose failure to invite his black sheep son-in-law Śiva to his sacrifice costs him his head. I argued that in this myth we have not only a scapegoat in the form of the Pentheus-like figure of Dakṣa-Prajāpati, destroyed by his daughter (rather than his mother, as is the case of Pentheus in *The Bacchae*) and accused of incest, but also the figure of the lycanthropic *homo sacer* in the form of Śiva, whose attack on the sacrifice bears a striking resemblance to the Vedic myth of Indra and the Yatis. I concluded from this that the content of what I call the Śaiva critique of sacrifice derives from the archaic two-sacrificer system that continues to haunt the classical one-sacrificer model.

Then I examined the second failed sacrificer myth, the story of the Śaiva king Jarāsaṃdha, whose purported plan to rule the world by sacrificing all its kings is foiled by Kṛṣṇa so that Yudhiṣṭhira can do precisely the same thing. In condemning one form of human sacrifice while setting the stage for another, far bloodier one, namely the battle at Kurukṣetra, Kṛṣṇa exposes the arbitrary nature of victim selection, allowing structural (or contingent) guilt to replace moral (or absolute) guilt, leading to the ultimate failure of the *Mahābhārata*'s sacrificial war. Next, I recounted the story of the churning of the ocean, in which the gods and the demons form a temporary alliance to obtain the draught of immortality through a subtle but destructive form of sacrifice.

The chapter ended with the existential critique of sacrifice as presented in the story of Karṇa, the doomed sixth Pāṇḍava whose heroism contains elements of the Śaiva and Vaiṣṇava critiques. Karṇa is a representative of the expelled *homo sacer*, not only because he exists in the liminal space between divine and human, between Pāṇḍava and Kaurava, but because, like the classical Indo-European *homo sacer*, he can be killed, *but not sacrificed*. Both his ascension to Heaven upon his death, which sets him apart from all the other victims of the *Mahābhārata* war, and his refusal to name himself as a participant in the sacrifice of battle demonstrate this fact. But unlike the Śaiva *homo sacer*, Karṇa does not come back to haunt or destroy the sacrifice but performs the Vaiṣṇava function of exposing its empty structure, refusing to be either a victim or a persecutor, creating his own separate dharma instead.

In the fifth chapter, "Meaning: The Secret Heart of the Sacred," I returned to the central elements of the Śaiva and Vaiṣṇava critiques of sacrifice, namely the excluded middle and the arbitrary nature of victim selection, this time in a discussion of the structure of riddles and rituals. From this discussion, I moved on to an examination of the *brahmodya*, the verbal contest that occurs as part of the sacrifice and that preserves the logic of exclusion and the agonistic nature of archaic ritual. I demonstrated that the analogical philosophical tradition that emerges out of this verbal contest, which requires one to uncover the hidden connections that make ritual action effective, resurrects the excluded *homo sacer* in the form of the *bandhu*, or the connection.

Then, after an examination of how the story of Śiśupāla conflates the critique of sacrifice with historical tensions between Kṣatriyas and Brahmins and Śaivas and Vaiṣṇavas, I demonstrated a ritual and philological connection between the Indo-Iranian poet-priest called the Kavi and the Greek *pharmakon*, both of which represent the "poisoned gift." From this connection, I moved on to a discussion of how Derrida's critique of the sacrificial-substitutional form of classical thought and all that follows from it can be extended to understanding Indian myth and philosophy, a possibility I demonstrated through a reading of the myths of the Bhargava sage Cyavana, the story of the birth of poetic language in the *Rāmāyaṇa*, and a rereading of the Śunaḥśepa story. Finally, I concluded with a comparison of the indigenous theory of sacrifice developed by the Pūrva Mīmāṃsā school of philosophy and the contemporary writings of Speculative Realists, especially Quentin Meillassoux.

Now that I have summarized the arguments of the book so far, I want to conclude by examining the differences between Girard's interpretation of the Hindu critique of sacrifice and my own, and then suggesting how Girard's theory, supplemented by my analysis of the Hindu material, might be used to articulate an ethical position.

The Universal Singularity against the *Mahāpralāya*

In *Sacrifice*, Girard argues that one place in the Hindu tradition where one can clearly see the decoding of sacrifice is in the description of the *soma* offering (*agniṣṭoma*) in the *Śatapatha Brāhmaṇa*. Although the *soma* pressing necessitated by the rite is literally the pressing of a plant between stones to extract the juice, it is made to look like the killing of a victim: The god Soma is enthroned as a king, he cuckolds the sacrificer, and before he (in the form of the plant) is pressed between the stones, they are dyed red to appear as if covered in blood. More than its personification as a sacrificial victim, or even its hallucinogenic, ecstasy-producing properties, *soma* is the sacrificial substance par excellence because it as much natural as it is cultural, functioning as a kind of transcendental signifier in its own way and thereby allowing the *soma* ritual to continue unaffected long after the *soma* plant was lost. As Joel Brereton observes, "Already in the later Vedic period, sacrificers were using various plants to perform the *soma* rite . . . [such] substitutions were possible because *soma* is as much the product of the words, chants, and acts of the ritual as it is the juice of a plant."[1] But what arouses Girard's interest is the fact that in the liturgy of the *soma* offering, the Adhvaryu priest pressing the *soma* plants is advised to "think of his enemy" when doing so, or in the absence of an enemy, to "aim his thoughts at a stalk of grass."[2] The entire verse reads as follows:

> When preparing to crush [the *soma* with the pressing-stone], let [the Adhvaryu priest] have in his mind someone he hates, [thinking] "With this I strike so-and-so, not you!" Whoever kills a human Brahmin here is surely deemed guilty. How much more so for one who strikes [Soma], for Soma is a god. Nevertheless they do kill him when they press him. They kill him with that [stone]. Therefore he rises from there, therefore he lives, and no guilt is incurred. But if he hates no one, let him think of a blade of grass and no guilt is incurred.[3]

For Girard, this passage is absolutely crucial and his interpretation of it is worth quoting in full:

> *There is here, by all evidence, a full and complete revelation of the real function of sacrifice.* It is no ordinary sacrifice, to be sure, but the sacrifice of a god. What the text recommends to the sacrificer to protect him from his victim is to think expressly of the one whom he truly desires to kill, the one whom he would perhaps kill if it were not forbidden.
>
> *Because the sacrificial victim is here deemed even more precious than the being for whom it is substituted, the ordinary sense of the substitution is inverted; by articulating this inversion the text reveals the real function of sacrifice.* It is a strategy for preventing enemies from killing each other by furnishing them with alternative victims. Nothing could be more astonishing than the revelation of this game made possible by the illusion, cleverly maintained, that the violence perpetrated against the god is the more real and more fearsome of the two. During this charade the truth appears suddenly, a flash of lightning in the sky of sacrifice before all sinks back into the night.
>
> The text confirms our essential intuition. Sacrifice is a strategy for preventing violence from spreading throughout the community, for diverting toward an expendable victim the dangerous disorder that the murder of a personal enemy would precipitate were it allowed. *Sacrifice is an attempt to outwit the desire for violence by pretending, as far as possible, that the more*

> *dangerous and therefore more fascinating victim is the one being sacrificed rather than the enemy who obsesses us in everyday life. The ancient Brahmins understood that, between the violence of men and that of sacrifice, there exists a rapport which is no less essential for being concealed, and the text explicitly formulates this truth.* Of all the sacrificial reflections on sacrifice, this one, I think, is the most revealing of all.[4]

In this passage Girard explicitly argues that the Brāhmaṇas demonstrate an awareness of sacrifice's true nature that removes them from the realm of archaic religion and places them in the realm of revelation. But as we have seen in our examination of the tradition, and as Girard seems to have intuited, there is much more to say on this point. I have demonstrated the presence of three types of sacrificial critique in Hindu myth, ritual, and philosophy. We have detected a Śaiva critique that is visible the myths of Indra and the Yatis and Dakṣa's sacrifice. We have observed a Vaiṣṇava critique that is visible in the myths of Jarāsaṃdha and Śiśupāla. And we have also uncovered an existential critique that combines elements of both and can be found above all in the story of Karṇa. It is in Karṇa's story that we can clearly see the presence of what Girard sees in the intuitions of Baudelaire and Hölderlin, namely the assertion that "'universal singularities' are possible, can be free of resentment and are aware of the radical truth that is in the process of emerging out of the general panic."[5]

Karṇa's apotheosis calls to mind another apotheosis, this one decidedly negative: the transformation of humanity from a species into a force of nature, a transformation that marks our own *yugānta* ("turning of the age") from the Holocene epoch to the Anthropocene, in which human activity threatens the very natural conditions that made human life on this planet possible. This coming ecological apocalypse is not the fiery (or watery) end of humanity, but something more like the literal meaning of the word, serving as a revelation of the universality of the human. Postcolonial theorist Dipesh Chakrabarty illustrates this point powerfully in "The Climate of History: Four Theses," which are:

- THESIS 1: Anthropogenic Explanations of Climate Change Spell the Collapse of the Age-Old Humanist Distinction between Natural History and Human History

- THESIS 2: The Idea of the Anthropocene, the New Geological Epoch When Humans Exist as a Geological Force, Severely Qualifies Humanist Histories of Modernity/Globalization
- THESIS 3: The Geological Hypothesis Regarding the Anthropocene Requires Us to Put Global Histories of Capital in Conversation with the Species History of Humans
- THESIS 4: The Cross-Hatching of Species History and the History of Capital Is a Process of Probing the Limits of Historical Understanding[6]

The environmental crisis and the realization that countries like India and China, as they implement the industrial capitalist model that made the United States the wealthiest country in the world, present what will be the biggest environmental threat of the coming years, only underline Girard's point about how right myth-makers are not to distinguish between wars, plagues, and floods as natural or human-made. In her recent book, *Hegel, Haiti, and Universal History*, Susan Buck-Morss argues that it is in fact only in apocalyptic collapse that some kind of universal history can emerge, something that Girard might call the Kingdom of God:

> The definition of universal history that begins [to emerge] is this: rather than giving multiple, distinct cultures equal due, whereby people are recognized as part of humanity indirectly through the mediation of collective cultural identities, human universality emerges in the historical event at the point of rupture. It is in the discontinuities of history that people whose culture has been strained to the breaking point give expression to a humanity that goes beyond cultural limits. And it is in our empathic identification with this raw, free, and vulnerable state, that we have a chance of understanding what they say. Common humanity exists in spite of culture and its differences. A person's nonidentity with the collective allows for subterranean solidarities that have a chance of appealing to universal moral sentiment, the source today of enthusiasm and hope. It is not through culture, but through the threat of culture's betrayal that consciousness of a common humanity comes to be.[7]

It is following this point of "empathic identification" that I will return to Karṇa. In the epic, Karṇa's role is to stand in the place of the unrepresentable object that cannot be contained in the system because it is created as a byproduct of the system. He embodies ambiguous excess (Is he the superfluous 101st Kaurava or the equally superfluous sixth Pāṇḍava?) and stands against Kṛṣṇa, the self-transcending embodiment of the sacrificial system (whose unstoppable all-consuming violence is, paradoxically, humanity's only hope for peace) as the thing that it can neither contain nor annihilate. Whether or not the epic authors ever intended it, Karṇa's story has the potential to be a model of a non-mimetic existential heroism, giving us a figure who completely rejects the sacrificial model and exists inside it only as a symbol of its emptiness and, what is more, who cannot really be destroyed by it because he never participated in its game, a universal singularity against the universal dissolution of the *mahāpralāya.*

"Cast away illusions, prepare for struggle:"[8] Indian Universal History

At the end of Christopher Nolan's 2008 superhero blockbuster *The Dark Knight*, Batman, the movie's protagonist, tells his friend inside the police force, Commissioner Gordon, to publicly blame him for the crimes committed by Harvey Dent, a righteous and reform-minded district attorney tortured and corrupted into becoming an insane criminal by the villainous Joker. With Batman taking responsibility and going into exile for the murders Dent committed as the disfigured Two-Face, only he and Commissioner Gordon will know the truth and the public will be allowed to remember their beloved district attorney as a hero. Batman explains in his martyrdom speech:

> You either die a hero or live long enough to see yourself become the villain. I can do those things because I'm not a hero, not like Dent. [Let them think that] I killed those people. That's what I can be. I'm whatever Gotham needs me to be. You'll hunt me. You'll condemn me. Set the dogs on me. Because that's what needs to happen. Because sometimes the truth isn't good enough. Sometimes people deserve to have their faith rewarded.[9]

In his discussion of the enormous popularity of the film, released during the last months of Barack Obama's 2008 election campaign and in the midst of the spiraling global economic meltdown, Slavoj Žižek asks the following question: "[Why], at this precise moment, this renewed need for a lie to maintain the social system?"[10] He concludes that the crisis of late capitalism has triggered an ideological regression and that *The Dark Knight*'s popularity stems from the fact that the film "touches a nerve in our ideologico-political constellation: the undesirability of truth."[11]

"Those who claim that the human animal is wicked simply want to tame it and turn it into a morose wage-earner or a depressed consumer,"[12] writes Alain Badiou, reminding us of the pitfalls of the pessimistic view of human nature, of which John Milbank and Hans Boersma have accused Girard, saying that his placing violence at the heart of culture is tantamount to the claim that humanity is doomed without some kind of social control.[13] But of course, this is a misrepresentation of Girard, who quotes from his beloved Hölderlin at the end of the introduction to *Battling to the End*: "But where danger threatens / That which saves from it also grows."[14] It is worthwhile to quote the rest of this stanza from "Patmos," here translated by Scott Horton:

> God is near
> Yet hard to seize.
> Where there is danger,
> The rescue grows as well.
> Eagles live in the darkness,
> And the sons of the Alps
> Go fearlessly over the abyss
> Upon bridges simply built.
> Therefore, since the peaks
> Of Time are heaped all about,
> And dear ones live close by,
> Worn down on the most separated mountains—
> Then give us innocent waters;
> Give us wings, and the truest minds
> To voyage over and then again to return.[15]

Like Žižek, Girard utterly rejects the idea of protecting the lie to preserve the social order, instead turning to a positive view of the apocalypse and the non-mimetic Kingdom of God as preached by Jesus. But as the radical Catholic priest Alfred Loisy wrote in *L'évangile et l'église* in 1902, six years before his excommunication by Pope Pius X, "*Jésus annonçait le Royaume et c'est l'Église qui est venue* (Jesus came preaching the Kingdom, and what arrived was the Church)."[16] Like Badiou, Girard also rejects the universalization of scapegoating, which amounts to the scapegoating of humanity, and which is precisely what he accuses Freud of doing in universalizing the Oedipus complex instead of uncovering the innocence of Oedipus.[17] It is true that the floodgates of mimetic violence are opened and Girard argues that Christianity has made this possible by demystifying the sacrifice, but this poison also contains within it the cure. The powerful idea that can combat all the dangers is that of catholicity, the legacy not of Jesus, but of Paul, which completes Jesus's message of love and forgiveness with the message of universal truth. For Girard, it is unequivocally the Universal Roman Catholic Church that is the "last *Internationale*."[18] The question is: Where does this leave Hinduism?

Like the Napoleonic Europe that serves as the background for Girard's discussion of Clausewitz in *Battling to the End*, postcolonial India has seen its share of the escalation to extremes, from the Partition in 1947, to the assassinations of Mahatma Gandhi, Indira Gandhi, and Rajiv Gandhi, to the Union Carbide disaster in Bhopal in 1985, to periodic outbreaks of communal violence, to the nuclear stalemate of India and Pakistan. Religion is often the scapegoat for India's violence, but this is far too easy an answer. Religion, especially the anti-Muslim sentiments of right-wing Hindu movements like those responsible for the murder of 1,180 people in the 2007 anti-Muslim riots in Gujarat, has played a powerful part, but it is a religion that has grown directly out of secularism. As Girard argues, "Those who believe in the defeat of religion are now seeing it reappear as the product of that very demystification, but what is being produced is something sullied and demonetized, and frightened by the revelation of which it was the object."[19]

Ashis Nandy, one of the few Indian thinkers to have seriously engaged Girard's ideas, argues that communalism and secularism are "disavowed doubles," locked in what Girard would most certainly call a mimetic rivalry:

> Secular historians assume that the past of India has been bloody and fanatic, that the Hindus and the Muslims have been fighting for centuries, and that the secular state has now brought to the country a modicum of peace. They believe that the secular faiths—organized around the ideas of nation-state,

> scientific rationality, and development—are more tolerant and should correct that history (despite the more than 110 million persons killed in man-made violence in this century, the killing in most cases justified by secular faiths, including Baconian science and Darwinism in the case of colonialism, biology in the case of Nazism, and science and history in the case of communism). The Hindu nationalists believe that, except for Hinduism, most faiths, including the secular ones, are intolerant. But they do not celebrate that exception. They resent it; it embarrasses them. *They, therefore, seek to masculinize Hinduism to combat and, at the same time, resemble what according to them has been the style of the dominant faiths, which the Hindu nationalists see as more in tune with modern science and technology and, above all, scientized history*. At the same time, they insist that the history produced by their opponents, the Indian secularists, is not adequately scientific. *They believe, as their historically minded opponents do, that there is an implicit science of violence that shapes history and history itself gives us guidance about how to tame and use that violence for the higher purposes of history through the instrumentalities of the modern nation-state*. Like their opponents again, the Hindu nationalists are committed to liberating India from its nasty past, by acquiring access to the state in the name of undoing the past with the help of the same kind of history. The secular historians have done it in the past; the Hindu nationalists are hoping to do so in the future.
>
> In this "historical" battle, the two sides understand each other perfectly. One side has attacked only pseudo-secularism, not secularism; the other has attacked the stereotypy of minorities, never the "universal" concepts of the state, nationalism, and cultural integration that underpin the colonial construction of Hinduism that passes as Hindutva ["Hinduness"]. *It is a Mahābhāratic battle between two sets of illegitimate children, fathered by nineteenth-century Europe and the colonial empires, who have escaped from the orphanage of history.*[20]

Nandy astutely observes the ways in which secularism and communalism function as enemy twins, vainly attempting to control the violence of history, but without the means to do so.

I have been arguing for a unique critique of sacrifice in the Hindu tradition, visible in narratives like the *Mahābhārata* and philosophical systems like Pūrva Mīmāṃsā. And they are present in all those places, but we must face the fact that, probably because Hinduism never developed anything like a Church, these ideas were never mobilized and deployed in the world the way the Christian revelation was. To find an analogous moment in Hinduism, we must search out the period in which some Hindus, in imitation of Christianity, sought to remake their tradition into a world religion, the very period which gives rise to the "disavowed doubles" of secularism and communalism. And so we turn to the nineteenth century Hindu reformers, such as Swami Vivekananda and Sarvepalli Radhakrishnan, recently denigrated by Indologists and anthropologists as the men whose privileging of the esoteric and highly intellectual form of Hinduism known as Vedānta has produced hopeless distortions, as it effaces and repudiates the traditional and popular forms of religiosity practiced by most people calling themselves Hindus. In their attempts to turn Hinduism into a world religion, the argument goes, the nineteenth century reformers laid the groundwork for the highly selective and essentializing version of Indian religious history endorsed by the reactionary Hindu fringe we encountered in the introduction, banning books and attacking scholars. But I am persuaded by the recent call by Andrew J. Nicholson to reassess Vivekananda's and Radhakrishnan's legacy. Vedāntic universalism seems to me, much like the *pharmakon*, both a poison and a cure. On the last page of his book *Unifying Hinduism*, Nicholson attempts to rescue the universalizing force of the Hindu reformers from the forces of communalism:

> Hindu communalism has at its ideological foundations the need to completely elide differences within specifically circumscribed Hindu parameters. At the same time, it exaggerates differences between Hindu and non-Hindu, specifically with regard to the Muslims and Christians who have replaced Buddhist and Jainas in the discourses that enable Hindu self-identity. Yet contemporary Hinduism also contains universalizing, globalizing tendencies: the global Hinduism of the heirs of Radhakrishnan and Vivekananda is one that transcends national boundaries and that understands Hindu philosophical truth as a legacy that belongs to all nations equally. As Vivekananda wrote, "No man, no nation, my son, can hate others and live; India's doom was sealed the day they invented the word *mlechcha* [*sic*][21] and stopped from communion with others."[22]

Nicholson alludes to a possible "third way" (or perhaps a middle way, to follow the Buddha) that "acknowledges differences between religions as real (unlike the universalists) but sees those differences as potentially enriching Hinduism, rather than threatening to destroy it (as the communalists do)."[23] But I think Nicholson misses an opportunity here. As an antidote to the enemy twins of secularism and communalism, Vivekananda's call to abandon the politics of *mleccha*-making seems to be a more radical choice than the multiculturalism of liberal democracy, which cannot grasp the power of the *homo sacer* that is so forcefully present in the Śaiva critique of sacrifice. It is only by becoming the *mleccha* ourselves, by becoming the *homo sacer*, that we can overcome scapegoating. But, fortunately or unfortunately, this is not a choice we have to make, since the alienating forces of global capitalism are well on the way to making *homines sacrī* of us all. As Žižek writes in a 2009 article in the *New Left Review*:

> The predominant liberal notion of democracy also deals with those excluded, but in a radically different mode: it focuses on their inclusion, as minority voices. All positions should be heard, all interests taken into account, the human rights of everyone guaranteed, all ways of life, cultures and practices respected, and so on. The obsession of this democracy is the protection of all kinds of minorities: cultural, religious, sexual, etc. The formula of democracy here consists of patient negotiation and compromise. What gets lost in this is the position of universality embodied in the excluded. The new emancipatory politics will no longer be the act of a particular social agent, but an explosive combination of different agents. What unites us is that, in contrast to the classic image of proletarians who have 'nothing to lose but their chains,' we are in danger of losing everything. The threat is that we will be reduced to an abstract, empty Cartesian subject dispossessed of all our symbolic content, with our genetic base manipulated, vegetating in an unliveable environment. This triple threat makes us all proletarians, reduced to 'substanceless subjectivity,' as Marx put it in the *Grundrisse*. The figure of the 'part of no part' confronts us with the truth of our own position; and the ethico-political challenge is to recognize ourselves in this figure. In a way, we are all excluded, from nature as well as from our symbolic substance. Today, we are all potentially *homo sacer*, and the only way to avoid actually becoming so is to act preventively.[24]

Vivekananda's Vedāntic call for an end to scapegoating and *mleccha*-making, though it may come from a philosophy highly influenced by the religious sensibilities of the colonial masters, comes very close to embracing the Hindu critique of sacrifice we have seen throughout the tradition, from the Vedas to the *Mahābhārata*. Oddly enough, it would seem then that Hinduism's war against the "powers and principalities" of communal violence and nationalism really is found precisely where Girard expected it to be: in the philosophical tradition emerging from the Upaniṣads. Perhaps it is after all in Vedānta, the "End of the Veda," that we begin to see the possibility for Yajñānta, the "End of Sacrifice."

Notes

Introduction

1. "India's Gift to the World," *Brooklyn Standard Union*, February 27, 1895.
2. Axel Michaels, *Hinduism: Past and Present*, trans. Barbara Harshav (Princeton, NJ: Princeton University Press, 2004), 32.
3. Brian K. Smith, *Reflections on Resemblance, Ritual, and Religion* (New York: Oxford University Press, 1989), 13–14.
4. Thus "Brāhmaṇic" would refer to something related to the texts and "Brahminical" would refer to something related to the people.
5. Michael Witzel, "Vedas and Upaniṣads," in *The Blackwell Companion to Hinduism*, ed. Gavin Flood (Malden, MA: Blackwell Publishing Ltd., 2003), 68.
6. G. S. Mudur, "Caste Barriers Not Older than 2000 Years—Indians Mated Across Ethnic Groups until 2nd Century: Study," *The Telegraph*, August 9, 2013, http://www.telegraphindia.com/1130809/jsp/nation/story_17213287.jsp.
7. Tracing one Vedic lineage will help to illustrate the structure of the corpus: The Taittirīya branch of the Black *Yajur Veda* contains the *Taittirīya Saṃhitā*, the *Taittirīya Brāhmaṇa*, the *Taittirīya Āraṇyaka*, and the *Taittirīya Upaniṣad*.
8. David N. Lorenzen, *Who Invented Hinduism: Essays on Religion in History* (New Delhi: Yoda Press, 2006), 2.
9. We should note, though, that the period in which Roy considered himself a "Hindu Unitarian" was between the years 1824 and 1828, well after he coined the word.
10. Lorenzen, *Who Invented Hinduism*, 36.

11. *Mensonge romantique et vérité romanesque* (Paris: Grasset, 1961); *Deceit, Desire and the Novel: Self and Other in Literary Structure* (Baltimore: Johns Hopkins University Press, 1966). The more accurate French title translates to something more like "Romantic Lie and Novelistic Truth."

12. *La violence et le sacré* (Paris: Grasset, 1972); *Violence and the Sacred* (Baltimore: Johns Hopkins University Press, 1977).

13. *Des choses cachées depuis la fondation du monde* (Paris: Grasset, 1978); *Things Hidden since the Foundation of the World: Research undertaken in collaboration with Jean-Michel Oughourlian and G. Lefort*, eds. Stephen Bann and Michael Leigh Metteer (Stanford, CA: Stanford University Press, 1987).

14. Again, the French title, *Achever Clausewitz: Entretiens avec Benoît Chantre* (Paris: Carnets Nord, 2007), translates to "Completing Clausewitz," which gives a much better idea of the project the book undertakes. *Battling to the End: Conversations with Benoît Chantre* (East Lansing: Michigan State University Press, 2010).

15. Mark Johnston, *Saving God: Religion after Idolatry* (Princeton, NJ: Princeton University Press, 2009), 161.

16. This gives a rather ominous subtext to the old saying "Two's company, three's a crowd."

17. J. P. Mallory and Douglas Q. Adams, *The Oxford Introduction to Proto-Indo-European and the Proto-Indo-European World* (New York: Oxford University Press, 2006), 412.

18. Terry Eagleton expresses the idea with admirable lucidity in *Literary Theory: An Introduction* (Minneapolis: University of Minnesota Press, 1983), 131:

> [Western philosophy] has yearned for the sign which will give meaning to all others . . . for the anchoring, unquestionable meaning to which all our signs can be seen to point (the 'transcendental signified'). A great number of candidates for this role—God, the Idea, the World Spirit, the Self, substance, matter and so on—have thrust themselves forward from time to time. Since each of these concepts hopes to found our whole system of thought and language, it must itself be beyond that system, untainted by its play of linguistic differences. It cannot be implicated in the very languages which it attempts to order and anchor: it must be somehow anterior to these discourses, must have existed before they did. It must be a meaning, but not like any other meaning just a product of a play of difference. It must figure rather as the meaning of meanings, the lynchpin or fulcrum of a whole thought-system, the sign around which all others revolve and which all others obediently reflect.
>
> That any such transcendental meaning is a fiction though perhaps a necessary fiction—is one consequence of the theory of language I have outlined. There is no concept which is not embroiled in an open-ended play of signification, shot through with the traces and fragments of other ideas. It is just that, out of this play of signifiers, certain meanings are elevated by social ideologies to a privileged position, or made the centres around which other meanings are forced to turn.

19. René Girard, *Things Hidden since the Foundation of the World*, eds. Stephen Bann and Michael Leigh Metteer (Stanford, CA: Stanford University Press, 1987), 102–103.

20. Girard, *Things Hidden*, 103.

21. See David Dawson, *Flesh Becomes Word: A Lexicography of the Scapegoat or, the History of an Idea* (East Lansing: Michigan State University Press, 2013).

22. René Girard, *Sacrifice*, trans. Matthew Patillo and David Dawson (East Lansing: Michigan State University Press, 2011), 10.

23. Girard, *Sacrifice*, 87.

24. Alan Cameron, *The Last Pagans of Rome* (New York: Oxford University Press, 2011), 65.

25. See Herman D'Souza, *In the Steps of St. Thomas* (Pune: Yeravda Prison Press, 1964).

26. Wendy Doniger, *The Hindus: An Alternative History* (New York: Penguin Press, 2009), 339.

27. Doniger, *Hindus*, 367.

28. Girard, *Sacrifice*, 87–88 (italics added).

29. Swami Venkatesananda, *Vasiṣṭha's Yoga* (Albany: State University of New York Press, 1993), 34.

30. Hayden White, "Ethnological 'Lie' and Mythical 'Truth,'" *Diacritics* 8:1, Special Issue on the Work of René Girard (Spring 1978), 2.

31. Jesse Goldhammer, *The Headless Republic: Sacrificial Violence in Modern French Thought* (Ithaca, NY: Cornell University Press, 2005), 107.

32. Ivan Strenski, *Theology and the First Theory of Sacrifice* (Boston: Brill, 2003), 204 (italics added).

33. Strenski, *Theology*, 65.

34. Girard, *Violence and the Sacred*, 222.

35. Strenski, *Theology*, 205.

36. David Frankfurter, *Evil Incarnate: Rumors of Demonic Conspiracy and Ritual Abuse in History* (Princeton, NJ: Princeton University Press, 2006), 213.

37. Girard, *Sacrifice*, 82.

38. Raymund Schwager, "The Theology of the Wrath of God," in *Violence and Truth: On the Work of René Girard*, ed. Paul Dumouchel (Stanford, CA: Stanford University Press, 1988), 52.

39. Girard, *Things Hidden*, 221–222.

40. Girard, *Things Hidden*, 221.

41. Girard, *Things Hidden*, 221.

42. All Bible verses are taken from Wayne A. Meeks, et al., *The HarperCollins Study Bible*, New Revised Standard Edition with the Apocryphal/Deuterocanonical Books (New York: HarperCollins, 1993).

43. Girard, *Sacrifice*, 45.

44. And yet there is still something about the advent (or the event) of Christianity that undeniably and irreparably destabilizes the deep structure of Indo-European ideology in a seismic shift Nietzsche calls the transvaluation of values and Girard calls the revelation of the scapegoat mechanism. This is nowhere more apparent than in the modern mythology of the American Dream. Where a century ago, in the world so magnificently recorded in the writings of Marcel Proust, F. Scott Fitzgerald, and Evelyn Waugh, it was desirable to conceal one's humble origins, it is now vital that one conceal one's elevated origins. In the contemporary era, people are more likely to invent a phony rags-to-riches story for themselves than claim descent from some blue-blooded aristocracy. Although Nietzsche's point of view is more complex than this, he essentially treats the slave morality of Christianity as a disaster for the most part, while for Girard it is a

relative bad thing and an absolute good thing. And unlike de Maistre, Girard has no interest in propping up a sacrificial system, no matter how stable, productive, and secure a society it produces. Girard's Christianity is a complete rejection of sacrificial violence in all its guises. But he also recognizes that by destroying the power of the sacrificial system, Christianity has opened the floodgates of mimetic violence and put the world in imminent danger of apocalyptic destruction. But locating the total revelation of the scapegoat victim in the Gospels—a set of texts written by humans, authorized by human institutions and edited with an eye to some very worldly concerns—is to grant them a non-human origin, which is a theological and not a scholarly position. If we were to read Girard atheologically, we could render his argument in these terms: The sacrificial system that arises as result of the spontaneous founding murder always contains the seeds of its own destruction. Around the beginning of the first millennium C.E. these seeds of destruction began to bear fruit that has been ripening ever since. In other words, the same system that brought humanity as we know it into the world may ultimately be responsible for ushering it out in what the Sanskrit Purāṇas call the *mahāpralaya* or "great dissolution." In fact, we will soon see that the picture Girard's argument paints is very close to the classical Indian conception of time.

45. Lucien Scubla, "The Christianity of René Girard and the Nature of Religion," trans. Mark Anspach, in *Violence and Truth: On the Work of René Girard*, ed. Paul Dumouchel (Stanford, CA: Stanford University Press, 1988), 178.

46. Robert Hamerton-Kelly, "Response" (presented at the Symposium on René Girard and World Religions at the Graduate Theological Union, Berkeley, California, April 14–16, 2011).

47. René Girard, "Tiresias and the Critic," in *The Structuralist Controversy: The Languages of Criticism and the Sciences of Man*, eds. Richard Macksey and Eugenio Donato (Baltimore: Johns Hopkins University Press, 1975), 20.

48. René Girard, "Generative Scapegoating; Girard Paper: Discussion," in *Violent Origins: Ritual Killing and Cultural Formation*, ed. Robert G. Hamerton-Kelly (Stanford, CA: Stanford University Press, 1987), 140.

49. Girard, "Discussion," 141.

50. Girard, "Discussion," 141.

51. Robert Ackerman, *J. G. Frazer: His Life and Work* (New York: Cambridge University Press, 1987), 171.

52. J. G. Frazer, *Balder the Beautiful Volume I: The Fire Festivals of Europe and the Doctrine of the External Soul*, part 7 of *The Golden Bough: A Study in Magic and Religion*, 3rd ed. (Project Gutenberg, May 4, 2004), e-book #12261.

53. Jonathan Z. Smith, "When the Bough Breaks," *History of Religions* 12:4 (May 1973): 371.

54. Ackerman, *J. G. Frazer*, 189.

55. Girard, *Sacrifice*, 66.

56. Girard, *Things Hidden*, 251.

57. Krishnan Ramaswamy, Antonio de Nicolas, and Aditi Banerjee, "Invading the Sacred: An Analysis of Hinduism Studies in America," http://invadingthesacred.com/content/view/13/33/.

58. McComas Taylor, "Mythology Wars: The Indian Diaspora, 'Wendy's Children' and the Struggle for the Hindu Past," *Asian Studies Review* 35:2:06 (2011): 149.

59. H. Nagarajao, November 12, 2010, "Dissapointing and full of manufactured and manipulated

lies," review of *The Hindus: An Alternative History* by Wendy Doniger, *Amazon.com*, http://www.amazon.com/review/R34UOB82P8FNWX/ref=cm_cr_pr_perm?ie=UTF8&ASIN=1594202052&nodeID=&tag=&linkCode=.

60. Aseem Shukla, "Whose History Is It Anyway?" *Washington Post*, March 2010, http://onfaith.washingtonpost.com/onfaith/panelists/aseem_shukla/2010/03/whose_history_is_it_anyways.html.

61. Girard, *Things Hidden*, 251.

62. Shiv Sena spokesman Raj Thackeray did later apologize for the incident, to his credit. "Raj Thackeray Apologizes to Bahulkar," *The Times of India*, December 29, 2003, http://articles.timesofindia.indiatimes.com/2003-12-29/pune/27195967_1_sanskrit-references-sena-mla-deepak-paigude-sanskrit-scholar-shrikant-bahulkar.

63. Alain Badiou, *Saint Paul: The Foundation of Universalism* (Stanford, CA: Stanford University Press, 2003), 1.

64. Badiou, *Saint Paul*, 14.

65. Badiou, *Saint Paul*, 44.

66. Slavoj Žižek, *Living in the End Times* (New York: Verso, 2010), 21.

67. For an interesting comparison of Žižek and Girard, see Frederiek Depoortere, *Christ in Postmodern Philosophy: Gianni Vattimo, René Girard and Slavoj Žižek* (London: T & T Clark, 2008).

68. The temple in question was built during the period of the Medang kingdom from the eighth to the tenth centuries, between four and seven centuries after the arrival of Hindu missionaries in the region. Nearby stands the Buddhist complex of Candi Sojiwan, attesting to the Hindu-Buddhist fusion that the Medang adopted as its state religion.

69. Roy E. Jordaan and Robert Wessing, "Construction Sacrifice in India, 'Seen from the East,'" in *Violence Denied: Violence, Non-Violence and the Rationalization of Violence in South Asian Cultural History*, ed. Jan E. M. Houben and Karel R. Van Kooij (Boston: Brill, 1995), 215.

70. Ramacandra Kaulācāra, *Śilpa Prakāśa: Mediaeval Orissan Sanskrit Text on Temple Architecture*, trans. Alice Boner and Sadāśiva Rath Śarmā (Leiden, Netherlands: Brill, 1966), 77.

71. Jordaan and Wessing, "Construction Sacrifice," 238.

72. The terms *astika* and *nāstika* respectively refer to the "pro" and "con" positions of a Sanskrit philosophical debate.

73. Girard takes his version of the story on pages 89–91 from Sylvain Lévi's French translation in *La doctrine du sacrifice dans les Brâhmanas* (Paris: Ernest Leroux, 1898), 118–120, translated here into English:

> Manu had some vessels. If they clattered, all the Asuras who heard the clatter ceased to exist that day. Now, there were in those days among the Asuras two Brahmins, Tṛṣṭa and Varutri. The Asuras said to those two, "Cure us of this evil." The two Brahmins said, "Manu, you are a sacrificer. Faith is your God. Give us these vessels." He gave them to them and they destroyed them by means of fire. A bull licked the flames and the [power of the] sound entered into him. If it bellowed, all the Asuras who heard it bellowing ceased to exist that day. Tṛṣṭa and Varutri said, "Manu, you are a sacrificer. Faith is your God. We will sacrifice this bull for you." They sacrificed the bull for him and the [power of the] voice passed into the wife of Manu. If she spoke, all the

Asuras who heard her ceased to exist that day. Tṛṣṭa and Varutri said, "Manu, you are a sacrificer. Faith is your God. We will sacrifice your wife for you." They splashed her with water, led her around the fire, and prepared the wood and the grass.

Indra observed, "These two hypocrites among the Asuras deprive Manu of his wife." Passing himself off as a Brahmin, Indra approached and said, "Manu, you are a sacrificer. Faith is your God. I want to sacrifice for you." [Manu asked,] "Who are you?" "A Brahmin," [Indra replied]. "What is the use of asking after the father of a Brahmin or his mother? If you can find in him the sacred science, that is his father, that is his grandfather." [Manu asked,] "What will be the offering?" "These two Brahmins," [replied Indra]. [Manu asked,] "Am I the lord of these two Brahmins?" "You are their lord," [Indra answered]. "Whosoever offers hospitality is the lord of his guests." He advanced to destroy the other altar. [The false Brahmins] brought the wood and the grass. They said [to Indra], "What are you doing there?" [Indra answered,] "I am sacrificing for Manu." "With what?," [they asked]. "With you," [said Indra]. They knew then that it was Indra. They threw down the wood and the grass and ran away. . . . Manu said to Indra, "Complete my sacrifice, that my sacrifice not be lost." He said to [Manu], "What you desire by sacrificing her you will have, but leave this woman." And he let his wife go.

74. Joseph Townsend, *The Character of Moses Established for Veracity as an Historian, Recording Events from the Creation to the Deluge* (London: M. Gye, et al., 1816), 76, as quoted in "Adam Clarke's Bible Commentary–Romans 9," http://www.godrules.net/library/clarke/clarkerom9.htm (italics added).

75. Kṛṣṇadāsa Kavirāja, *Caitanya Caritāmṛta of Kṛṣṇadāsa Kavirāja: A Translation and Commentary*, ed. Tony Stewart, trans. Edward C. Dimock, Jr. (Cambridge, MA: Harvard University Press, 2000), 826–828.

76. Adam Clarke, *The New Testament of Our Lord and Savior Jesus Christ: The Text in the Authorized Translation with a Commentary and Critical Notes*, http://www.godrules.net/library/clarke/clarke.php#commentary.

77. Adam Clarke, *The New Testament.*

78. Adam Clarke, *The New Testament.* Never mind that Christ himself says in Matthew 10:35, "I have come to set a man against his father, and a daughter against her mother, and a daughter-in-law against her mother-in-law."

79. Hugh B. Urban, *Tantra: Sex, Secrecy, Politics, and Power in the Study of Religion* (Berkeley: University of California Press, 2003), 81.

80. René Girard, *The Scapegoat* (Baltimore: Johns Hopkins University Press, 1986), 15. Accounts of the murder of British women and children abounded in reports of the Sepoy Mutiny of 1857, which Queen Victoria's government used as a pretext to institute the Viceregency in 1858, taking India away from the British East India Company and putting it under the direct control of the Crown. See especially the accounts of the siege at Cawnpore (Kānpur) treated in Jan Morris, *Heaven's Command: An Imperial Progress*, vol. 1 of *The Pax Britannica Trilogy* (Boston: Mariner Books, 2002), 230–236.

81. As Hugh Urban has shown without citing Girard directly, these stereotypes are omnipresent in the accounts of not only the Thugees, but of Tantric religion (often associated with the worship of the goddess Kālī) in general, remarking, "While reading these accounts, it is difficult for a modern reader not to be reminded of medieval Inquisitors' accounts of witchcraft, or the Christian Fathers' accounts of the perverse rituals of certain Gnostic heresies." The loss of social cohesion

(a symptom of the sacrificial crisis) also attends the onset of the Thugee scare. Urban quotes John Malcolm's assessment that at the time of the Thugee persecution, "[the] native states were disorganized and society on the verge of dissolution; the people crushed by despots, the country overrun by bandits. . . . [G]overnment had ceased to exist; there remained only oppression and misery" (Urban, *Tantra*, 83). The perverse sexuality of Tantra is a well-worn cliché, but for an example of the Sadean excesses conjured up by the British imagination, we can look at the account of a Tantric rite, quoted by Urban, from Elizabeth Sharpe's sensational occult novel *Secrets of the Kaula Circle* (London: Luzac, 1936) in which the author describes a Dionysian Tantric ritual that climaxes on page 47 with "a perfect orgy of bestiality."

82. Urban, *Tantra*, 82.

83. Felix Padel, *The Sacrifice of Human Being: British Rule and the Konds of Orissa* (New York: Oxford University Press, 1995), 33–34.

84. Padel, *Sacrifice*, 111.

85. Padel, *Sacrifice*, 110–112.

86. Lata Mani, *Contentious Traditions: The Debate on* Sati *in Colonial India* (Berkeley: University of California Press, 1998), 2. This situation recalls certain aspects of the contemporary debate about abortion, in which politicians and activists who fight to protect the lives of the unborn show little concern for the children of unwanted pregnancies once they are born and placed into the foster care system.

87. H. T. Colebrooke, *Essays on History, Literature and Religions of Ancient India* (London: Williams and Norgate, 1858), 35–36.

88. Urban, *Tantra*, 5–6.

89. To give the reader an idea of Winternitz's place in the Indological tradition (or *parampara* in Sanskrit), he was the teacher of Heinrich Lüders, who went on to train Vishnu S. Sukthankar, the Indian scholar appointed by the Bhandarkar Oriental Research Institute as the general editor of the *Mahābhārata* critical edition project in 1925. The methods of interpreting Sanskrit texts developed by Winternitz were used by Bhandarkar to determine how to construct a critical edition from the hundreds of regional *Mahābhārata* texts, and that critical edition is the text that the vast majority of Indologists have been using for better or worse since it was completed in 1966.

90. Maurice Winternitz, *A History of Indian Literature Volume One: Introduction, Veda, Epics, Purāṇas and Tantras* (Delhi: Motilal Banarsidass, 1981), 162.

91. *The Veda of the Black Yajus School Entitled Taittirīya Sanhitā*, Harvard Oriental Series 18, trans. A. B. Keith (Cambridge, MA: Harvard University Press, 1914), cxxxviii.

92. Keith, *Taittirīya Sanhitā*, cxxxix.

93. Winternitz, *History of Indian Literature*, 199.

94. See H. H. Wilson, "On the Sacrifice of Human Beings as an Element of the Ancient Religion of India," *Journal of the Royal Asiatic Society* 13 (1852), and F. Max Müller, *A History of Ancient Sanskrit Literature so Far as It Illustrates the Primitive Religion of the Brahmans*, 2nd ed. (London: Williams and Norgate, 1860), 419. The question must not have been the cause of too much contention between them, though, since Müller dedicated his work to Wilson "as a token of admiration and gratitude by his pupil and friend."

95. A debate that closely parallels the one about human sacrifice is the debate about the killing of

cows in Ancient India. Like the pastoral Nuer tribe observed by Evans-Pritchard, the Brahmin clans also see cows as a kind of parallel human society. This is true at least in the etymology of the word for a Brahmin clan, *gotra*, a term for a cow stall derived from the Sanskrit word *go* (cognate with our "cow"). The issue of cow killing has long been a point of contention between Hindus and meat-eating Muslims in India and the idea of the "holy cow" is one of the great clichés about Hinduism. The basis of this cliché was demonstrated when the historian D. N. Jha presented his evidence for widespread practice of eating beef in early Hinduism in *The Myth of the Holy Cow* (London: Verso, 2002) and his book was greeted with outrage.

96. The Colloquium on Violence & Religion has done much to amend this mischaracterization in recent years, including a Symposium on René Girard and World Religions at The Graduate Theological Union in Berkeley in April 2011 and a book panel on *Sacrifice* with Francis X. Clooney, Katherine McClymond, David Dawson, and this author at the 2012 American Academy of Religion conference in Chicago.

Rivalries

1. For a fuller account of European scholars' assessments of the Brāhmaṇas, see Wendy Doniger, *Tales of Sex and Violence: Folklore, Sacrifice, and Danger in the* Jaiminīya Brāhmana (Chicago: University of Chicago Press, 1985), 3–9; Brian K. Smith, *Reflections*, 30–46; and Herman W. Tull, "F. Max Müller and A. B. Keith: 'Twaddle,' the 'Stupid' Myth, and the Disease of Indology," *Numen* 38:1 (June 1991): 27–58.

2. F. Max Müller, *Chips from a German Workshop, Vol. I: Essays on the Science of Religion* (New York: Charles Scribner's Sons, 1891), 113.

3. Arthur A. MacDonnell, *A History of Sanskrit Literature* (London: William Heinemann, 1900), 32.

4. W. D. Whitney, "Eggeling's Translation of the *Çatapatha Brāhmaṇa*," *American Journal of Philology* 3:12 (1882): 393.

5. *The Śatapatha-Brāhmaṇa, According to the Text of the Mâdhyandina School, Part I, Books I and II*, trans. Julius Eggeling, volume 12 of *Sacred Books of the East*, ed. F. Max Müller (Oxford: Clarendon, 1882), ix. Eggeling goes on to explain that he has undertaken this "rather thankless task" at the request of none other than F. Max Müller himself, then general editor of the 50-volume *Sacred Books of the East* series, of which the rest of the *Śatapatha-Brāhmaṇa* takes up volumes 26, 41, 43, and 44.

6. Eggeling, *Śatapatha-Brāhmaṇa*, ix.

7. Girard, *Sacrifice*, 10–11.

8. Girard, *Sacrifice*, 10.

9. "People have complained that books about Vedic ritual, and ritual generally, are tedious and dull. This is often true and always due to the fact that ritual activities should be seen and heard, not read about. Witnessing the live performance of one ritual provides more understanding than the study of dozens of monographs" (Frits Staal, "What Is Happening in Classical Indology?—A Review Article," *The Journal of Asian Studies* 41:2 [Feb. 1982]: 281). Having read a number of scholarly studies on Vedic ritual and observed only one in the form of a Full-moon Iṣṭi performed in a Brahmin's smoke-filled living room in Pune in 2001, I can only express qualified skepticism at what looks like the naivety of this statement. Be that as it may, Frits Staal, who died at the age of 81 on February 19, 2012, during the writing of this book, was a prodigious scholar whose

contribution to the field is incalculable. I could not have written this book were I not able to stand on the shoulders of giants like Staal.

10. There are two types of Vedic rites. The *śrauta* or solemn rites require three fires (the *dakṣina* or southern fire, the *gārhapatya* or householder's fire, and the *āhavanīya* or offering fire) and a team of priests from all the branches of the Veda. The *gṛhya* or domestic rites only require one fire and a domestic priest or chaplain called a *purohita*. Unless noted otherwise, we will only be discussing the solemn rites here.

11. Staal, "What Is Happening," 280.

12. Girard, *Violence and the Sacred*, 6.

13. Smith, *Reflections*, 46–47.

14. Smith, *Reflections*, 44.

15. René Girard, "The Evangelical Subversion of Myth," in *Politics and Apocalypse*, ed. Robert Hamerton-Kelly (East Lansing: Michigan State University Press, 2007), 45.

16. Girard, "Evangelical Subversion," 45.

17. Girard, "Evangelical Subversion," 45.

18. See Hamerton-Kelly's Girardian critique of Hegel in *Sacred Violence: Paul's Hermeneutic of the Cross* (Minneapolis: Fortress Press, 1992), 199–207, and Girard's own critique of Freud in *Things Hidden*, 352–392.

19. Roberto Calasso, *The Ruin of Kasch*, trans. William Weaver and Stephen Sartarelli (Cambridge, MA: The Belknap Press of Harvard University Press, 1994), 158.

20. Girard, *Sacrifice*, 20.

21. Rose Vincent, *The French in India: From Diamond Traders to Sanskrit Scholars*, trans. Latika Padgaonkar and Rose Vincent (Bombay: Popular Prakashan, 1990), 22.

22. François Charpentier, *Discours d'un fidèle sujet du roy touchant l'establissement d'une compagnie françoise pour le commerce des Indes orientales: adressé à tous les français* (Paris: 1665), 7.

23. It is now called Putuccēri, but still retains some of the trappings of a French colony to the present day, including an unofficial designation as *La Côte d'Azur de l'Est*.

24. Hermann Kulke and Dietmar Rothermund, *A History of India* (New York: Routledge, 2010), 228.

25. And recently traced, using the computer models of evolutionary biology, to eighth millennium B.C.E. Anatolia (now Turkey), where agriculture developed in the wake of the last glacial age. Predictably, many linguists remain unconvinced, mostly because the unanimous Indo-European evidence of words for the parts of the wagon, including the wheel, and for copper, excludes dates before the late fourth millennium B.C.E., when we have the earliest evidence of these two technologies. Remco Bouckaert, et al., "Mapping the Origins and Expansion of the Indo-European Language Family," *Science* 24:337:6097 (August 2012): 957–960. See also Edwin F. Bryant, *The Quest for the Origins of Vedic Culture: The Indo-Aryan Migration Debate* (New York: Oxford University Press, 2001).

26. "The *Sanscrit* language, whatever be its antiquity, is of a wonderful structure; more perfect than the *Greek*, more copious than the *Latin*, and more exquisitely refined than either, yet bearing to both of them a stronger affinity, both in the roots of verbs and the forms of grammar, than could possibly have been produced by accident; so strong indeed, that no philologer could examine them all three, without believing them to have sprung from some common source, which, perhaps,

no longer exists; there is a similar reason, though not quite so forcible, for supposing that both the *Gothic* and the *Celtic*, though blended with a very different idiom, had the same origin with the *Sanscrit*; and the old *Persian* might be added to the same family" (Sir William Jones, *Discourses Delivered before the Asiatic Society: And Miscellaneous Papers, on the Religion, Poetry, Literature, etc., of the Nations of India* [London: C. S. Arnold, 1824], 28).

27. Bruce Lincoln, *Theorizing Myth: Narrative, Ideology, and Scholarship* (Chicago: University of Chicago Press, 1999), 85–88.

28. Jean-Sylvain Bailly, *Lettres sur l'origine des sciences et sur celle des peuples de L'Asie* (Paris: Frères Debure: 1777), 51.

29. Bryant, *Quest for the Origins of Vedic Culture*, 18.

30. Claudine Leblanc, annotated bibliographic entry on Foucher d'Obsonville and Maridâs Poullé, ed. and trans., *Bagavadam ou Doctrine divine; ouvrage indien canonique, sur l'être suprême, les dieux, les géants, les hommes, Bhāgavata-Purāna* (Paris: Tillard, 1788) in "Bilingual Annotations" to "French Books on India: From Dupleix to Decolonization v. 1," ed. Guy Deleury et al., http://www.liv.ac.uk/soclas/research/Peripheralvoices/french-books/Bilingual_annotations.pdf.

31. The Vellajas technically belonged to the Śūdras, the lowest of the four classes of classical Indian ideology. But despite the official doctrines on caste hierarchy, it was not in practice unusual for Śūdras to attain high estates as far back as the late Vedic period, when the Śūdra Nanda dynasty overthrew the Śiśunagas in the fifth century B.C.E.

32. Jaques Weber, "Chanemougam, 'King of French India': Social and Political Foundations of an Absolute Power under the Third Republic," *Economic and Political Weekly* 26:6 (Feb. 9, 1991): 301.

33. Weber, "Chanemougam," 301.

34. Weber, "Chanemougam," 301.

35. Vincent, *French in India*, 145–146.

36. Girard, *Sacrifice*, 11.

37. My thanks go to William Johnsen for pointing out that Lévi is listed in the bibliography of *Violence and the Sacred*, though not in the index, suggesting that Girard may have picked up on something that he meant to make more of later.

38. The official reason given for the rejection was his young age, although his 18-year-old classmate Henri Berr had no trouble being admitted.

39. Ivan Strenski, "Zionism, Brahminism and the Embodied Sacred: What the Durkheimians Owe to Sylvain Lévi," in *The Sacred and Its Scholars: Comparative Methodologies for the Study of Primary Religious Data*, eds. Thomas A. Idinopulos and Edward A. Yonan (New York: Brill, 1996), 20.

40. Roland Lardinois, *L'invention de l'Inde: Entre ésotérisme et science* (Paris: CNRS Éditions, 2007), 225.

41. Strenski, "Zionism," 23.

42. Strenski, "Zionism," 29.

43. Strenski, "Zionism," 26.

44. Strenski, "Zionism," 26.

45. And if Girard bashes the idea of irreducible cultural difference, he does so no more than Alain Badiou, the reigning grand master of French intellectuals.

46. D. Némedi, W. S. F. Pickering, and H. L. Sutcliffe, "Durkheim's Friendship with the Philosopher Octave Hamelin: Together with Translations of Two Items by Durkheim," *The British Journal of Sociology* 46:1 (Mar., 1995), 114.

47. Lardinois, *L'invention*, 224.

48. Howard Murphy, "Some Concluding Anthropological Reflections," afterword to *On Prayer* by Marcel Mauss, W. S. F. Pickering, and Howard Murphy (New York: Bergahn Books, 2003), 139.

49. Tim Jenkins, "Marcel Mauss's Essay *On Prayer*: An Important Contribution on the Nature of Sociological Understanding," *Revue du MAUSS permanente* (Nov. 6, 2008), http://www.journaldumauss.net/spip.php?article418.

50. Lardinois, *L'invention*, 224.

51. Lévi, *La doctrine*, 133.

52. Strenski, "Zionism," 34.

53. Wendy Doniger, *The Origins of Evil in Hindu Mythology* (Berkeley: University of California Press, 1976), 58.

54. Girard, *Sacrifice*, 17.

55. Lévi, *La doctrine*, 74.

56. Girard, *Things Hidden*, 52.

57. Girard, *Sacrifice*, 21.

58. The "family books" of the *Ṛg Veda*, which is divided into ten books or *maṇḍalas* ("circles"), are so called because they are each attributed to a Vedic Brahmin clan descended from an eponymous seer, or *ṛṣi*. The second book is attributed to the Gṛtasamadas, the third to the Viśvāmitras, the fourth to the Vāmadevas, the fifth to the Atris, the sixth to the Bharadvājas and the seventh to the Vasiṣṭhas.

59. According to the Sanskrit rule of phonetics called *saṃdhi*, when you pronounce a short *a* just before another short *a* or a long *a* the result is a lengthening of the vowel. Thus we get the formula *a + asura = āsura*.

60. Aryan from the Vedic word *arya*, or "noble," is the name used for themselves by the people who brought the Veda into India. Its close Indo-European cognates are seen today in the place names Iran and Éire (Ireland).

61. Stanley Insler, "Review of *ÁSURA in Early Vedic Religion*, by Wash Edward Hale," *Journal of the American Oriental Society* 113:4 (Oct.–Dec., 1993): 596.

62. For a philologically informed discussion, see Calvert Watkins, *How to Kill a Dragon: Aspects of Indo-European Poetics* (New York: Oxford University Press, 1995), 297–440.

63. *The Rig Veda: An Anthology; One Hundred and Eight Hymns Selected, Translated and Annotated by Wendy Doniger* (New York: Penguin Classics, 1981), 110–111.

64. The image of Indra hurling his lightning bolt at Vṛtra and causing the waters to fall from his belly is strongly reminiscent of a thunderstorm, leading many to conclude that this is a nature myth.

65. It may never have been part of the Veda to begin with. Many Vedic hymns seem to refer to

a mythology that was known to all, and perhaps for this reason it never became part of the memorized tradition. We may be trying to piece together *Hamlet* from *Rosencrantz and Guildenstern Are Dead*. Or, conversely, we may be trying to reconstruct a biography of the title character from *Waiting for Godot*.

66. Abel Bergaigne, *La religion védique d'après les hymnes du* Rig-Véda (Paris: P. Vieweg, 1878), 139–149.

67. Tvaṣṭṛ is the craftsman of the gods.

68. *The Rig Veda*, 150.

69. Girard, *Sacrifice*, 54.

70. Hermann Oldenberg, *The Religion of the Veda*, trans. Shridhar B. Shroti (Delhi: Motilal Banarsidass, 1988), 154n91.

71. Henri Hubert and Marcel Mauss, *Sacrifice: Its Nature and Functions*, trans. W. D. Halls (Chicago: University of Chicago Press, 1964), 154n476.

72. F. B. J. Kuiper, "Four Word Studies," *Indo-Iranian Journal* 15:3 (Sept. 1973), 183.

73. Madeleine Biardeau, *Le sacrifice dans l'inde ancienne*, ed. Charles Malamoud (Paris: Presses universitaires de France, 1976), 90.

74. As the slayer of Vṛtra, Indra is also a creator deity. He is described making firm the earth and settling the mountains in *ṚV* 2.12.2, and separating and supporting the heavens and the earth after slaying Vṛtra in 5.29.4 and 7.23.3.

75. This is a play on words based on the word *pra-sū*, which means literally, "to set into motion" and the resemblance of the agentive form (*prasavitṛ*) to the name of the god, Savitṛ. This pun seems to be the only reason why Bṛhaspati would return to Savitṛ for help because presumably, if Savitṛ had the power to render this hazardous material harmless, it would not have blinded him moments before. This preference on the part of the Brāhmaṇa authors for nonsensical stories and folk etymologies is doubtless part of what frustrated Eggeling over the course of his enormous translation project. Also, the word *pra-sū* literally means "to set in motion" or "to impel," but from the context of the story, it is here referring to some kind of magical augmentation. So I have opted for the word "enchant," and in doing so, firmly planted in my mind the image of Mickey Mouse causing mops to magically clean the floor to the tune of Paul Dukas's *The Sorcerer's Apprentice*.

76. *ŚB* 1.7.4.1–8. The Brāhmaṇas are concerned with providing origins (some more fanciful than others) for each element of the sacrifice, from ritual actions to specific chants. Novelist and Oxford philologist J. R. R. Tolkien wrote in the foreword to the second edition of *The Lord of the Rings* that his thousand-page epic fantasy was "primarily linguistic in inspiration and was begun in order to provide the necessary background of 'history' for Elvish tongues" (J. R. R. Tolkien, *The Lord of the Rings* [Boston: Houghton Mifflin, 1994], xv. To the consternation of many of his devoted readers who wanted to see it as an allegory about the Second World War or a synthesis of northern European heroic epics, Tolkien was insistent that the main purpose of the story was to explain the diffusion and development of all the languages and dialects in his imagined Elvish language family. In a way not wholly dissimilar, the authors of the Brāhmaṇas present us with a rich mythology, borrowing from earlier Vedic mythemes and some that are unknown to us, in order to explain a ritual to themselves and each other. The section of the *Śatapatha Brāhmaṇa* that contains this story is a commentary on the performance of the new- and full-moon offerings of grain and milk. The great myths of the Brāhmaṇas are, in some ways, secondary in the minds of the authors to the less dramatic rituals they purport to explain.

77. My translation is partially based on Doniger's translation in *The Rig Veda*, 30–31.

78. Another place where the sacrifice of Prajāpati entered Western discourse on salvation is the 1950 tract by Anubhavanand Keshav Ray Sharma Mandapaka, also called *Sacrifice*. In it, the author argues that the Vedas foretell the sacrifice of Christ and are evidence of the truth of the Gospels:

    > Vedas declare sacrifice as the only way for salvation. 'Dharmani prathamani' means that sacrifice is most important of all our duties.
    >
    > 'Yagyo vay bhuvanasya nabhih'—Sacrifice is the base of the world.
    >
    > 'Yagye sarvam pratishtitham'—Through sacrifice all things can be obtained.
    >
    > 'Yagyo vay sutram nouh'—Sacrifice is a boat by which life can be driven smoothly.
    >
    > 'Yagyem va deva divangatah'—Gods got to heaven only through sacrifice.
    >
    > 'Ritasya nah pathinay ati vishvani durita'—Get saved through sacrifice.

    The tract concludes with the message:

    > In this anointed person, the sacrifice of repentance which can save sinners is completed. All these things clearly states [*sic*] that this is the anointed one of God through whom sinners can get salvation of their souls. This anointed one is none other than JESUS.
    >
    > Purushsukt says, 'Nanya panthah vidhyatey nyayah'—'Even by the thousands of good works you can not get to heaven, except through Brahmdev who gave Himself as sacrifice.'

    So there is none other than 'JESUS' who can save you from your sins.

    "Vedas Foretell about the Sacrifice of Christ," *In Search of Peace Free Online Magazine* 3:17 (Nov. 11, 1999), http://insearchofpeace.org/3v17issue.htm#2.

    Evangelical Christians have since identified this tract as the source of the "Prajapati Heresy," for a hellfire-and-brimstone rant about which, see Johnson C. Philip, "Prajapathi [*sic*] Heresy: A History; How Hinduism Made Inroads into Brethren Assemblies through The Trechery [*sic*] of Prominant [*sic*] Men," http://www.biblebeliever.co.za/Brethren%20Assemblys/Brethren%20 Information/Prajapathi_Heresy.htm.

79. There must be some wry humor behind these words.

80. Girard, *Sacrifice*, 46–48 (italics added).

81. Girard, *Sacrifice*, 48.

82. Perhaps significantly, Lévi notes on page 21 of *La doctrine du sacrifice* that it is the Kauśītaki "which, often distinguished by a moral tendency, does not dare suppress the traditional incest, but transfers it from Prajāpati to his sons."

83. Deborah A. Soifer, *The Myths of Narasiṁha and Vāmana: Two Avatars in Cosmological Perspective* (Albany: State University of New York Press, 1991), 30.

84. Viṣṇu is especially identified with the beheading of the sacrifice and the Pravargya rite (as in *ŚB* 14.1), an association we will treat at length in chapter five.

85. *MBh* 6.26.7: *Yadā yadā hi dharmasya glānir bhavati bhārata/ abhyutthānam adharmasya tadā 'tmānaṁ sṛjāmy aham.*

86. Smith, *Reflections*, 40.

87. Soifer, *Narasiṁha and Vāmana*, 128–129.

88. Analogous to his Greek and Norse counterparts Zeus and Odin, Indra is a shape-shifting god.

And just as Odin is given to wandering the earth as a beggar, so Indra often appears in the epics and the Purāṇas in the shape of a poor Brahmin. Soifer also mentions a story inside the Vāmana story from the *Skanda Purāṇa* where Indra disguises himself as a Brahmin and visits Bali's father Virocana and when the latter offers him anything he wants, including his own head, Indra demands Virocana's head with the crown on it (Soifer, *Narasiṁha and Vāmana*, 133).

89. Soifer, *Narasiṁha and Vāmana*, 35.

90. Girard distinguishes his project from Durkheim's: "Durkheim lacked the concrete means of showing that religion, far from being merely parasitic as we have believed since Voltaire, is really the generative force behind human culture. It is unfair to dismiss Durkheim either as a man who 'reduces' religion to the social, or as a 'mystic' who reduces the social to the religious. Durkheim will always remain vulnerable to these symmetrical charges, however, because something is needed to fulfill his program which he himself lacked. In my opinion, of course, this something is the mimetic cycle and unanimous victimage mechanism" ("Interview: René Girard," *Diacritics* 8:1, Special Issue on the Work of René Girard [Spring 1978]: 36).

91. Incidentally, *The Prince and the Pauper* is a variant of the European folk tale of Bearskin, in which a man is forced to live as an outsider because of a pact with the Devil (Aarne-Thompson motif type 361 [Antti Aarne and Stith Thompson, *The Types of the Folktale: A Classification and Bibliography* (Helsinki: Soumalainen Tiedeakatemia, 1961)]) and is closely associated with the period of exclusion or wandering which a king is forced to undergo as part of his coronation ritual. In the *Mahābhārata*, the Pāṇḍavas must live as beggars in the wilderness for twelve years.

Priests and Kings, Oaths and Duels

1. In India, we can speak of the *techne* of Vedic ritualism and the *episteme* of Brāhmaṇic speculation. As we move forward in the period of the composition of Vedic literature, *techne* becomes ever more consigned to ritual manuals like the *Kalpa-Sutras* and *episteme* becomes the main concern of the Upaniṣads.

2. Girard, *Violence and the Sacred*, 90.

3. Gerard Loughlin, "René Girard (b. 1923): Introduction," in *The Postmodern God: A Theological Reader*, ed. Graham Ward (Malden, MA: Blackwell Publishing, 1997), 96.

4. For a discussion of the larger controversy about the supposed racist and anti-Semitic overtones in Dumézil's work, see Lincoln, *Theorizing Myth*, 121–137; Carlo Ginzburg, "Germanic Mythology and Nazism: Thoughts on an Old Book by Georges Dumézil," in *Clues, Myths, and the Historical Method*, trans. John and Anne Tedeschi (Baltimore: Johns Hopkins University Press, 1989), 126–145; and Didier Eribon's book-length response, *Faut-il brûler Dumézil? Mythologie, science et politique* (Paris: Flammarion, 1992). From reading his work and in light of his close association with the Jewish scholars Lévi, Mauss, Durkheim, and Granet, I do not believe Dumézil's theories are tainted by anti-Semitism.

5. Georges Dumézil, *Mitra-Varuna: An Essay on Two Indo-European Representations* (New York: Zone Books, 1988), 13.

6. C. Scott Littleton, "Gods, Myths and Structures: Dumézil," in *The Edinburgh Encyclopedia of Continental Philosophy*, ed. Scott Glendinning (Edinburgh: Edinburgh University Press, 1999), 560.

7. Marcel Mauss, *The Gift: The Form and Reason for Exchange in Archaic Societies*, trans. W. D. Halls (New York: W. W. Norton, 1990), 3.

8. He had also attended the epochal conference organized by Girard at Johns Hopkins in 1966 at which Jacques Derrida delivered his seminal essay, "Structure, Sign, and Play in the Discourse of the Human Sciences," and Girard delivered "Tiresias and the Critic."

9. Girard, *Violence and the Sacred*, 41.

10. Girard, *Things Hidden*, 113.

11. Girard, *The Scapegoat*, 66–67.

12. Early on in their discussion, Dumézil's structural theory of myth is put to Girard by Jean-Michel Oughourlian as an objection to the possibility of finding the origin of religion: "Others, such as Georges Dumézil, maintain that the only contemporary method capable of producing results is the 'structural' method, and that this method can operate only with material already symbolized, with structures of language, and not with over-generalized principles such as the sacred, etc." (Girard, *Things Hidden*, 4).

13. Girard, *Violence and the Sacred*, 1.

14. Georges Dumézil, *Flamen-brahman* (Paris: P. Geuthner, 1935), 93–94.

15. Davíd Carrasco, *City of Sacrifice: The Aztec Empire and the Role of Violence in Civilization* (Boston: Beacon Press, 1990), 84.

16. *BrP* 73.22.

17. Dumézil, *Mitra-Varuna*, 19.

18. Dumézil, *Mitra-Varuna*, 178–179.

19. Dumézil, *Mitra-Varuna*, 178.

20. *ŚB* 4.1.4.1–4.

21. *ŚB* 4.1.4.8.

22. And killing Vṛtra in violation of a compact is only one of Indra's three great sins. The other two are the killing of the Brahmin Viśvarupa and the seduction of the forest sage's wife Ahalyā. He is only able to regain his status when the gods perform a Horse Sacrifice on his behalf and he casts off the guilt of his sin and distributes it among the trees, mountains, earth, and women. Dumézil identifies the "three sins of the sovereign" as three crimes against each of the top three functions, resulting in a corresponding loss or fall and ending in the ultimate destruction of the sinner. He first sees this pattern in the myths of Indra, Heracles, and the Scandinavian hero Starkarðr-Starcatherus, but later drops Indra and Heracles in favor of the *Mahābhārata* villain Śiśupāla and the Roman warrior king Tullus Hostilius. Hiltebeitel argues for the re-inclusion of Indra in the list of the sinning sovereigns and suggests that, "as a mythical theme, Indra's three sins may well be an Indian invention" (Alf Hiltebeitel, *The Ritual of Battle: Krishna in the* Mahābhārata [Albany: State University of New York Press, 1990], 230).

23. For a more recent study of these institutions in medieval Christendom see Peter Brown, "Society and the Supernatural: A Medieval Change," in *Society and the Holy in Late Antiquity* (Berkeley: University of California Press, 1982), 307–317.

24. It is instructive here to note the way in which the titles of Lea's volumes on the oath and the duel, *The Wager of Law* and *The Wager of Battle*, recall the language of Pascal's famous wager. Though far from being the naïve bargain it is often made out to be, Pascal's wager still fails to escape the trap of sacrificial thinking. Why would God care if anyone believes in him, except in an archaic theology of divine wrath?

25. Edward Peters, Introduction to *The Duel and the Oath*, by Henry Charles Lea (Philadelphia: University of Pennsylvania Press, 1974), 5.

26. Henry Charles Lea, *The Duel and the Oath* (Philadelphia: University of Pennsylvania Press, 1974), 25 (italics added).

27. Lea comes to this conclusion by examining oaths as they function in the legal literature of medieval Europe, and one would come to the same conclusion when looking at the Sanskrit legal literature. But an unmediated form of the oath is also present in Sanskrit mythology. Two of the most famous instances are Sītā's oath witnessed by Agni testifying to her purity while held prisoner by demon king Rāvaṇa in the epic *Rāmāyaṇa* and the Buddha's oath witnessed by the Earth to have made all the great acts of generosity required for Buddhahood in the story of his enlightenment.

28. Girard has never made a systematic analysis of the oath or the contract with one exception. Before his discovery of mimetic desire and while he was teaching at Bryn Mawr, Girard wrote a fascinating study of marriage ceremonies and vows from the archives of his own hometown, called "Marriage in Avignon in the Second Half of the Fifteenth Century" (*Speculum* 28:3 [July, 1953]: 485–498).

29. Girard and Chantre, *Battling to the End*, 29.

30. Girard and Chantre, *Battling to the End*, 29.

31. Lea, *Duel and the Oath*, 104.

32. Friedrich Nietzsche, *The Antichrist*, in *The Portable Nietzsche*, ed. and trans., Walter Kaufmann (New York: Penguin Books, 1954), 643. But lest we take this as an endorsement of Manu's hierarchical ordering of society, Nietzsche also wrote in his notebooks later edited together as *The Will to Power*:

> The whole book is founded on the holy lie. . . . We find a species of man, the priestly, which feels itself to be the norm, the high point and the supreme expression of the type man: this species derives the concept "improvement" from itself. It believes in its own superiority, it wills itself to be superior in fact: the origin of the holy lie is the *will to power*. . . .
>
> Power through the lie—in the knowledge that one does not possess it physically, militarily—the lie as a supplement to power, a new concept of "truth."
>
> It is a mistake to suppose an *unconscious and naive* development here, a kind of self-deception—Fanatics do not invent such carefully thought-out systems of oppression—The most coldblooded reflection was at work here; the same kind of reflection as a Plato applied when he imagined his "Republic." . . .
>
> We possess the classic model in specifically *Aryan* forms: we may therefore hold the best-endowed and most reflective species of man responsible for the most fundamental lie that has ever been told—That lie has been copied almost everywhere: *Aryan influence* has corrupted all the world. (Quoted in Walter Kaufmann, *Nietzsche: Philosopher, Psychologist, Antichrist*, 4th ed. [Princeton, NJ: Princeton University Press, 1974], 302)

33. Giorgio Agamben, *The Sacrament of Language: An Archaeology of the Oath (Homo Sacer II, 3)* (Stanford, CA: Stanford University Press, 2011), 20–21.

34. Patricia Lawrence documents a contemporary example of this practice in her fieldwork among ethnic Tamils suffering under the Sinhalese police state during the Sri Lankan civil war of the 1990s between the Christian, Hindu, and Muslim LTTE rebel forces, or Tamil Tigers, and the

Sinhalese-speaking Buddhist majority government. In 1996, Lawrence interviewed 19-year-old Tamil man Kumāravēlu, a resident of the village of Paduvankarai, a stronghold of the LTTE. When Kumāravēlu was arrested and tortured at the Palpody prison camp, he made a vow to the goddess Kāḷi (Sanskrit Kālī) that if he were released, he would perform the *muḷḷakāvaṭi* (*vaṭi* from Sanskrit *vrata*), in which the devotee swings from hooks inserted into his back. Patricia Lawrence, "Kāḷi in a Context of Terror: The Tasks of the Goddess in Sri Lanka's Civil War," in *Encountering Kālī: In the Margins, at the Center, in the West*, ed. Jeffrey J. Kripal and Rachel Fell McDermott (Berkeley: University of California Press, 2003), 108–110.

35. In terms of the Indo-European trifunctional ideology, when Agamben asserts the primacy of the oath and the binding powers of speech, he affirms the Brahminical hierarchy, in which the Brahmins with their control of speech rule over the Kṣatriyas with their weapons. In the mythic representations we have been looking at so far, we have seen some conflicting models of the relation of kingship and priesthood in the divine and human realms. At some moments, we see Mitra and Varuṇa opposed to each other as the first and second functions, but when the figure of Mitra-Varuṇa is collapsed into the first function deity Varuṇa, we see him opposed to Indra, as in the case of the story of Śunaḥśepa (which we will examine below). And in other moments, like the *Ṛg Veda* story of Indra enticing Agni to defect from the side of the demons, we see Agni and Indra representing the first and second functions, respectively. Dumézil offers one possible explanation for this constant shifting between the religio-magical sovereignty of the first function and the politico-military sovereignty of the second. After introducing Marcel Granet's strict structuralist idea of a system that "corresponds to a type of mind that pushes to the extreme the recognition and use of *contrasts*," Dumézil adds: "A second characteristic is also common to at least a very large number of these contrasts: not only are they antithetical, they are also *rhythmic*, which is to say, subject to a system of alternations, of which the seasons provide the most typical natural example" (Dumézil, *Mitra-Varuna*, 176). Another example of this rhythmic alternation, though not a natural one, is the tragic dialogue of the Greek *stichomythia* from Euripides' *Phoenician Women*, which Girard examines in *Violence and the Sacred*.

36. Agamben, *Sacrament of Language*, 65.

37. Agamben, *Sacrament of Language*, 66.

38. Agamben, *Sacrament of Language*, 69.

39. Agamben, *Sacrament of Language*, 68.

40. Agamben, *Sacrament of Language*, 69.

41. Agamben, *Sacrament of Language*, 70.

42. Agamben, *Sacrament of Language*, 70.

43. J. C. Heesterman, *The Inner Conflict of Tradition: Essays in Indian Ritual, Kingship, and Society* (Chicago: University of Chicago Press, 1985), 75.

44. Agamben, *Sacrament of Language*, 70–71.

45. Lea, *Duel and the Oath*, 102.

46. Lea, *Duel and the Oath*, 107.

47. Girard, *Things Hidden*, 144–148.

48. For an idea of how the Christian conception of divinity begins to unravel this institution, consider this infamous passage from Gottfried von Strassburg's thirteenth century poem *Tristan* (I.15737–15740), in which a character complains about Isolde's perjury going unpunished: "Thus

it was made manifest and confirmed to the world that Christ in his great virtue is as pliant as a windblown sleeve [*da wart wol goffenbseret und al der werlt bewseret, daz der vil tugenthafte Krist winthschaffen alse ein ermel ist* . . .]" (Gottfried von Strassburg, *Tristan*, ed. Karl Marold [Leipzig, Germany: Edward Avenarius, 1906], 219).

49. Sukumari Battacharji, "Varuṇa," in *Encyclopedia of Religion*, ed. Lindsey Jones, vol. 14 (Detroit: MacMillan Reference USA, 2005), 9525.

50. Lea, *Duel and the Oath*, 187–188.

51. In-depth discussions of Śukra, the priest of the demons, can be found in Wendy Doniger, *The Origins of Evil in Hindu Mythology* (Berkeley: University of California Press, 1976), passim; Georges Dumézil, *The Plight of a Sorcerer*, eds. Jaan Puhvel and David Weeks (Berkeley: University of California Press, 1986), 25–50; and Herman Lommel, "Kāvya Uçan," in *Mélanges de linguistique offerts à Charles Bally* (Genève: 1939), 209–214.

52. *MBh* 1.71.5–10.

53. Dumézil's comment on this situation hits the nail on the head: "The priestly assistants of belligerents are rivals to be sure, but they themselves are not at war; class or professional solidarity is stronger than the fleeting circumstances or contractual obligations that oppose them" (Dumézil, *Plight of a Sorcerer*, 29).

54. *MBh* 1.71.54.

55. Dharma, *artha*, and *kāma*, the three goals of human life in classical Hinduism.

56. *MBh* 1.72.16.

57. Dumézil, *Plight of a Sorcerer*, 34.

58. *MBh* 1.73.10–11.

59. Vṛka is cognate with the modern Swedish word *varg*, which the fantasy author and philologist J. R. R. Tolkien gives (in the Old Norse form of *warg*) to the demonic wolf creatures in his *Lord of the Rings* saga.

60. David Gordon White, *Myths of the Dog-Man* (Chicago: University of Chicago Press, 1991), 93.

61. Stephanie W. Jamison, *The Ravenous Hyenas and the Wounded Sun: Myth and Ritual in Ancient India* (Ithaca, NY: Cornell University Press, 1991), 69–72.

62. *Troilus and Cressida* act 1, scene 3.

63. Jamison, *Ravenous Hyenas*, 51.

64. The *Mahābhārata* conflates this story with that of Śukra and Kaca in 1.71.26 when the demons hand Kaca over to the Sālāvṛkeyas.

65. Jamison, *Ravenous Hyenas*, 57.

66. Jamison, *Ravenous Hyenas*, 111.

67. Jamison, *Ravenous Hyenas*, 55.

68. Theodore Proferes uses a philological analysis of the text to argue that "Makha" is some kind of reference to the sacrificial victim:

> With the mention of *makha* we stumble upon a subject that has puzzled Indologists in the past. I will not enter into the question here, but will merely point out the reference to 'the head of makha' (*makhásya śírah*) among the *yajuḥ* formulas belonging

to the same portion of the Agnicayana liturgy which we have linked, via the *tvāya* gerunds, to [the legendary court priest] Tura Kāvaṣeya. It is by no means clear what '*makha*'s Tura Kāvaṣeya' means in the present Khila verse. Perhaps it reflects a mythical connection between Tura and Dadhyañc on the grounds that both possessed an esoteric 'knowledge of the head of the sacrificial victim,' amounting to a knowledge of how to find a proper substitute for it. The important point here is that the Khila verse associates Tura with this *makha* whose head plays a role in the Agnicayana liturgy, while according to Vādhūla the Kuru lords—in whose service Tura composed, according to [the *Aitareya Brahmaṇa*]—were renowned for their Agnicayana rite since they possessed 'the knowledge of the head of the sacrificial victim.' (Theodore Proferes, "Kuru Kings, Tura Kāvaṣeya, and the *-Tvā́ya* Gerund," *Bulletin of the School of Oriental and African Studies, University of London* 66:2 [2003]: 214)

69. Quoted in Jonathan Z. Smith, "The Bare Facts of Ritual," *History of Religions* 20:1–2, Twentieth Anniversary Issue (Aug.–Nov., 1980): 113.

70. Jamison, *Ravenous Hyenas*, 127–128.

71. Tamar C. Reich, "The Interruption of the Sacrifice and the Verbal Contest: Three Different Epic Interpretations of a Pair of Vedic Motifs," in *Language, Ritual and Poetics in Ancient India and Iran: Studies in Honor of Shaul Migron*, ed. David Shulman, 136–160 (Jerusalem: The Israel Academy of Sciences and Humanities, 2010), 149–153.

72. For a study of the werewolf cult in Greece, see Walter Burkert, *Homo Necans: The Anthropology of Ancient Greek Sacrificial Ritual and Myth*, trans. Peter Bing (Berkeley: University of California Press, 1983). For a more general study, see Priscilla K. Kershaw, *The One-Eyed God: Odin and the (Indo)Germanic* Männerbünde, Journal of Indo-European Studies Monograph No. 36 (Washington, DC: Journal of Indo-European Studies, 2000); and for an idiosyncratic but fascinating study of the werewolf, see Robert Eisler, *Man into Wolf: An Anthropological Interpretation of Sadism, Masochism, and Lycanthropy; A Lecture Delivered at a Meeting of the Royal Society of Medicine* (New York: Greenwood Press, 1951).

73. In the *Ṛg Veda* the Maruts are the sons of Rudra, the relatively minor outsider deity who becomes the pan-Indian god Śiva in the post-Vedic period. Like Indra, they are storm deities invoked to bring rain as well as fierce warriors. Their Indra-like function caused mythmakers to link Indra and the Maruts in the later Vedic literature, giving Indra the epithets Marutvat ("Attended by Maruts") and Marudgaṇa ("Attended by the Host of Maruts").

74. White, *Myths of the Dog-Man*, 15–16.

75. Kenneth R. Stow, *Jewish Dogs: An Image and Its Interpreters: Continuity in the Catholic-Jewish Encounter* (Stanford, CA: Stanford University Press, 2006), xiv and passim.

76. J. C. Heesterman, "Vrātya and Sacrifice," *Indo-Iranian Journal* 6 (1962): 7.

77. White, *Myths of the Dog-Man*, 99.

78. Bruce M. Sullivan, "Tantroid Phenomena in Early Indic Literature: An Essay in Honor of Jim Sanford," *Pacific World: Journal of the Institute of Buddhist Studies* 3:8 (Fall 2006): 17.

79. Heesterman, "Vrātya and Sacrifice," 19.

80. J. C. Heesterman, "Warrior, Peasant and Brahmin," *Modern Asian Studies* 29:3 (July 1995): 653.

81. A verse composed in *anuṣṭubh* meter consists of thirty-two syllables arranged into four sets of eight.

82. A verse composed in *satobṛhatī* meter consists of forty syllables arranged into sets of twelve, eight, twelve, and eight.

83. A verse composed in *bṛhatī* meter consists of thirty-six syllables arranged into sets of eight, eight, twelve, and eight.

84. On this difficult passage I have followed Caland exactly.

85. *Pañcaviṃśa-Brāhmaṇa: The Brāhmaṇa of Twenty-five Chapters*, trans. Willem Caland (Calcutta: Asiatic Society of Bengal, 1931), 454–460.

86. S. N. Biswas, "Ober das Vrātya Problem in der Vedischen Ritualliteratur," *Zeitschrrift der Deutschen Morgenlamdische Gesellschaft* 105 (1955): 53.

87. Heesterman, "Vrātya and Sacrifice," 8.

88. There may be a fruitful comparison to be made between the concepts of *viṣama* and *sama/śama* and the Old Norse legal concepts of *odd* and *jafn* explored in William Ian Miller, *An Eye for an Eye* (New York: Cambridge University Press, 2006).

89. Heesterman, "Vrātya and Sacrifice," 9.

90. In an important Śaiva myth, Śiva also swallows a noxious poison produced in the churning of the ocean in order to protect the gods from it. He holds it in his throat, which turns it blue and earns him the name Nīlakaṇṭha, "The Blue-throated One."

91. The word used for food here is *anna*, which elsewhere in the Vedas refers to the mystical form of food that sustains the universe.

92. Carlo Ginzburg, *The Night Battles: Witchcraft and Agrarian Cults in the Sixteenth and Seventeenth Centuries* (New York: Penguin Books, 1985), 15 (italics added).

93. Ginzburg, *The Night Battles*, 29–30. For a revival of this myth, see Neil Gaiman, *The Graveyard Book* (New York: HarperCollins, 2008).

94. Giorgio Agamben, *Homo Sacer: Sovereign Power and Bare Life* (Stanford, CA: Stanford University Press, 1998), 104–107.

95. Gregory Schopen, "The Buddha as a Businessman: Economics and Law in Old Indian Religion," paper presented at the 106th Faculty Research Lecture at the Freud Playhouse, UCLA, March 10, 2009, http://www.uctv.tv/shows/The-Buddha-as-a-Businessman-Economics-and-Law-in-an-Old-Indian-Religion-16444.

96. This marginality also comes into play in the figure of Harlequin, early on identified with Wotan and the Wild Hunt, who later becomes the stock figure in the Italian *commedia dell'arte* that the audience can see while he remains invisible to the other characters in the play. For an interesting take on this figure see *Harlequin* (*Dark Forces* in the U.S. release) DVD, dir. by Simon Wincer (1980; Synapse 2008). The main character's first name is Gregory (probably a reference to Rasputin, whose legend provides some of the material for the story) and last name is Wolfe and he adopts the disguise of Harlequin in a key scene in which it is revealed that his image does not show up on video.

97. Heesterman, "Warrior, Peasant and Brahmin," 651.

98. Heesterman, "Warrior, Peasant and Brahmin," 651.

99. Doniger, *Origins of Evil*, 322.

100. Doniger, *Origins of Evil*, 327.

101. *BhP* 4.14.40.

102. *Niṣāda* also refers to outcastes and those excluded from the social order in general.

103. *BhP* 4.15.3.

104. Heesterman, "Warrior, Peasant and Brahmin," 654.

105. Girard, *Sacrifice*, 55–56.

106. Girard, *Sacrifice*, 56.

107. *TS* 6.1.11.1.1–7. In this and other passages it is difficult to know whether *soma* refers to the plant or the god.

108. A recent news story brought to my attention by Afroz Taj suggests a modern real-life parallel to the Śunaḥśepa story.

> A ganja and bhang addict posing as a tantrik was arrested by Mathura police on Monday, after his three children complained that their father used to extract blood from their bodies with the help of a blade and/or syringe to offer to the goddess, police said. DSP Kayam Singh said, the tantrik Netra Pal was married to a woman Maya, who left him two years ago, when she found that her husband had first cut off her finger to offer the goddess and then planned to 'sacrifice' her. On Sunday, as [Netra Pal] tried to extract blood from his son Sanju, the three children managed to run to a neighbouring village Gaidalpur and told people about this. The villagers beat up [Netra Pal] and handed him over to the police. Says Sanju: 'Our father used to beat us with sticks if we protested. He used to extract blood from our bodies to offer to the goddess.' DSP Kayam Singh said the tantrik used to remain cool during the day, but after intake of ganja or bhang, he used to become a devil with his own children. ("Mathura Dracula Held for Offering Children's Blood to the Goddess," *India TV News*, September 27, 2011, http://www.indiatvnews.com/crime/news/Mathura-Dracula-Held-For-Offering-Children-s-Blood-To-Goddess-183.html)

Professor Taj also reported that several Pandits in India were publicly defending Netra Pal's actions, since the children were his to do with as he saw fit, but I have not yet seen evidence of this. The article also seems to attribute the actions of the "Mathura Dracula" to his ingestion of marijuana (*ganja* and *bhang*) and suggests that any connection to religion, "tantrik" or otherwise, must be fraudulent.

109. David Dean Shulman, *The Hungry God: Hindu Tales of Filicide and Devotion* (Chicago: University of Chicago Press, 1993), 87.

110. *AB* 7.15.8.

111. *AB* 7.16.2.

112. Shulman, *Hungry God*, 91.

113. Shulman, *Hungry God*, 93.

114. Shulman, *Hungry God*, 94.

115. 1 John 2, 10–11, quoted in Girard, *Things Hidden*, 277.

116. Shulman, *Hungry God*, 100.

117. *Rām* 1.61.16, quoted in White, *Myths of the Dog-Man*, 83.

118. Heesterman, "Warrior, Peasant and Brahmin," 654.

119. In his thorough account of the Kāpālikas David N. Lorenzen states that the accounts of the Kāpālikas practicing human sacrifice are very likely true, given its history in India, but it is hard not to see the stereotyped accusations against the sect as another form of the scapegoat's crimes: "[It] is difficult to doubt that the Kāpālika's practised human sacrifice. The purpose of the rite was to appease and gratify a wrathful and blood-thirsty deity. The idea of the victim as a scapegoat is less explicit, but is inherent, in any case, in the very concept of sacrificial propitiation." (*The Kāpālikas and the Kālāmukhas: Two Lost Śaivite Sects* [Berkeley: The University of California Press, 1972], 86)

120. *AB* 7.17.4–6.

121. White, *Myths of the Dog-Man*, 84.

122. White, *Myths of the Dog-Man*, 79–80.

123. White, *Myths of the Dog-Man*, 78–79.

124. René Girard, *I See Satan Fall Like Lightning* (Maryknoll, NY: Orbis Books, 2001), 22.

Epic Variations on a Mimetic Theme

1. *MBh* 1.56.33.

2. Girard, *Sacrifice*, 56.

3. Tamar C. Reich, "Sacrificial Violence and Textual Battles: Inner Textual Interpretation in the Sanskrit *Mahābhārata*," *History of Religions* 41:2 (Nov. 2001): 143.

4. Reich, "Sacrificial Violence," 143.

5. Girard, *The Scapegoat*, 95.

6. Girard, *The Scapegoat*, 95.

7. John D. Caputo, *The Prayers and Tears of Jacques Derrida: Religion without Religion* (Bloomington: Indiana University Press, 1997), 139.

8. Mauss, *The Gift*, 71.

9. Georges Dumézil, "La terre soulagée," in *Mythe et épopée* I (Paris: Gallimard, 1968), 31–257.

10. For a fuller treatment of this material, see Brian Collins, "Headless Mothers, Magic Cows, and Lakes of Blood: The Parsaśurāma Cycle in the *Mahābhārata* and beyond" (PhD Diss., University of Chicago, 2010).

11. In *MBh* 1.127.12 Duryodhana alludes to a figure named Dadhīci whose bone is used to make the thunderbolt with which Indra defeats the demons.

12. Girard, *Sacrifice*, 50–51.

13. Roberto Calasso, *Ka: Stories of the Mind and Gods of India*, trans. Tim Park (New York: Alfred A. Knopf, 1998), 45–46.

14. Doniger, *Origins of Evil*, 129.

15. Hartmut Scharfe, *The State in Indian Tradition* (Leiden, Netherlands: Brill, 1989), 145n164.

16. Gurchuran Das, "Changing Rules of Dharma," *The Times of India*, November 30, 2008, http://timesofindia.indiatimes.com/home/opinion/gurcharan-das/men-ideas/Changing-rules-of-dharma/articleshow/3774379.cms?.

17. For a discussion of American post-9/11 jurisprudence in light of the lycanthropic *homo sacer* see Michael E. Moore, "Wolves, Outlaws and Enemy Combatants," in Eileen A. Joy, Myra J. Seaman, Kimberly K. Bell, and Mary K. Ramsey, eds., *Cultural Studies of the Modern Middle Ages* (New York: Palgrave Macmillan, 2007), 217–236.

18. Giorgio Agamben, *State of Exception* (Chicago: University of Chicago Press, 2005), 2.

19. *The Laws of Manu*, trans. Wendy Doniger and Brian K. Smith (New York: Penguin, 1991), lviii.

20. Carl Schmitt, *Political Theology: Four Chapters on the Concept of Sovereignty*, trans. Charles Schwab (Cambridge, MA: MIT Press, 1985), 36.

21. *The Laws of Manu*, lviii.

22. This retelling is taken from *MBh* 2.12–22.

23. J. A. B. van Buitenen, "Introduction," in *The Mahābhārata, Volume 2, Book 2: The Book of Assembly; Book 3: The Book of the Forest* (Chicago: University of Chicago Press, 1975), 16–17.

24. Van Buitenen translates the phrase *manuṣyāṇāṃ samālambhaḥ* in 2.20.9 as "human sacrifice," but this translation gives the impression that Kṛṣṇa may be using the term *Puruṣamedha*. The phrase more properly translates to "the taking hold of human beings as sacrificial victims."

25. *MBh* 2.20.6–12.

26. Van Buitenen, "Introduction," 23.

27. See Alf Hiltebeitel, *Rethinking the* Mahābhārata*: A Reader's Guide to the Education of the Dharma King* (Chicago: University of Chicago Press, 2001), 92–97 and passim.

28. As Hiltebeitel points out, Ugraśravas's name means "Frightful to Hear" while the name of his father, Lomaharṣaṇa, translates to "Hair-raising" (*Rethinking the* Mahābhārata, 96).

29. A traditional Indian butter churn is not the "up-and-down" type of churn found in America, but uses a central pole mounted with paddles that is rapidly turned clockwise and counterclockwise (the same kind of motion used to start a fire) with a rope wrapped around the pole. A large butter churn would be operated by two people, each holding one end of the rope.

30. *MBh* 1.16.12–27.

31. Girard and Chantre, *Battling to the End*, x.

32. *MBh* 1.126.9.

33. *MBh* 1.126.10.

34. *MBh* 1.126.33.

35. *MBh* 1.127.6–7.

36. *MBh* 1.127.24.

37. In a poignant moment, he does, however, promise to only kill Arjuna of all the Pāṇḍavas so that no matter who won the duel Kuntī would still have five sons left.

38. This story is missing from the critical edition of the text, which has Karṇa fail along with all the other suitors, but is well attested in the northern recensions. See Stephanie W. Jamison, "Penelope and the Pigs: Indic Perspectives on the 'Odyssey,'" *Classical Antiquity* 18:2 (Oct., 1999), 246. In Gurchuran Das's exploration of morality in the epic, he follows the story of Karṇa's humiliation at the *svayaṃvara* with a positively Proustian anecdote from his own youth about a similarly humiliating meeting with a snobby girl from his class at one of Simla's Raj-era clubs shortly after

India's Independence (*The Difficulty of Being Good: On the Subtle Art of Dharma* [New York: Oxford University Press, 2009], 158–159).

39. The first duel between Viśvāmitra and Vasiṣṭha ended the same way.

40. Girard, *Violence and the Sacred*, 290.

41. Girard, *Violence and the Sacred*, 287.

42. Girard, *Violence and the Sacred*, 292.

43. Dhṛṣṭadyumna was in fact born from a fire sacrifice performed by his father in order to have a son who would be able to kill Drona, the beloved preceptor of both the Kauravas and the Pāṇḍavas in their childhood, bound by duty to fight for the Kauravas.

44. Also in fulfillment of a vow Bhīma made at the same time he vowed to smash Duryodhana's thighs.

45. *MBh* 5.139.29b-54.

46. See chapter two.

47. Some strains of Hindu physiology believe the *ātman* is contained in the head, which is why Hindu funeral rites sometimes require the son to smash the head (*kapāla kriyā*) of his father's burning corpse to set his spirit free to go to Heaven or his next birth.

48. *MBh* 8.69.17.

49. See James L. Fitzgerald, "Bhīṣma beyond Freud: Bhīṣma in the *Mahābhārata*," in *Gender and Narrative in the* Mahābhārata, ed. Simon Brodbeck and Brian Black (New York: Routledge 2007), 189–207.

50. See Otto Rank, *The Myth of the Birth of the Hero: A Psychological Interpretation of Mythology*, trans. F. Robbins and Smith Ely Jelliffe, Nervous and Mental Disease Monograph Series No. 18 (New York: The Journal of Nervous and Mental Disease Publishing Company, 1914).

51. Aditya Adarkar, "Karṇa in the *Mahābhārata*" (PhD diss., University of Chicago, 2001), 8.

52. There may be more to this than meets the eye. The three temptations of Jesus (turning a stone into bread, calling upon his angels in front of the Temple, becoming the universal monarch) all correspond to Dumézil's three sins of the sovereign—one against each of the three Indo-European functions. For a detailed exposition, see Riccardo Di Giuseppe, "Trifunctional Structure in the Desert Temptations: G. Dumézil, L. Dumont and the Christ" (paper presented at the annual meeting of the Colloquium On Violence & Religion, Innsbruck, Tyrol, Austria, June 18–21, 2003).

53. Girard, *I See Satan Fall Like Lightning*, 182. Comparing Kṛṣṇa to Satan will no doubt offend some Hindus. But there are many other characters in the epic, Karṇa included, who say much the same thing. And in more recent times, suspicion has fallen upon the seemingly war-mongering rhetoric of the *Gītā*, prompting some prosecutors in Tomsk, Russia, to push for a ban on the sale of the text in late 2011. The case went to court but was dismissed on December 28, 2011.

54. *MBh* 8.68.34–38.

55. René Girard, "Racine, Poet of Glory," in *Mimesis and Theory: Essays on Literature and Criticism, 1953–2005*, ed. Robert Doran (Stanford, CA: Stanford University Press, 2008), 99.

56. See chapter four.

57. Girard, "Racine," 107.

58. Hamerton-Kelly, *Sacred Violence*, 204.

59. Girard, "Racine," 103.

60. Girard, "Racine," 108.

61. We should note, however, that after his death Duryodhana is described as a good and righteous king beloved by his subjects.

62. T. S. Eliot, *East Coker* (London: Faber, 1940).

63. Adarkar, "Karṇa," 112.

64. As a baby, Kṛṣṇa escapes the infanticidal rage of his uncle Kaṃsa and grows up to kill his murderous father-figure and assume his true identity as the embodied god Viṣṇu.

65. Another reason for Karṇa's departure from the tragic hero pattern is the *Mahābhārata* itself, which contains more of what Girard (after Simone Weil) calls the anthropology of the Gospels than the *katharsis* of Greek tragedy. As David Shulman argues: "[There] is no escape built into [the epic] from its relentless, bleak vision. It presents itself not as a work of art, but as reality itself. No boundary marks off this text from the world. Even in recitation, it functions not as purveyor of dramatic illusion, nor as an imaginative venture in narrative, but as the vehicle of what might properly be termed 'realistic' insight" (David Dean Shulman, "Toward a Historical Poetics of the Sanskrit Epics," *International Folklore Review* 8 [1991]: 11).

66. Bruce M. Sullivan, "The Ideology of Self-Willed Death in the Epic *Mahābhārata*," *Journal of Vaishnava Studies* 14:2 (Spring 2006): 73.

67. Badiou, *Saint Paul*, 97.

68. Rāvaṇa is actually a *rākṣasa* rather than an *asura*, but I have called him a demon here because his role as the rival of Rāma is analogous to the traditional opposition of the demons to the gods. And his learning, religiosity, and righteousness make it clear he is more like a god than a flesh-eating goblin like a *piśāca* or a blood-drinking *vetāla*.

69. Karṇa's apotheosis also recalls the story from the *Jaiminīya Brāhmaṇa* in which the sacrificer Sthūra is killed by enemies who have come to destroy his sacrifice, after which one of the survivors witnesses him ascending to Heaven (*JB* 2.297–99; Heesterman, *Inner Conflict of Tradition*, 85–86 and 99; Reich, "Interruption of the Sacrifice," 141).

70. I could go on at some length about the mimetic elements of this story in the Sanskrit version of the epic, but I have already said that this book will not repeat Girardian interpretations of Hindu myths ad nauseam. For more on the Śūrpaṇakhā episode, see Kathleen M. Erndl, "The Mutilation of Śūrpaṇakhā," in *Many* Rāmāyaṇas*: The Diversity of a Narrative Tradition in South Asia*, ed. Paula Richman (Berkeley: University of California Press, 1991), 67–88.

71. *Rām* 3.32.

72. Bernard Schweizer, *Hating God: The Untold Story of Misotheism* (Oxford: Oxford University Press, 2011).

73. It may speak to France's inclination to favor southern India, where they had a colonial presence, that the *fin de siècle* artist Fernand Cormon painted the scene in tragic fashion in his 1875 work, "The Death of Ravana, King of Lanka." The same title was earlier used by the fourth century South Indian grammarian Bhatti for his poetic retelling of the *Rāmāyaṇa* intended to demonstrate to his students the grammatical structure of Sanskrit.

74. M. S. Purnalingam Pillai, *Tamil Literature* (Thanjavur, India: Tamil University, 1985), 224.

Meaning: The Secret Heart of the Sacred

1. Girard, *Things Hidden*, 100.

2. Girard, *Things Hidden*, 100.

3. Bertrand Russell, "The Philosophy of Logical Atomism," in *The Collected Papers of Bertrand Russell*, vol. 8, *The Philosophy of Logical Atomism and Other Essays, 1914–19*, ed. John G. Slater (New York: Routledge, 1986), 228. This is expressed mathematically as "R={x:x not in x}. Then R in R if R not in R." Ludwig Wittgenstein regarded this paradox as a false one because he rejected the idea of mathematical sets, later proposing the idea of "family resemblances" to replace set theory, an idea sometimes used to describe the relationship between the various South Asian traditions collectively referred to as Hinduism.

4. Harry Falk, *Bruderschaft und Würfelspeil: Untersuchungen zur Entwicklungsgeschichte des vedischen Opfers* (Freiburg, Germany: H. Falk, 1986), 181–187; Don Handelman and David Dean Shulman, *God Inside Out: Śiva's Game of Dice* (New York: Oxford University Press, 1997), 35.

5. Handelman and Shulman, *God Inside Out*, 35.

6. *ŚB* 2.1.13.

7. Don Handelman, "Traps of Trans-formation: Theoretical Convergences between Riddle and Ritual," in *Untying the Knot: On Riddles and Other Enigmatic Modes*, eds. Galit Hasan-Rokem and David Shulman (New York: Oxford University Press, 1996), 53.

8. Girard, *Things Hidden*, 103.

9. Sigmund Freud, *Jokes and Their Relation to the Unconscious*, trans. James Strachey (New York: W. W. Norton, 1989), 34n37.

10. Richard Salomon, "When Is a Riddle Not a Riddle? Some Comments on Riddling and Related Poetic Devices in Classical Sanskrit," in *Untying the Knot: On Riddles and Other Enigmatic Modes*, eds. Galit Hasan-Rokem and David Shulman (New York: Oxford University Press, 1996), 169.

11. Sunthar Visuvalingam, "Towards an Integral Appreciation of Abhinava's Aesthetics of Rasa" (2002), 50.

12. This connection is apparent in the episode of the haunted pool from the third book (Araṇyaka Parvan) of the *Mahābhārata*, in which Yudhiṣṭhira and his brothers spend twelve years of exile in the forest as a consequence of losing the ritual dicing match. We are already within the ritual structure here, since the Pāṇḍavas' exile corresponds to the king's ceremonial period of exclusion before his coronation in the *rājasūya*. In marching order, the five brothers arrive at a pond where a hidden Yakṣa (a kind of water sprite) commands them not to drink without answering his questions. One by one, beginning with the Aśvin twin Nakula, each brother ignores the voice and drinks the water before dropping dead in his tracks. When Yudhiṣṭhira finally arrives to find the bodies of his brothers strewn about the pond, he heeds the Yakṣa and answers a long series of riddles. (Here is a representative Q&A from *MBh* 3.297.58–59: Q: "How is a man dead, how is a kingdom dead, how is a death ritual dead, how is a sacrifice dead?" A: "A man is dead when poor, a kingdom is dead when kingless, a death ritual is dead without a learned Brahmin, a sacrifice is dead without payment.") When Yudhiṣṭhira has answered all the questions, the Yakṣa gives him leave to drink and offers to raise one of his brothers from the dead. Surprisingly, Yudhiṣṭhira chooses the comparatively unimpressive Pāṇḍava Nakula over the mighty warriors Arjuna and Bhīma. When asked why, he explains that Nakula and Sahadeva are the sons of his father's second wife Mādrī and the law of non-cruelty (*ahiṃsa*) dictates that he must make sure each woman has at least one

son alive. At this selfless act, the Yakṣa identifies himself as the god Dharma, the embodiment of law and order and Yudhiṣṭhira's divine father.

13. *Rig Veda*, trans. Doniger, 78.

14. Stephanie W. Jamison, *Sacrificed Wife/Sacrificer's Wife: Women, Ritual, and Hospitality in Ancient India* (New York: Oxford University Press, 1996), 73.

15. Heesterman, *Inner Conflict of Tradition*, 71.

16. Heesterman, *Inner Conflict of Tradition*, 75.

17. Axel Michaels, "Perfection and Mishaps in Vedic Rituals," in *When Rituals Go Wrong: Mistakes, Failure, and the Dynamics of Ritual*, ed. Ute Hüsken (Leiden, Netherlands: Brill, 2007), 123.

18. John Milbank, "Stories of Sacrifice," *Contagion: Journal of Violence, Mimesis, and Culture* 2 (Spring 1995): 94.

19. The homophonic resemblance of *nāstika* and "gnostic" is pure magnificent coincidence.

20. René Girard, *Job: The Victim of His People*, trans. Yvonne Freccero (London: Athlone Press, 1987), 97.

21. Girard, *Violence and the Sacred*, 67.

22. J. C. Heesterman, *The Broken World of Sacrifice: An Essay in Ancient Indian Ritual* (Chicago: University of Chicago Press, 1993), 45.

23. Heesterman, *Broken World of Sacrifice*, 227n6.

24. Heesterman, *Broken World of Sacrifice*, 75.

25. Jean-Pierre Dupuy, "Totalization and Misrecognition," in *Violence and Truth: On the Work of René Girard*, ed. Paul Dumouchel (Stanford, CA: Stanford University Press, 1988), 76.

26. *ṚV* 10.130.3. There are some insights on mimesis and the Vedic creation hymns to be found in Barbara Mikolajewska, *Creation Hymns of the* Rig Veda (New Haven, CT: The Lintons' Video Press, 1999).

27. Dupuy, "Totalization and Misrecognition," 77.

28. Kimberley C. Patton, *Religion of the Gods: Ritual, Paradox, and Reflexivity* (New York: Oxford University Press, 2009), 9.

29. M. S. Bhat, *Vedic Tantrism: A Study of the* Ṛgvidhāna *of Śaunaka with Text and Translation; Critically Edited in the Original Sanskrit with an Introductory Study and Translated with Critical and Exegetical Notes* (Delhi: Motilal Banarsidass, 1987), 106.

30. *ṚV* 1.164.34–35.

31. Jan E. M. Houben, "The Ritual Pragmatics of a Vedic Hymn: The 'Riddle Hymn' and the Pravargya Ritual," *Journal of the American Oriental Society* 120:4 (Oct.–Dec., 2000): 502.

32. *The Pravargya Brāhmaṇa of the Taittirīya Āraṇyaka*, trans. Jan E. M. Houben (Delhi: Motilal Banarsidass, 1991), 4–6.

33. Houben, "Ritual Pragmatics," 513.

34. Houben, *Pravargya Brāhmaṇa*, 4.

35. Julius Eggeling in the introduction to *ŚB*, vol. 5, xlviii.

36. Heesterman, *Broken World of Sacrifice*, 168.

37. Houben, "Ritual Pragmatics," 529.

38. Houben, "Ritual Pragmatics," 529.

39. Girard, *Sacrifice*, 40.

40. Girard, *Sacrifice*, 40.

41. Heesterman, *Broken World of Sacrifice*, 71.

42. The *Vādhūla Brāhmaṇa* takes its name from the Brahmin clan of Vātula, of which the Bhṛgus are a subgroup. It is also connected to the Kuru warrior clan, a nomadic pastoral-raiding clan in the old Aryan style that Heesterman connects to the Vrātyas.

43. Stephanie W. Jamison and Michael Witzel, "Vedic Hinduism," in *The Study of Hinduism*, ed. Arvind Sharma (Columbia: University of South Carolina Press, 2003), 73.

44. Heesterman, *Broken World of Sacrifice*, 74.

45. In this case, "Indra" is more of a title meaning "Lord" than a proper noun.

46. This reference comes from *The Çrautasūtra of Kātyāyana with Extracts from the Commentaries of Karka and Yājñikadeva*, ed. Albrecht Weber (Berlin: Dümmler, 1856). But for the sake of consistency, I have transliterated the title as *Kātyāyana Śrauta Sūtra*. This and all other transliterations conform to the International Alphabet of Sanskrit Transliteration, which renders the unvoiced palatal sibilant (*ç* in some older systems of romanization) as *ś*.

47. *BŚS* 10.9.8.

48. Heesterman, *Inner Conflict of Tradition*, 50–53.

49. Heesterman, *Inner Conflict of Tradition*, 47.

50. Heesterman, *Inner Conflict of Tradition*, 47.

51. Heesterman, *Inner Conflict of Tradition*, 48.

52. See Collins, "Headless Mothers," 100–158.

53. Heesterman, *Inner Conflict of Tradition*, 215n15.

54. *The Rig Veda*, trans. Doniger, 32n18.

55. Girard, *Sacrifice*, 37.

56. Heesterman, *Broken World of Sacrifice*, 8.

57. Heesterman, *Broken World of Sacrifice*, 45.

58. Dawson, *Flesh Becomes Word*, 80.

59. Girard, *Things Hidden*, 278.

60. Girard, *Violence and the Sacred*, 37.

61. Heesterman, *Broken World of Sacrifice*, 48.

62. Heesterman, *Broken World of Sacrifice*, 91.

63. Like the Vrātyas, Indra and Śiva are both excluded from the sacrifice and blamed for some unforgivable sin, usually Brahminicide. In the earliest layer of the *Ṛg Veda*, Indra, like his human counterparts among the Āryan tribes, is both warrior and priest-poet. In fact, the great

warrior-god Indra and the Bṛhaspati, the *purohita* of the gods, are two aspects of the same figure. But at a later stage, the great god of the sacrifice is identified as Prajāpati and the Brahmins (in the role of *nāstikas*) heap abuse on Indra accusing him of Brahminicide. Śiva's exclusion from the sacrifice and its disastrous consequences are recounted in the famous myth of Dakśa's sacrifice.

64. René Girard, "Lévi-Strauss, Frye, Derrida and Shakespearean Criticism," *Diacritics* 3:3 (Autumn 1973): 36.

65. For a further discussion of the *pharmakos*, see Walter Burkert, *Structure and History in Greek Mythology and Ritual* (Berkeley: University of California Press, 1979), 59–78.

66. Girard, *Violence and the Sacred*, 94–95.

67. Todd M. Compton, *Victim of the Muses: Poet as Scapegoat, Warrior, and Hero in Greco-Roman and Indo-European Myth and History* (Washington, DC: Center for Hellenic Studies, 2006), 3.

68. Compton, *Victim of the Muses*, 221.

69. Georges Dumézil, *The Stakes of the Warrior*, trans. David Weeks and ed. Jaan Puhvel (Berkeley: University of California Press, 1983), 14–15.

70. One can see in this story a close parallel to the death of Baldr treated by Dumézil and Girard.

71. Dumézil, *Stakes of the Warrior*, 15.

72. The text describes Yudhiṣṭhira speaking to Bhīṣma "as Indra might speak to Bṛhaspati," drawing a direct connection between the Pāṇḍavas' sacrificial struggle against their enemies to the gods' sacrificial struggle against the demons.

73. *MBh* 2.37.5b–14.

74. *MBh* 2.41.1–4.

75. Dumézil, *Stakes of the Warrior*, 57.

76. It should not escape us that Samothrace was home to one of the most famous sacrificial cults in the ancient world.

77. Jarrod L. Whitaker, *Strong Arms and Drinking Strength: Masculinity, Violence, and the Body in Ancient India* (New York: Oxford University Press, 2011), 48.

78. Jan Gonda, "Some Riddles Connected with Royal Titles in Ancient Iran," in *Selected Studies Volume I: Indo-European Linguistics* (Leiden, Netherlands: E. J. Brill, 1975), 444.

79. J. A. F. Roodbergen, "Notes to Canto 1," in *Mallināthaʼs Ghaṇṭāpatha on the Kirātārjuniya I–VI* (Leiden, Netherlands: Brill, 1984), 378.

80. Joseph T. Shipley, *The Origins of English Words: A Discursive Dictionary of Indo-European Roots* (Baltimore: Johns Hopkins University Press, 1984), 182.

81. Dumézil, *Flamen-brahman*, 93–94.

82. Gananath Obeyesekere, "Sorcery, Premeditated Murder, and the Canalization of Aggression in Sri Lanka," *Ethnology* 14:1 (Jan. 1975): 22n2.

83. Dumézil, *The Plight of a Sorcerer*, 43.

84. Compton, *Victim of the Muses*, 221.

85. Quoted in Ellison Banks Findly, "*Mántra kaviśastá*: Speech as Performative in the Ṛgveda," in

Understanding Mantras, ed. Harvey P. Alper (Albany: State University of New York Press, 1989), 24.

86. On another level, Odin and Thor also represent the contractual-binding and martial sides of the first function, as do Mitra and Varuṇa. In this and many other myths, all three functions contain elements of the others.

87. Dumézil, *Stakes of the Warrior*, 77.

88. In *MBh* 6.33.32 Kṛṣṇa famously proclaims to Arjuna, "I am time grown old, on a path of world destruction, born to annihilate the cosmos. Even without you, all these warriors arrayed in hostile ranks will cease to exist. Therefore, arise and win glory! Conquer your foes and fulfill your kingship! They are already killed by me. Merely be my instrument, the archer at my side!"

89. Reich, "The Interruption of the Sacrifice," 139.

90. This is laid out most clearly in chapter twelve of the *Gītā*.

91. See James Fitzgerald, "The Great Epic of India as Religious Rhetoric: A Fresh Look at the *Mahābhārata*," *Journal of the American Academy of Religion* 51:4 (Dec. 1983): 626: "The figures of authority and nobility in the old order appear to be helpless in the face of the divisive evil. . . . And when the new order is presented as deriving from, authorized by, and in fact founded by the powerful god Nārāyaṇa-Viṣṇu . . . the new order he initiates cannot be opposed."

92. Hiltebeitel, *Rethinking the* Mahābhārata, 214.

93. The text uses the word *grāma*, originally a cattle raiding party and later a village.

94. Girard, *Things Hidden*, 402.

95. In the *Pañcaviṃśa Brāhmaṇa*, Cyavana is a descendant of Dadhyañc.

96. Robert P. Goldman, *Gods, Priests, and Warriors: The Bhṛgus of the* Mahābhārata (New York: Columbia University Press, 1977), 54.

97. We also see in this story what can be read as rough outline of the paradigmatic goddess myth of India in which the gods temporarily cede their power to a "tame" goddess like Pārvatī so that she can kill a powerful demon (typically the Buffalo Demon Mahiṣa) and take the fearsome form of Kālī only to watch her grow drunk with bloodlust and threaten to destroy the whole world until Śiva is called in to calm her by lying down in front of her. The first recordings of this myth model do not come until the middle of the first millennium C.E., but what suggested this admittedly anachronistic interpretation to me is the line from verse 35, "Behold the forms of Sūryā that only a Brahmin can purify" (*Sūryāḥ paśya rūpaṇi tāni brahmā tu śundhati*), which seems to identify the demonic Kṛtyā as a form of the beneficent goddess Sūryā, who requires a priest's intervention to pacify her. One other equally insubstantial but provocative piece of evidence for this bit of speculation is the later use of "Kṛtyā" to denote a fierce goddess who receives blood sacrifices as Kālī does; I say it is insubstantial because the usage appears only in Sanskrit lexicons and is not attested outside of them.

98. Girard, *Violence and the Sacred*, 166.

99. Jacques Derrida, *Dissemination*, trans. Barbara Johnson (London: Athlone Press, 1981), 90.

100. Stephanie W. Jamison, *The* Rig Veda *between Two Worlds* (Paris: Collège de France, 2007), 124.

101. The word "unbound" here is a reference to the literal unbinding of Śunaḥśepa, which is the key moment in his story. But it also refers to *Oedipus Unbound*, the title of a collection of Girard's essays on Oedipus. In the title of that book, the "unbinding" refers to the process of prying the

story of Oedipus loose from the psychoanalytic framework in order to gain a new perspective on it. But there is a third type of unbinding that is also relevant to this discussion: "unbound" in the sense of "unraveled." It is to this kind of "unbound" that Alain Badiou refers when he writes, "As far as nihilism is concerned, we shall acknowledge that our epoch bears witness to it precisely in the way that by nihilism we understood *the rupture of the traditional figure of the bond*, unbinding as a form of being of all that pretends to be of the bond" (*Manifesto for Philosophy*, trans. and ed. Norman Madarasz [Albany: State University of New York Press, 1999], 55).

102. Compton, *Victim of the Muses*, 216.

103. Derrida, *Dissemination*, 77.

104. A. K. Ramanujan, "The Indian Oedipus," in *Oedipus: A Folklore Casebook*, ed. Lowell Edmunds and Alan Dundes (New York: Garland, 1983), 254.

105. Michael Witzel, "Vedas and Upaniṣads," in *The Blackwell Companion to Hinduism*, ed. Gavin Flood (Oxford: Blackwell Publishing Ltd., 2003), 69.

106. Derrida, *Dissemination*, 77.

107. Girard, *Violence and the Sacred*, 297.

108. Edwin Gerow, "Indian Poetics," in *Scientific and Technical Literature, Part II*, vol. 5 of *A History of Indian Literature*, ed. Jan Gonda (Wiesbaden, Germany: Otto Harrassowitz, 1977), 13.

109. The line, *Rām* 1.2.14, reads: '*māniṣāda pratiṣṭhāṃ tvam agamaḥ śāśvatīḥ samāḥ / yat krauñcamithunād ekam avadīḥ kāmamohitam.*'

110. Ch. Vaudeville, "*Rāmāyana* Studies I: The *Krauñca-Vadha* Episode in the Vālmīki *Rāmāyaṇa*," *Journal of the American Oriental Society* 83:3 (Aug.–Sep. 1963): 330n9.

111. Giuliano Boccoli, "The Incipits of Classical Sargabandhas," in *Śāstrārambha: Inquiries into the Preamble in Sanskrit*, ed. Walter Slaje, volume 62 of *Abhandlungen für die Kunde des Morgenlandes* (Berlin: Deutsche Morgenländische Gesellschaft, 2008), 193.

112. *MS* 1.1.5.

113. José Pereira, *Hindu Theology: A Reader* (Garden City, NY: Image Books, 1976), 98–99.

114. It is the word *śabda* that Catholic missionaries use to translate the *logos* of Jesus Christ when they attempt to formulate an Indian Christian Theology. See Robin H. S. Boyd, *India and the Latin Captivity of the Church: The Cultural Context of the Gospel* (New York: Cambridge University Press, 1974), 77. But in the Sanskrit translation of the Gospel of John done by Baptist missionaries in the nineteenth century, *logos* becomes *vāda*, a word that has the specific sense of "speech" (William Carey et al., *The New Testament of Our Lord and Savior Jesus Christ in Sanscrit: Translated from the Greek by the Calcutta Baptist Missionaries with Native Assistants*, 2nd edition [Calcutta: 1851], http://www.sanskritweb.net/sansdocs/#BIBLE).

115. This formulation of an eternal correspondence also occurs much later in the *Kāvyālaṅkāra* ("The Jewel of Poetry") of the seventh century C.E. philosopher of poetics Bhāmaha, who defines *kāvya* as *śabdarthau sahitau*, "word and meaning united." Bhāmaha's work is more indebted to the epistemologies of the Nyāya and Vaiśesika schools than the Mīmāṃsā, but it points back toward the *kavi*.

116. Francis X. Clooney, *Thinking Ritually: Rediscovering the Pūrva Mīmāṃsā of Jaimini* (Vienna: De Nobili Research Library, 1990), 25.

117. For a good overview of the movement, see Levi Bryant, Nick Srnicek, and Graham Harmon, eds., *The Speculative Turn: Continental Materialism and Realism* (Melbourne: re.press, 2011).

118. As Meillassoux has it: "[Suppose] that by 'construction' I refer instead to the mechanisms by which an archaeologist has set up a dig site in order to excavate some ruins without damaging them. In this case the 'constructions' (a complex of winches, sounding lines, scaffolding, spades, brushes, etc.) are not destined to *produce* an object, as in the case of architecture. On the contrary, they are made with a view to *not* interfere with the object at which they aim: that is to say, excavating the ruins without damaging them, in unearthing them 'as is,' and not as modified or even destroyed by the impact of the excavation tools. Thus, mathematics and experimental sciences can certainly be human 'constructions': but this does not prove that they are such in the sense of architectural construction rather than archaeological 'discovery' (in the manner in which one speaks of 'the discovery of ruins or of a treasure')." (Quoted in Graham Harman, *Quentin Meillassoux: Philosophy in the Making* [Edinburgh: Edinburgh University Press, 2011], 167–168)

119. Joseph Dauben, *Georg Cantor, His Mathematics and Philosophy of the Infinite* (Cambridge, MA: Harvard University Press, 1979), 147.

120. Clooney, *Thinking Ritually*, 131–137.

121. Veena Das, "Language of Sacrifice," *Man* 18:3 (Sep. 1983): 447; Harman, *Quentin Meillassoux*, 52.

122. Quentin Meillassoux, *After Finitude: An Essay on the Necessity of Contingency*, trans. Ray Brassier (New York: Continuum, 2008), passim.

123. Meillassoux, *After Finitude*, 26.

124. There is something of Plato's *Symposium* here as well, in which the desire for a beautiful object is transmuted into the desire for beauty itself.

125. Clooney, *Thinking Ritually*, 211.

126. Das, "Language of Sacrifice," 445 (italics added).

127. Das, "Language of Sacrifice," 446.

128. William K. Mahoney, *The Artful Universe: An Introduction to the Vedic Religious Imagination* (Albany: State University of New York Press, 1998), 3.

129. Das, "Language of Sacrifice," 447.

130. Francis X. Clooney, "Sacrifice and Its Spiritualization in the Christian and Hindu Traditions: A Study in Comparative Theology," *The Harvard Theological Review* 78:3/4 (July–Oct. 1985): 380.

131. Heesterman, "Warrior, Peasant and Brahmin," 654.

Yajñānta: The End of Sacrifice

1. Joel Brereton, "Soma," in *Encyclopedia of Religion*, ed. Lindsey Jones, vol. 12 (Detroit: MacMillan Reference USA, 2005), 8522.

2. Girard, *Sacrifice*, 56.

3. *ŚB* 3.9.4.17.

4. Girard, *Sacrifice*, 56–57 (italics added).

5. Girard and Chantre, *Battling to the End*, 197.

6. Dipesh Chakrabarty, "The Climate of History: Four Theses," *Critical Inquiry* 35 (Winter 2009): 201.
7. Susan Buck-Morss, *Hegel, Haiti, and Universal History* (Pittsburgh: University of Pittsburgh Press, 2009), 133.
8. The title of an August 14, 1949, article written by Mao Zedong in response to the U.S. State Department's white paper on China-U.S. Relations.
9. *The Dark Knight*, DVD, dir. by Christopher Nolan (Warner Brothers, 2008).
10. Žižek, *Living in the End Times*, 61.
11. Žižek, *Living in the End Times*, 61.
12. Alain Badiou, *Pocket Pantheon: Figures of Postwar Philosophy*, trans. David Macey (London: Verso, 2009), viii.
13. Depoortere, *Christ in Postmodern Philosophy*, 84–85.
14. Quoted in Girard and Chantre, *Battling to the End*, xvii.
15. Friedrich Hölderlin, "Patmos," trans. Scott Horton, *Harper's Magazine*, July 16, 2007, http://harpers.org/archive/2007/07/hbc-90000528.
16. Alfred Loisy, *L'évangile et l'église* (Paris: Alphonse Picard et Fils, 1902), 111.
17. Girard, *Sacrifice*, 74.
18. Girard and Chantre, *Battling to the End*, 199.
19. Girard and Chantre, *Battling to the End*, 198.
20. Ashis Nandy, "History's Forgotten Doubles," *History and Theory* 34:2, Theme Issue 34: World Historians and Their Critics (May 1995): 64–65 (italics added).
21. The word *mleccha*, used to refer to foreigners, is the Sanskrit equivalent of "barbarian," meaning one who babbles.
22. Andrew J. Nicholson, *Unifying Hinduism: Philosophy and Identity in Indian Intellectual History* (New York: Columbia University Press, 2010), 204.
23. Nicholson, *Unifying Hinduism*, 204.
24. Slavoj Žižek, "How to Begin from the Beginning," *New Left Review* 57, May-June 2009, http://newleftreview.org/II/57/slavoj-zizek-how-to-begin-from-the-beginning.

Bibliography

Primary Texts in Sanskrit, French, and English

Aitareya-Āraṇyaka. Translated by A. B. Keith. Oxford: Clarendon Press, 1969.

Aitareya-Brāhmaṇa. On the basis of the edition by Th. Aufrecht, *Das Aitareya Brāhmaṇa. Mit Auszügen aus dem Commentare von Sāyaṇācārya und anderen Beilagen*. Bonn, Germany: 1879. Entered, converted and edited in Wordcruncher format by Fco. Javier Martínez García. Erlangen, Germany, and Madrid: 1991–1992. TITUS version by Jost Gippert. http://titus.uni-frankfurt.de/texte/etcs/ind/aind/ved/rv/ab/ab.htm. [*AB*]

Aitereya Brāhmaṇa. With the *Vṛtti Sukhapradā* of Ṣaḍguruśiṣya. Edited by R. Anantakriṣṇa Śāstri. University of Travancore Sanskrit Series No. cxlix. Trivandrum, India: Bhaskara Press, 1942.

Bacchae of Euripides, The. Translated by C. K. Williams. New York: Farrar, Strauss and Giroux, 1990.

Bagavadam ou Doctrine divine; ouvrage indien canonique, sur l'être suprême, les dieux, les géants, les hommes. Translated by Foucher d'Obsonville and Maridâs Poullé. Paris: Tillard, 1788.

Baudhāyana Śrauta Sutra, Belonging to the Taittirīya Saṃhitā, The. Edited by Willem Caland. Calcutta: Asiatic Society, 1904. [*BŚS*]

Bhaktirasāmṛtasindhu of Rūpa Gosvāmin. Translated by David L. Haberman. Delhi: Motilal Banarsidass, 2003.

Bhat, M. S. *Vedic Tantrism: A Study of the* Ṛgvidhāna *of Śaunaka with Text and Translation; Critically*

Edited in the Original Sanskrit with an Introductory Study and Translated with Critical and Exegetical Notes. Delhi: Motilal Banarsidass, 1987.

Brahmā-Purāṇa, Adhyayas 1–246. Input by Peter Schreiner and Renate Soehnen-Thieme for the Tuebingen Purana Project. http://gretil.sub.uni-goettingen.de/gretil/1_sanskr/3_purana/brahmap/brahmpau.htm. [*BrP*]

Caitanya Caritāmṛta of Kṛṣṇadāsa Kavirāja: A Translation and Commentary. Edited by Tony Stewart and translated by Edward C. Dimock, Jr. Cambridge, MA: Harvard University Press, 2000.

Calasso, Roberto. *Ka: Stories of the Mind and Gods of India*. Translated by Tim Park. New York: Alfred A. Knopf, 1998.

———. *The Ruin of Kasch*. Translated by William Weaver and Stephen Sartarelli. Cambridge, MA: The Belknap Press of Harvard University Press, 1994.

Carey, William, et al. *The New Testament of Our Lord and Savior Jesus Christ in Sanskrit*. 2nd ed. Calcutta: 1851.

Clarke, Adam. *The New Testament of Our Lord and Saviour Jesus Christ*. Edited by Daniel Curry. New York: Phillips and Hunt, 1883.

Çrautasūtra of Kātyāyana with Extracts from the Commentaries of Karka and Yājñikadeva, The. Edited by Albrecht Weber. Berlin: Dümmler, 1856.

Doniger, Wendy. *Tales of Sex and Violence: Folklore, Sacrifice, and Danger in the* Jaiminīya Brāhmaṇa. Chicago: University of Chicago Press, 1985.

Eliot, T. S. *East Coker*. London: Faber, 1940.

Gopatha Brāhmaṇa of the Atharva Veda in the Original Sanskrit, The. Edited by Rājendralāla Mitra and Harachandra Vidhyābhushaṇa. Bibliotheca India, New Series, nos. 215 and 252. Calcutta: Asiatic Society of Bengal, 1872.

Hölderlin, Friedrich. "Patmos." Translated by Scott Horton. *Harper's Magazine*, July 16, 2007. http://harpers.org/archive/2007/07/hbc-90000528.

Kaulācāra, Ramacandra. *Śilpa Prakāśa: Mediaeval Orissan Sanskrit Text on Temple Architecture*. Translated by Alice Boner and Sadāśiva Rath Śarmā. Leiden, Netherlands: Brill, 1966.

Kauśītaki Brāhmaṇa (or Śaṃkhāyana Brāhmaṇa). Based on the edition by E. R. Sreekrishna Sarma. Verzeichnis der orientalischen Handschriften in Deutschland, Supplement 9.1. Wiesbaden, Germany: 1968. Input by Muneo Tokunaga, 1995. http://gretil.sub.uni-goettingen.de/gretil/1_sanskr/1_veda/2_bra/kausibru.htm.

Kāvyālaṅkāra of Bhāmaha. Translated by P. V. Naganatha Sastry. Delhi: Motilal Banarsidass, 1991.

Kṛttibāsa. *Rāmāyaṇa*. Edited by Subodhacandra Majumdāra. Calcutta: Aruṇacandra Majumdāra at Deva Sāhitya Kuṭīra Pvt. Ltd., 1985.

Laws of Manu, The. Translated by Wendy Doniger and Brian K. Smith. New York: Penguin, 1991.

Mahābhārata, The. Translated by J. A. B. van Buitenen. 3 volumes. Chicago: University of Chicago Press, 1973–1978.

Mahabharata in Sanskrit: Parallel Devanagari and Romanization, The. Edited by Muneo Tokunaga and John D. Smith. http://www.sacred-texts.com/hin/mbs/index.htm.

Mahābhārata: Text as Constituted in Its Critical Edition, The. Pune, India: Bhandarkar Oriental Research Institute, 1976. [*MBh*]

Mahābhārata The, Volume 7, Book 11: The Book of the Women; Book 12: The Book of the Peace, Part One. Translated by James L. Fitzgerald. Chicago: University of Chicago Press, 2004.

Mallināthas Ghaṇṭāpatha on the Kirātārjuniya I–VI. Translated by J. A. F. Roodbergen. Leiden, Netherlands: Brill, 1984.

Mānava Śrauta Sutra Cayana. Edited by J. M. van Gelder. Leiden, Netherlands: A. W. Sijthoffs Verlagsgesellschaft, 1921.

Meeks, Wayne A., et al. *The HarperCollins Study Bible*. New York: HarperCollins, 1993.

Milton, John. *Paradise Lost: An Authoritative Text, Backgrounds and Sources, Criticism*. Edited by Scott Elledge. New York: W. W. Norton, 1993.

Mīmāṃsā Sūtras of Jaimini, The. The Sacred Books of the Hindus, vol. 27, parts 1–8. Edited by B. D. Basu. Allahabad, India: Sudhindra Nath Vasu, 1923. [*MS*]

Ovid. *Metamorphoses*. Translated by Charles Raeburn. New York: Penguin Classics, 2004.

Pañcaviṁśa-Brāhmaṇa. Electronic edition by Martin Kümmel, Arlo Griffiths, and Masato Kobayashi, March 31, 2005; TITUS version by Jost Gippert, Frankfurt a/M, August 30, 2009. http://titus.uni frankfurt.de/texte/etcs/ind/aind/ved/sv/pb/pb.htm.

Pañcaviṃśa-Brāhmaṇa: The Brāhmaṇa of Twenty-five Chapters. Translated by Willem Caland. Calcutta: Asiatic Society of Bengal, 1931.

Pereira, José. *Hindu Theology: A Reader*. Garden City, NY: Image Books, 1976.

Pravargya Brāhmaṇa of the Taittirīya Āraṇyaka, The. Translated by Jan E. M. Houben. Delhi: Motilal Banarsidass, 1991.

Rig Veda: An Anthology; One Hundred and Eight Hymns Selected, Translated and Annotated by Wendy Doniger, The. New York: Penguin Classics, 1981.

Rigveda: Metrically Restored Text, The. Edited by Karen Thomson and Jonathan Slocum. http://www.utexas.edu/cola/centers/lrc/RV/RV00.html. [*ṚV*]

Śatapatha-Brāhmaṇa, According to the Text of the Mâdhyandina School, The. Translated by Julius Eggeling. 5 volumes. Volumes 12, 26, 41, 43, and 44 of *Sacred Books of the East*, edited by F. Max Müller. Oxford: Clarendon, 1882–1900.

Śatapatha-Brāhmaṇa, Mādhyandina Śākha. Encoded by H. S. Ananthanarayana and W. P. Lehmann, 1971. Input by John Robert Garner, 1996–2010. http://vedavid.org/index-sutra.html. [*ŚB*]

Satwalekar, Shripad Damodar. *Yajurvediya Maitrāyaṇī-Saṃhitā*. Bombay: Aundh Svadhyayamandala, 1940.

Shakespeare, William. *Troilus and Cressida*. Edited by Kenneth Muir. Oxford World's Classics. New York: Oxford University Press, 1982.

Sharpe, Elizabeth. *Secrets of the Kaula Circle*. London: Luzac, 1936.

Sparreboom, M., and J. C. Heesterman. *The Ritual of Setting up the Sacrificial Fires According to the Vādhūla School: Vādhūlaśrautasūtra 1.1.–1.4.* Vienna: Verlag der Österreichischen Akademie der Wissenschaften, 1989.

Śrauta Sūtra of Āpastamba, Belonging to the Taittirīya Saṃhitā, with the Commentary of Rudradatta, The. Edited by Richard Garbe. Calcutta: Asiatic Society, 1881–1902.

Śrauta Sūtra of Āśvalāyana, with the Commentary of Gárgya Náráyana, The. Edited by Rāmanārāyana Vidyāratna. Calcutta: Asiatic Society, 1874.

Śrīmad-bhāgavata-purāṇam. Searchable file of complete Sanskrit text for researchers. http://www.sanskritweb.net/sansdocs/#BHAGPUR. [*BhP*]

Taittiriya Brāhmaṇa, The. With the Commentary of Bhattabhaskaramisra. Edited by A. Mahadeva Sastri and L. Srinivasacharya. Government Sanskrit Series: Bibliotheca Sanskrit No. 38. Mysore, India: Government Branch Press, 1908.

Texts of the White Yajur Veda: Translated with a Popular Commentary, The. Translated by Ralph T. H. Griffith. Benares, India: E. J. Lazarus and Co., 1899.

Tolkien, J. R. R. *The Lord of the Rings*. Boston: Houghton Mifflin, 1994.

Townsend, Joseph. *The Character of Moses Established for Veracity as an Historian, Recording Events from the Creation to the Deluge.* Bath, England: M. Gye, et al., 1816.

Vālmīki-Rāmāyana, The. Edited by Chandulal Sakaralal Patel. Baroda, India: Oriental Institute, 1975. [*Rām*]

Veda of the Black Yajus School Entitled Taittirīya Sanhitā, The. Translated by A. B. Keith. Harvard Oriental Series 18. Cambridge, MA: Harvard University Press, 1914.

Venkatesananda, Swami. *Vasiṣṭha's Yoga*. Albany: State University of New York Press, 1993.

Verne, Jules. *La maison a vapeur: voyage a travers l'Inde septentrionale*. 2 vols. Paris: Hetzel, 1880.

Vira, Raghu, and Lokesh Chandra. *Jaiminīya Brāhmaṇa of the Sāma Veda, Volume I.* Sarasvati Vihara Series, vol. 31. Lahore, Pakistan: The International Academy of Indian Culture, 1937. [*JB*]

Viṣṇudharmottara Purāṇa. Bombay: Venkateśvara Steam Press, 1912.

von Strassburg, Gottfried. *Tristan*. Edited by Karl Marold. Leipzig, Germany: Edward Avenarius, 1906.

Weber, Albrecht. *The Vajasaneyi-Saṃhitā in the Mādhyandina and the Kānva-Śākhā.* With the Commentary of Mahidhara. Chowkhamba Sanskrit Series 103. Berlin: 1849. http://titus.uni-frankfurt.de/texte/etcs/ind/aind/ved/yvs/ts/ts.htm. [*VS*]

———. *Die Taittirîya-Saṃhitâ.* Edited by Makoto Fushimi. Leipzig, Germany: Brockhaus, 1871–1872. http://titus.uni-frankfurt.de/texte/etcs/ind/aind/ved/yvs/ts/ts.htm. [*TS*]

Yogavāsiṣṭha-Mahā-Rāmāyaṇa of Vālmīki. With the Commentary *Vāsiṣṭha-Mahā-Rāmāyaṇā-Tātparyaprakāśa*. Edited by W. L. S. Pansikar. Bombay: 1918.

Secondary Sources

Aarne, Antti, and Stith Thompson. *The Types of the Folktale: A Classification and Bibliography*. Helsinki: Suomalainen Tiedeakatemia, 1961.

Ackerman, Robert. *J. G. Frazer: His Life and Work*. New York: Cambridge University Press, 1987.

Adarkar, Aditya. "Karṇa in the *Mahābhārata*." PhD diss., University of Chicago, 2001.

Agamben, Giorgio. *Homo Sacer: Sovereign Power and Bare Life*. Stanford, CA: Stanford University Press, 1998.

———. *State of Exception*. Chicago: University of Chicago Press, 2005.

———. *The Sacrament of Language: An Archaeology of the Oath (Homo Sacer II, 3)*. Stanford, CA: Stanford University Press, 2011.

Badiou, Alain. *Manifesto for Philosophy*. Edited and translated by Norman Madarasz. Albany: State University of New York Press, 1999.

———. *Saint Paul: The Foundation of Universalism*. Stanford, CA: Stanford University Press, 2003.

———. *Pocket Pantheon: Figures of Postwar Philosophy*. Translated by David Macey. London: Verso, 2009.

Bailly, Jean-Sylvain. *Lettres sur l'origine des sciences et sur celle des peuples de L'Asie*. Paris: Frères Debure, 1777.

Battacharji, Sukumari. "Varuṇa." In *Encyclopedia of Religion*, edited by Lindsey Jones, vol. 14, 9524–9525. Detroit: MacMillan Reference USA, 2005.

Bergaigne, Abel. *La religion védique d'après les hymnes du* Rig-Véda. Paris: P. Vieweg, 1878.

Biardeau, Madeleine. *Le sacrifice dans l'inde ancienne*. Edited by Charles Malamoud. Paris: Presses universitaires de France, 1976.

Billot, Frédéric-Florentin. *L'Inde, L'Angleterre et la France*. Paris: Dentu, 1857.

Biswas, S. N. "Ober das Vrātya Problem in der Vedischen Ritualliteratur." *Zeitschrrift der Deutschen Morgenlamdische Gesellschaft* 105 (1955): 53.

Boccoli, Giuliano. "The Incipits of Classical Sargabandhas." In *Śāstrārambha: Inquiries into the Preamble in Sanskrit*, edited by Walter Slaje, 183–205. Volume 62 of *Abhandlungen für die Kunde des Morgenlandes*. Berlin: Deutsche Morgenländische Gesellschaft, 2008.

Bouckaert, Remco, et al. "Mapping the Origins and Expansion of the Indo-European Language Family." *Science* 24:337:6097 (August 2012): 957–960.

Boyd, Robin H. S. *India and the Latin Captivity of the Church: The Cultural Context of the Gospel*. New York: Cambridge University Press, 1974.

Brereton, Joel. "Soma." In *Encyclopedia of Religion*, edited by Lindsey Jones, vol. 12, 8521–8522. Detroit: MacMillan Reference USA, 2005.

Bryant, Edwin F. *The Quest for the Origins of Vedic Culture: The Indo-Aryan Migration Debate*. New York: Oxford University Press, 2001.

Buck-Morss, Susan. *Hegel, Haiti, and Universal History*. Pittsburgh: University of Pittsburgh Press, 2009.

Cameron, Alan. *The Last Pagans of Rome.* New York: Oxford University Press, 2011.

Caputo, John D. *The Prayers and Tears of Jacques Derrida: Religion without Religion.* Bloomington: Indiana University Press, 1997.

Carrasco, Davíd. *City of Sacrifice: The Aztec Empire and the Role of Violence in Civilization.* Boston: Beacon Press, 1999.

Chakrabarty, Dipesh. "The Climate of History: Four Theses." *Critical Inquiry* 35 (Winter 2009): 197–222.

Charpentier, François. *Discours d'un fidèle sujet du roy touchant l'establissement d'une compagnie françoise pour le commerce des Indes orientales: adressé à tous les français.* Paris: 1665.

Clarke, Adam. *The New Testament of Our Lord and Saviour Jesus Christ: The Text in the Authorized Translation with a Commentary and Critical Notes.* New York: G. Lane and C. B. Tippett, 1846.

Clooney, Francis X. "Sacrifice and Its Spiritualization in the Christian and Hindu Traditions: A Study in Comparative Theology." *The Harvard Theological Review* 78:3/4 (July –Oct. 1985): 361–380.

———. "Jaimini's Contribution to the Theory of Sacrifice as the Experience of Transcendence." *History of Religions* 25:3 (Feb. 1986): 199–212.

———. "Why the Veda Has No Author: Language as Ritual in Early Mīmāmsā and Post-Modern Theology." *Journal of the American Academy of Religion* 55:4 (Winter 1987): 659–684.

———. *Thinking Ritually: Rediscovering the Pūrva Mīmāṃsā of Jaimini.* Vienna: De Nobili Research Library, 1990.

Colebrooke, H. T. *Essays on History, Literature and Religions of Ancient India.* New Delhi: Cosmo Publications, 1977.

Collins, Brian. "Headless Mothers, Magic Cows, and Lakes of Blood: The Parsaśurāma Cycle in the *Mahābhārata* and Beyond." PhD diss., University of Chicago, 2010.

Compton, Todd M. *Victim of the Muses: Poet as Scapegoat, Warrior, and Hero in Greco-Roman and Indo-European Myth and History.* Washington, DC: Center for Hellenic Studies, 2006.

Crooke, William. *The Popular Religion and Folklore of Northern India.* Westminster, England: Archibald Constable, 1896.

Dark Knight, The. DVD. Directed by Christopher Nolan. Warner Brothers, 2008.

Das, Gurchuran. *The Difficulty of Being Good: On the Subtle Art of Dharma.* New York: Oxford University Press, 2009.

———. "Changing Rules of Dharma." *The Times of India*, November 30, 2008. http://timesofindia.indiatimes.com/home/opinion/gurcharan-das/men-ideas/Changing-rules-of-dharma/articleshow/3774379.cms?.

Das, Veena. "Language of Sacrifice." *Man* 18:3 (Sep. 1983): 445–462.

Dauben, Joseph. *Georg Cantor, His Mathematics and Philosophy of the Infinite.* Cambridge, MA: Harvard University Press, 1979.

Dawson, David. *Flesh Becomes Word: A Lexicography of the Scapegoat or, the History of an Idea.* East Lansing: Michigan State University Press, 2013.

Death Takes a Holiday. DVD. Directed by Mitchell Leisen. Paramount, 1934.

Deleury, Guy, et al. "Bilingual Annotations" to "French Books on India: From Dupleix to

Decolonization v. 1." http://www.liv.ac.uk/soclas/research/Peripheralvoices/french-books/Bilingual_annotations.pdf.

Depoortere, Frederiek. *Christ in Postmodern Philosophy: Gianni Vattimo, René Girard and Slavoj Žižek.* London: T & T Clark, 2008.

Derrida, Jacques. *Dissemination.* Translated by Barbara Johnson. London: Athlone Press, 1981.

Doniger, Wendy. *The Origins of Evil in Hindu Mythology.* Berkeley: University of California Press, 1976.

———. *Splitting the Difference: Gender and Myth in Ancient Greece and India.* Chicago: University of Chicago Press, 1999.

———. *The Hindus: An Alternative History.* New York: Penguin Press, 2009.

D'Souza, Herman. *In the Steps of St. Thomas.* Pune, India: Yeravda Prison Press, 1964.

Dumézil, Georges. *Flamen-brahman.* Paris: P. Geuthner, 1935.

———. "La terre soulagée." In *Mythe et épopée* I., 31–257. Paris: Gallimard, 1968.

———. *The Destiny of a King.* Translated by Alf Hiltebeitel. Chicago: University of Chicago Press, 1973.

———. *The Stakes of the Warrior.* Translated by David Weeks and edited by Jaan Puhvel. Berkeley: University of California Press, 1983.

———. *The Plight of a Sorcerer.* Edited by Jaan Puhvel and David Weeks. Berkeley: University of California Press, 1986.

———. *Mitra-Varuna: An Essay on Two Indo-European Representations.* New York: Zone Books, 1988.

Dupuy, Jean-Pierre. "Totalization and Misrecognition." In *Violence and Truth: On the Work of René Girard,* edited by Paul Dumouchel, 75–100. Stanford, CA: Stanford University Press, 1988.

Eagleton, Terry. *Literary Theory: An Introduction.* Minneapolis: University of Minnesota Press, 1983.

Falk, Harry. *Bruderschaft und Würfelspeil: Untersuchungen zur Entwicklungsgeschichte des vedischen Opfers.* Freiburg, Germany: H. Falk, 1986.

Findly, Ellison Banks. "*Mántra kaviśastá*: Speech as Performative in the Ṛgveda." In *Understanding Mantras,* edited by Harvey P. Alper, 15–47. Albany: State University of New York Press, 1989.

Fitzgerald, James. "The Great Epic of India as Religious Rhetoric: A Fresh Look at the Mahābhārata." *Journal of the American Academy of Religion* 51:4 (Dec. 1983): 626.

Frankfurter, David. *Evil Incarnate: Rumors of Demonic Conspiracy and Ritual Abuse in History.* Princeton, NJ: Princeton University Press, 2006.

Frazer, J. G. *Balder the Beautiful Volume I: The Fire Festivals of Europe and the Doctrine of the External Soul.* Part 7 of *The Golden Bough: A Study in Magic and Religion.* 3rd ed. Project Gutenberg: May 4, 2004. E-book #12261.

Freud, Sigmund. *Jokes and Their Relation to the Unconscious.* Translated by James Strachey. New York: W. W. Norton, 1989.

Gerow, Edwin. "Indian Poetics." In *Scientific and Technical Literature, Part II.* Volume 5 of *A History of Indian Literature,* edited by Jan Gonda. Wiesbaden, Germany: Otto Harrassowitz, 1977.

Ginzburg, Carlo. *The Night Battles: Witchcraft and Agrarian Cults in the Sixteenth and Seventeenth Centuries.* New York: Penguin Books, 1985.

Girard, René. *Mensonge romantique et vérité romanesque*. Paris: Grasset, 1961.

———. *Deceit, Desire and the Novel: Self and Other in Literary Structure*. Baltimore: Johns Hopkins University Press, 1966.

———. *La violence et le sacré*. Paris: Grasset, 1972.

———. "Lévi-Strauss, Frye, Derrida and Shakespearean Criticism." *Diacritics* 3:3 (Autumn 1973): 34–38.

———. "Tiresias and the Critic." In *The Structuralist Controversy: The Languages of Criticism and the Sciences of Man*, edited by Richard Macksey and Eugenio Donato, 15–21. Baltimore: Johns Hopkins University Press, 1975.

———. *Violence and the Sacred*. Baltimore: Johns Hopkins University Press, 1977.

———. *Des choses caches depuis la foundation du monde*. Paris: Grasset, 1978.

———. "Interview: René Girard." *Diacritics* 8:1, Special Issue on the Work of René Girard (Spring 1978): 31–54.

———. *The Scapegoat*. Baltimore: Johns Hopkins University Press, 1986.

———. "Generative Scapegoating; Girard Paper: Discussion." In *Violent Origins: Ritual Killing and Cultural Formation*, edited by Robert G. Hamerton-Kelly, 106–145. Stanford, CA: Stanford University Press, 1987.

———. *Job: The Victim of His People*. Translated by Yvonne Freccero. London: Athlone Press, 1987.

———. *Things Hidden since the Foundation of the World: Research Undertaken in Collaboration with Jean-Michel Oughourlian and G. Lefort*. Edited by Stephen Bann and Michael Leigh Metteer. Stanford, CA: Stanford University Press, 1987.

———. *I See Satan Fall Like Lightning*. Maryknoll, NY: Orbis Books, 2001.

———. "The Evangelical Subversion of Myth." In *Politics and Apocalypse*, edited by Robert Hamerton-Kelly, 29–49. East Lansing: Michigan State University Press, 2007.

———. "Racine, Poet of Glory." In *Mimesis and Theory: Essays on Literature and Criticism, 1953–2005*, edited by Robert Doran, 96–124. Stanford, CA: Stanford University Press, 2008.

———. *Sacrifice*. Translated by Matthew Patillo and David Dawson. East Lansing: Michigan State University Press, 2011.

Girard, René and Benoît Chantre. *Achever Clausewitz: Entretiens avec Benoît Chantre*. Paris: Carnets Nord, 2007.

———. *Battling to the End: Conversations with Benoît Chantre*. Edited by Benoît Chantre. East Lansing: Michigan State University Press, 2010.

Di Giuseppe, Riccardo. "Trifunctional Structure in the Desert Temptations: G. Dumézil, L. Dumont and the Christ." Paper presented at the annual meeting of the Colloquium on Violence & Religion, Innsbruck, Tyrol, Austria, June 18–21, 2003.

Godfather, The. DVD. Directed by Francis Ford Coppola. Paramount, 1972.

Goldhammer, Jesse. *The Headless Republic: Sacrificial Violence in Modern French Thought*. Ithaca, NY: Cornell University Press, 2005.

Goldman, Robert P. *Gods, Priests, and Warriors: The Bhṛgus of the* Mahābhārata. New York: Columbia University Press, 1977.

Gonda, Jan. "Some Riddles Connected with Royal Titles in Ancient Iran." In *Selected Studies Volume I: Indo-European Linguistics*, 432–447. Leiden, Netherlands: Brill, 1975.

———. "Vedic Gods and the Sacrifice." *Numen* 30:1 (Jul. 1983): 1–34.

Hamerton-Kelly, Robert. *Sacred Violence: Paul's Hermeneutic of the Cross*. Minneapolis: Fortress Press, 1992.

———. "Response." Presented at the Symposium on René Girard and World Religions at the Graduate Theological Union, Berkeley, California, April 14–16, 2011.

Handelman, Don. "Traps of Trans-formation: Theoretical Convergences between Riddle and Ritual." In *Untying the Knot: On Riddles and Other Enigmatic Modes*, edited by Galit Hasan-Rokem and David Shulman, 37–61. New York: Oxford University Press, 1996.

Handelman, Don, and David Dean Shulman. *God Inside Out: Śiva's Game of Dice*. New York: Oxford University Press, 1997.

Harman, Graham. *Quentin Meillassoux: Philosophy in the Making*. Edinburgh: Edinburgh University Press, 2011.

Heesterman, J. C. "Vrātya and Sacrifice." *Indo-Iranian Journal* 6 (1962): 3–37.

———. *The Inner Conflict of Tradition: Essays in Indian Ritual, Kingship, and Society*. Chicago: University of Chicago Press, 1985.

———. *The Broken World of Sacrifice: An Essay in Ancient Indian Ritual*. Chicago: University of Chicago Press, 1993.

———. "Warrior, Peasant and Brahmin." *Modern Asian Studies* 29:3 (July 1995): 637–654.

Hiltebeitel, Alf. *The Ritual of Battle: Krishna in the* Mahābhārata. Albany: State University of New York Press, 1990.

———. *Rethinking the* Mahābhārata: *A Reader's Guide to the Education of the Dharma King*. Chicago: University of Chicago Press, 2001.

Houben, Jan E. M. "The Ritual Pragmatics of a Vedic Hymn: The 'Riddle Hymn' and the Pravargya Ritual." *Journal of the American Oriental Society* 120:4 (Oct.–Dec. 2000): 499–536.

Hubert, Henri, and Marcel Mauss. *Sacrifice: Its Nature and Functions*. Translated by W. D. Halls. Chicago: University of Chicago Press, 1964.

Insler, Stanley. "Review of *ÁSURA in Early Vedic Religion*, by Wash Edward Hale." *Journal of the American Oriental Society* 113:4 (Oct.–Dec. 1993): 595–596.

Jamison, Stephanie W. *The Ravenous Hyenas and the Wounded Sun: Myth and Ritual in Ancient India*. Ithaca, NY: Cornell University Press, 1991.

———. *Sacrificed Wife/Sacrificer's Wife: Women, Ritual, and Hospitality in Ancient India*. New York: Oxford University Press, 1996.

———. "Penelope and the Pigs: Indic Perspectives on the 'Odyssey.'" *Classical Antiquity* 18:2 (Oct. 1999): 227–272.

———. *The* Rig Veda *between Two Worlds*. Paris: Collège de France, 2007.

Jamison, Stephanie W., and Michael Witzel. "Vedic Hinduism." In *The Study of Hinduism*, edited by Arvind Sharma, 65–113. Columbia: University of South Carolina Press, 2003.

Jenkins, Tim. "Marcel Mauss's Essay *On Prayer*: An Important Contribution on the Nature of

Sociological Understanding." *Revue du MAUSS permanente* (Nov. 6, 2008). http://www.journaldumauss.net/spip.php?article418.

Johnston, Mark. *Saving God: Religion after Idolatry*. Princeton, NJ: Princeton University Press, 2009.

Jones, Sir William. *Discourses Delivered before the Asiatic Society: And Miscellaneous Papers, on the Religion, Poetry, Literature, etc., of the Nations of India*. London: C. S. Arnold, 1824.

Jordaan, Roy E., and Robert Wessing. "Construction Sacrifice in India, 'Seen from the East.'" In *Violence Denied: Violence, Non-Violence and the Rationalization of Violence in South Asian Cultural History*, edited by Jan E. M. Houben and Karel R. Van Kooij, 211–247. Boston: Brill, 1999.

Kaufmann, Walter. *Nietzsche: Philosopher, Psychologist, Antichrist*. 4th edition. Princeton, NJ: Princeton University Press, 1974.

Kuiper, F. B. J. "Four Word Studies." *Indo-Iranian Journal* 15:3 (Sept. 1973): 179–204.

Kulke, Hermann, and Dietmar Rothermund. *A History of India*. New York: Routledge, 2010.

Lardinois, Roland. *L'invention de l'Inde: Entre ésotérisme et science*. Paris: CNRS Éditions, 2007.

Lawrence, Patricia. "Kāḷi in a Context of Terror: The Tasks of the Goddess in Sri Lanka's Civil War." In *Encountering Kālī: In the Margins, at the Center, in the West*, edited by Jeffrey J. Kripal and Rachel Fell McDermott, 100–123. Berkeley: University of California Press, 2003.

Lea, Henry Charles. *The Duel and the Oath*. Philadelphia: University of Pennsylvania Press, 1974.

Lévi, Sylvain. *Le théâtre indien*. 2 vols. Paris: Émile Bouillon, 1890.

———. *La doctrine du sacrifice dans les Brâhmanas*. Paris: Ernest Leroux, 1898.

———. "La Régéneration Religieuse." *Archives israëlites* 61 (1900): 181.

———. "Rituel du Judaisme." *Archives israëlites* 61 (1900): 62.

Lincoln, Bruce. *Theorizing Myth: Narrative, Ideology, and Scholarship*. Chicago: University of Chicago Press, 1999.

Littleton, C. Scott. "Gods, Myths and Structures: Dumézil." In *The Edinburgh Encyclopedia of Continental Philosophy*, edited by Scott Glendinning, 558–568. Edinburgh: Edinburgh University Press, 1999.

Loisy, Alfred. *L'évangile et l'église*. Paris: Alphonse Picard et Fils, 1902.

Lorenzen, David N. *The Kāpālikas and the Kālāmukhas: Two Lost Śaivite Sects*. Berkeley: The University of California Press, 1972.

———. *Who Invented Hinduism: Essays on Religion in History*. New Delhi: Yoda Press, 2006.

Loughlin, Gerard. "René Girard (b. 1923): Introduction." In *The Postmodern God: A Theological Reader*, edited by Graham Ward, 96–104. Malden, MA: Blackwell Publishing, 1997.

MacDonnell, Arthur A. *A History of Sanskrit Literature*. London: William Heinemann, 1900.

Mahoney, William K. *The Artful Universe: An Introduction to the Vedic Religious Imagination*. Albany: State University of New York Press, 1998.

Mallory, J. P., and Douglas Q. Adams. *The Oxford Introduction to Proto-Indo-European and the Proto-Indo-European World*. New York: Oxford University Press, 2006.

Mandapaka, Anubhavan, and Keshav Sharma. "Vedas Foretell about the Sacrifice of Christ." *In Search of Peace Free Online Magazine* 3: 17 (Nov. 11, 1999). http://insearchofpeace.org/3v17issue.htm#2.

Mani, Lata. *Contentious Traditions: The Debate on* Sati *in Colonial India*. Berkeley: University of California Press, 1998.

"Mathura Dracula Held for Offering Children's Blood to the Goddess." *India TV News*, September 27, 2011. http://www.indiatvnews.com/crime/news/Mathura-Dracula-Held-For-Offering-Children-s-Blood-To-Goddess-183.html.

Mauss, Marcel. *The Gift: The Form and Reason for Exchange in Archaic Societies*. Translated by W. D. Halls. New York: W. W. Norton, 1990.

Meillassoux, Quentin. *After Finitude: An Essay on the Necessity of Contingency*. Translated by Ray Brassier. New York: Continuum, 2008.

Michaels, Axel. *Hinduism: Past and Present*. Translated by Barbara Harshav. Princeton, NJ: Princeton University Press, 2004.

———. "Perfection and Mishaps in Vedic Rituals." In *When Rituals Go Wrong: Mistakes, Failure, and the Dynamics of Ritual*, edited by Ute Hüsken, 121–132. Leiden, Netherlands: Brill, 2007.

Milbank, John. "Stories of Sacrifice." *Contagion: Journal of Violence, Mimesis, and Culture* 2 (Spring 1995): 75–102.

Mill, James. *The History of British India*. London: Baldwin, Cradock and Joy, 1818.

Mitra, Rājendralāla. "On Human Sacrifices in Ancient India." *Journal of the Asiatic Society of Bengal* (1876).

Mudur, G. S. "Caste Barriers Not Older than 2000 Years—Indians Mated Across Ethnic Groups until 2nd Century: Study." *The Telegraph*, August 9, 2013. http://www.telegraphindia.com/1130809/jsp/nation/story_17213287.jsp.

Müller, Friedrich Max. *A History of Ancient Sanskrit Literature so Far as It Illustrates the Primitive Religion of the Brahmans*. 2nd ed. London: Williams and Norgate, 1860.

———. *Chips from a German Workshop, Volume I: Essays on the Science of Religion*. New York: Charles Scribner's Sons, 1891.

Murphy, Howard. "Some Concluding Anthropological Reflections." Afterword to *On Prayer*, by Marcel Mauss, W. S. F. Pickering, and Howard Murphy, 139–154. New York: Bergahn Books, 2003.

Nandy, Ashis. "History's Forgotten Doubles." *History and Theory* 34:2, Theme Issue 34: World Historians and Their Critics (May 1995): 44–66.

Némedi, D., W. S. F. Pickering, and H. L. Sutcliffe. "Durkheim's Friendship with the Philosopher Octave Hamelin: Together with Translations of Two Items by Durkheim." *The British Journal of Sociology* 46:1 (Mar. 1995), 107–125.

Nicholson, Andrew J. *Unifying Hinduism: Philosophy and Identity in Indian Intellectual History*. New York: Columbia University Press, 2010.

Nietzsche, Friedrich. *The Antichrist*. In *The Portable Nietzsche*, edited and translated by Walter Kaufmann, 565–656. New York: Penguin Books, 1954.

Obeyesekere, Gananath. "Sorcery, Premeditated Murder, and the Canalization of Aggression in Sri Lanka." *Ethnology* 14:1 (Jan. 1975): 1–23.

———. *The Work of Culture: Symbolic Transformation in Psychoanalysis and Anthropology*. Chicago: University of Chicago Press, 1990.

Oldenberg, Hermann. *The Religion of the Veda.* Translated by Shridhar B. Shroti. Delhi: Motilal Banarsidass, 1988.

Padel, Felix. *The Sacrifice of Human Being: British Rule and the Konds of Orissa.* New York: Oxford University Press, 1995.

Parpola, Asko. "Human Sacrifice in India in Vedic Times and Before." In *The Strange World of Human Sacrifice*, edited by Jan M. Bremmer, 157–177. Leuven: Peeters, 2007.

Patton, Kimberley C. *Religion of the Gods: Ritual, Paradox, and Reflexivity.* New York: Oxford University Press, 2009.

Peters, Edward. Introduction to *The Duel and the Oath*, by Henry Charles Lea, 5–10. Philadelphia: University of Pennsylvania Press, 1974.

Pillai, M. S. Purnalingam. *Tamil Literature.* Thanjavur, India: Tamil University, 1985.

Proferes, Theodore. "Kuru Kings, Tura Kāvaṣeya, and the *-Tvā́ya* Gerund." *Bulletin of the School of Oriental and African Studies, University of London* 66:2 (2003): 210–219.

"Raj Thackeray Apologises to Bahulkar." *The Times of India*, December 29, 2003. http://articles.timesofindia.indiatimes.com/2003-12-29/pune/27195967_1_sanskrit-references-sena-mla-deepak-paigude-sanskrit-scholar-shrikant-bahulkar.

Ramanujan, A. K. "The Indian Oedipus." In *Oedipus: A Folklore Casebook*, edited by Lowell Edmunds and Alan Dundes, 234–262. New York: Garland, 1983.

———. "Poetics and Pragmatics in the Vedic Liturgy for the Installation of the Sacrificial Post." *Journal of the American Oriental Society* 123:2 (Apr.—Jun. 2003): 317–350.

Puhvel, Jaan. "Victimal Hierarchies in Indo-European Animal Sacrifice." *The American Journal of Philology* 99:3 (Autumn 1978): 354–362.

Ramaswamy, Krishnan, Antonio de Nicolas, and Aditi Banerjee. "Invading the Sacred: An Analysis of Hinduism Studies in America." http://invadingthesacred.com/content/view/13/33/.

Raynal, Guillaume-Thomas François. *Histoire philosophique et politique des établissements et du commerce des Européens dans les deux Indes.* 4 vols. Amsterdam: 1770.

Reich, Tamar C. "Sacrificial Violence and Textual Battles: Inner Textual Interpretation in the Sanskrit *Mahābhārata*." *History of Religions* 41:2 (Nov. 2001): 142–169.

———. "The Interruption of the Sacrifice and the Verbal Contest: Three Different Epic Interpretations of a Pair of Vedic Motifs." In *Language, Ritual and Poetics in Ancient India and Iran: Studies in Honor of Shaul Migron*, edited by David Shulman, 136–160. Jerusalem: The Israel Academy of Sciences and Humanities, 2010.

Roodbergen, J. A. F. "Notes to Canto 1." In *Mallinātha's Ghaṇṭāpatha on the Kirātārjuniya I–VI*, 369–525. Leiden, Netherlands: Brill, 1984.

Russell, Bertrand. "The Philosophy of Logical Atomism." In *The Collected Papers of Bertrand Russell.* Volume 8, *The Philosophy of Logical Atomism and Other Essays, 1914–19*, edited by John G. Slater. New York: Routledge, 1986.

Salomon, Richard. "When Is a Riddle Not a Riddle? Some Comments on Riddling and Related Poetic Devices in Classical Sanskrit." In *Untying the Knot: On Riddles and Other Enigmatic Modes*, edited by Galit Hasan-Rokem and David Shulman, 168–178. New York: Oxford University Press, 1996.

Scharfe, Hartmut. *The State in Indian Tradition.* Leiden, Netherlands: Brill, 1989.

Schmitt, Carl. *Political Theology: Four Chapters on the Concept of Sovereignty*. Translated by Charles Schwab. Cambridge, MA: The MIT Press, 1985.

Schopen, Gregory. "The Buddha as a Businessman: Economics and Law in Old Indian Religion." Paper presented at the 106th Faculty Research Lecture at the Freud Playhouse, UCLA, March 10, 2009. http://www.uctv.tv/shows/The-Buddha-as-a-Businessman-Economics-and-Law-in-an-Old-Indian-Religion-16444.

Schwager, Raymund. "The Theology of the Wrath of God." In *Violence and Truth: On the Work of René Girard*, edited by Paul Dumouchel, 44–52. Stanford, CA: Stanford University Press, 1988.

Schweizer, Bernard. *Hating God: The Untold Story of Misotheism*. Oxford: Oxford University Press, 2011.

Scubla, Lucien. "The Christianity of René Girard and the Nature of Religion." Translated by Mark Anspach. In *Violence and Truth: On the Work of René Girard*, edited by Paul Dumouchel, 161–178. Stanford, CA: Stanford University Press, 1988.

Shipley, Joseph T. *The Origins of English Words: A Discursive Dictionary of Indo-European Roots*. Baltimore: Johns Hopkins University Press, 1984.

Shukla, Aseem. "Whose History Is It Anyway?" *Washington Post*, March 2010. http://onfaith.washingtonpost.com/onfaith/panelists/aseem_shukla/2010/03/whose_history_is_it_anyways.html.

Shulman, David Dean. "Toward a Historical Poetics of the Sanskrit Epics." *International Folklore Review* 8 (1991): 9–17.

———. *The Hungry God: Hindu Tales of Filicide and Devotion*. Chicago: University of Chicago Press, 1993.

Smith, Brian K. *Reflections on Resemblance, Ritual, and Religion*. New York: Oxford University Press, 1989.

———. *Classifying the Universe: The Ancient Indian Varṇa System and the Origins of Caste*. New York: Oxford University Press, 1994.

Smith, Brian K., and Wendy Doniger. "Sacrifice and Substitution: Ritual Mystification and Mythical Demystification." *Numen* 36:2 (Dec. 1989): 189–224.

Smith, Jonathan Z. "When the Bough Breaks." *History of Religions* 12:4 (May 1973): 342–371.

———. "The Bare Facts of Ritual." *History of Religions* 20:1–2, Twentieth Anniversary Issue (Aug.–Nov. 1980): 112–127.

Soifer, Deborah A. *The Myths of Narasiṁha and Vāmana: Two Avatars in Cosmological Perspective*. Albany: State University of New York Press, 1991.

Staal, Frits. "What Is Happening in Classical Indology?—A Review Article." *The Journal of Asian Studies* 41:2 (Feb. 1982): 269–291.

———. *Rules without Meaning: Ritual, Mantras, and the Human Sciences*. New York: P. Lang, 1989.

Stow, Kenneth R. *Jewish Dogs: An Image and Its Interpreters: Continuity in the Catholic-Jewish Encounter*. Stanford, CA: Stanford University Press, 2006.

Strenski, Ivan. "Zionism, Brahminism and the Embodied Sacred: What the Durkheimians Owe to Sylvain Lévi." In *The Sacred and Its Scholars: Comparative Methodologies for the Study of Primary*

Religious Data, edited by Thomas A. Idinopulos and Edward A. Yonan, 19–35. New York: Brill, 1996.

———. *Theology and the First Theory of Sacrifice.* Boston: Brill, 2003.

Sullivan, Bruce M. "The Ideology of Self-Willed Death in the Epic *Mahābhārata*." *Journal of Vaishnava Studies* 14:2 (Spring 2006): 61–79.

———. "Tantroid Phenomena in Early Indic Literature: An Essay in Honor of Jim Sanford." *Pacific World: Journal of the Institute of Buddhist Studies* 3:8 (Fall 2006): 9–20.

Taylor, McComas. "Mythology Wars: The Indian Diaspora, 'Wendy's Children' and the Struggle for the Hindu Past." *Asian Studies Review* 35:2:06 (2011): 149–168.

Thompson, George. "The Brahmodya and Vedic discourse." *Journal of the American Oriental Society* 117:1 (Jan.—Mar. 1997): 13–37.

Tull, Herman W. "F. Max Müller and A. B. Keith: 'Twaddle,' the 'Stupid' Myth, and the Disease of Indology." *Numen* 38:1 (June 1991): 27–58.

Urban, Hugh B. *Tantra: Sex, Secrecy, Politics, and Power in the Study of Religion.* Berkeley: University of California Press, 2003.

Vaudeville, Ch. "*Rāmāyana* Studies I: The *Krauñca-Vadha* Episode in the Vālmīki *Rāmāyaṇa*." *Journal of the American Oriental Society* 83:3 (Aug.–Sep. 1963): 327–335.

Vincent, Rose. *The French in India: From Diamond Traders to Sanskrit Scholars.* Translated by Latika Padgaonkar and Rose Vincent. Bombay: Popular Prakashan, 1990.

Visuvalingam, Sunthar. "Towards an Integral Appreciation of Abhinava's Aesthetics of Rasa." 2002. http://www.svabhinava.org/abhinava/Sunthar-integral/.

Watkins, Calvert. *How to Kill a Dragon: Aspects of Indo-European Poetics.* New York: Oxford University Press, 1995.

Weber, Albrecht. "Uber Menschenopfer bei den Indern der vedischen Zeit." *Zeitschrift der Deutsche Morgenländische Gesellschaft* 18: 262–287. Reprint *Indische Streife* Band 1: 54–89. Berlin: Nicholaisch Verlagsbuchhandlung, 1868.

Weber, Jaques. "Chanemougam, 'King of French India': Social and Political Foundations of an Absolute Power under the Third Republic." *Economic and Political Weekly* 26:6 (Feb. 9, 1991): 291–293, 295–297, 299–302.

Whitaker, Jarrod L. *Strong Arms and Drinking Strength: Masculinity, Violence, and the Body in Ancient India.* New York: Oxford University Press, 2011.

White, David Gordon. *Myths of the Dog-Man.* Chicago: University of Chicago Press, 1991.

White, Hayden. "Ethnological 'Lie' and Mythical 'Truth.'" *Diacritics* 8:1, Special Issue on the Work of René Girard (Spring 1978): 2–9.

Whitney, William Dwight. "Eggeling's Translation of the *Çatapatha Brāhmaṇa*." *American Journal of Philology* 3:12 (1882): 393.

———. *The Roots, Verb-forms and Primary Derivatives of the Sanskrit Language.* Delhi: Motilal Banarsidass, 2000.

Wilson, Horace Hayman. "On the Sacrifice of Human Beings as an Element of the Ancient Religion of India." *Journal of the Royal Asiatic Society* 13 (1852): 96–107.

Winternitz, Maurice. *A History of Indian Literature Volume One: Introduction, Veda, Epics, Purāṇas and Tantras*. Delhi: Motilal Banarsidass, 1981.

Witzel, Michael. "Vedas and Upaniṣads." In *The Blackwell Companion to Hinduism*, edited by Gavin Flood, 68–101. Malden, MA: Blackwell Publishing Ltd., 2003.

Žižek, Slavoj. "How to Begin from the Beginning." *New Left Review* 57 (May–June 2009). http://newleftreview.org/II/57/slavoj-zizek-how-to-begin-from-the-beginning.

———. *Living in the End Times*. New York: Verso, 2010.

Index

A

Acts of Saint Thomas, 14
Adarkar, Aditya, 169, 171, 172–173
Agamben, Giorgio: on oath, 84, 98–102, 104, 135, 232; on state of exception, 151–153; and work on *homo sacer*, 122, 184
Agni, 92, 144, 167, 269n35; allied with demons, 63–67, 69–70, 77
Ahura Mazdā, 64
Aitareya Āraṇyaka, 192
American Dream, 255n44
Angoulvant, Gabriel Louis, 54
anthropogenesis, 99–101
āpaddharma, 152–153
Āpastambha Śrauta Sūtra, 120
Aquinas, Thomas, 2
Āraṇyakas, 6
Aristotle, 163–164, 173
Arjuna, 107, 173; and *Bhagavad Gītā*, 70, 81, 145, 153; and Karṇa, 161–163, 165–168
Aryans, 65, 92, 263n60; and Buddhism, 57; migration hypothesis of, 209; and sacrificial contest, 77, 105
asuras. See *devas* vs. *asuras*
Aśvaghosha, 14
Āsvalāyana Śrauta Sūtra, 137–138
Aśvamedha, 32–33, 39, 40, 79, 103, 192; in *Mahābhārata*, 139, 148
Asya Vamāsya. *See* "Riddle of the Sacrifice"
Augustine, 2

B

Badiou, Alain, 246, 247, 262n45, 283n101; *Saint Paul: The Foundation of Universalism*, 28–29, 174; and "Speculative Realism," 230
Bahulkar, Shrikant, 28
Bailly, Jean-Sylvain, 52–53, 54
Bali, 77–78, 79–80, 90–91
Bataille, Georges, 17, 88
Battacharji, Sukumari, 103
Baudelaire, Charles, 243
Baudhāyana Śrauta Sutra, 113, 197
Benandanti, 120–121, 132
Bergaigne, Abel, 59, 67
Bhagavad Gītā, 70, 80–81, 145, 153, 156, 213; and American scholarship on Hinduism, 26; and avatar doctrine, 76; and attempted ban in Russia, 276n53
Bhāmaha, 283n115
Bhāravi, 210
Bhatti, 278n73
**bhlagh(s)-men*, 84, 86–88, 129–130, 202, 210,

212, 223
Bhuvaneśvarī, 31
Biardeau, Madeleine, 41, 71
Bible, 23; Gospels, 13–15, 18–21, 24, 82, 131, 256n44; New Testament, 28–29, 34–35, 48, 132, 141, 159; Old Testament, 14, 19, 41, 99, 103, 132, 184
Billot, Frédéric-Florentin, 53
Biswas, S. N., 118
Boas, Franz, 60
Boccali, Giuliano, 228
Boersma, Hans, 246
Brāhmaṇas, 3–4, 6, 8, 39, 43–49, 55, 58, 60–61, 70, 75, 82, 202, 264nn75–76; *Aitareya Brāhmaṇa*, 40–41, 63, 76, 110, 127, 151; early European reactions to, 44–46, 55, 126; *Gopatha Brāhmaṇa*, 63; *Jaiminīya Brāhmaṇa*, 133, 151, 215, 217–119, 277n69; *Kauśītaki Brāhmaṇa*, 76; *Pañcaviṃśa Brāhmaṇa*, 115–118; *Śatapatha Brāhmaṇa*, 45, 63, 71, 75, 76, 77, 93, 95, 125, 129, 150, 185, 193–194, 197, 215–217, 221, 241–242; *Taittirīya Brāhmaṇa*, 63; *Vādhūla Brāhmaṇa*, 32, 196, 280n42
Brahmins, 4, 5–7, 15, 20, 34, 37, 45, 53, 61, 73, 79, 80, 89–90, 94–95, 105, 107, 114–115, 124–125, 130; vs. Kṣatriyas, 83–84, 92, 93–94, 127, 129, 133–134, 197, 215, 269n35; as sacrificial victims, 210–211
brahmodyas, 182–183, 187, 192, 211
Brereton, Joel, 241
Bṛhaspati, 105–106, 109, 227, 264n75, 281n63
Buber, Martin, 181–182
Buck-Morss, Susan, 244
Buddhism, 2, 78, 97, 112, 187, 229–230; and Sylvain Lévi, 57–58
Buitenen, J. A. B. van, 154, 155
Burkert, Walter, 31, 55, 228

C

Caillois, Roger, 182
Caitanya Caritāmṛta, 34
Caland, Willem, 32, 118
Calasso, Roberto, 1–2, 49, 149–150
Cameron, Alan, 13
Cantor, Georg, 230
Caputo, John D., 141
Carrasco, David, 89
caste system, 53–54
Chakrabarty, Dipesh, 243–244
Chanemougam, 53–54
Chantre, Benoît, 55, 97
Charpentier, François, 50
Christianity, 8, 13–14, 16–18, 22, 23, 25, 58, 255n44, 269n48; Girard on, 100–101, 131, 247, 255n44; Heesterman on, 200–201; in India, 14–15, 265n78, 283n114
Clarke, Adam, 34–35
Clausewitz, Carl von, 9, 97, 247
Clive, Robert, 50–51
Clooney, Francis X., 230, 231, 233
Colbert, Jean-Baptiste, 50
Colebrooke, Henry Thomas, 39–40
Compton, Todd M., 203, 211
Cormon, Fernand, 278n73
Coutouly, Charles, 54–55
cows, sacred, 259n95
Crooke, William, 32
Cyavana, 198, 214–221, 223–224

D

Dadhyañc, 198
Das, Gurchuran, 152, 276n38
Das, Veena, 231–232
deconstruction, 141
Derrida, Jacques, 11–12, 21, 141, 223–226; on *pharmakos*, 202, 211
Descartes, René, 12
devas vs. *asuras*, 76–82, 90, 108, 195–198; in *Mahābhārata*, 143, 159; in *Sacrifice*, 62–65; and Śukra, 105–106
Devayānī, 106–109
dharma, 75–76, 80, 124, 152–153, 160, 173–174, 201; and *ṛta*, 232
Dharma (deity), 146–147
Dharmadāsa, 186
Diderot, Denis, 52
Don Quixote (Cervantes), 13
Doniger, Wendy, 26–28, 67, 75, 153, 175, 199
duels, 84, 102–105, 186
Dumézil, Georges, 22, 83, 125, 202, 211, 215, 267n22, 269n35, 270n53; background, 85–86; on **bhlagh(s)-men*, 84, 86, 87, 129–130, 210–211, 234; controversial views of, 266n4; on Kaca myth, 108; on Mitra, 92; on Śiśupāla, 203–204, 208, 212; structural theory of myth, 267n12; on trifunctional model of culture, 84, 87, 88, 143; and "ultrahistory," 209
Dupleix, Joseph François, 50–51

Dupuy, Jean-Pierre, 191, 195
Durgā, 31, 32
Durkheim, Émile, 44, 56–57, 85–86; and Girard, 81, 88, 195, 266n90; and Mauss, 59–60
dveṣabhakti, 174–175, 178
Dyutāna, 116, 119

E

Eagleton, Terry, 254n18
Eggeling, Julius, 45, 194
Eliade, Mircea, 18
Eliot, T. S., 172, 173, 180
Enlightenment, 43, 48, 49, 58, 81
ethnocentrism, 23–28, 57
Euripides: *The Bacchae*, 38, 151, 239; *Heracles*, 189; *The Phoenician Women*, 269n35

F

Falk, Harry, 184
Frankfurter, David, 18
Frazer, James George, 24–25, 60
Freud, Sigmund, 49, 186, 247
Frye, Northrop, 202

G

games of chance, 182–183, 184
Gandhi, Indira, 2, 247
Gandhi, Mohandas Karamchand, 2, 247
Gandhi, Rajiv, 2, 247
Ganeśa, 2, 26
Gāthas, 64
Gautrekssaga, 203
Geertz, Clifford, 28
Gerow, Edwin, 226–227
Ghatotkaca, 137–138
Ginzburg, Carlo, 120, 136
Girard, René: on anthropologists, 1, 23–25; *Battling to the End*, 9, 49, 97, 159, 246, 247, 254n14; and Brāhmaṇas, 9, 43–44, 46, 48, 49, 55, 74–75, 81, 93, 125, 149, 243; on Christianity, 14, 23, 131, 191, 200, 256n44; *Deceit, Desire and the Novel*, 8, 181; defines sacrifice, 242–243; on Derrida, 11–12, 226; on Dumézil, 87; on Durkheim, 266n90; "The Evangelical Subversion of Myth," 48; existential ethics, 174; as historian of religion, 16–21; on "Hymn of Puruṣa," 199–200; *Job*, 189; on *Mahābhārata*, 139; "Marriage in Avignon in the Second Half of the Fifteenth Century," 268n28; *Oedipus Unbound*, 283n101; "Racine, Poet of Glory," 170–171; *Sacrifice*, 3, 9, 13, 18, 20, 25, 30, 31, 42, 46, 49, 55, 74, 81, 91, 125, 149, 195, 241–243; *The Scapegoat*, 36, 87, 140; similarities with Agamben, 102; *Things Hidden since the Foundation of the World*, 8–9, 11–12, 64, 87; "Tiresias and the Critic," 21–22; *Violence and the Sacred*, 8, 16, 64, 85, 87, 103, 163–164, 189, 202–203, 210. *See also* mimetic theory; sacrificial victims; scapegoating
Gnosticism, 14, 45, 230, 233, 258n81
Goldhammer, Jesse, 16–17
Goldman, Robert, 219
Gonda, Jan, 210
Gosvāmin, Rūpa, 178
Goumain, Captain, 54
Granet, Marcel, 85–86
Greek mythology, 19, 22, 70, 210
Griffin, John Howard, 82

H

Hale, Wash Edward, 65
Hamelin, Octave, 59
Hamerton-Kelly, Robert, 21, 171
Handelman, Don, 184, 185
Hare Krishnas, 34
Hariścandra, 34, 127–128, 129, 133
Haug, Martin, 192
Heesterman, Jan C., 41, 48, 77, 118–119, 122, 131, 180, 213, 235; on *brahmodyas*, 187–188; on relationship between sacrifice and ritual, 101, 102, 105, 115, 189–190, 191, 194, 200–201; on riddles, 187, 196; on sacrificial heads, 196, 197–198; on Vena-Pṛthu myth, 124; on Vrātyas, 114
Hegel, Georg Wilhelm Friedrich, 59, 100, 187; and Girard, 49, 97, 170–171
Heidegger, Martin, 12, 18, 141
Hiltebeitel, Alf, 41, 214, 267n22
Hindu mythology, 2–3, 15, 20, 62–82, 90–91, 180
Hinduism, 2–3, 6–8, 15–16, 26, 30, 57–58, 247–251, 278n3; revelation in, 156, 229–230
Hobbes, Thomas, 152
Hölderlin, Friedrich, 243, 246
Homeric epics, 163, 175, 210
homo sacer, 75, 84, 99, 104, 122, 135, 155, 157, 184, 223, 234, 250; lycanthropic, 147, 151–153, 180, 202, 239
Horse Sacrifice. *See* Aśvamedha

Houben, Jan E. M., 193, 194–195
Hubert, Henri, 57, 59, 70, 84–85, 88, 231
human sacrifice. *See* sacrificial victims
"Hymn of Puruṣa," 199–200

I

India: European presence in, 15, 31–33, 50–55, 81, 258nn80–81, 277n73; recent history of, 2, 247
Indra, 44, 63–71, 75–76, 78, 79–82, 90–92, 94–96, 108–109, 126–127, 129, 133, 197, 202, 264n74, 265n88, 267n22, 271n73; in *Jaiminīya Brāhmaṇa*, 218; in *Mahābhārata*, 143, 148, 158, 167, 219–220; in *Ṛg Veda*, 269n35, 281n63; as Sālāvṛkī, 80, 109, 112; in *Taittirīya Saṃhitā*, 126, 196–197; and Yatis, 110–112, 121, 149, 151
Invading the Sacred, 26
Islam, 58

J

Jagannāth, 34, 37
Jaimini, 228, 229–233, 235
Jainism, 2, 112, 187
Jamison, Stephanie, 109–110, 186–187, 223
Jesus, 13, 17, 198, 246–247, 276n52; birth of, 19–20; Heesterman on, 200; and Karṇa, 169, 171
Jewett, Robert, 23
Johnston, Mark, 9
Jones, William, 52
Jordaan, Roy E., 30–31
Judaism, 8, 56–58

K

Kabir, 237
Kaca, 106–108
Kafka, Franz, 111, 183
Kālī, 31, 35, 143, 282n97
Kālidāsa, 13, 228–229
Kant, Immanuel, 230
karma, 160, 214
Karṇa. See *Mahābhārata*
katharsis, 163–164, 277n65
Kathāsaritsāgara, 13
Kātyāyana Śrauta Sūtra, 197
kavis, 209–212, 221, 224
kāvya, 210, 226–229, 283n115
Kāvya Uśanas. *See* Śukra
Keith, A. Berriedale, 40
kingship, 64, 81, 84, 91, 122–125, 210, 269n35
Kojève, Alexandre, 170–171
Kripal, Jeff, 26
Kṛṣṇa, 19, 34, 53, 70, 76, 81; in *Mahābhārata*, 139, 144–146, 153–156, 165–167, 169, 172–173, 205–209, 212–213, 282n88; Satan and, 169, 276n53
Kṛttibāsa, 34
Kṛtyās, 221–223, 282n97
Kṣatriyas, 5, 53, 80, 83–84, 92, 107–108; in *Mahābhārata*, 143, 154–155, 160, 162, 168–169, 174. *See also* Brahmins
Kulke, Hermann, 51

L

Laine, James, 28
Lang, Andrew, 24
Lardinois, Roland, 56–57
Lawrence, Patricia, 268n34
Laws of Manu, The, 29, 83, 114, 192, 268n32; and *āpaddharma*, 153; and oaths, 97–98
Lea, Henry Charles, 84, 96–97, 102, 104
Lefort, Guy, 55
Lévi, Daniel, 55
Lévi, Sylvain, 22, 44, 55–63, 67, 112; and Dumézil, 85–86, 92, 266n4; and Mauss, 59–60, 85; and *Sacrifice*, 9, 13, 46, 49, 55, 74, 81, 125, 238, 257n73; and Zionism, 56–58
Lévi-Strauss, Claude, 47, 87, 99, 183, 190
Loisy, Alfred, 247
Lorenzen, David, 7, 274n119
Lucretius, 1
Luther, Martin, 57, 141

M

MacDonnell, Arthur A., 44
Mack, Burton, 55
Mahābhārata, 4, 6, 15, 67, 70, 76, 93, 95, 106, 111–112, 113, 123, 134, 137–174, 179–180, 209, 211–214, 215, 219, 227, 239–240, 248, 277n65; haunted pool episode in, 278n12; and mimetic theory, 136, 137, 141–142; narrative devices, 139, 142–143, 157, 160, 173; plot summary, 143–147; and sacrifice, 139–140, 145, 147, 151–160, 171–172, 177; story of churning of ocean, 70, 142, 157–160, 167, 180; story of Dakṣa, 138, 147–151, 185; story of Jarāsaṃdha, 142, 154–156; story of Karṇa, 107–108, 138, 142, 143–144, 161–174, 178–179, 240, 243, 244–245, 275n38; story

of Śiśupāla, 154, 204–209, 211–214; textual history, 259n89
Mahadeva, 14
mahāpralaya, 33, 157, 245, 256n44
Mahoney, William K., 232
Maistre, Joseph de, 16–17, 36, 235, 256n44
Maitrāyaṇī Saṃhitā, 63, 110, 151
Makha, 111, 193, 198, 270n68
Malamoud, Charles, 190
Mallinātha, 210
Mānava Śrauta Sūtra, 197
Mānavadharmaśāstra. See *Laws of Manu, The*
Mandapaka, Anubhavanand Keshav Ray Sharma, 265n78
Mani, Lata, 38
Männerbund, 112–113, 120
Mauss, Marcel, 22, 47, 57, 59–60, 67, 70, 84–85, 88, 231; on *Mahābhārata*, 142–143
Meillassoux, Quentin, 230–231, 284n118
Meillet, Antoine, 85, 86
Michaels, Axel, 3, 188
Milbank, John, 188, 246
Mill, James, 52
Milton, John, 172, 174
Mīmāṃsā, 8
mimetic desire, 9–10, 18, 43, 48, 49, 81, 93, 108, 134, 141–142, 191; and "metaphysical desire," 233
mimetic doubling, 134, 182, 188
mimetic rivalry, 12, 43–44, 49–50, 83, 92, 104, 178, 188, 202, 247; of communalism and secularism, 247; of France and England, 49–50; of gods and demons, 62–63, 78, 80, 81, 108; in Gospels, 18, 20; of Karṇa and Arjuna, 162; in sacrificial crisis, 9–10, 182–183; of Viśvāmitra and Vasiṣṭha, 133–135
mimetic theory, 3, 7–10, 41, 95, 104, 136, 141; antagonism toward, 43–44, 81; criticism of, 16–22; and Hinduism, 49–50, 180, 184; as radicalized Durkheimianism, 195
Miśra, Śālika Nātha, 228–229
Mitra, 129, 135, 269n35; and Varuṇa, 91–94, 126, 150, 211; and Vṛtra, lynching of, 94–96, 125
Mitra, Rājendralāla, 32
movies: *The Dark Knight*, 245–246; *Death Takes a Holiday*, 138; *The Godfather*, 79; *Harlequin (Dark Forces)*, 272n96
Müller, F. Max, 31, 41, 43, 44, 59, 127, 140, 226
myth, function of, 12–13, 18–19, 139–140, 189, 201, 213, 267n12

N

Nandy, Ashis, 247
Nārada, 127, 133
Nicholson, Andrew J., 249–250
Nietzsche, Friedrich, 191; and Christianity, 13, 23, 255n44; and *The Laws of Manu*, 98, 268n32

O

oaths, 84, 125, 135, 268nn27–28; anthropogenic, 96–102; in India, 104
Obeyesekere, Gananath, 139–140
Oedipus myth. *See* Sophocles
Oldenberg, Hermann, 70
Oughourlian, Jean-Michel, 11, 55
Ovid, 33

P

Padel, Felix, 36–38
Pāṇini, 210, 227
Paraśurāma, 107–108
Pārvatī, 148, 229
Pascal, Blaise, 267n24
Patton, Kimberly, 192
Peters, Edward, 96
pharmakos/pharmakon, 202–203, 215, 221; and Kavi, 211; and *logos*, 224–225
Pillai, M. S. Purnalingam, 179
Plato, 12, 202, 215, 225–226, 284n124
Poe, Edgar Allan, 198
poetics, Indian. See *kāvya*
postcolonial studies, 7, 26, 28–29, 36–37, 38–39
Poullé, Maridâs, 53
Prajāpati, 19, 64, 71–76, 82, 91, 149–151, 194, 198, 264n78, 281n63
prakṛti, 93, 229
Proferes, Theodore, 270n68
prohibitions, 12–13, 99, 142
Purāṇas, 6, 7, 33, 39, 78–79, 82, 130; *Bhāgavata Purāṇa*, 53, 76, 79, 124; *Brahmā Purāṇa*, 79, 90–91; *Bṛhaddharma Purāṇa*, 123–124; *Devībhagavāta Purāṇa*, 133; *Kūrma Purāṇa*, 79; *Matsya Purāṇa*, 80; *Skanda Purāṇa*, 77, 79, 151, 227; *Vāmana Purāṇa*, 79; *Viṣṇu Purāṇa*, 179; *Visnudharmottara Purāṇa*, 79
Puruṣa, 20, 71, 72–76, 79, 82, 88–91, 183–184, 195, 199, 202, 210, 214, 229
Puruṣamedha (human sacrifice), 30, 39–40, 127, 275n24
Pūrva Mīmāṃsā, 228–233, 249

R

Racine, Jean-Baptiste, 170–171
Radhakrishnan, Sarvepalli, 249
Rāma, 76, 174–177
Ramanujan, A. K., 225
Rāmāyaṇa, 6, 32–34, 76, 130, 131, 174–179, 227–228; *Krauñcavadha* episode, 227–229
Rank, Otto, 169, 173
Raudrī, 31
Raynal, Guillaume-Thomas François, 52
Reich, Tamar, 112, 139, 140
religion vs. knowledge, 189
Renou, Louis, 223
"Riddle of the Sacrifice," 186, 192–193, 194–195, 199
riddles, 130, 185–187, 278n12
ritual, 12–13, 15, 61, 63–64, 74, 84, 94, 101–102, 105, 110, 113–114, 182–183, 188–190, 260nn9–10; meaninglessness of, 46–49; and Pūrva Mīmāṃsā, 228, 229, 233
Rohita, 127, 130
Romanticism, 49, 174
Roodbergen, J. A. F., 210
Rothermund, Dietmar, 51
Roy, Rammohan, 7
ṛta, 232
Rudra, 65, 71–72, 149–151, 208, 271n73
Russell, Bertrand, 184, 185–186

S

sacrifice: in Aztec culture, 89; and beheaded/headless motif, 193–198, 218; in Christianity, 8–9, 13–14, 17–18, 80, 101, 189–190; in Hinduism, 6, 15, 30–31, 35, 37–40, 57, 61, 69–70, 74, 76–78, 80, 83, 88–91, 95, 101–102, 105, 113–115, 125, 130, 137–138, 184–202, 208, 234–235, 251; incomplete nature of Vedic, 184–185; intoxication and, 69, 196, 220; Jaimini on, 232–233, 235; as mediation, 47, 201; as origin of culture, 3, 12; as origin of religion, 84–85, 122
sacrificial mechanism, 80, 125, 171, 189, 200, 213
sacrificial victims, 10–11, 15, 16–17, 61, 74, 77, 82, 88, 128, 164–165, 171, 182, 199, 214, 242–243; human sacrifice and, 30–39, 69, 88–89, 127, 132, 156, 197, 238, 274n119; as transcendental signifier, 11–12, 149, 183, 199, 241, 254n18
sacrificial violence, 9, 10, 14, 17, 21, 31, 63–64, 101, 125, 140, 159, 185, 222, 232, 242, 247, 256n44
Said, Edward, 23
Śaiva sect, 7, 132, 149; critique of sacrifice, 147, 151–153, 155–157, 179–180, 250; mythology, 151, 185, 208–209
Śāktism, 7, 8
Sālāvṛkī. *See* Indra
Saṃhitās. *See* Vedas
śamitar, 137–138, 165–166
saṃsāra, 16
Sanskrit language, 261n26, 263n59
Sanskrit mythology. *See* Hindu mythology
Śarmiṣṭhā, 108–109
sati, 29, 38
Sattra sacrifice, 37, 113
Śaunaka, 192
Savitṛ, 72
Scandinavian mythology, 87, 203–204, 211–212, 265n88, 282n86
scapegoating, 8, 10, 13–14, 18, 49, 64, 71, 74, 119, 123, 132, 151, 155–156, 188, 235, 247, 250–251, 255n44; of Rāvaṇa, 179; of Thugees, 36–38. *See also* sacrificial victims
Scharfe, Hartmut, 152
Schmitt, Carl, 18, 151–152, 184
Schopen, Gregory, 122
Schwager, Raymund, 19
Schweizer, Bernard, 178
Scubla, Lucien, 21
Shakespeare, William, 7, 13, 109–110, 202
Shipley, Joseph Twadell, 210
Shukla, Aseem, 27
Shulman, David, 127, 129, 130–131, 184, 185, 277n65
Śilpaśāstra texts, 30–31
Śiva, 2, 7, 26, 78, 202, 208, 209, 229, 272n90, 281n63; and Dakṣa, 142, 147–149, 151; and Rudra, 65. *See also* Śaiva sect
Sleeman, William, 35–36
Smith, Brian K., 3, 7, 47–48
Smith, Jonathan Z., 24–25, 55, 111
Smith, Wilfred Cantwell, 7
smṛti, 6
sociology, French, 55–56, 58, 88
Soifer, Deborah, 77, 78–80
soma: beverage, 4, 65, 68–69, 93–95, 182, 193, 194, 196, 219–220; plant, 125–126, 128–129,215–216, 241–242
Soma (god), 63–64, 70, 93–94; as sacrificial victim, 125–126, 241, 242; on side of demons, 66–67

Sonnerat, Pierre, 53
Sophocles: *Oedipus Rex*, 18, 131, 149, 156, 166, 173, 185, 186, 203, 225, 247, 283n101; *The Women of Trachis*, 189
"Speculative Realism," 230
Spencer, Baldwin, 60
śrauta. *See* ritual
Śrī, 67, 144, 159
śruti, 4
Staal, Frits, 15, 46–47, 48, 190, 260n9
Starkarðr, 203–204, 211–212, 214
stoma, 69
Stow, Kenneth, 112
Strenski, Ivan, 17, 56–57
structuralism, 21, 55, 87, 202, 217
Śukra, 78–79, 105–109, 110, 135, 211, 214
Sullivan, Bruce, 113–114, 173–174
Śunaḥśepa, 84, 86, 126–133, 135, 137, 174, 191, 202, 224–226
Sūtras, 6
suttee. See *sati*

T

Taittirīya Saṃhitā, 79, 126, 196–197; and story of Viṣṇu's dwarf avatar, 77, 90; Viśvāmitra and Vasiṣṭha in, 133
Tantra, 39–40, 258n81
Tari Pennu, 37
Taylor, McComas, 26–27
Thackeray, Raj, 257n62
Thugee cult, 35–36, 258n81
Tillich, Paul, 173
Tolkien, J. R. R., 264n76, 270n59
Townsend, Joseph, 32–35, 126
transcendental signifier. *See* sacrificial victims
Twain, Mark, 82, 266n91
twins, 13, 14, 33, 64
Tylor, Edward Burnett, 60

U

universal history, defined, 244
Upaniṣads, 6, 15, 230, 232, 251
Urban, Hugh, 41, 258n81
Uṣas, 71–72

V

Vādhūla Anvākhyāna or *Sūtra*. *See* Brāhmaṇas
Vaiṣṇava sect, 7, 90, 153; critique of sacrifice, 138, 147, 155–157, 179–180, 213; mythology, 76, 78, 147
Vajasaneyī Saṃhitā, 40
Vālmīki, 33, 176, 219, 227–229. See also *Rāmāyaṇa*
Vāmana, 76–77, 79–81, 90–91, 109, 147
varṇa system, 5, 80, 86, 118, 124, 262n31; created by sacrifice of Puruṣa, 73; and oaths, 98. *See also* Brahmins; Kṣatriyas
Varuṇa, 34, 63–64, 66–67, 70, 80, 91–94, 150, 211; as enforcer of oaths, 98–99, 103, 126–129, 133
vas kavi, 211
Vasiṣṭha. *See* Viśvāmitra
Vaudeville, Charles, 227
Vedānta, 6, 249, 251
Vedas, 3–6, 8, 21, 39, 82, 95, 99, 101, 122, 142, 225, 228–230, 232–233, 263n65; *Atharva Veda*, 4, 5, 65, 73, 119–120, 123, 193; *Ṛg Veda*, 4, 5, 8, 64–74, 76–77, 88, 92, 95, 110–111, 118–119, 123, 128, 133, 192–193, 211, 215, 221–222, 263n58; *Sāma Veda*, 4, 5, 73, 118, 193; *Yajur Veda*, 4, 5, 6, 8, 45, 73, 76, 110, 193. *See also* "Hymn of Puruṣa"; "Riddle of the Sacrifice"
Velankar, H. D., 211–212
Vena-Pṛthu myth, 123–125
Verne, Jules, 53
Viṣṇu, 7, 44, 70–71, 75–82, 90–91, 94, 109, 147, 194, 265n84; in *Mahābhārata*, 143, 144, 159–160
Viśvāmitra, 128–129, 130–131; rivalry with Vasistha, 132–136, 163, 182
Vivekananda, 2, 249–251
Vrātyas, 84, 113–120, 125, 132, 137, 152, 163, 184, 192, 202, 213, 280n42
Vṛṣaparvan, 109
Vṛtra, 65–71, 75, 77, 93–96, 125, 148
Voltaire, 53, 54, 266n90
von Strassburg, Gottfried, 270n48
Vyāsa, 157. See also *Mahābhārata*

W

Weber, Albrecht, 31, 109
Weil, Simone, 237
werewolves, 109, 121
Wessing, Robert, 30–31
Wheeler, James Talboys, 40
Whitaker, Jarrod, 209
White, David Gordon, 109, 112–113, 133, 152
White, Hayden, 16
Whitney, William Dwight, 44–45
Wikander, Stig, 143
Wilson, Horace Hayman, 41, 127

Winternitz, Moritz, 40, 127, 259n89
Wittgenstein, Ludwig, 234–235, 278n3
Witzel, Michael, 4
wolf-warriors, 109, 121
Woodruffe, Sir John, 40

Y
yajña. *See* sacrifice
Yāska, 227
Yogavāsiṣṭha, 16

Z
Zend Avesta, 209
Žižek, Slavoj, 29, 246, 250
Zoroaster, 209